Forever Tandem

A Love Story with Ancillary Passion for the Foreign Service

Interviews by Charles Stuart Kennedy with
David T. Jones
March 16, 1999-March 19, 2002
and
Teresa Chin Jones
July 2, 2007-August 10, 2007

Diplomatic Oral History Series
Association for Diplomatic Studies and Training

Copyright © 2011 by David & Teresa Jones.

ISBN:	Softcover	978-1-4653-7921-4
	Ebook	978-1-4653-7922-1

All rights reserved. No part of this book may be reproduced or transmitted in any form or by any means, electronic or mechanical, including photocopying, recording, or by any information storage and retrieval system, without permission in writing from the copyright owner.

This book was printed in the United States of America.

To order additional copies of this book, contact:
Xlibris Corporation
1-888-795-4274
www.Xlibris.com
Orders@Xlibris.com
81873

Forever Tandem

CONTENTS

Foreword: The ADST Diplomatic Oral History Series 17

PART I: THE GIRL FROM NOVASIBIRSK
TERESA CHIN JONES

Chapter 1:   How It All Happened 21

    Born in the USSR of Chinese Diplomatic Parents 21
    Parents 21
    Tashkent Time 27
    Communist Takeover of China—Escape from Russia 31
    Interlude in Sweden—and then to the United States 32
    Growing up in America—New Jersey Style 34
    The Role of Religion in Chinese Life 37
    Chinese History and Folklore 39
    Thinking of Politics and Nixon's Opening to China 42

Chapter 2:   Academics and the University of
                  Pennsylvania (1959-1966) 44

    Why Penn? 44
    Friends and Studies at Penn 45
    On to the PhD 47

Chapter 3:   Working for the Department of
                  Agriculture (1966-1968) 52

    Tobacco Labs in Philadelphia 52
    Chromatography 53

Chapter 4:   It's Paris—and Motherhood! (1969-1971) 55

Chapter 5: Back to the United States—
Vineland and Washington (1971-1972) 57

    Teaching in Vineland.. 58
    And Then to Washington 59

Chapter 6: Entering the Foreign Service (1974) 60

Chapter 7: First Assignment—ACDA (1974-1976) 63

    Verification Technology Issues 63
    Binary Chemical Weapons.. 64
    Chemical, Biological, and Radiological (CBR) Warfare 64
    Three Mile Island and Nuclear Reactor Vulnerability 65
    Destroying a Nuclear Reactor—How To . . .
       (or the Osirak Story).. 66
    India's "Peaceful" Nuclear Explosion.. 66
    And Learning about Interagency (and Intragency) Backbiting 66
    Soviet Attitudes and Their Technology 67

Chapter 8: Some Perspective and a "Tour" of Leave without
Pay (1976-1978) 69

Chapter 9: Belgium, Family, and Margaret (1978-1980) 72

    The Advent of Margaret 73
    Ambassador Robert Strausz-Hupé at NATO 73
    Working at the Consulate and the Flemings vs. the Walloons..... 74
    Visa Cases that I Have Known 75
    The Pedophile Culture in Belgium 78
    The Problems of Holtzman 79
    The Fallout of the Iranian Revolution for Embassy Brussels 80
    Dealing with the Congress.. 81
    Summing Up as Consul in Brussels—What I Learned................ 81

Chapter 10: Back to Mother State—This Time as a Science
Officer (1980-1982) 84

    Nonproliferation and Nuclear Export Controls 85
    The Pakistani Nuclear Program, Mr. "Theft" Khan, and Vela 86
    President Carter and Poisonous Nuclear Politics.......................... 87
    Work Environment at State—the "Best of Intentions".................. 87

The "South Atlantic Event" and Nuclear Analysis 88
SLIFERS 89
Dealing with the Soviets—Problems/Problems 89
The Interagency Policy Battles Over Export Control 90

Chapter 11: The Intelligence and Research Bureau and
Politicized Intelligence (1982-1985) 93

INR's Director: Hugh Montgomery: An Intelligence
Professional 93
State's Science and Technology Committee 94
Working Environment in INR and the Intelligence
Community 95
Telephone Technology 95
Personalities and Politics 96
East West Trade and COCOM 96
Supercomputers—Not So "Super" 97
Soviet-Europe Gas Pipeline Project 99
Summing Up in INF and Abramowitz as INR Director 100
Human Relations and Some of My Principles for FS Work 102

Chapter 12: The Trials of East West Trade in Export
Controls (1985-1987) 104

COCOM Again—and Agencies Differences of View 104
Operations and "Chicken Herding" in East-West Trade 105
Chemistry and East-West Trade—Some Parallels 106
On Being a Science Officer 108
The Soviets and Biological Warfare 110
High Speed Integrated Circuits and Designing
Nuclear Weapons 110
Detecting Nuclear Submarines and the "Toshiba" Problem 111
The Italian Hughes Helicopter Diversion to North Korea 113

Chapter 13: Economics Training and a Cox Sabbatical (1987) 115

The Econ Course: Pluses and (Many) Minuses (1987) 116
Some Personalities from the Economics Course 118
Understanding Promotion Panels 119
Una Chapman Cox Sabbatical—a Special Gift to the
Foreign Service (1988) 121
Recruiting for State: the Hunt for Visible Minorities 122

The Damage from Affirmative Action 124

Chapter 14: Back to OES and Technology
             Cooperation (1988-1990) 126

    Scope of International Agreements 126
    AAAS Fellows at State 127
    A Maze of Circular 175 Memos.. 128

Chapter 15: A Bit of French Training (1991-1992) 134

Chapter 16: Board of Examiners—Selecting the Next FSO
             Generation (1992) 136

    The Examination Process 136
    Case Study Method 137
    The Candidates—a Mixed Bag of Qualifications................................. 139

Chapter 17: A Northern Exposure—Montreal, Canada................................ 141

    Canada after the Collapse of National Unity Efforts........................... 142
    Quebec Separatists.. 143
    Economic Factors in the Separation Issue 144
    The French Fact(or) 145
    Anti-Americanism in Ottawa School... 147
    Atlantic Provinces Have Their Own Attitudes 147

Chapter 18: On to Ottawa—Two Years as Embassy
             Science Counselor (1994-1996) 149

    Scandal in National Institute of Health Grant 149
    The Failures of Canadian "Universal" Health Care............................. 150
    The Boundary Waters Treaty/Commission and
        Environmental Controls 151
    Perspectives on Polluting the St. Lawrence River 152
    Some Representative Bilateral Water Issues.. 152

Chapter 19: Home Again: Washington and
             Mother State (1996-1998) 154

    On Being a CAO for Seniors.. 154
    Appointment of Ambassadors.. 157

EEO as a Problem 159
A FOIA Finale 160

Chapter 20:   Comments on the Foreign Service 162

Retirement Seminar/Career Transition and Retirees............................... 162
The Foreign Service Journal and Foreign Service Writers 163
The American Foreign Service Association. 163
Foreign Service Elitism—and Science Officers...................................... 164
Impressions of Secretaries of State... 164
Some Closing Comments... 165

PART II: THE BOY FROM SCRANTON
DAVID T. JONES

Chapter 21:   Preludes—Growing Up and Getting
              Started with Life 169

Born and Raised in Scranton, Pennsylvania 169
Penn—A Legacy as I Follow Family Footsteps 173
Meeting and Marrying the Girl from Novasibirsk.................................. 178
Military Service—and a Korean Experience... 179
Another Image of Asia—Japan 186
Again, Penn.. 186
The Slow Progress Toward the Foreign Service 187
Those Initial Foreign Service Experiences and
   the 83rd A-100 Class... 190

Chapter 22:   Every Young FSO Should Have a Tour in Paris 193

The Environment: Embassy and Paris 194
The French—and Their Challenges... 195
The French Establishment... 197
The French and the "American Challenge" 198
Some Local French Staff.. 200
The Atmospherics of the Era—Demonstrations.................................... 202
Wine Wars 203
More Rotation in Paris—and the Political Section
   the Stars Fell Upon 204
Ambassadors: Changing of the Guard from Shriver
   to Watson 206

    The French, the D-Day Anniversary, and Their Attitudes.................208
    Parents Are We! 211
    Communism and the French..212

Chapter 23:   An Interlude—Leave Without Pay and the Foreign
                 Service Opens to Married Women 214

Chapter 24:   The Intelligence and Research Bureau—
                 Wrestling with Koreans...217

    ROK Leader Park Chung Hee and Action in Korea............................218
    North Koreans and the Regular Fear of Resumed War......................219
    Assessing North Korea and the Foreign Broadcast
        Information Service 219
    Koreans Pushing the Economic Envelope..221
    The China Factor—a New Dimension for the
        Republic of Korea..223
    . . . and Also the Japanese 223

Chapter 25:   The NATO Desk and the Beginning of the
                 Core of My Career...226

    Some Personalities: At US Mission NATO and in EUR/RPM...........226
    Committee on the Challenges of Modern Society: NATO's Kinder Face
        and CSCE 227
    The NATO Political Committee and the Nuclear
        Planning Group..229
    The Philosophy and Psychology of Nuclear Weapons.......................230
    Thinking about the Soviets—Not Very Subtle..................................233
    The "All Volunteer" U.S. Army and Its Challenges 233
    Internal NATO National Politics..235
        —Portugal...235
        —France 235
        —NATO "Neutrals" 236
        —Italy...237
        —Greece and Turkey (the Never-ending Feud).....................237
    The Never Ending Threat..239

Chapter 26:   Moving from the Desk to the Field: US Mission
                 NATO as NATO's Engine 242

    The US Mission at NATO: Structure and Operations.......................242

The Carter Transition in 1977 and the
  Ouster of Strausz-Hupé 244
The Hallmark of the Era: the Neutron Bomb and Nuclear Deterrence in
  Europe 248
Nuclear Capable Missiles—a Discussion 249
European Attitudes, Nuclear Weapons Deployments, Carter's
  Inexplicable Decision Not to Deploy ER Weapons, and
  Consequent European/U.S. Attitudes 251
The SALT II Treaty 254
The Soviets in Afghanistan—and Not in Poland 254
The INF Issue Evolves from Nuclear Force Modernization—
  Background 256
European Angst 256
Special Group (SG) and High Level Group (HLG) Activity 257
European Logic and Concerns 257
Creating a "Second Track" for an INF Decision 258
The December 12, 1979 Decision Meeting on
  INF Deployments 259
Starting to Implement the December 12 Decision—
  Refighting the Fights 261
The "Mansfield Amendment" and Conventional
  Force Reductions 262
Afghanistan and U.S. Hostages in Tehran—U.S. Attitudes 264
A Personal Sidebar 265

Chapter 27:   A New Area and a New Problem: Cyprus 267

Reviewing the Bidding: Greeks and Turks and
  Turks and Greeks 267
Peace Efforts: Seeking an Answer to the Cyprus Problem 269
UN Special Representative Hugo Gobbi 271
The Advent of the Special Cyprus Coordinator, Reg Bartholomew 272
Raul Denktash and Why Not to Make a Deal 273
Greek Cypriots: Clerides and Kyprianou 274
Congressional Interest in Cyprus—An Illustration
  of U.S. Domestic Politics 274
Student Scholarship Programs 275
The Missing—Politics and Personal Anguish 276
Turkish Military Coup 277

Chapter 28:   Preserving Our Bases in Greece—Once More
              with Bartholomew 279

Greek President Karamanlis..279
The Base Negotiations and Their Issues..280
Why PASOK?..281
Bartholomew and the Base Negotiations: A Tour de Force................281
Switching Special Cyprus Coordinators: Chris
    Chapman Takes Over..282
Our Bases in Greece: An Individual Assessment 283
Proper Prior Preparation Prevents 284
The Negotiations: A Unique Approach 285
Concepts for Base Negotiations..286
But What Did PASOK Want?..287
USG Negotiating Tactics and Approaches: Round by Round 289
Some Personal Touches..294
Security as a Subset of Our Problems..295
Addressing the Greek Media and Avoiding Its Traps 296
U.S.-Greek Relations as Reflected in the Congress.............................297
Some Final Thoughts on Greece and Our Bilateral Relations..........298

Chapter 29: Interlude—A (Temporary) Child of the Hill
             as a Pearson Fellow 300

A Pearson with Senator Hart (D-Colorado)..301
Contribution to Hart's Policies 302
Hart's Personality and Style 302
Jerusalem Issue Defines My Relationship in the Office 305
Feminism and Females as a Force on the Hill—and for Hart............306
Pearson Fellows and Relations with State..307

Chapter 30: A Year with the Greeks..309

More Papandreou..309
    —Our Battered Bilateral Relations 309
    —Greek Terrorism 310
Nuclear Powered Warships and other Nuclear Problems....................311
Greek Domestic Politics and Elections..312
A Personal Sidebar and the EUR/SE Office Director.......................313
Day-to-Day on the Desk 314
    —Greek Area Handbook...315

Chapter 31: Deputy for Theater Military Policy—
             My PM Experience Begins 316

The Political-Military Affairs Bureau—Organization
and Personalities 317
TMP's Responsibilities and My Work Load 318
    —A Day in the Life of 320
Working the Special Consultative Group 321
National Security and the Philosophy of Arms Control 322
The Soviet Union, Gorbachev, and the INF Negotiations 323
USG Internecine Bureaucratics: ACDA, DOD, JCS, NSC 324
Pie in the Sky: World Without Nuclear Weapons 328

Chapter 32: End Game for the Geneva INF Negotiating Team
              and Senate Ratification 331

U.S. Delegation Structure and Personalities 333
Some Rituals within the Delegation and with the Soviets 334
Attitudes and Concerns During the INF End Game 335
    —Intelligence Concerns: Where Are the Missing Missiles? 337
Grinding Onward—Team Spirit 338
    —The Famous Photo: The Delegation in Exile 339
Wordsmithing the Russian Language 342
Signing Ceremony in the Delegation and Getting Home 342

Chapter 33: Obtaining Senate Treaty Ratification—
              Not Half the Fun 345

Trying to Educate the Senate in Advance for the Treaty 345
Domestic Political Tensions in Play 346
USG Organization for the Ratification Process 347
Questions, Questions, Questions 348
Senator Jesse Helms and His Ritualistic Rejection 349
Suffering under Sofaer 349
Senate Testimony and Treaty Analysis—the Nunn Objections 350
    —The "Double Negative." 351
    —"Futuristics" 351
Forcing the Ratification Action to a Conclusion 353
Wrapping It Up and Winding It Down—INF
    Aftermath and Assessment 354

Chapter 34: Another Interlude—An Una Chapman Cox Sabbatical 357

The Cox Legend and How the Sabbatical Operates 358
What Did David Do? 359

Travels with Cox..362
An INF Manuscript...363
Battling Over the Next Foreign Service Assignment 363

Chapter 35:   Foreign Affairs Advisor (POLAD) for the Army.....................365

POLADS: Who and What They Are and Where to Find Them 365
On Being a POLAD...367
   —A Hypothetical Visit by a Foreign Army Chief 369
Some Substantive Issues..371
   —Panama..371
   —The Fall of the Berlin Wall and the Slow-Motion Disintegration
       of the USSR..374
   —Conventional Forces in Europe 374
   —Reforger 375
   —Burden sharing..376
The Changing Army 376
Examples of Senior Officer Excellence..378
The Gulf War: Saddam Hussein and the Kuwait Invasion 379
Army Attitudes about Desert Shield/Desert Storm and Its Tactics 382
   —Colin Powell..382
   —Norman Schwarzkopf..383
   —Barry McCaffrey...385
Military Relations with China 386
The Israelis—and Egyptians and Jordanians 387
The Conference of American Armies: Western
   Hemispheric Armed Forces..389
Indians and Pakistanis 390
The Clarence Thomas Affair and Resultant
   Workplace Attitudes 391

Chapter 36:   Oh Canada—A Defining Tour 393

U.S. Ambassadors in Canada...393
   —Teeley..393
   —Blanchard..394
On Being the Political Counselor 397
Status of the Relations 399
Unpopular Tories..400
Dealing with the Government in Waiting..401
   —The Lloyd Axworthy Factor...402

Comments on Canada: Operating Environment 403
    —Differences Between Canadians and Americans 406
Canadian Foreign Affairs Structures and Some Bilateral Issues 406
NORAD as a Keystone of the U.S.-Canadian Military Relationship .. 410
The Clinton Administration and the Canadian Government 410
National Unity and the Quebec Separatist Issue 412
Meech Lake and the Charlottetown Accord/National
    Referendum 414
End of the Tories and the National Election 416
Prospects for Bilateral Relations with the
    Liberals and Liberal Attitudes 421
Results of the 1993 Election 426
Preston Manning, Reform, and the Canadian West 427
    —The New Democratic Party 428
Bilateral Relations with the Liberals after the 1993 Election 429
    —Cruise Missiles 432
    —Haiti 433
    —A Much-Needed Civil Aviation Agreement 434
    —Salmon 434
Clinton's Visit to Canada: Some Atmospherics 435
The Quebec Sovereignty Referendum 437
Aftermath of the Sovereignty Referendum 446

Chapter 37: Back to Washington—End of Active Duty and
    into Retired Action 448

First, last, and always to each other: David to Teresa; Teresa to David.

To list all of the family, friends, and colleagues who have made us who we are and contributed to our lives would be superfluous. We appreciate all and forget none.

A journey of 10,000 years begins with a single day.

Forever Tandem

FOREWORD

The ADST Diplomatic Oral History Series

For 235 years, extraordinary men and women have represented the United States abroad with courage and dedication. Yet their accomplishments in promoting and protecting American interests often remain little known to their compatriots. The Association for Diplomatic Studies and Training (ADST) created the Diplomatic Oral History Series to help fill this void by publishing in book form selected transcripts of interviews from its Foreign Affairs Oral History Collection.

The text contained herein acquaints readers with the distinguished service of David Taylor Jones and Teresa Chin Jones, senior career Foreign Service officers who specialized in arms control, science policy, economic negotiations, intelligence, and political analysis. We are proud to make their interviews available through the Diplomatic Oral History Series.

ADST (*www.adst.org*) is an independent nonprofit organization founded in 1986 and committed to supporting training of foreign affairs personnel at the State Department's Foreign Service Institute and advancing knowledge of American diplomacy. It sponsors books on diplomacy through its Memoirs and Occasional Papers Series and, jointly with DACOR, the Diplomats and Diplomacy Series. In addition to posting oral histories under "Frontline Diplomacy" on the website of the Library of Congress, ADST manages an educational website at *www.usdiplomacy.org*.

Kenneth L. Brown
President
Association for Diplomatic Studies and Training

PART I

THE GIRL FROM NOVOSIBIRSK

TERESA CHIN JONES

CHAPTER 1

How It All Happened

Q: You go by "Terry"?

JONES: Yes.

Q: Well, Terry, let's start at the beginning. When and where were you born?

Born in the USSR of Chinese Diplomatic Parents

JONES: I was born on November 30, 1941, in Novosibirsk, USSR.

Q: All right. So we want to figure out how you came to be born in the USSR in Novosibirsk.

Parents

JONES: Well, in the summer of 1941, Hitler invaded the Soviet Union. My father was a Chinese diplomat assigned to the Republic of China embassy in Moscow. They sent all the diplomatic dependents to Novosibirsk for safety. My mother still remembers going on the train to Novosibirsk, which was packed with diplomats and their children, and looking at the endless troop trains going in the other direction. She didn't think too many of those troops ever made it home again.

Q: These were the Siberian divisions that were brought in that sort of turned the tide in the battle for Moscow.

JONES: Well, they were a never-ending stream of men. Once my then-expectant mom and dad got to Novosibirsk, they settled in nicely, but on November 30, she fell down a flight of icy stairs. She was eight months pregnant when I was born. Even Chinese coming from wartime China were horrified at the sanitation standards at the hospital. Doctors didn't wash their hands and wore their outside boots into surgery.

It was no surprise when Mom developed peritonitis—considered 100 percent lethal before antibiotics or even sulfa drugs existed. But fortunately, at this point in time Stalin wanted the Nationalists as friends, so Malenkov (the Soviet minister of foreign affairs) listened to my father's complaints about the total incompetents dealing with my mother and actually ordered one of the better surgeons in Moscow to go there and take care of her. With no antibiotics, they could only operate to drain the pus from the infection, at a rate of two operations a week. She was down to about 80 pounds after several months, and she had weakened so much that they were sure she was dying.

A good friend of hers, a Polish-Chinese wife of a Chinese diplomat and a very devout Catholic, managed to somehow find a priest to give my mother last rites and to baptize me Teresa, after her favorite saint. She also gave my mother the very last of her holy water from Lourdes which she had gotten years ago when on a pilgrimage.

My mother then came out of the coma. As my mother told us, she dreamt that she had died and was greeted by a little boy and a little girl carrying a lantern—spirits whom traditional Chinese believed were there to escort dead souls to judgment. She prepared to go when she heard a loud voice tell her "Not your time"—thus shocking her out of her coma.

She still had months of hospitalization during which her Russian became superb. She was twenty years old and a high school graduate, which made her a very well-educated Chinese woman for that time. By the time she came out of the hospital she could read *War and Peace* easily in Russian, she could go to plays, and she could bargain for food in the bazaars.

Q: But first, let's take your family. What do you know about your father's family? What was the family name, and where did they come from?

JONES: My father's family name is Chin (Qin), which is written as the same Chinese character as the Chin emperor. But since the Chin emperor's name wasn't Chin, the actual family descent was from a well-known Chinese Robin Hood, who was not a Sherwood Forest prototype. I was told he was a courier who fell ill while waiting for a response to his message. His horse, his armor, his sword all got taken to pay for his care. Once recovered, he wanted to retrieve his sword, a family heirloom. The locals said, "Well, too bad. The sword has been bought by a bandit king in the mountains. You will have to go get it from him." He went to take the sword by force from the bandit king, but ended by talking and drinking with his newfound soul mate. They talked, and then talked some more; then they drank, and drank some more. This is a hard liquor region of China—just look at all those bronze wine vessels from Chinese tombs in the Smithsonian. My ancestors had a world technological lead in distilling alcohol.

In the end, they became partners and controlled that area for years and years. They were brought back into legality only because the emperor got caught in a ravine in some local battle and sent out passenger pigeons carrying the message, "Whoever comes to my aid gets instant pardon and control of your land." They joined the mob that rescued the emperor and that was it. That is my father's family backdrop.

The family village, according to my parents, is just a little south of Shanghai Guan, the gateway of invasions in the Great Wall. They were sent there when the Great Wall was built. It was basically a military settlement, where the soldiers and their families would forever after defend China against the barbarian hordes on the other side of the gate. However, the Great Wall was not just a barrier. It was a customs control method. You were able to staff a much larger area across extremely mountainous terrain with a smaller number of troops manning watch towers. Then you could collect tariffs. People had to have passports. There is nothing like a literate bureaucracy. Eventually, people intermarried across the wall, and within a few generations my father's region of China was no longer rice-eating. They ate something called mantou, a steamed bread. You probably can find it downtown at Tony's Mongolian Barbecue. It looks like sort of a donut, except the hole isn't complete. The whole region developed a unique culture.

My father's family was basically agricultural. They owned their land. In the north of China, women were valued, as the hard life meant that men outnumbered women, and a man had to pay a bride price—usually land. So I grew up with all of the family legends, including role models of strong, independent women. My favorite was a member of Dad's family who was sent for an arranged marriage to a man in the south of China to seal a partnership. She journeyed there with her maids who were also her bodyguards—my guess is they were impressive lasses as northern Chinese are larger than southern Chinese (for example, my baby brother is six feet, four inches, and weighs two hundred pounds, and what I lack in height, I make up for in a solid build). Anyway, she arrived to find that she was not to be wife number one but a tertiary wife. Instead of either accepting it or committing suicide in protest, she and her maids beat up everyone in sight and marched back north with every item of value that they could carry. She went on to marry successfully in her own region, where no one would dare "dis" her by offering her an inferior position.

Q: Would you say the size difference was maybe because of the Mongolian stock?

JONES: Oh, I doubt it. There were people born with brown hair rather than black Chinese hair. You had to be generally pretty physically strong to survive. From what my father said of his uncles, he was the runt of the family at five feet, eight inches and 180 pounds of solid muscle. They also used their fists a lot. He grew up basically in Harbin, Manchuria, when his father, my grandfather, brought him into the city for an education. His father was the village success. The village paid for his father's education and he ceded all his inheritance to the rest of the family. His father eventually became one of the judges in what the Chinese call the northwest territory, which included Manchuria and was headquartered in Harbin, the territorial capital.

Q: Was the Dowager Empress the ruler at the time?

JONES: This was just a little after. China was already a republic. My parents always considered themselves followers of Sun Yat-sen but had no particular love for either Chiang Kai-shek (president of China at the time) or his Kuomintang (the National People's Party). In fact, my father had a bilingual education, as he was groomed from the start for a diplomatic career (this meant junior and high school and university study in both Russian and Chinese). His deal with his father was to finish this education, at which point his father would pay for his engineering training in Japan—but the Japanese invasion of Manchuria ended that alternative.

Q: Where did he get educated?

JONES: At Beijing University, my father got his degree bilingually in both Russian and Chinese. He could do a legal brief in Russian, and since Russian was taught by émigrés, his grammar was often superior to the Russian spoken and written in the Soviet Union. He spent a fair amount of time in the Soviet Union correcting the Soviets' Russian.

Q: Did you ever find out why he was trained in Russian?

JONES: That was the focus for the very far north of China, just as learning English was the focus for Chinese in Canton and Shanghai. Those were the people they dealt with much more, the people they saw. I was not surprised when the Chinese and the Russians had a falling out, since the only group of Chinese that actually knew Russia and spoke Russian well never got along with them well. Harbin was melting pot in which Russian-speaking and Chinese-speaking and Japanese-speaking street gangs lived to beat on each other.

Dad was pretty much assigned to diplomatic service. When Manchuria was taken, and right after he graduated from college in 1937 he was invited to serve in the Chinese Air Force to help Russian pilots train the Chinese. This was well before Flying Tigers were active. They flew ancient World War I vintage planes. My father wanted to be a pilot. If he had succeeded, I wouldn't be here because only two people survived in the original training class. He and his best friend both survived because they had washed out due to high blood pressure, which knocked them out during dives. Both did their tours as interpreters. They went from airfield to airfield in China.

We were told stories, like the Japanese bombing one of their airfields in the middle of the night. The whole group of them managed to leap out of their quarters, run across the airfield, vault over a wall for safety, but afterward none of them could crawl back over the wall, and it took two men to get my father back over the wall.

Q: How did your father move from the air force into the diplomatic service?

JONES: There were very few educated Chinese, so when they needed him in the Ministry of Foreign Affairs, he was told to join the diplomatic service. It was a very small service, especially the Russian speakers, who all knew each other. I think the Chinese ambassador to Moscow had been a professor of my father's at Beijing University. In late 1939, he was assigned to the Soviet Union. In the Chinese Foreign Service, you had to pay your family's travel expenses. He and my mother had married by that time. He was 25 and she was 20.

Her father was basically the equivalent of the assistant secretary for Russian affairs. But that had nothing to do with the marriage. In fact, while they were still in Peking [Beijing], their families had tried to arrange a marriage between them because the fathers knew each other; each of my parents screamed, "No! Over my dead body!" They were modern Chinese.

But as China lost more and more territory, the government moved to Chungking. My mother had to escape with her mother to the wartime capital, Chungking. There she met my father at a reception. She was a beautiful young woman and had no shortage of suitors, and she was used to admiration. When they met, instead of flowery compliments, his only statement was, "Don't tell me you are Fatso's daughter." Her father was the legendary fattest member of the Chinese Ministry of Foreign Affairs. He easily weighed in at 300 pounds and could only fly in American planes because he had to be able to get through the door.

Q: At this particular point, where was your parents' allegiance? Were they ardent Kuomintang supporters? How did this work?

JONES: They did not support Kuomintang. Basically, Kuomintang was the bulwark for people from Chiang Kai-shek's regime in China. Being a northerner, my father was definitely out of it. Politically, I would say they were original supporters of Sun Yat-sen, which was a slightly different focus and party. My father got in the Kuomintang's bad books when he refused their intelligence service's request to report on his colleagues. They did not think Chiang Kai-shek was personally corrupt, but he was surrounded by deeply corrupt officials and staff. At the same time, spending years in the Soviet Union and seeing Stalin's rule made them fervent opponents of communism.

Tashkent Time

After Novosibirsk, my father was sent to be the number-two person at the Chinese consulate general in Tashkent. I have only vague memories left of growing up in the Tashkent consulate general compound. The consul general was also named Chin and was also from Northern China. It was a busy post, as there were large numbers of Chinese, probably illegal laborers, who got into trouble with the Soviet government. For example, at that time it was the easiest thing in the world to obtain Soviet citizenship You went in to get a ration card, they put your thumb on a card, and they told you, "You are now a Soviet citizen." So there was a whole lot of pleading and begging at the consulate.

The area itself was strongly Muslim, and the locals often looked very Asian, probably as a result of centuries of Mongolian control. Even under Stalin, the crime rate was very high—for example, the policeman in front of the consulate gate was murdered. For security, the consulate bought a half wolf—half dog hybrid from the city zoo. Thus growing up, I had the strongest impression that dogs kept their tails between their legs and howled.

Q: Nothing like exposure to Stalinist Russia . . .

JONES: The Chinese Foreign Service tour was ten years, with rotations among the consulates. All I remember was that my father had also served at Khabarosk. Of course, he started in Moscow and went to Habarovsk because we have photos of me as a scrawny little one-and-a-half-year old. He arrived in Tashkent around 1944 and stayed until 1949, when we were declared persona non grata by the Soviets after the Chinese government fell in 1949. The first place he could get out was through Finland. From Helsinki you could to Sweden. Once we were in Sweden they were at a loss—the Chinese embassy in Sweden had also been abandoned by the government. There was no government left and no contact from the

Ministry of Foreign Affairs. They and the other Chinese diplomats who made it out of the Soviet Union at the same time were embittered by this. Their attitude was that a government that had abandoned them did not deserve any loyalty.

Q: *Do you recall your father's experience through tales you were getting or something else? All during this time people from the Republic of China, Chiang Kai-shek's regime, were in the Soviet Union while the Soviets were supporting the Communist Party of China, including Mao and others, and were sending agents there. How was this playing with the Chinese diplomats, watching their host country trying to subvert their own country?*

JONES: Chinese diplomats followed old and ancient traditions. From well before the time of the Warring States, which preceded the Qin emperor, envoys did their duties for their rulers as best as they could. The *Art of War*, by Sun Tzu, also stressed the importance of intelligence, and all diplomats were responsible for getting all the information they could and reporting honestly. I remember my father would go out into the hills, and talk to the various groups. Remember he was not only Russian speaking, he looked exactly like the locals and the locals liked him—at least they liked him better than the "white Russians" who represented Stalin's repression.

Q: *This was in Tashkent.*

JONES: Yes, Tashkent. They had very close relations to the different groups We still have photographs of my father wearing a ceremonial Cossack bandolier, and as a little kid I remember going with my father to different places. He often complained that he sent in endless reports of Soviet help to Chinese Communists across the Sino-Soviet border and they were all ignored. Stalin did not control Kazakhstan except in the cities through the commissars. For years, commissars met with unfortunate accidents if they did things the locals didn't like. It was a very Moslem society. The women wore chadors. It was very dangerous to be a policeman because thieves would disguise themselves with chadors. If you stopped a thief and you caught a man in a chador, you were a hero. If you were wrong, they cut your throat. I remember being with my mother when she personally caught a pickpocket. The wolf-dog turned out to be very effective in keeping theft down.

Q: *Did you learn to speak Tajik?*

JONES: I spoke Russian. By age seven, I had learned to read, write, and speak Russian. My parents tried to teach me Chinese, and I still speak Mandarin but forgot the ideograms as soon as I had memorized them. When we came to the United States, the focus was on learning English.

Q: Did you go to school while you were there?

JONES: No. The Soviets started school very late, age eight for kindergarten. I could have been put into a preschool, but my parents and the Chinese at the consulate had no desire to raise a group of little world communists. So, they hired tutors who usually had been tutors under the czar. I remember a very strict woman who had a hard hand with a yardstick if you didn't pay attention. But she taught us the basics.

We were a very small community—definitely not an American-style consulate. This is one where the offices and living quarters were pretty much one. The office was on the other side of the bedroom wall. There were no indoor toilet facilities and no running water. Winter or not, you either had your chamber pot or you galloped out to the outhouse in the yard.

It was an earthquake area, and there was one really severe earthquake that I remember. We were all saved by the huge old-fashioned brass bed. Everyone got under the bed, and then the ceiling came down. Almost 10,000 people died in a nearby town (Almaty). As diplomats, we were allotted about 500 grams of meat for a family of four each month, so to supplement our diet, the consulate turned to a sideline: raising chickens. The kids had a chance to watch all the hens and the two roosters, who gave us a cockfight a day—one rooster was too stupid not to challenge, and the other rooster was just strong enough to win the match but not destroy the opponent. We got rice from China, but as a result of corruption along the way, the 100 pounds of rice would arrive with 70 pounds of rice in it and 30 pounds of everything else. So the wives' diplomatic tea consisted of pouring the rice out on a huge table and picking the stones from rice grains.

Q: Do you recall your father and other members of the staff and the family following events particularly after the end of World War II, with the Chinese civil war and the long and slow collapse of the Republic of China, and wondering what was going to happen?

JONES: I have some scattered memories, or at least memories of what I was told. One time, Chiang Kai-shek's son visited the consulate general, which resulted in the death of a couple of extra chickens.

None of the quarters had kitchens. The kitchen was in the center of the courtyard and a Chinese cook did all the food preparation. He was invaluable, as was evident when he was hit by a car and couldn't work for a couple of months. The wives had to put their hands to cooking. This meant using the old-fashioned, wood-fired stove, where your little stove lid weighed about ten pounds. Indeed, I will say that massive indigestion occurred, as all these women who had never cooked in their lives tried different things. I still remember a lady trying to make dim sum (gyoza), where you have to make the dough that's rolled into little wrappers for the dim sum. In her case, she added a little water. It was too watery so she added more flour. Then it was too dry so she added more water. Eventually it took three strong men to roll a hunk of batter that was the size of a human torso. The collective farm system meant that there was never any food in the stores. The markets had food grown on little private plots, but that was really expensive. The official exchange rate had no relationship to the real exchange rate. If it were not for the rubles that the Chinese locals exchanged for U.S. dollars, we would never have been able to afford the bazaar prices.

We saw lots of drunks in diplomatic entertaining. In fact, I forgot to mention that as a kid I remember seeing them set the table for the diplomatic entertaining. No women involved. They had a bottle at each place setting for the entertaining. As my father described it, they would toast the friendship between the countries, they would start by toasting friendship between the countries, and eventually the toasts would descend to Stalin's body parts. By then half of them were under the table. The kids always ran around looking for Mr. Hu to be carried out first, as he weighed about 115 pounds. My father, however, and the consul, being northern Chinese, had been weaned on this Chinese moonshine, called Kaoliang wine (eighty proof). The only time I tasted it, I thought it was kerosene.

I just remember some childhood events. It was not a terribly healthy place. At one point, they found that there was an infestation of lice of every conceivable sort, body, hair. The Chinese solution was to shave everyone's head, boy or girl, and DDT everything—the rooms, the house, the bedding, the people. We still have a picture of me as a very short-haired kid.

Local hygiene was tricky because a lot of the women believed in washing their hair with buttermilk—glossy hair, but enough to gag one downwind. In order to avoid diplomatic incidents caused by ordering consulate employees to change these habits, they offered the maids free perms. They bribed one of the former pre-Communist-regime hairdressers (a few pounds of sugar did the trick, and he cut their hair, washed it, and permed it. To keep their lovely new hairdos, they had to wash often, and no buttermilk. My child's-eye view of Chinese diplomatic life was very different.

Q: Did you have little Kazakh kids to play with you?

JONES: No, we played with each other. I still remember losing a fight and coming crying to my parents. My father's comment was, "You have teeth, don't you?" So the next time he picked on me, I bit him, and after that we got along.

Communist Takeover of China—Escape from Russia

Q: Then you were moved and sent off to Finland, and then off to Sweden. For a kid, this must have been pretty traumatic, wasn't it?

JONES: No, it's not traumatic if you are with your parents and they say OK, it is time to go. Remember, my standard of living was improved by going to Sweden. I remember being curious about going back to China. China didn't exist for me. I was born in the Soviet Union. My baby brother was born in Tashkent. In fact, he was named after the doctor that told my mother that, given her peritonitis, she would never be able to have children. My brother was named was Nikolai Ivanovich Chin. It is now Nicholas Chin.

I just remember a very long train ride, plus having all of your clothes tied at the ankles and wrists—keeps the train's bedbugs off of you. We ended up at a plane. I remember the plane to Helsinki because it had no heat. It was a converted World War II military plane. I remember a group of Russians dressed in heavy fur coats building a little fire on the plane so that they could keep themselves warm. Then, of course, in Helsinki we went on a Swedish plane. As the Chinese government had paid my father in U.S. dollars and he had an account in Switzerland for his savings, we had survival funds. The government took care of everything, as the Soviet infrastructure was both unusable and untrustworthy.

Q: When you say "the government," it was . . .

JONES: The Chinese government. It was owned by the Chinese government. The whole consulate set of buildings and yard. This is a more Middle Eastern—looking structure. All I remember is the extremely high wall surrounding the inner courtyard. Once we even met an American diplomat who was traveling through. My father actually still remembers his name. The only common language they had was Russian. He had just barely enough Russian to communicate with the Chinese. They don't remember anything about him, except that he was a jolly sort. He also borrowed some money from the consul general. I don't think he ever repaid it. So that was it.

Interlude in Sweden—and then to the United States

Q: So what happened you were in Sweden for a while?

JONES: We waited almost a year for news, for permission, or for orders. Finally, we were issued transit visas to the United States. If things didn't work out, my parents planned to try to reach Hong Kong; but on the trip over, the Korean War started and Taiwan was still incommunicado and a mess, so New York City it was. We left from Oslo on a freighter called the *Mormarcrio* (10,000 tons). I still remember that trip because my brother got into the toilet paper and we had toilet paper streamers all over the ship.

Q: Then where did you go in the United States? This would have been . . .

JONES: 1950. We arrived on 4th of July weekend. We had friends, the former consul general at Tashkent had already come to the United States. He had cashed in all of his family wealth, and signed some sort of a deal for an apartment. Everyone thought that he was horribly taken advantage of because he paid $30,000 for a ninety-year lease on this apartment in Riverside Drive, which had I think four bedrooms, three bathrooms, servant's quarters, the works. Then later they forced him to buy it for another $10,000. We then managed to find someplace to stay while my father ran around trying to figure out what to do. I remember all of us staying in one room in an apartment in the West Riverside Drive area.

Q: Well, there was the . . .

JONES: He couldn't go back to China.

Q: But Taiwan had diplomatic relations with the Americans.

JONES: Yes, except there was no place for anyone, and by then they had started shooting people in mainland China. People in my father's family were executed by people's courts because they had owned a few acres of land. My father was very lucky that he was ejected from the Soviet Union. Some of his colleagues never made it out and were never heard of again. I still have a copy of a picture, which includes one of "a communist spy" in their midst. She was, by the way, the only woman with a figure and nicely dressed, and she later married a very high-level Communist official and even became a [government] minister. The ones that came to the United States had all lost family members. The person whom I remember most was Mr. Hu, the communicator, or telegraph operator. His father and brother had been shot in China. A Mr. Liu also came to New York, also a Russian-speaking Chinese.

My parents had to learn English. My mother worked in a jewelry factory in New York while my father scouted out possibilities. It was a factory where she glued fake pearls to earring backs. Eventually my father got a driver's license and bought a black 1950 Plymouth, which was absolutely the ugliest car I have ever seen. My father learned to pilot it in eight hours of lessons, and passed the driver's exam. Then he drove to New Jersey and bought a chicken farm in Dorothy, New Jersey. So we moved there. We were like aliens from outer space, with no fellow Asians in the area, but, fortunately, there was a community of Russian-speaking Orthodox Jews there who helped us settle.

Growing up in America—New Jersey Style

Q: How about you? When did you move to New Jersey?

JONES: In 1950 we arrived. It was July. My birthday is in November, so I was eight and a half when we arrived. We moved to New Jersey within a year, eight or nine months later after arriving in New York.

Q: Well, during this year and a half what you are doing? You have not had any formal education.

JONES: I had tutoring in Russian while in Russia. While we were in Sweden, my mother continued teaching us in Chinese, and teaching us mathematics. In New York, they took me to the public school, which was just across Broadway. That is the only thing I remember of it. My mother asked, "Should she be put in first grade?" They said, "Well she is too old." So they put me in third grade. I learned English in about three months. After about three months, I was put into fourth grade. I still remember that the school was in such bad shape, you went up and down the fire escapes after classes because the hallways weren't always passable. I remember very nice teachers, and ended up with a serious New York accent as a result. The kinds were a mixed group. Chinese kids get a lot more math at any age, so I never had a problem with the math. Learning English was fairly difficult, and I got into a fair number of fights because the Chinese upbringing I had was not the pacifist type. It was the northern, make yourself heard with a baseball bat if you have to.

But once we were in Dorothy, New Jersey, we went to the local middle school and to the local junior high. My father farmed, and had the chicken farm for several years. Remember the Korean War had started. My parents came from the generation that expected World War III any time—especially since they knew what the Soviets were like and how aggressive the Soviets were. That was why they had left Sweden. It was just too close to the Soviet Union. Plus my mother didn't want us to become little Swedes. Nothing against the Swedish, but she was bothered by the fact that she would see Swedish drunks drinking alone at the bars—very different from the loud Russian drunks.

Q: Ok, you are now in New Jersey. How long, from when to when, were you in New Jersey?

JONES: We got there, I am sure, in '52. Actually we stayed in New Jersey, though we moved from Dorothy to Buena Vista and then to Vineland in '56. In '59, I finished high school. I got a scholarship for a chemistry degree at the University of Pennsylvania and went on from there. I had chosen what they call an "iron rice bowl" career—hopefully war and recession proof.

Q: OK, we will go to '52 then. When you start, it is '52 to '59.

JONES: My father's brains were not affected by his lack of English, and he could spot economic trends. As soon as I could read the *Wall Street Journal*, I would help translate it. He began investing in the early '50s. He saw that after the Korean War, the farms were going to have trouble. He sold the farm then, and he and my mother both worked at Kimble Glass (now Owens-Illinois) making laboratory glassware. First he worked four shifts, and later it was three. My mother did two shifts until, finally, she joined the packing department. She continued working there until I was almost finished with college. Then, when she thought she had acquired enough English to go back to school, she did so and got a nursing degree.

Q: Let's talk about school early on. You say there was an Orthodox Jewish community in the area. How was school? Were they Orthodox in the school?

JONES: It was a standard public school and a very small town so that the post office, the mayor, the gas station, the only grocery were one building. I had no idea what Orthodox really meant at that point.

Q: What was the name of the place?

JONES: Dorothy, New Jersey. Now it is a bit larger. The farms averaged ten to fifteen acres.

Q: Is this the famous truck gardens area?

JONES: No, this was a chicken farm area, with lots and lots of chickens, and corn for the chickens. The school was about a mile walk from our house. The schoolhouse was so small that two grades would share a room. I think it stopped at fourth grade, because for fifth and sixth grades I went to Belcoville by bus. For junior high, I attended J. P. Cleary Junior High in

Buena Vista. There, one teacher made all the difference. I was still a slow reader in English. An English teacher, Orlando Canale, who was learning how to teach speed-reading, noticed I was moving my lips when I read. So he took it upon himself to teach me speed-reading as he studied it himself. At the end of a year of extra lessons, I had achieved an average of about 600 to 700 words a minute with about 90 percent comprehension. That made all the difference.

Q: This was in high school?

JONES: Not yet. I was in seventh grade.

Q: Let's go back even before then. How did you find the teaching and the students in this small town with two classes in a room?

JONES: Quite sufficient. Basically, first I am Chinese, and Chinese kids are taught to be very respectful of teachers because education was your only hope. This is an attitude set from a millennia of history and an educated bureaucracy, and based on that great Chinese examination system. The teachers were good, and I absorbed the material. My parents kept wondering why there wasn't any homework, because there wasn't. I didn't even notice math was really anything until I got algebra, and then it was kind of fun.

Q: How about the student body?

JONES: Kids, farm kids. I remember one family that was very poor. Not a single one of them had clothes that fit, and people would regularly donate clothes to them. There was a Russian émigré family, the Valentines. The son and daughter were very nice kids; they taught me to play musical chairs.

Q: Did you find that being Chinese made it that different? I mean, was it such a mix that the kids didn't focus on this at all?

JONES: They didn't much. I will say that in high school it made somewhat more difference. In junior high, there were a couple of kids that decided to pick on me, and there was some nasty stuff written on blackboards. I thought it wasn't worth it to bother my parents. Despite my small size, I slammed the ringleader into a locker and said that it wasn't going to be fun to pick on me, because even if I died doing it, I was going to fight back. After that, they found other prey. Unfortunately, one of the kids they found to pick on was a Jewish kid called Richard Yanowitz. Now, I was small, but he was even smaller than I was, a skinny, freckled kid who was very bright. After they found out it wasn't any fun picking on me—it was more or less like picking on a Rottweiler—they did horrible things to him. Years later, I think he still had the scars. Even though he went on to university, he washed out. I heard that later he had all sorts of problems.

Sometimes it's easier knowing you are indeed different. My parents told us: "You are different. You are a different race. You are a different culture. You are going to start all over again." My father said his career problems were not his fault, and that was his comfort. The only thing we had was intelligence. You would always be welcome when you specialized in areas such as medicine, science and engineering, where they needed your skills. Knowing that I was different made it easier to adapt and to keep what I wanted of my own culture. I did have a bit of luck, as I followed a family pattern of maturing very slowly, very late, and very, very gradually. As a result, in high school I was not bothered by the hormonal storms that were wiping out my classmates. A good half of them had to get married after high school. It made it easier to concentrate on whatever I wanted to. Slow maturation made it very much easier to focus on physics problems.

The Role of Religion in Chinese Life

Q: In the first place, did you grow up with a religion?

JONES: Not really. My parents were basically agnostic Confucians. That means that they believed that there probably was a God, but they figured that as God created everything, he was above all these little squabbles. Chinese don't have a history normally of killing each other for religion. It was normal to kill for land, wealth, revenge, or domination. They were familiar with Buddhism, which they explained to me, but which my father and mother felt was too negative a religion. To them, Buddhism was a way to explain the inequities and injustices of life, and to convince you to take it until the next time around. They had great respect for Christianity based on what they saw in China. They described parts of China so poor that the people didn't even have dogs. Even there, the Catholics had set up orphanages.

The Chinese had more problems with Protestants, because my parents had been raised in a culture of celibate clergy. The idea is if you devote your life to something, then devote your life to something. They could not see how someone who had family responsibilities could actually give to God what was necessary and still care for the family. Remember, Chinese family obligations were very strong and demanding. So if you were a minister and had a son, they couldn't see how you couldn't favor your own son, because that is what you were supposed to do. Therefore, it made reconciling your religious sermons and your private lives difficult. There was a certain humor too.

According to my mother her family had a rotating altar at the entryway depending on the religion of the guest, just to be polite. This is the same spirit that leads to Hong Kong weddings with six religions officiating. They never got the various denominations straight. It took them years to get Jews and Christians straight.

In one anecdote, a Methodist bishop was giving a talk in quite good Chinese—in fact, even deceptively good Chinese—but every once in a while he would slip up. The Chinese thought his mastery of the tones was very good. He was a hell-and-damnation type of preacher and said, "And Christ will march to victory at the head of the banners of heaven." Manchu military units followed banners (similar to the Roman eagles). Well, the Chinese term for concubines is "tzidze" (high tone) and the Chinese term for banners was "tzidze" (low tone), so what the Chinese heard was Christ will march to victory at the head of the concubines of heaven. So they asked, "We didn't know you were that liberal. How many?" And he said, "Thousands." Well, he may have made converts, but it sure confused a whole lot of Chinese.

We had a very strong Confucian ethical background. Confucius had the view that if you are a human being, you act like you have certain duties, responsibilities. Honor is very important. Honesty is very important. My mother transmitted Chinese culture to me with the usual tales. In fact, I have written a book, *Tales of the Monkey King*, based on the stories she told my brother and me and our children.

Judaism they understood as a contract between God and the tribes. So whatever the contract required, that was fine with them. They were neither pro—nor anti-Semitic, and liked or disliked people pretty much on the basis of what they were like rather than the group to which they belonged. They had a vague understanding of Christianity. As for Catholics, they understood the structure of the religion but thought the pope was nuts on birth control. Both my brother and I went to a local Methodist Sunday school because our mother wanted us to learn a little more about Christianity in the culture. We got a little ticket for attendance, and if you got enough tickets you got a free Bible. My brother won all the tickets available in some incredible game of marbles and still has that Bible.

I believed that a good person would do good deeds and their duty not because of heaven or hell, but because that was human.

Chinese History and Folklore

Q: So there weren't family gods or something like this around?

JONES: Oh no, my parents were rebels of their generation. They thought that China had been held back severely by its attitudes. The Opium War and the Boxer Rebellion were wake up calls. They were very much for modernization. My father was strong on women being able to take care of themselves. My mother was certainly able to take care of herself. After all, at the age of sixteen, my mother was able to make it from Beijing to Chungking with her my grandmother in a 2,500-mile river boat trip. She was not the pampered darling of the family, although her father, my grandfather, did well. He (my maternal grandfather) took a Russian wife and tried to abandon my grandmother, his Chinese wife and his daughter (my mother), except that his mother, my grandmother's mother-in-law, refused to let him. He gave them an allowance, which according to my mother was approximately what fed the family dog—a pampered pet.

All I can say is that my family had scholars on both sides, so that my brother and I inherited great test-taking genes, which we passed on to our children. Along with that, we probably lost all entrepreneurial and money-making genes.

Q: Were you getting through the family a feeling—I don't know how to put this, because I don't mean it in a pejorative sense—that the Chinese were almost a chosen race? Not a master race—that is a bad term—but, in other words, a superior race? Was there feeling that Chinese were better, or not. Were you picking up any of that?

JONES: It was an odd mixture. No, we were not taught Chinese were racially superior or inferior, because basically that isn't something for which we could take credit. We are born what we are born. An evil person did evil, regardless of ethnic background; a good person did good deeds. My parents were very strong on what you achieve. They thought the Chinese patterns of behavior were civilized and, like other Chinese of their class, they willing to accept anyone as equal or superior to Chinese, depending on their behavior.

This is historical. There was a person called Matteo Ricci, who was a Jesuit missionary sent to convert the Chinese. He had such tremendous success that his actual writings are still in Chinese archives (under the Chinese name Li Madou); he was accepted because he had turned into a Chinese mandarin. This created a problem for the pope, who found the Jesuits were becoming more Chinese and less Jesuit. The next missionaries he sent were Dominicans, which is why the Chinese are not all Catholics. If they had kept it up with the Jesuits, there was a chance there would have been a Catholic China.

There was respect for certain behavior patterns, for certain attitudes, a value for education. There was the recognition that life isn't that easy, so you have to use what assets you had. At the same time, you had to make an ethical choice. Things like the *Art of War,* by Sun Tzu, are taught as children's stories.

For example, good manners are taught with the tale of a ferocious war leader who was assassinated by his tailor because lost his temper; he yelled at and terrified his tailor so much that the tailor stabbed him. Their ideas were well in line with the Biblical admonition to be gentle as doves and as wise as serpents. Of course, as for stories of diplomatic derring-do, all through Chinese history there are thousands of examples of people who were able to save themselves and others by using their intelligence and understanding of the human mind.

My favorite is an instance when, long, long, ago, an emperor told the newly named district magistrate to stop human sacrifice in an area of China where the rivers flooded every year. And every year the locals would get young men and women, bedeck them in jewels, and toss them in. But the emperor couldn't use force to change their ways, as he had no troops to send. The magistrate's solution was very elegant. He went to the villages and asked, "Have you been doing this a long time?" They answered, "As far as man can remember, for centuries." Then he asked, "Do the rivers flood?" "Oh yes, the rivers have flooded every year," they replied. He said: "You are obviously sending the wrong kind of men and women. How do you know what the river god likes? Did he ever come out and tell you?" "No," they answered. He said, "Well, send the priests." He ordered all the priests tossed in. At about the halfway point, the surviving priests confessed they had been taking the jewels. That was an elegant solution.

Q: Did any literature—I use the term very broadly—that is, any genre or books, particularly strike you as a young girl?

JONES: We had the standard texts: *Ivanhoe, Tale of Two Cities,* and much Shakespeare. I think we had *Romeo and Juliet, Julius Caesar, Hamlet,* and *Macbeth.* I vaguely remember thinking Romeo and Juliet were idiots. You have to remember, I was headed for science. I liked the other plays. I liked Dickens, and actually read several Dickens books. Then I hit *Pickwick Papers* and decided this was written for people from outer space, not me. At age fifteen, I discovered Agatha Christie, Robert Heinlein (science fiction), and *Scientific American.* I was a library hound.

Q: Did you have a Carnegie library?

JONES: Yes, in Vineland, New Jersey, not more than a mile and a half from our house, so I could walk to it. We always took out the maximum limit of books, but I read a lot of science books also.

Q: Did any particular things in science interest you? I am talking about as a young kid.

JONES: I started with astronomy. Kids often start with astronomy. I liked biology, and I placed eighth in a New Jersey contest on it ages ago. I enjoyed it. I wanted something where I could think originally. Physics I enjoyed, but didn't have an instinct for it. Chemistry seemed to me the perfect science: It had enough theory, it had enough mathematics and logic and order, and enough strange stuff. It was also extremely practical, with direct industrial and manufacturing applications. As I said earlier, I was a descendant of test takers, and my college boards showed that mathematics and science were my strong suits. I was good in English, but I never felt any interest in continuing in it—it was not enough of an iron rice bowl.

Q: You might explain for someone reading this what you mean by "iron rice bowl."

JONES: OK. In China, your way of making a living is called your rice bowl. It is how you feed yourself. If you can only make your living by, let's say, sheer labor and have no special skills, then you have a clay rice bowl—one that is easily shattered. In a society which has a long history of wars, revolutions, natural disasters, an iron rice bowl is one where you carry your skills with you. The skills could be medicine, science, engineering, anything in demand and hard to master, a harder-to-shatter rice bowl. The term is similar to the Chinese for strong-minded females: "steel butterflies."

Thinking of Politics and Nixon's Opening to China

Q: Well, I often use the term, as when somebody comes in and proposes something, you have to be careful that you are not breaking too many rice bowls. You are upsetting the order of things, and you'd better have something effective. I was just wondering whether your parents, when they got into American society early on, did they have any political party favorites or not?

JONES: Oh yes. They are lifelong Republicans, because they felt they owed Richard Nixon for the opening to China. Until Nixon resumed contacts with China, it was illegal for Chinese to send money to their relatives. My mother still had a mother in China who certainly would have starved to death. The only thing she could do was to contact Chinese in New York City who were friends of friends. They had relatives who did business in Hong Kong and so had renminbi (Chinese Yuan) bank accounts. She would hand U.S. dollars to them for the relatives and ask for their help to keep an elderly woman from starving to death, and so earn merit in heaven. She never asked what commission they took, if any, but she kept her mother alive. She had letters from her mother saying that they were all right for that month. It was not just her mother, as her mother had adopted another relative's abandoned daughter and was raising her.

My parents also felt very strongly that the United States was not as wise as it should be in dealing with China. China could be a counterweight to the Soviet Union. My father was probably as anti-Communist as you could be.

When Nixon opened to China, they said, "This is a man who knows what he is doing." Also when they came to the United States in 1950, the most anti-immigrant, anti-Chinese people were the Democrats. People have forgotten that, as Democrats are very liberal today. Then, they were the ones who spoke of the "yellow terror." In 1950, people in the New York City subway would catcall my father, as they saw no difference between the different kinds of Asians.

When I was a senior in high school, I was interviewed for the university by a local Irish-American businessman who told me that when he was a kid, he and his friends used to chase after a Chinese laundry man, calling him names. Now he saw it as proof of how stupid children can be. I also think that he compensated by giving me a rave review that got me a scholarship to Penn.

I also learned that if you brood on your wrongs or on your slights, there is no way to move ahead. My parents basically taught us that if someone calls you a Chink, get over it—the best comeback is success. Perspective is important. Chinese saw quite enough bias by Chinese against other Chinese, or blacks against blacks, or Welsh against Welsh. In Vineland, New Jersey, you had Puerto Rican farmhands who, while legal and U.S. citizens, were still exploited by the local chicken farmers. You had families of blacks. You had poor whites. History has enough examples—think of the Protestant-Catholic conflicts.

Vineland was an Italian-American town. The local lore is that in the 1900s the Poles and the Italians had it out in Junior Police Field, and the Italians won Vineland and the Poles won Millville, leading to an eternal football rivalry between the high schools. At the school, I had wonderful teachers. I had friends. In fact, some of my friends (a pair of Polish-German American twin girls) felt more left out than I did. I knew I was different, so I didn't expect to be in the local social and dating circles, but they really felt ostracized. Remember, I didn't date. I wasn't interested in dating, and my parents really wanted me to concentrate on my studies.

CHAPTER 2

Academics and the University of Pennsylvania (1959-1966)

Q: What about chemistry? Coming out of rural New Jersey, I wouldn't think you would get the best chemical training.

JONES: The U.S. education system was wonderful as the great equalizer. The high school principal was a woman named Miss Rossi. She had dedicated her life to Vineland High School, which had about four hundred students with about thirty-five college prep students. She made sure that the chemistry teachers, the physics teachers, and the math teachers had master's degrees in their field. She wasn't going to take second best. We entered every state contest there was. I think I placed in every field, chemistry, biology, and physics. The teachers often used college textbooks to strengthen our background. So when I got to the University of Pennsylvania, it was no problem at all.

Q: You were at the University of Pennsylvania from 1959.

JONES: Nineteen hundred fifty-nine through 1963 for undergraduate, but when I was in undergraduate school, I took a year of graduate work.

Why Penn?

Q: Let's talk about the University of Pennsylvania now. When you got there in 1959, what was it like? I mean how did you see it?

JONES: It was a very good environment, especially for a woman, because I was in the women's dorms. The college for women was separate from the college for men, not for classes but administratively. We were told that we had higher SATs than the college for men. The other women were not there to get their "MRS." It was also very international. We had a couple of Hong Kong students who were really amazing. We had a layer of old Philadelphia, but I was there after Grace Kelly and her sisters had been students.

Friends and Studies at Penn

Q: The Kellys came from mainline Philadelphia. Well, they weren't really mainline, they were Irish upstarts.

JONES: True, Kelly Construction parking garages at least didn't collapse. I found friends. I never joined a sorority, because I was never interested. You have to remember the BS chemistry program was so rigid—I could have graduated after two and a half years if you just counted courses. We had a lot of lab work. Of course, I had close friends in the chemistry group. We started with five women and ninety-five men. We graduated five women and ten men. I met Dave right at the start. He was a buddy first.

Q: He is your husband. What is his middle initial?

JONES: T. David Taylor Jones. Right after I met him, he told me it was like Davey Jones's locker. I thought of him as David Locker for weeks. For freshman year, I promised my parents to date only Chinese kids, but it turned out that I had turned into an American in the interim and was a bit too much of a chemist for the lads.

Q: Did you concentrate in the field of chemistry?

JONES: Yes. I selected a graduate adviser who was the youngest professor—a man called Ed Thornton—and who specialized in physical organic chemistry, a new field which applied physical chemistry thinking methods to organic problems. I liked organic and I liked physical chemistry, and this way I didn't have to choose.

Q: Were you pointed toward anything?

JONES: Not really, except for the bias in favor of an iron rice bowl. The idea was that you do best what you do best at. My parents had just one rule, because you have no idea what your kids are going to be good at. So they came up with the idea that whatever it is, just do your best at it, even if it is going to be the best hairdresser in Vineland. They also recognized, though, that Vineland was a small town where being related to someone made a big difference. It was probably easier, in fact, to get a degree in neurosurgery than to get into the Plumbers Union, unless you had an uncle in the union. So they felt that we had to leave Vineland to succeed. The university was wonderful. I had a full scholarship, plus I had a scholarship from the high school, so I think my parents were out of pocket $300 a year for my university education.

Q: In high school and in university, did you have summer jobs or evening jobs or anything like that?

JONES: I did. The first summer before college and the first year of college, I worked at a local food-flavoring firm in Vineland called Limpert Brothers. They had one chemist who needed an assistant. He was a huge, humongous Swede, who probably could have lived until 110 except that he drank, the result (he said) of having married the hardest heart and the prettiest ankles in New York City. We did flavoring research, which gave him an excuse to order a lot of absolute ethanol for use as a solvent. He used some for experiments and some for his drink mixes. The only books he had around were Samuel Pepys's diaries. As I watched different experiments, I got a chance to read all about the plague in London.

Later, I had other summer jobs. I had the standard lab tech jobs at American Cyanamid and Atlantic Refining. I did well and ended up first in the Penn chemistry program at the end of four years. I also had a teaching fellowship at Penn, so it was easy to just continue there, especially since David was still there and we were engaged.

I was so glad I chose Penn, although I had scholarship offers from MIT [Massachusetts Institute of Technology], where I would have been one of seventeen females cloistered in a special dorm. I turned down Barnard, as they required zoology for a chemistry degree and I disagreed. Penn may not be the most glamorous of the Ivies, but it retained some of the original Ben Franklin ethic there. It was much more relaxed about a lot of things. Penn and Columbia were among the first Ivies to admit Chinese. So among the Chinese community, they had a much higher reputation than Harvard or Princeton and Yale because they had a reputation of fairness.

On to the PhD

Q: As you were doing this and looking around, irrespective of the Chinese factor, what about the female factor? Were you feeling that the cards were stacked against women, particularly in the sciences and things like that?

JONES: No, actually when I was a graduate student, I was in a group with five women in a graduate research group of twelve. All five of us got our PhDs within two years of each other. One day, we just sat around talking about being women PhD candidates in chemistry. We were all very different personalities. One could have been a concert pianist, one could take your car apart and rebuild it, one could have been a fashion model and was a married fashionista with a child. What we had in common was the conviction that we would be good at chemistry. The nicest thing about science is that you could prove you belonged by being good at it. When you got 100, you got 100—they couldn't take it away from you. We all passed our graduate prelim exams one after another and that was it. If guys wanted to complain about it, they could complain all they wanted, but it didn't change our abilities. We quickly worked out a division of labor for the lab.

Keep in mind that American graduate students do their own glass work, their own welding, and their own soldering. It might be harder for the women to move nitrogen tanks, but we could do it with the right equipment. But if you had a colleague who was having a desperately hard time attaching glass joints to each other, we could trade. All the women seemed to do better than the men at the fine glass work. It was pre—women's lib movement, and we were all less self conscious about feminism, self realization, and whatnot. And if someone stepped out of line, it was up to the target, female or not, to make clear objections. Every once in a while, we had someone who did step out of line. There would be a ferocious reaction, the male body parts would be re-glued, and life would continue. But science graduate students are not like humanities graduate students in one way. Basically, humanities graduate students, like Dave's fellow political science and international relations graduate students, all competed against each other. For science, we had problems to fight, the things that would keep us from getting our doctorates, so we helped each other much more. In the end, we pretty much typed each other's dissertations, including helping with the English for foreign students. In one case, we each did one chapter, and so the student ended with a dissertation of eleven chapters written in eleven different styles.

Q: I don't run across many people in higher science in doing these interviews because of the nature of the Foreign Service. What did you do your dissertation on?

JONES: The dissertation was on the solvolysis mechanism of methyl chloralmethyl ether. In other words, when something reacts with a solvent, it's easier to model it mathematically, as the solvent molecules are overwhelmingly more numerous than the reactant, so you can count its concentration as a constant. Normally, when you try to do a study of two things reacting, you have to follow through time the changes in concentration and so on of two elements. By putting it into a solution and using the solution as one of the reactants, you make it easier on yourself—a sort of kung fu of the mind. We had certain theories on how something happened. In order to determine if the model was correct, I replaced the hydrogen atoms with the deuterium atoms. Because deuterium is twice the molecular weight of hydrogen, it means all the molecular vibrations are different, just as it would be if you had a violin string and put a weight on it. I had a National Institutes of Health fellowship for my research, so I was an instructor for just one year. As an instructor, I had my first run-in with a different culture. I had a Turkish student who refused to admit he was being taught by a woman—I was "Mister Chin" to him for the entire course. He also always wanted to negotiate the grades, but didn't like my policy of regrading an entire test and not just one question.

I had another student who was a Black Panther, full Afro, attitude, and sandals. I got him out of the sandals by asking him if he really wanted to replace all of his toenails after they rotted off when the lye spilled on them. I finally had to take him to one side and said: "Look whatever my ancestors did, they didn't do it to your ancestors. Whatever your ancestors did, they didn't do it to mine. So I have nothing to do with all of this, and if everyone else in the world disappeared, I don't think you want to give up penicillin, plastic, steel, alloys. The point is learning these skills. I don't care about the rest of it." Actually, he turned out to be pretty good.

Q: Then you got your PhD when?

JONES: I got my PhD in November of 1966. I had to get it a little bit earlier because I had a job lined up in the Department of Agriculture. The government was a stickler for having the degree first. They wouldn't hire me at the pre-PhD level and then wait a semester. I didn't bother going to the graduation in May because I had a set of experiments to finish.

Q: Did you mention the Black Panthers? Did the winds of the civil rights movement and affect you? Was the chemistry department sheltered or out of the loop?

JONES: No. We had two African-American graduate students in our group, Al Smith and Malcolm Pope, just on my floor. They were very different personalities. Malcolm Pope was difficult, pushy aggressive, a classic male chauvinist and a fantastic chemist. He got total respect, no doubt about it. Because if he was right and you were wrong, he would stuff it up your nose with a smile. Al was much more genial. He had been in the Air Force. He had much more people skills. He had more problems with the chemistry, as he had been out of college a while.

The Penn system required you to pass a cumulative exam in your field on anything in your field, and to be accepted as a PhD candidate, you had to pass seven or you failed. This meant that in addition to the graduate courses you took, you read like a maniac in everything in your field. There was no assurance that you could get away with just knowing organic chemistry. You had to know heterocyclic chemistry. You had to know polymer chemistry. You had to know all sorts of physical chemistry. Al was close to not making it, and filed a civil rights action. He had flunked six cumulative exams. So the seventh one was going to be the determining one. The particular professor who gave the next one shelved the issue by passing everyone—no names on the exams.

In the women's dorms, we had one African-American girl who, like me, was a scholarship kid; her name was Inez Qualles. She was warm and friendly, and she was a skillful seamstress who made extra money with her tailoring skills. There would be a line ten people long in front of her door before any kind of dance. She became a teacher. There was another one, Muriel Garland, who was a short, feisty, very dark African American, one who had finished all of her chemical engineering requirements in three years. She was brilliant, as smart as she was difficult. Her favorite ploy was to tell gross anatomy stories at the dorm dinner table where we ate family style. She then got the dessert servings of her nauseated tablemates.

Muriel and I got along. I met her because she had a radio that played too loud, so I told her I couldn't stand it, and she had better turn it down or I was going to smash her radio. She said, "You know, you talk to me like a person." I said, "Of course I talk to you like a person. You are." She said she got so tired of people tiptoeing around her being nice to the poor little black kid. She would rather be disliked for herself. Thus, we became friends.

The Political Scene in the 1960s

Q: You were there during the election in 1960 between Kennedy and Nixon. Did you get caught up in this at all?

JONES: Only to the extent that I stood on the sidewalk looking like everyone else when Nixon's motorcade went by. I may have been there when Kennedy's came by. The way people seemed to idolize Kennedy bothered me. I guess I had an ingrained suspicion of following any charismatic leader, especially of having family dynasties. China had 4,000 years of bad family dynasties. I was also opposed to any hereditary aristocracy, as were my parents. We were raised with that. In an old Chinese folk tale, there was a man who was the son of a shoemaker who became a duke. People made fun of his very humble origins. He said, "Look, which is better? To be a duke who is the son of a shoemaker, or the other way around?"

Q: So, on this, I take it you came around out of the whole educational side with a very positive attitude.

JONES: Absolutely. Oh, we did have Vietnam War protesters. The head of the department was a Quaker—Charles Price, president of the American Chemical Society. He had worked at Oak Ridge National Laboratory on the atom bomb project. Though a Quaker, he said no one was going to have any rights as a Quaker if we lost WWII. He patented a lot of things, so he was quite a wealthy man and had a yacht, which his graduate students enjoyed. At the time, the organic chemistry department was considering whether to accept an army project to develop better incapacitants, that is, chemicals that allowed you to avoid shooting people in tunnels, as they would be so dizzy puking out their guts you could capture them. So in some ways, it was considered humane. About seventy students decided to oppose this. Until the TV cameras showed up, they sat around, and then they went around in circles with big signs accusing the chemistry department of killing babies and so on. Marching in a circle allowed the cameras to fool the audience as to the actual number of protesters. Charles Price was so mad at the demonstrators, he not only accepted that Army project, he accepted six others.

But Penn was not an activist campus; it definitely was not like Berkeley. The students were pretty wrapped up in their own affairs. We lost friends in the Vietnam War, and I thought the treatment meted to the Nam vets was shameful. I married on December 12, 1964, just a month before my husband was sent to Korea. He went right after his master's degree in international relations. He had passed the Foreign Service exam as a senior and was all set on his future career. We married very quickly, with just a month of preparation, so that I would be covered by all the military spousal benefits before he went to Korea. I just continued my graduate work, no distractions.

CHAPTER 3

Working for the Department of Agriculture (1966-1968)

Tobacco Labs in Philadelphia

Q: Then you graduated and got your PhD and immediately went to work for the government.

JONES: Yes, for the Department of Agriculture in Wyndmoor on the outskirts of Philadelphia in something called the pyrolysis lab, where they looked at the mechanisms behind what was produced in tobacco smoke. We tried to identify the specific mechanisms that produced the various carcinogens. Most people don't realize this, but you can get the same lung cancer if you smoked dried lettuce. It is not the tobacco plant. It is the smoke from burning plant material. You could smoke wood chips. You could smoke rutabaga peels. The smoke included complex aromatic hydrocarbons called benzopyrenes, which were carcinogenic.

Science and science statistics can be mushy—we are all bell curved. Some will be very susceptible to carcinogens and others aren't at all. Scientific training allows you to step aside from the problem, break it down in elements. That is its strength. A weakness is that when you take a problem and break it down into elements, you simplify it. When you simplify it, automatically there are errors which are introduced. This is why, in all the whoop-de-do over global climate change, honest scientists sound like they are made of mush. They know there is much that they don't know. I felt sorry for former Secretary of Defense Rumsfeld when he was criticized for saying that the unknown unknowns were important. The science training I had gave me a very much more practical way of looking at problems and problem solving. Agriculture worked out very nicely. I worked for a man who was an Orthodox Jew, so he had all these restrictions once the days became shorter. He and I cut a deal. He could leave early on Fridays and I could leave early on Monday, so we were very happy. I had two technicians, and I did what I could to train them. So it worked.

Chromatography

Q: When you were working with the Department of Agriculture on tobacco, were you feeling any pressure because this was the time everybody in WWII used to call cigarettes "coffin nails." No big surprise, but there had been this tremendous idea put forward by the tobacco industry and by the smokers trying to discount all this. Were you feeling any of the pressure on this?

JONES: No, because our research was totally different. I was developing new methods of using liquid chromatography, gas chromatography. Chromatography is basically something that depends on the fact that if you have a mix of different compounds, and you put a gas through them, or a liquid, the flow rate—the rate at which they will be carried into a medium—differs depending on the molecular weight and the characteristics of the compound, and the characteristics of the substrate. This is all back in the dark ages, with no computers. The first computer work I did was for my dissertation, where I had to learn machine language programming to do nonlinear statistical error analysis. We were not the tobacco industry. We were not involved with tobacco farmers.

Q: The Surgeon General's report came out in '64.

JONES: The surgeon general's report was very straightforward. It said that if you smoked two packs a day for twenty years, you had roughly one in eight chances of developing lung cancer. But if you were the type who smoked three cigarettes a day or five a week, then your body took care of it unless you were very cancer prone. They have studies in which they rubbed tobacco tar on shaved rats. When they rubbed the tar on the skin, tumors came out. Then some bright scientist decided to leave out the tar and just rub the rats, and the tumors came out. It turned out that it was a strain of rats that got tumors the minute you looked at them sideways. We had other studies that compared very heavy smoke inhalation by a whole group of rats, and not a single one died of lung cancer. Of course, they died because they were asphyxiated by too much smoke. So you had a certain amount of cheating, but on the whole the science was very clear. The question was one of personal choice. It had not gotten to the level here now. It still was that old adage, it depends on you. Not everyone who smokes gets lung cancer. Some of the ones who get lung cancer may be more susceptible to certain diseases. Some of them get maybe some sort of emphysema, which is an awful way to go. That is the way humans are structured. There is a great deal that needs to be known. The thing that always struck me about the Foreign Service or any humanities is that the problems are much more complex than any I have ever encountered in science. Science allows you to break it down. You can't break down, let's say, Kazakh-Turkmenistan relations into a formula.

Q: You did this for how long?

JONES: I was at the Wyndmoor agricultural research labs for two years. Once David entered the Foreign Service, I transferred to the Department of Agriculture lab in D.C. and worked in the dairy lab. That was basically analysis using gas chromatography to identify different flavor chemicals.

CHAPTER 4

It's Paris—and Motherhood! (1969-1971)

Q: You and David are now married, and David is entering the Foreign Service. Let's see how a scientist views American foreign policy, Foreign Service life, and all that. This is 1968.

JONES: In 1968 and part of '69, David was in the Foreign Service finishing his A-100 training, waiting for his assignment. I was finishing up at the Department of Agriculture. We were planning a family. I had arranged for a post-doctorate at Institut Pasteur in Paris because I had a professor who was French and who had helped arrange it. I would not be paid, so I was definitely welcome. I was going to embark on the diplomatic life. I never in 10,000 years would have imagined myself as a Foreign Service officer.

In 1969, after French language training, David was assigned as a rotational junior officer at the U.S. Embassy, Paris. This was the assignment that set the pattern of his entire career in the Foreign Service, and that resulted in my taking the Foreign Service test and entering in January 1974. The post doctorate was arranged through a University of Pennsylvania professor, Madeleine Jouillie. It was complicated by the fact that I was pregnant and expecting twins, though I didn't know it until hours before they were born. As a result, I was certainly enormously pregnant even in the early months.

At Institute Pasteur, I had two PhD candidates who were wonderful young men but very different from U.S. graduate students. They always waited for technicians to do the actual lab work while they thought great thoughts. It did wonders for my French to speak and give presentations in French, but my accent must have troubled them, as they kept urging me to go Alliance Française for classes.

I had little knowledge of Foreign Service work, though I did meet the science counselor, who was pleasant and on the periphery of the embassy. I still remember him talking about a sniffer system to detect acetic anhydride produced by heroin labs—alas, acetic anhydride reacts with water to produce vinegar. So an overflight of the Marseille to Nice area only managed to map all the French restaurants. As an embassy wife and one who spoke French, I was guaranteed a seat next to some minor Francophone contact. It was fun, and I quickly learned that the perfect icebreaker was to ask about the cheeses, the wine, and the politics of France. David loved the work and worked for people who became friends and who eventually set him onto a political-military arms-control track. It also ultimately got him the promotion into the Senior Foreign Service, with the success of the Intermediate Nuclear Forces Treaty. One of his supervisors also mentioned me in David's efficiency report and suggested that I take the F.S. [Foreign Service] exam, which they had just opened for spouses.

The twins were a total surprise and inspired me to ask for an anesthesiologist in perfect French as soon as I heard there were two in there. In fact, I was so ignorant that I had had labor pains all night before they induced labor. Boy, did I worry when I heard the midwife say "two heads, I feel two heads." I remember praying fervently for "two bodies please, two bodies." There was no ultrasound then. We had twin girls, each about five and a half pounds, named Martha (after David's mom) and Lisa (after my mom). I tied up the washing machines at the embassy apartments for months doing diapers. I used to take notes on who did what. I also improved my French by watching TV. They had all the presidential candidates giving speeches all the time. As a result, I began to think that sentences were supposed to begin with "Je constate . . ."

CHAPTER 5

Back to the United States—Vineland and Washington (1971-1972)

Q: Let's hear more on life after Paris.

JONES: In 1969, we got back to the States. After a year in Vineland, New Jersey, where David took a year's leave to finish up his graduate degree, I was a substitute mathematics teacher for the high school and thinking of either going to medical school or taking the F.S. test.

Coming back to the States was interesting in reentry terms. I still remember my parents were in shock at those bald little things, their grandchildren, who weren't toilet trained yet. So they did a twenty-four-hour Chinese special toilet-civilizing routine, which is probably why the twins turned into engineers.

Q: When you came back, how long were you back in Washington?

JONES: It was '72 before we came back to Washington. I don't have the exact dates. But from '71 to '72, we were in Vineland, New Jersey, where I got a job doing substitute teaching of mathematics at the local high school. This was working for the same woman who taught me math. Any chemist, particularly if you go on to graduate school, takes enough mathematics to teach high school—in fact, we had much more math the average math teacher did. Then I thought of teaching as a possible second career; I took extra courses so at least I would be certified as a teacher in New Jersey. I found out what education classes were like. I even did some student teaching, which was fine in Vineland.

Earlier, in college, my best friend and I had another friend who had a disastrous romantic collapse. As a result, she couldn't do her homework. She had education classes. So the two of us did her homework for three months, even though we didn't have time to read the books. We would pick a paragraph and write an essay. I don't know how they didn't catch us. Deanna was an English major, so her writing was elegant, with beautiful choice of words, and at least 700 words long for a 500-word essay, whereas mine was filled with every factoid I could find, and I could barely stretch it to 430 words.

Teaching in Vineland

The three months of teaching I did was very interesting. For the bright kids, algebra was no problem, but I had one girl who just couldn't get the idea. I put her though the paces using numbers, and at about seventy repeats, she got the idea what the little letter symbols did. But my best class and my best story is when I taught the general math class. They were practically counting on their toes. No one had taught them the multiplication tables. I was horrified. This was tenth grade. Not only that, a couple of them were clearly under the influence of drugs. There was no discipline, no dress code. I had one girl who was a gorgeous girl, but she wore transparent blouses with transparent underwear. These were boys aged fifteen to seventeen. They were having enough problems getting their brains in gear. I had no disciplinary power. So one day, I wore three sweaters and opened all the windows. Pretty soon she covered up. I threw out the textbook. I taught them how to add, subtract, multiply, and divide. And I had one kid, Salvatore, who came to me and said his uncle was really connected and his uncle was going to call me because I wasn't treating him well. That was because I was giving him zeroes, as he wasn't doing his work.

That night I got a call I from a male who identified himself as Salvatore's uncle, and who asked why was I being mean to Salvatore. I said, "If Salvatore were a loan shark, he wouldn't know how to charge five percent on a $100 loan." The uncle said, "Really?" I said, "Yes." The next day Salvatore was all dressed up in a white shirt and told me, "My uncle told me to be very respectful." And he did his homework. There is probably a loan shark in New Jersey that is my fault.

At the same time, our twin daughters were growing more and more capable of taking everything apart—they were clearly born engineers. They also ate everything living or dead and now should be immune to all parasites on their travels.

And Then to Washington . . .

We had been remarkably frugal. Of course, we had the money I had made in the Department of Agriculture, so when we came to Washington we were able to buy a house at a time when it was actually more expensive to rent than to buy.

So I was very busy just surviving. David actually found our Arlington home—I had no time to join him and house hunt. Our major requirement was to have a house that was close to the department. We got an old brick colonial house very nearby, and he spent the next ten years picking broken glass out of the yard.

CHAPTER 6

Entering the Foreign Service (1974)

Q: How did things develop after that when you moved to Washington? When you moved to Washington, it would be '71 or so?

JONES: In '72 we moved to Washington. Then I took the F.S. exam.

Q: In '72.

JONES: I think it was '72, because it took them a year to get me my security clearances, because they couldn't find my landing card from when I came to New York City at the age of eight and a half. Fortunately, they eventually did find it. I had no problems with the written part because I had read, as you know, all of David's textbooks when I ran out of reading material in Paris. It was standard general knowledge. They also had put in some science knowledge, which is pretty much what any science student would know.

They scheduled me for an oral. During the oral, they did not ask me a single question having to do with science. At the end of three hours, I suggested that maybe they could make up their minds based on what they had heard already. I had already decided at the time that if I didn't make it in, the one alternative portable career would have been medicine, so I would have gone to medical school. At that point they passed me. Although the man that told me I passed said he was really of two minds because he thought I had a flippant attitude. I may have been a little more humorous than the average candidate, but it worked out well.

I knew I would be starting in January of '74 with my A-100 class. By then, you were coned. I had picked the consular cone because I figured that the Department of State, when David was back at State, was so short of anyone with any technical literacy that there would always be a good assignment, an assignment more ambitious Foreign Service colleagues might not want. Overseas, they were always short of consular officers. I had seen enough of David doing consular work, as well as the work in the consular section in Paris. I used to chat with all the locals. I could see they needed a lot of people. They were front line, and it looked reasonably interesting. That was it. I was now a full-fledged junior officer.

Q: With your A-100 course, what was your impression of it, the people and the training?

JONES: We were very lucky because they came in cones, so there was no fratricidal competition. There were also U.S. Information Agency (USIA) officers. There were only 22 of in the class. We had a Foreign Service weekend at Harper's Ferry as part of the training. Our bus broke down on the way to Harper's Ferry right in front of the DC liquor store. None of had had breakfast. So the more enterprising members of the class went in and bought a couple of gallons of really cheap Gallo wine. They got back on the bus, and they partied. I sat next to a fellow Chinese American in the USIA, Richard Gong, who highly disapproved of this, and I knew that with an empty stomach, I had better pass. One of the most boisterous members of the class, whose name I will not mention because he is recently retired and full of years and dignity, managed to pull his sailor hat down over his ears, giving him the look of someone who had an IQ the same as his shoe size. Unfortunately, he led the charge by falling off the top step of the bus (wine in hand) in front of our instructor. What a nightmare group we must have appeared.

I roomed with a very attractive blond USIA officer who went out with another member of the class. They must have had fun, as I had to help her to bed at two a.m. The next morning, you could tell who had partied, as they were all green.

I thought the training was very well done. At the end of it we would get assignments. We teased each other a lot. We had one member of the class who was a firm believer that women should stay at home. His wife was a Taiwanese Chinese. We had a woman called Gladys Rogers from the State Department talk about women's issues. One of the points she made is if you have a wife staying at home and something happens to you, what happens to your spouse. So a wife's ability to earn a living was very important to the whole family. At the end of it, we asked him what he thought of that. He said, "I am going to get more insurance." He was not going to change.

At that time, the State Department just had a science bureau, and Gladys Rogers felt that women were underrepresented in that bureau. When it came to assignments, I had a call from the science bureau, who said they would love to have me. They didn't have a position yet, but they had a place I could sit. I thought, this is nuts. This is not the way I intend to do things.

CHAPTER 7

First Assignment—ACDA (1974-1976)

I found out that the Arms Control and Disarmament Agency [ACDA] actually hired science PhDs to be physical science officers, and they also accepted Foreign Service detailees. So I interviewed with them. They were happy to put this freebie into their nuclear weapons and advanced weapons technology section.

Verification Technology Issues

The logic is simple. Before you can do arms control, you have to be able to anticipate new weapons. You also have to understand enough of the technology if you are dealing with nonproliferation to do something about it. And you have to be able to verify. All of these were technical issues. So my first two years in the Foreign Service had absolutely nothing to do with the State Department, except as a member of another agency. I did notice that the State Department could use more science literacy, because basically the problem was not a Foreign Service officer who didn't know, admitted that he or she didn't know, and then called the right expert. The danger lay in Foreign Service officers who thought they knew but didn't. Facility with a few acronyms did not equal understanding. Invariably, they could be made to look very stupid in interagency meetings; even sadder, they didn't even know they looked stupid.

My portfolios involved terrorism, nuclear terrorism, radiological warfare, high-energy lasers, particle beam weapons, and so on.

Q: How did you find the ACDA team you were working with?

JONES: Well, they were fellow science types. One had in fact gotten his PhD at MIT from my adviser's adviser, J. C. Swain, known far and wide as J. C. Swine. Bob Mikulak was a fellow chemist. The other one was Pierce Cordon. He was a physicist who had also gone to the University of Pennsylvania at one point, where he lost his calling for the priesthood. So they were bachelors. They were very nice. I also shared an office at one point with John Boright, a PhD in physics. We were "techies," and it gave us a chance to learn basically about the structure of arms control and political military issues. This was useful, as you couldn't isolate the technical from the issue.

I also learned about the edit and reedit culture in government. I had a boss who literally would rewrite phone messages. It was valuable being able to see how the State Department operated from the outside. I dealt a lot with the political-military bureau on arms control issues.

Binary Chemical Weapons

I had a chance to represent ACDA for the national security decision memorandum meetings on "binary" chemical weapons. Binary refers to chemical weapons in which the active ingredients are separated, so it is after you shoot the shell or drop the bomb that the rotation breaks a barrier between them, and you mix it. It is a bit inefficient but safer to transport.

Chemical, Biological, and Radiological (CBR) Warfare

Q: CW is chemical warfare.

JONES: I generally did CBR [chemical, biological, radiological] warfare.

Q: Particularly at the time—it still remains a certain threat—the Soviets were supposed to be quite far ahead and a tremendous threat in chemical warfare.

JONES: Oh yes, and one of the things in chemical warfare is that if both sides use it, they handicap each other, because you have to wear the protective gear. We had some experience in developing incapacitants, which had been used in Vietnam. They were going into persistent chemical agents, nerve agents. It was something where Bob Mikulak and I were very much dedicated to having a convention to ban these things. We had already had the biological weapons convention, but it only covered research. Governments can cheat. Who knew what the Soviets were actually doing.

I also did a lot of projects for Rear Admiral Thomas Davies. Dr. Robert Buckheim, a mathematician, was his number two. It amused them to regularly send me to odd places. He would call his buddies and say he was sending his favorite Welshman, "Terence Jones." Then I'd show up. So I'd call back and say, "You had better get your security clearances through because I am sitting in the guardhouse at Livermore Labs." However, I enjoyed the technical aspects.

Three Mile Island and Nuclear Reactor Vulnerability

Q: Well, just to get a feel for the time, were we looking at terrorism coming from outside the Soviet Union, the PLO [Palestine Liberation Organization] or any other group? Was that an issue?

JONES: It was then. It was always an issue in a sense, because as soon as you have a nuclear power reactor, there would be security concerns. I actually worked with a group from Oak Ridge National Laboratory to see what would happen if one actually destroyed a nuclear power reactor. Since we had no research money, I took an MIT study on the probabilities of different failures in a nuclear reactor [using event trees]. If you have terrorist action, let's say, they manage to get in and produce a loss of coolant, which is the most severe accident that can happen, then I could assign a probability of one to that loss of coolant event tree. Our results said that nuclear reactors were not vulnerable in the physical sense because of their containment structures. So yes, you could create a true mess, but it would all stay inside, just as it really did at Three Mile Island. Three Mile Island is a major success despite all the brouhaha at the time. There was no China syndrome. Hollywood is better suited for propaganda than realism.

Nuclear waste can be extremely radioactive, and any terrorist who didn't care about living could think of using it. Nuclear wastes are contained in nuclear fuel rods, which are designed to withstand the interior of a nuclear reactor. You don't just blow it up and get a poisonous cloud to kill millions. Even Chernobyl damage was limited.

Destroying a Nuclear Reactor—
How To . . . (or the Osirak Story)

We found that, essentially, nuclear reactors were economically vulnerable, because to cause a "crash" in a nuclear reactor, you did not need to get the reactor; you could just get transformer stations outside of the reactor. We also had studies from Oak Ridge which gave a blow-by-blow account of how to destroy a nuclear reactor using conventional weapons, such as by breaching containment with something like a 2,000-pound bomb and then following with a second precision-guided munition. The Israelis in fact did exactly that when they got rid of the Osirak reactor in Iraq. [Osirak was a small research reactor with ninety-three percent highly enriched uranium fuel rods supplied by the French.]

India's "Peaceful" Nuclear Explosion

Q: Did you get any feeling of being too far removed from the diplomatic process—the interface between ACDA and the State Department and its work on nonproliferation?

JONES: State really wasn't paying a much attention to nonproliferation at the time. ACDA, I would say, was considerably more in step when the Indian explosion occurred—the so-called PNE, or peaceful nuclear explosion. ACDA had more dedicated technical people who had close ties with the International Atomic Energy Agency [IAEA] safeguard experts. State had a counterpart nonproliferation group, who were with the Bureau of Oceans and International Environmental and Scientific Affairs. Later, nonproliferation moved to the Bureau of Political-Military Affairs. What I did was get a chance to see the interagency process, which was useful though very slow. ACDA's problems originated in a massive purge that had taken place years ago and which still left many hard feelings.

And Learning about Interagency (and Intragency) Backbiting

Q: This is going from the Johnson administration to the Nixon.

JONES: Yes, ACDA was just still recovering. Some people had managed to hide out and save their careers, but there were people with grudges against others, there were people who wouldn't speak to each other, there were people who had temper tantrums because they found out their ceramic agency seal was smaller than someone else's ceramic agency seal. They had lawyers, very dedicated and often very blind to anything but their own little line of thought. Some sincerely believed that if you changed a semicolon, atoms would stop fissioning.

Soviet Attitudes and Their Technology

Q: How did you feel about the bureaucratic wars and all that when you came out of arms control?

JONES: I thought it was normal in the sense that from my point of view, it was healthy to have a bureaucracy where people could speak up. Admittedly, the end result resembled a sort of puree, taking little bits from six different agencies. It was better than any alternatives. No one was going to be marched out and shot for their views.

My view was formed by my experience as a little girl in the Soviet Union. I remembered watching a May Day parade with my mother. There was beautiful music, troops all over the place, and girls all wearing their best. They were all chanting "Stalin is our mother, Stalin is our father, Stalin is our brother." My mother turned to me and said: "That is the real evil. It is not enough they have your body, that you are working for them, that you are doing everything that the state demands. They want your soul." I remembered that. Even when people disagreed strongly with me, their ability to do so was a reflection of the health of the system. At that point, I had a more mature understanding of human interactions. I had seen the way testosterone could nix sense. That included the women, who seemed to have the same testosterone attacks.

Q: During this time you were in ACDA, how did you view the Soviet Union?

JONES: I viewed the Soviet Union as an entity that was not interested in the ultimate survival of the UN [United Nations], the United States, or its way of life. I had lived there and knew all about the lousy shoes and ill-fitting clothes they made. I even heard that when a shoe factory broke its form for the right foot, to meet quotas, they just doubled the number of left-footed shoes. I focused mostly on Soviet military technical capabilities, such as whether they could do high-energy lasers, whether they could do particle beam weapons, whether they could leap enough to threaten our survival.

Q: As I recall, there was much talk about lasers and particle beam weapons, where the Soviets were considered to be preeminent in this.

JONES: They were very good, partially because we didn't know how good. Just to be on the safe side, we had to make the kind of assumptions that had them as a bigger threat. They were very strong in building tough, rugged, and reliable power sources. They did something like that using magneto-hydrodynamic generation. When you want to have a laser beam come out at a very high energy, you have to provide an input at a very high energy very fast, making it a weapons laser.

CHAPTER 8

Some Perspective and a "Tour" of Leave without Pay (1976-1978)

Q: Your ACDA comments sound like in a way—and I don't mean to be disparaging—the carryover from what I understand, and I haven't experienced it, the academic world. You know the academic fights can get very nasty over minor things.

JONES: Yes. But I always was under the assumption that it was the people. I could never accept the mantra that the end justifies the means; instead, I believed that the means can forever corrupt the ends. One thing science teaches you is that if you don't know, you know that you don't know. That means you duct tape your lips and you stop, and you try to understand before you speak.

At 33, I was one of the oldest people in my A-100 class, so as I almost felt like a dorm mom for the class. I felt that the only thing I could take to the Foreign Service that would be of value is a sense of professionalism. Without a strong sense of ethics—remember my Confucian background—you can justify anything. I was not quite as ambitious as the normal Foreign Service officer; a career as a diplomat would be interesting and useful, but that had not been my be-all and end-all. This made being part of a tandem team with two careers easier to balance. Covering twin college tuitions were more of a motivator than achieving confirmation or deification as an ambassador.

I was perfectly willing to let David's career take priority on assignments, as it was much tougher to get good political cone assignments. I had a wonderful two years at ACDA and moved without regrets.

At the time, assignment systems were straightforward. They sent David to NATO [North Atlantic Treaty Organization]. He was at EUR-Regional Political-Military Affairs during the time I was in ACDA. His NATO assignment was a four-year assignment: one year as the executive officers and three years as a political-military officer. I talked to the assignments people and took leave without pay for two years, followed by two years as a vice consul in the Brussels consular section.

Q: In Brussels?

JONES: In Brussels. This way there was no conflict of interest. A consular officer and a political-military officer at NATO did not overlap.

Q: When you were in ACDA, who was the head of ACDA at the time?

JONES: In fact, I think it was Fred Iklé.

Q: Did you ever run across Linda Gallini?

JONES: Oh yes, she was just starting.

Q: I just finished a long set of interviews with Linda.

JONES: Yes, she was very interesting, a very bright and attractive blonde.

Q: She stayed there the whole time. It is interesting, because I got from her something you never get from the normal Foreign Service because she was civil service the whole time. The idea of a group of people—this was a family with all sorts of, you know, the problem uncle and all that. But the point was they worked as a family because they had been doing this for years. In the Foreign Service, you have to make best buddies within two years because one of you will be gone after that.

JONES: Actually, at the same time you don't carry baggage. Let's say the fact that you and someone else had a feud over a parking place at the embassy disappears when they have left. Actually, it was ironic. One of my final preretirement assignments was as a counseling and assignments officer. This is in '96, at the State Department. I represented all science officers. They had a position in IAEA into which they wanted to parachute someone. My job required me to ensure that a qualified Foreign Service science officer got the assignment. So when I saw her again, she said that they absolutely had to have someone with nuclear experience, IAEA experience with a PhD in physics. I said, "I have the person," who was then placed there over their protests. Later, I found out the head of our mission to IAEA had a favorite he wanted to bring in from the outside.

Q: Screwing up the system, screwing up the arrangement.

JONES: Yes, so that failed, and then they tried a second choice who was a younger person in INR [Bureau of Intelligence and Research], but who had no science background. So they had to eat their own words. But I had gotten the director general's decision that we could not violate the rules, especially since this person literally had every single qualification, plus some, and was a science officer. So we did it. Later, I met the person who was in IAEA, who was unfortunately shafted by the whole procedure. He asked me how they could have achieved it. I said, "Well, if I were on the other side of the fence, I would have advised them to reclassify the position. After you reclassify the position, it is much easier to parachute someone. But otherwise the way you went about it was the very worst possible way."

CHAPTER 9

Belgium, Family, and Margaret (1978-1980)

Q: So you and David are off to Brussels, Belgium, when?

JONES: We basically went off in '76. We came back in '80. So I had two years leave without pay, a chance to get to know my twins better. We were really fortunate—Martha and Lisa were very bright and very healthy.

Q: So you already had the baby.

JONES: I had Margaret, born in '77.

Q: Your third child.

JONES: Yes, the third baby.

Q: Did she have hair?

JONES: No. By something in the genetic mix they eventually had beautiful heads of hair, but it had my parents worried for years. After all, little Asian babies are born with long black fuzz.

Q: OK, how did you do the two years you were in? You only had a dose in a way, not so much of the Foreign Service but of a major element of diplomacy, and that is the arms problem.

JONES: And bureaucratics.

The Advent of Margaret

Q: Well then, Brussels—let's take the domestic side. How did you find being a Foreign Service wife again, with three children and all.

JONES: First, I had two for a while, and it was nice to have time with Martha and Lisa, although I did have nine months of morning sickness with Margaret. David just took over the house of his predecessor in a small Belgian village called Everberg, an easy drive to NATO. This saved us a lot of fuss and bother.

I am pretty indifferent to interior decoration. If I did a house myself, it would probably look like a lab with drain traps in the floor so everything could be hosed down. The girls were at a very good age at age six, and they were discovering engineering skills. They used dental floss to launch their Barbies from the third floor stairs to greet their daddy, practically decapitating him. They set up pulley systems and had never played with Barbie dolls without building elevators for them. Now [2011] one is a radiologist with a M.D./PhD from Johns Hopkins and an undergraduate and master's in electrical engineering; and the other has a PhD in chemical engineering from Cornell, plus leading her class at Penn engineering, and is doing leading-edge work at Intel—so they did turn out to be engineers. Even the baby (Margaret), who was also toilet trained in record time by my parents at the age of one, also got a dual engineering/Wharton finance degree. She is married, works at a hedge fund and she and her husband are proud parents to David Alexander Marshalleck—our grandson born in February 2011.

Ambassador Robert Strausz-Hupé at NATO

Q: Did you get involved in the social life of the embassy?

JONES: I did get involved in the NATO mission social life, but as a spouse. Dave was the executive officer and Ambassador Strausz-Hupé had once been a professor of his at Penn. I even attended one of his lectures when I was an undergraduate and they were allowed to bring guests. I remember thinking he was going to fall off the speaker's platform, the podium, because he had a habit of grabbing it at the sides and leaning forward. You would see the whole structure start shaking. Though he had a reputation for being a terror to his executive officers, he was very good to David. There were no extra demands.

His wife had died a year earlier and, one time at NATO when they had thirteen at a table, I remember being called in on an emergency basis to attend. This was to prevent thirteen being at a table. I got to know some of the other wives. One of them, Elisabeth Pendleton, lived right across from the American school. We had decided on the American school, as I knew our girls liked structure—the more American, the better. I also knew what it was like to learn a foreign language as a child. As a result, I did the usual mother activities with groups such as Girl Scouts. I helped with some overnight events, where I basically escorted little girls to the bathroom all night. That was it.

Q: Well in '78 you started the consular tour at the embassy.

JONES: At the embassy. I was the sole vice consul. The consul was Jim Lassiter, and he had a family emergency, so two months after I was there, I was in charge. The family emergency back took him months to resolve. Then he was back just a few months before going on to another assignment in Bucharest. While he was in the U.S., one of my first tasks was to ban his wife from the section, as she had been using the consular employees to take her dogs sixty miles to SHAPE [Supreme Headquarters Allied Powers Europe] in Mons, Belgium, for vet care. That was a no-no. So I decided if ever I was canned by the Foreign Service, it would be because I was doing the right thing, and not for tolerating the wrong thing. Fortunately, he was actually grateful that I had done it. I did endless visa interviews, visits with prisoners.

Working at the Consulate and the Flemings vs. the Walloons

We had wonderful Foreign Service nationals [FSNs]. It took them a while to figure out that I could understand their rapid-fire French. Fortunately, by the time they figured it out, I had also figured out that two groups had not been on speaking terms for fifteen years and had been passing notes to each other in the section.

Q: Within the section?

JONES: Within the section, the Flemings and the Walloons did not get along well. I also realized that not only could I save money if I eliminated overtime during the summer months, but I wouldn't have to work overtime myself. Fortunately, I was able to offer the FSNs early departure to catch their trains if they finished their work. Amazingly enough, we only had two hours of overtime for my entire tenure. I would say production went up about 30 percent.

We had one logjam at the old automated visa lookout systems, which no one wanted to do. You basically typed out the information and sent it on a tape to the department the way communicators used to send cables. So I suggested that we all do it. Any time somebody walked by that pile of passports, we did ten of them. First, I did the first ten and kept doing it as promised; eventually, we completely eliminated backlogs and made the whole system much faster.

Our consul at the time had come back from the States and used to bring his dogs to the office. One of them was named Pita. He would let his dogs out via a sliding door to an inside garden, but they weren't very obedient when he called. With this two-way system, we could hear him screaming, "Lie down! I told you stay on the couch, Pita." They would wonder.

But consular work was very much about just running things and doing the best you could. You know that you had a real impact. I was glad that I kept my word to the assignments people and did not jump at an offer from the DCM [deputy chief of mission] at NATO to take a science position on the Committee for Challenges in Modern Society.

Visa Cases that I Have Known

The consular work was very interesting. I now have a life time of consular stories, none of which I would dare write up, because I am sure they would recognize themselves.

Q: One of the things I try to gather here are some of the consular stories. Let's take arrest cases. You don't have to mention names.

JONES: I probably don't remember the names. Ever since I have done things where other people's privacy is involved, I try very hard to forget all the names.

Q: Which is a very good practice.

JONES: So nothing is ever going to slip because it has long since been erased.
OK, one of my arrest cases convinced me that the master criminal image is definitely wrong. A young man decided to go to Amsterdam buy some hashish, which he was going to take to Germany and sell to American troops. He did not want to cross the German-Dutch border, which had antiterrorist patrols all over the place after a group of Japanese Red Army people had killed people at the Rome airport. So he decided to cross into Belgium at a place called Vise, and then into Germany. Well, hiding eleven pounds of hashish under your VW floor mat doesn't work, especially since Vise is one of these border crossings where they catch them all the time. I am not even sure the people who sold him the stuff didn't sell his name to the Belgians, so they got him.

I did go to his trial and discovered the difference between the European system and ours. There is no such thing as questioning or witnesses. A prosecutor got up and said, "Maximum penalty. This person deserves it. He is a swine." The defense got up and said, "Think of his poor mother, mercy." Anyway they sentenced him to five years, which, with good behavior, was more like three years. I visited him in jail in Liege. He could get work in prison and earned $150 a month while there. The only complaint he had was getting detergent hands from scrubbing the toilets, so I was able to convince the prison to give him rubber gloves.

For some reason, my counterpart in Antwerp had really bad arrest cases. He had pedophiles. Mine were really pretty harmless in comparison. I had another one who was a scam artist. He had convinced Belgians to give him their "black cash," cash they had hidden from the tax authorities. He told them he could buy and sell arms in Africa, making them tremendous amounts of money. What he really did was take the money. He was very careless and he forgot to pay his rent. In Belgium, that is something they would arrest you for. He didn't know any French. When they arrested him for not paying his rent, he had no idea why they arrested him, as he spoke no French or Flemish. So, at the police station, he said, "I confess." That they understood, and they let him go through the entire confession before they called a consular officer. By then, he had implicated several hundred Belgians. So the Belgian prosecutor was delighted. I noticed that they held him a full 71 hours and 52 minutes before they called me. We fielded a number of calls from worried Belgians. Eventually, he was deported from Belgium. He ended in Austria, and, the last I heard, he was running some scam there.

Q: Oh, yes, once a scammer, always a scammer. How about distressed Americans out of cash and that sort of thing, though it was a bit more in Antwerp?

JONES: Antwerp got a harder crowd, basically.

Q: Oh, boy. Did you have any problems as consular officer with the rest of the embassy saying, "This is the nephew of the prime minister's secretary, who is my best contact. You can't turn him down"? Or something like that. Did you get into this?

JONES: Yes, I had no problems with the political section. They just asked that any time I got a Zairian politician who was usually supported in Belgium by one of their parties for an interview, to also bring them in for the interview. That was easy. I had a requirement that they put it in writing. In other words, if they wanted special courtesy treatment, they had to write it down.

The only time I had problems was with a Filipino general and his sixteen-year-old secretary, who was gorgeous. They wanted a visa for her so that she could accompany the general on a trip to the states. I said, "You have to put it in writing. I am not going to issue and then find out this girl has disappeared and is being a working girl in New Orleans." So holding their noses all the way, I got this extremely cautiously worded request

Another time I had two Afghans who were automatic refusals—that is, out of district, no ties to Belgium—but they actually were connected to another part of the embassy. When I refused them, they finally said, "But we have a name we are supposed to call." Finally, they did get to the right section, and I never heard from them again.

Q: Well, in Antwerp was there the equivalent of what they have in Amsterdam, a red light district?

JONES: They did in Brussels, too.

The Pedophile Culture in Belgium

Q: That always creates a problem of robbery.

JONES: We had a certain number. The problem was with pedophiles, especially gay pedophiles. The first major visa refusal I had to make was against a man who wanted to import his Algerian adoptee, a little boy, to the United States. It sounded so fishy that I called the DEA [Drug Enforcement Administration] people and said, "Look, is there any information, just informally? I am not going to cite it." They told me this man was a professional. He had brought the boys regularly through legal adoptions. No one checked. No one cared. And then he would pretty much turn them out into the streets when they developed a mustache. So I turned him down. He was furious and said because of my turndown, it was going to cost him an enormous amount of money. He had to anchor offshore outside the territorial limit. But clearly there was a serious pedophile problem in Belgium, and it often surfaced in other nasty cases.

Q: Was there a system? Was this an American pedophile?

JONES: No, it was a Belgian pedophile. They had a seasonal trek. During the winter season in Miami, when rich Belgians went there, they went with their little boys.

Q: Was there a system in place where you could tell the immigration people, I mean send out essentially, we turned him down, but OK, this guy is a really bad guy?

JONES: What I did was in many cases, I would tell the DEA people this person tried to leave Belgium to go to the United States for this, and they would pass it to their police contacts. I mean I don't know what Belgian law was, but they certainly didn't seem to be doing anything about it. I think in the past few years—long after we left Belgium—they have had enough scandals in that area.

Q: I follow the French-Belgian news, and they have had some real pedophile problems.

JONES: Oh, yes. It is very much a class thing. If you are upper class, you just thought you had rights. We had one person we did a background check on and ended up with a police record a yard long. But he had all sorts of titles, had been invited to the ambassador's parties, had invited the ambassador to his chateau. In consular work, you began being suspicious of everything after a while.

The Problems of Holtzman

We also had the Holtzman Amendment, under which anyone who had been a Nazi, supported Nazis, or suppressed others during WWII was denied visas for life. Well, we had a large number of Belgians who had been sentenced to death after WWII for collaboration. The Belgians did it in a very interesting way: first they sentenced everyone to death, and then they went through each case and commuted the sentences of the ones that shouldn't be executed. We had one man saying that, yes, he did do all sorts of awful things, and he had a criminal record, but he did it as a criminal, not as a Nazi. So he robbed regardless of racial or ethnic origin.

We ended up with a person at NATO, a German. It was really tricky to tell. We regularly had fallout still from WWII. We had a very nice Belgian woman who had an arrest record for running a cathouse after WWII. Then she ran a very good restaurant instead. She had grandchildren in the United States, as her daughters had married the nice American soldiers who used to bring her hams. Every time she went to the United States, we had to get a waiver because she was 212 (a)(9) [felony record]. One time I had to translate and explain to the INS office that she had run a bordello. Their reply: "What is a bordello?" So I had to spell it out. They still didn't get it. I asked them to look it up in the dictionary. They didn't have a dictionary on hand. So I had to explain "bordello." All this time, I had forgotten we had gotten one of these cheap, lowest-bidder microphones, which amplified every sound on either side of the bulletproof glass and with a mediocre phone system, I ended virtually screaming. So when I finally finished the interview, I came out and saw a whole group lined up at the window waiting for the next act.

The Fallout of the Iranian Revolution for Embassy Brussels

Belgium was a very easy consular posting, especially when we got a large number of Iranians who came out after the shah fell. At this time, the U.S. hostages were still being held in Iran. My decisions were made easier because Iranians who made it to Belgium could benefit from all the Belgian refugee protections. No one was going to expel them or shoot them. I could handle them on a case-by-case basis without feeling that I was condemning someone to death. Belgian Iranians were no problem, as we had been issuing them visas on their Belgian passports for decades.

As for the others, at worst I was costing someone a week in New York City. Unattached males with passports that had been overwritten by the Iranian provisional authority with just a stamp were not good bets. Usually, the minute I turned them down they would threaten to cut my throat, and go into an anti-American tirade. My rule was if I were going to call for help, I was going to call for the Belgian guard. Better that a Belgian guard beats them up than a U.S. marine.

Q: I was interviewing a lady, Janet Folk, who was in London about this time. She was saying sometimes it was the flavor of the month with the Iranians, young men trying to get the hell out to the United States and not get into the Iranian army during the war with Saddam Hussein. They heard that Iranian Christians were getting special permission to go to the United States. She had one who came and said he was a Christian. She said, "I am a little bit confused, because I see by your passport that your first name is Mohammed."

JONES: We had a legend that there was a Farsi-speaking officer who had left Tehran right before the hostage takeover because he had suffered a nervous collapse from the stress of dealing with Iranian visa fraud. They sent him to London. Then, of course, the hostages were taken, and there he was in London under a window that said "Farsi-speaking officer." He had a chance to see all of his old cases. I do remember that we had had no guidance from State, although the hostages had been taken months ago. Every U.S. diplomatic post that had Iranians coming for visas was sending requests for guidance in vain. It was not a decisive administration in Washington.

Dealing with the Congress

Q: I was consul general in Naples at the time. We were left on our own.

JONES: Oh, yes, so we refused and we refused. Every refusal led to a congressional complaint. We had a rule then you had to answer a congressional within twenty-four hours; the cables were often classified. So that meant that *moi*—my little ten fingers—had to type the cable. My cable skills were awful. In those days, if you had to delete a letter, you typed one star after it, two stars for a line, and three stars for the whole paragraph. My cables went into the communications with a field of stars.

Summing Up as Consul in Brussels—What I Learned

Q: Well, then in 1980, whither? This is your consular assignment, and there you were pretty much it for a good part of the time. Did you find that your consular training helped, or was it just a matter of having books and manuals and you looked up the problem?

JONES: It was very helpful. They taught things you could not get from a book. The consular officers who did the training in the course provided sort of a basic ethical framework, which is fairness, honesty. When it came to U.S. citizen cases, which are really difficult because the U.S. citizens who often need help are not our finest examples. He gave us a special lecture saying: "This is the deal. A U.S. citizen with a U.S. passport is owed this by you. It doesn't matter if they are crazy, they are a murderers, whatever. It doesn't matter how poor they are, how old, whether they are the dregs of society. It doesn't matter. You have a duty. You don't just blow it off because this is a person you would never want to have anywhere near you normally." I found that helpful.

The local employees were extremely intelligent, all university trained and, in our section, bilingual in Flemish and French. On the phone, the person couldn't tell if you were a native Flemish speaker or a French speaker. That helped a lot. They knew the *Foreign Affairs Manual* ten times better than I did. I was only useful to them because I was their toxic waste dump. I only needed to see the bad cases. For things like a plane load of Belgian weight watchers going to New York City to buy cheap, big-sized clothes, they didn't need me. By '79 or a little before '79, I had a new consul.

Q: Who was that?

JONES: That was Robert J. Bel. He died a few years ago when he was consul in Jerusalem. His wife was Belgian. He had been a communicator and a former marine. In his earliest assignment in Belgium, he had been hit by a tram. The NATO hospital people assumed he was inoperable since he had been hit in the head, and that he was going to die, but his girlfriend at the time, and later his wife—I think her name is Marianne—found the best neurosurgeon in Belgium and saved his life. He was very good professional consular officer. He didn't want to be a DCM, he didn't want to be an ambassador, but he knew how to run things. He had a fund of great stories.

He had two sons. Occasionally, I would give him a ride home because it was right on the way back to Everberg. I would see his boys waiting for him. It was really very sweet. He was subject to epileptic attacks because of scars from his operation and was careful to prepare me for any attack. He was sort of very proper, very correct. I was always grateful that when there was a consular conference in Rome, he sent me. He said that he had an assignment in Rome for years, gave me the name of his favorite restaurant, which was wonderful.

So David came as the spouse to Rome, the Hotel Flora. I went to the consular conference, where you learned a great deal, not so much from the formal program but from the way people dealt with things. You need people to teach you. The same is true in science: It is an attitude. It is not just the technique.

Of course, I had hobby horses. I have a consular hobby horse. I had written the consular affairs bureau about a dozen times about paternity. DNA allows you to determine paternity. So a man should be able to come in and say this is my illegitimate child and this child is a U.S. citizen at birth because of my DNA. After all, we are agreed on sexual equality. Any woman who comes in and proves this is her baby transmits U.S. citizenship to her baby. Why not for men?

Q: All I can say is, as a consular officer, I am thinking "Oh, my God, it is the equivalent of Typhoid Mary. There could be Spermatozoa George, who is going out and sowing his seed all over the place, including by mail."

JONES: Yes. But the point is justice.

Q: That may be justice, but good God!

JONES: So I was the Typhoid Terry for this one.

CHAPTER 10

Back to Mother State—
This Time as a Science Officer (1980-1982)

Q: When you left there in 1980, where did you go?

JONES: Oh, the State Department—OES [Bureau of Oceans, Environmental, and Scientific Affairs] by then had a nuclear nonproliferation office. I knew John Boright. At that time, he did not have a position, but his colleague Mike Guhin had one for nonproliferation and export controls. So I went straight into that position. David had actually met my predecessor in that job, another science officer called Adrienne Stefan. From talking to her, he had gotten a very good idea of the demands of the job. So when I arrived, I was able to explain to Mike that while I would get all the work done, I had a rigid child-care schedule and would not just hang around to look good. If he didn't like that, John Boright was willing to swap officers. Dan Ujifusa was interested in more international work, and I had no problems with more technical safeguards work. Mike, to his credit said, "Oh, no problem." As it turned out, in my two years there, I think I had to stay late one night. That was it.

I stayed in the states for a long time, basically because of a medical clearance problem. I was also delighted to find out that the great mother lode of all science and technology assignments for the Department of State was in State itself. In embassies, there was more helping visiting delegations and less serious technical work.

Q: You were in the State Department starting in 1980, until when?

JONES: Until I went to Canada in '92, a long time ago.

Nonproliferation and Nuclear Export Controls

Q: So in the department you were assigned where, OES?

JONES: I served in a variety of offices. I had two years in OES, nuclear export controls. I was sort of the in-house technical expert. I found that nuclear engineering was basically chemistry, so the technical details made sense to me. Nuclear export controls require you to understand the peaceful uses so that you can understand how potential proliferators could use a "peaceful" program to achieve weapons capability.

Then I had three years in the Bureau of Intelligence and Research, where again I covered strategic technologies. Before you can do anything, you have to know what you are trying to anticipate. You can always have a shock from a sudden change in capabilities, let's say, satellites. The ability, for instance, to locate a nuclear missile submarine using its Kelvin wake in real time from space means that you can take out nuclear missile submarines, one leg of the triad. I enjoyed it a great deal, particularly work on the Science and Technology Intelligence Committee, which gave me a chance to travel to all the major Department of Energy [DOE] national labs—Sandia, Los Alamos, Livermore, and Oak Ridge. I found the DOE technical intelligence people to be first-rate, as they had real experience in the work while the CIA [Central Intelligence Agency] technical analysts tended to be stronger on academic credentials than on hands-on feel for their subjects. Understandably enough, DIA [Defense Intelligence Agency] analysts had a narrow and intense focus on what makes a real difference to troops in the field—number of tanks, location of tanks, and such.

Q: I want to move back to the OES. You say you had the issues of export control?

JONES: Yes, and nonproliferation also.

Q: What was going on in 1980 to '82 or so in that field that you were particularly concerned with?

JONES: Basically, the situation had become one of holding actions. In '74 the Indians had already set off a PNE, a peaceful nuclear explosion. So the cat was out of the bag. IAEA and its entire safeguard systems were beginning to look more like papier-mâché tigers than real tigers. There were no real consequences for a country in violating safeguards or setting off a nuclear explosion.

The Pakistani Nuclear Program, Mr. "Theft" Khan, and Vela

Nuclear programs take a long time, so we knew that a large number of countries had long-term programs to achieve nuclear weapons capabilities. A large number of companies, particularly in Europe, Italy and France, Portugal, Spain, and Germany, were very eager to make sales, and they really didn't care whether their special alloy steels were going into centrifuge systems. URENCO security had already been breached when Mr. Khan had stolen the centrifuge plans and taken them to Pakistan.

Q: He is sort of the genius . . . .

JONES: He was the father of the Pakistani nuclear program. He stole plans for the small centrifuges used by URENCO, which made catching them much harder. At the same time, I think this was before the South Atlantic event, where you had the Vela satellites pick up the signature double flash of a nuclear explosion. When an atomic bomb explodes, it heats the air. You have the initial flash of the explosion. Then the air is heated to such high temperatures that it is opaque until it cools off enough and you can see the light again, so it is a very particular double flash. And a Vela satellite, which was designed to give early warning for a ballistic missile launch, saw it. We did know that the South Africans were investing in the Becker nozzle uranium enrichment process, which is a process that depends on the fact that at certain speeds and under a magnetic field, the different uranium isotopes would end up with different arcs of curvature as they streamed out of a nozzle at supersonic speeds. So you can collect them with plates at different points. That one was extremely labor intensive, and extremely energy intensive, so it was more or less in the line of Oak Ridge gaseous diffusion plants, which can be easily seen, as the plant is almost a mile long, with the Tennessee Valley Authority electrical power plants feeding its energy needs.

President Carter and Poisonous Nuclear Politics

The work was very interesting. The politics were reasonably poisonous in the sense that when President Carter killed U.S. reprocessing of spent fuel to support his nonproliferation goals, this went a long way to killing the U.S. nuclear power program. These were the days before people were worried about global warming. And as allies, he had all the groups that were basically very antinuclear because they were very antideath, death being represented by radiation, even though light and heat area also radiation.

I worked with Bob Gallucci in OES. I will only say that if there was a way to believe intelligence and interpret it to fit his preconceptions, he did it. It was very innocent in a way, and he truly believed it would be a better world, the world he envisioned—but alas, my feelings at the time on all these programs was that they were doing exactly what the intelligence indicated they were doing. He and President Carter showed this kind of rosy vision of other intentions when first negotiating with the North Koreans. I understand that they completely ignored any intelligence contrary to their bias in favor of trusting the North Koreans.

Work Environment at State—the "Best of Intentions"

At the time in the State Department, there were always the people trained in political science or international relations who knew all about the great power moves, the history, and even games theory. They know how groups of people will work—they want power used for good and they were firm believers that the end justifies the means, forgetting that occasionally the means can corrupt the end. The sad thing, some were even unaware that they were stacking the deck and distorting the facts. The path to disaster can indeed be paved with the highest-minded intentions.

I will say that I was frankly well-shielded in my work. I was supposed to come up with a technical explanation. Most of my writing was actually just to make sure that the technical things were reasonably correctly written and that an elegant phrase didn't translate into inelegant physics. That was a lot of fun. I enjoyed it. I found my colleagues wonderful.

The "South Atlantic Event" and Nuclear Analysis

Q: Well, back to the Indian Ocean, the South Atlantic event, as it was called. What was the analysis that you were picking up? What was the "who did this and why"?

JONES: The analyses came in different directions. The straightforward analysis from the national labs was done by scientists, some of whom were old enough to remember when we did open-air testing. Even if it was the 50s and the instruments were crude, they had a very good feel for it. They couldn't find any other explanations, despite attempts to describe it as "double lightning" flashes. You rarely get two lightning flashes of the same intensity or duration. The flashes were mapped showing time on one axis and intensity of light on the other. The size of the peak and the relationship of the peaks to each other are a signature. There was a great deal of confrontation, argument back and forth. It didn't change the fact that no one knew. There were rumors.

To me, intelligence is very difficult in the sense that it is very much like early science. You have very little data. You try to make some sense out of what might be totally chaotic material. When you try to make that sense, you automatically bias it. So the only check you have is when you are proven wrong. You say well, if I am right and my theory is right, I will try this. When that blows up, you say, oh, maybe I didn't count that, and you try that. So with billions of tiny little steps, we marched forward toward plastics and to better thermal underwear and so on. This is a chemist's view. We are not much into big, giant theories. But it was very easy to see what you thought you should see. It is like bad proofreading. You see a sentence, and you see what should be there. You don't see the fact that you misspelled the president's name.

Q: You sound one note, but it is such an important event over this South Atlantic thing. In the first place, I would think that if you have got satellite pictures, you could take spectrums of what happened. I would think the whole thing would fit into—I mean, it sort of is or ain't a nuclear explosion.

JONES: The difficulty was these were Vela satellites. Vela satellites were designed to catch a warhead coming in. During the point where you would have a warhead burn, you would have a strong infrared signature. So they have filters on them. As a result, you are not getting 100 percent of the picture. Our data-handling processes were much less sophisticated then. There is always the danger of instrument error. You could, for instance, have had a double short for all anyone knew. Any time you are collecting light, you are depending on the fact that you have molecules at this end that react to a light flash, which can be converted into an electrical signal, which then can be recorded digitally. When something is recorded digitally, it depends on the resolution, which in turn is determined by how many little, itty-bitty pixels you have divided it into. So the technical people had every reason to continue chewing it over. I am sure they felt they still could until the year 3000. At the same time, the political people had to look for the political aspects or why and who.

SLIFERS

You don't need to do an open air explosion that can be detectable. We had become, and the Soviets also, world-class experts at doing it underground. We could test our warhead hardnesses by having concrete lined tunnels that went from the point of explosion to wherever we had the instruments. We even had instruments that you could put down the actual hole into which you lowered the explosive. They were called SLIFERS, "shorted location indicators by frequency of electrical resonance."

Dealing with the Soviets—Problems/Problems

While we were negotiating with the Soviets on the threshold test-ban treaty, the threshold being I think 150 kilotons, we needed verification that there was no cheating. The seismic signals are not enough to gauge the size of the explosion without knowing the geology. For example, if they set off an explosion in a cavern instead of a drill hole, the signal would be dampened and our estimate would be wrong. We offered, in the goodness of our hearts, to share the SLIFER technology with them so that we could get the data. In other words, we would end up with something attached to their explosive. The explosion would crush the cable and cause a short. A very high frequency magnetic signal would go up and down the cable and we could record the short formed as the cable was crushed by the explosive; this would then give us a picture of the explosion that was directly related to the size of the nuclear explosive.

The Soviets predictably said, "Never. Touch our thing? Absolutely never." In fact, DOE national labs sent ACDA an example of the SLIFER coupling unit for transmission by diplomatic pouch to Moscow. One of my unnamed colleagues managed to drop it, break it in two, and then more or less cram it back together. We figured they would be able to figure it out, as it was just a connection.

Q: What about Soviet technical capabilities?

JONES: They were very ingenious, good mathematicians. A computer works by the way you organize the bits. A "word," or byte, is eight bits. We had processors that could handle in those days 32 bits at that time, but the Soviets did not. The more that you can handle means that you can have more sophisticated programming, more parallel capabilities, and it makes for faster computation speeds. To compensate for this, they were able to do special architecture, in which they took what they called bit-slice, eight bits tied to another eight bits located somewhere else, tied to another one. So there was a lot of ingenuity. At the Smithsonian National Air and Space Museum [exhibit] that described the U.S. moon landing effort, they had a frieze that showed U.S. and Soviet space capabilities from Sputnik to the moon landing. First, we were way behind—remember the Vanguard catastrophe—and then, slowly, inexorably, we moved ahead, and finally we sped ahead. I could see why Gorbachev decided they couldn't win the technological arms race.

Alas, we have to keep in mind that people kill each other perfectly well with WWII surplus weapons.

The Interagency Policy Battles Over Export Control

In general, intelligence analysis is tricky and there were a whole lot of areas in which the politically directed people looked at things one way and called on the intelligence communities, especially the technical ones, to conform. The CIA was very politicized. They hired people with PhDs but little experience and sometimes little understanding of how their estimates could be distorted. They did not have enough working knowledge, and they were under immense pressure to produce things that would get them noticed, often in accord with the prevailing political desires.

Given this type of pressure, it was almost impossible for them not to be alarmists.

Q: *I would like to make sure I understand this, particularly the people who are doing this, because it is very important aspect. In science you have people who have the proper initials after their name and all, but often I take it they are not always the worker bees who are really down—I mean, they don't necessarily have the working knowledge of some of the things they are analyzing. Is that correct?*

JONES: Yes, in this way: You have to differentiate basic science, theoretical science, from technology. In science, you can become extremely expert in one area without even the ghost of knowledge in another. I will give you one example. This was when I was in an office dealing with export controls. We were dealing with the sale of certain kinds of machine tools that had multi-axis capabilities. The sellers, a big Italian company, were very interested in this sale. Selling machine tools is really big. It is not the machine tools that make you money; it is the service contract on those same machine tools. We said it could be used to improve Soviet tanks. The analyst who was doing this was very bright, a young woman, an engineer. But she never worked in the area. So she did not have the kind of background that made it possible for her to understand where the machine tools fit in tank-engine manufacture. So, perfectly honestly, she rang all the alarm bells which really made her political bosses happy. To get a clearer picture of an area where I was truly ignorant, I went to people who actually made this kind of tank, who used similar machine tools, and I said, "OK, what difference would it make if you had this capability?"

Their conclusions were totally different from hers. They said that it didn't make much difference, as the Soviets were already using this type of machine tool. It was not a miracle solution. Soviets were making tanks perfectly well with their existing tools and technology (something the DIA analysts strongly agreed with). This was the kind of understanding that the CIA analyst lacked.

My strongest asset was knowing that I didn't know. My ego survived this admission of ignorance nicely. And I knew where to find the people who were the real experts.

In another case, we had a furnace for draining off slag from melted aluminum, leaving the pure metal in the furnace. It is just a high-temperature furnace with a tap at the bottom. The DOD [Department of Defense] wanted to put an export control on it without any understanding of how these furnaces were used in general. The national lab experts were amused, as every jeweler in town used one of these furnaces.

CHAPTER 11

The Intelligence and Research Bureau and Politicized Intelligence (1982-1985)

INR's Director: Hugh Montgomery: An Intelligence Professional

Q: This is all the great advantage of the State Department—it has to be down to earth. There is not much time for any artsy fartsy.

JONES: No, I was lucky. This is not an area where State had any strong issues or sword to fall on. They had the standard view that whatever diplomatic game you played, you needed the strongest possible positions. Trying and failing could do more harm than not trying in many cases. No one wanted to look stupid.

As a dedicated anti-Communist, I was saddened to see CIA analysis weakened by the political "commissars." At the same time, the head of the Intelligence and Research Bureau at State was a WWII intelligence specialist called Hugh Montgomery, who really understood the uses of intelligence. He always backed honest analysis, even if he did not agree. Hugh Montgomery's view was: you got the best analysts you could, you gave them their head, and you kept them honest. He would back you all the way. He even backed me against accusations of racial prejudice by the East Asian bureau for analyses that reached conclusions on Chinese illegal technology transfer that differed from their ideas.

Q: What was that?

JONES: There were a lot valid reports of illegal Chinese technology transfer activities, which I wrote up with the conclusion that it was standard operating procedure for Chinese agents here and in any advanced country. It was no big deal—the French did the same thing here and in Paris as part of their commercial intelligence collection.

People did regularly accuse each other of clientitis or reverse clientitis when they loathed the country, for example, the North Korea desk. I was proud of the way that State held to its "big picture" positions. I was especially grateful to Hugh Montgomery for giving me a better understanding of how good intelligence works. He gave us regular lectures saying you don't use intelligence as a crutch. He explained the different time lines of intelligence, such as, for example "immediate" intelligence, which calls for an immediate response—for example, terrorists about to bomb a train. That's the DIA type of intelligence. In the same case, CIA may have been monitoring on a longer time line and noted that certain terrorist groups had been buying explosives for the past six months.

On practically my last day at INR, I attended a meeting in which the new director, Morton Abramowitz, spoke to us. He did the usual administration management 101 introduction and offered to hear our views on needs, resources, and actions. As I sat there and listened to my colleagues talk, I realized that he only listened enough to frame his rebuttal. I was saddened to see that change.

Science and Technology Committee

From 1982 to 1985, I represented the State Department on the Science and Technology Intelligence committee. My PhD was useful as a title, but proved nothing more than that I did one academic project well. So I saw my job as keeping the analyses as honest as possible. This meant footnoting dubious conclusions so thoroughly that by the time they saw the horrible mess, everyone would say, "Get me some aspirin; I don't want to read this." The footnotes were necessary. It is just as important to know that you don't know. Unknown unknowns can kill you.

Working Environment in INR and the Intelligence Community

Q: In fact, we are approaching the period now where all the technology in the world doesn't protect you from a suicide bomber. I am trying to get a feel for the dynamics. Correct me if I am wrong, but I get the feeling that you had your technical experts coming out of the CIA who in some ways were driven by the idea, saying this thing shouldn't get out. You are always safe doing that, whereas when you looked at it in myriad from INR or OES, you say, "Well, hell, it really doesn't make any difference."

Telephone Technology

JONES: Or it doesn't make sense. It got so bad, in fact, that Congress in the Export Administration Act added something called the Office of Foreign Availability, to be run under the Department of Commerce. What brought it to a head was the Chinese telephone system. The Chinese were ready to upgrade. They could upgrade the phones in several ways. For obvious reasons, those upgrades that went out into the air were preferable.

Q: We are talking about the National Security Agency.

JONES: Yes, and cell towers and so on. But those that had fiber optic links were much more complicated. There was something called time-division multiplexing, which allowed your call signal to be digitized, mixed with all the other call signals, and only reunited at the receiving point—obviously, this made for much higher transmission volumes, but also made it much harder for anyone trying to listen to the calls. In other words, you might think of telephone signals as a string of patterns with a little tag on them. They could break up this string into itty-bitty little pieces, and with the right capabilities, reunite them at the other end. So when you were speaking to your aunt in Tulsa, Oklahoma, you didn't notice any interruption, but they were able to pile into the same wires 10,000 other conversations with other people speaking. It was just a way to expand and also to harden systems.

Supposing a hurricane or a tornado took out one of the little nexuses between the two of you, the system would automatically reprogram itself so that it would go through Chicago instead. You would still be discussing something with your aunt. If the phone companies could not sell something to the Chinese that the Swedes, with no export restrictions, could, all our restrictions would do was hurt our own companies.

Personalities and Politics

The Department of Defense at the time had someone called Steve Bryen, who was one of Richard Perle's people—"the black prince." I used to remind people that the black prince was also Beelzebub, so they referred to him a bit less. Steve Bryan was very political. Once when he was trying to stop an American from traveling, he was so far out of line that the Customs guy (somewhat to the right of Genghis Khan) gave him a lecture on constitutionality. It made me very glad I worked in a system where he just couldn't say, "Take her out and have her shot."

East West Trade and COCOM

I coped. In the Office of East-West Trade, which was one of my final assignments, I chaired a working committee, the Economic Defense Advisory Committee II, which prepared all the position papers for COCOM, the Coordinating Committee for Multilateral Export Controls. DOD always wanted incredible, nonfeasible controls on everything. Commerce wanted to protect the U.S. technological lead and market share. State Department was usually caught between these two juggernauts. The White House had all sorts of true believers, who were very bright and very capable and very young, and still had not gotten the idea that they should rewrite all of the intelligence to fit their views.

This was a constant regardless of the administration's political party. It was very hard for many people to say no at more senior levels, because it really was their careers. It wasn't going to hurt Terry Chin Jones to have acted like a wet blanket in a meeting, saying you don't have the evidence, you don't have the evidence, and if you send people out as technical experts, they had better not be political hacks. We wanted strong positions for our delegations and saw no utility in political posturing to impress their bosses here.

You see, they wanted to send people they trusted. Fine, you always want people you can trust, but when you are going to something like COCOM, you are dealing with other countries that would send their top people. Think of a tank-factory specialist and a pet lieutenant colonel who only had his briefing notes in a major technical discussion. My view was that you never help any kind of a case without top people, especially when it came to science. In a technical discussion, especially one that means hundreds of millions, if not billions, of dollars in trade dealing with what they call red lines (that is, a line below which you could export without licenses and a line above which you had to go through the process), you needed to make really persuasive arguments. The export licensing process was horrible and, I believe, remains so to this day.

Supercomputers—Not So "Super"

Q: When talking about experts, you say the top person. But as a bureaucrat in a completely different field, the consular field, if you had something dealing with citizenship matters, if you had the consul general, you probably ended up with somebody who was removed from the process, and it would be better to have a consul or a vice consul who really was down there dealing with that particular subject and knew it. I would think this would pertain in science, too.

JONES: I will give you an example. There was serious concern about the access given to supercomputers by people from Red China and from certain Eastern European countries. The supercomputers have multiple uses. They are used for wind-tunnel analysis et cetera and weather prediction. So it was definitely a multiple-use thing. DOD argued for very stringent controls, and the State Political-Military Affairs assistant secretary was of like mind. I did not have enough background myself to make a strong argument, but we were very lucky. The Department of Energy had a person called Steve Hue, who was one of the original team with Seymour Cray who had created the first supercomputer.

Q: That was the Cray supercomputer.

JONES: Cray, who worked at Los Alamos. Hue was very familiar with it. He was a very hard-nosed Chinese-American engineer type, but a software genius. I brought him in to brief State Department on what exactly would be the risk of someone having access, let's say, to our Boulder, Colorado, NOAA supercomputer, to all the software, to everything, to do meteorological analyses. His view was that it wouldn't make much difference. The concept of parallel processing was already out. Once you knew it could be done, you were already dealing at a different level. And he argued that indeed, of course, you want to control access to these things and so on, but it was not anywhere near the make-or-break kind of situation that was presented. It was not anything like the analyses from several agencies, which I will not name, who basically said it was the end of the world and they would end up with a MIRV [multiple independently targeted reentry vehicle] warhead the size of your lunch pail.

Q: Excuse me, but would you name the agencies? I mean, time has gone on.

JONES: OK, it was basically, I would say, the CIA. In DOE, people worked with nuclear weapons all the time and had a very realistic view. They are far away from Washington, very careful of their caveats. They would say when they actually didn't know. DIA was highly specific. In other words, when it came to counting tanks, there was no better agency in the world. They paid attention to things that would make a difference if you were going to fly in troops. They want to know where the such-and-such unit is, where their headquarters are, how much electricity they are pulling from the local grid, and so on. They were down to earth. The CIA technical people were supposed to use their arguments to support the political views of their leaders. It was probably worst under CIA director William Casey. Once he came to a meeting of the Science and Technology Intelligence Committees subgroup that was going to do the Soviet military R&D [research and development] analysis. He not only attended, he ordered us to come up with the "right" conclusions. I was in shock. I don't think he knew there were non-CIA people there actually. But after he left, I said, "We will all do the most honest job that we can, and I will footnote up the wazoo if it isn't. They were just as horrified as I was. There were people who were there who were saying they had worked with totally horrible directors at CIA, in personnel terms, who had never ordered them to change the results.

Q: Did you get any feeling of what was behind almost all of this pressure, to limit as opposed to let it go?

JONES: There was almost no pressure to ease export controls The only pressure on the other side was what you would expect: improve the administration, speed up the case handling, improve what they call the import certificate delivery verification system so that you had a better way to check. Everyone agreed that the paperwork was horrible. I had a lot of sympathy for the analysts who were under the gun all the time, and I had no desire to ruin their careers. Even when they wrote impeccably honest national intelligence daily briefing items, the editors often jazzed it up and so made them alarmist and inaccurate.

Soviet-Europe Gas Pipeline Project

Q: Sure. I am told that if you were a businessman and checked into Paris, your briefcase was searched if you left it in your room.

JONES: There was one case dealing with Soviet plans to build a gas pipeline to sell natural gas to Western Europe. One of the best CIA analysts wrote a clear and balanced account, which concluded that we would be unable to change Soviet plans or European desires to have the pipeline, but that our adamant opposition would only kill any chances of any U.S. companies benefiting from contracts.

Q: Oh yes. This was a major contention point early on in the Reagan years.

JONES: As an economist, the CIA analyst was able to look at it from the economic linkage view. They supply, but you buy, and the two of you become like co-addicts. He sent us a draft and we cleared it without any problems. But he had to call us and pull it all back, and ended up transferring to another division when he refused to change his conclusions. CIA director William Casey personally rewrote and issued it. He was wrong. It may be patriotic, but it can be stupid if you guess wrong.

Q: Well, did you get any feel for the hierarchy within the State Department in what you were doing? I mean, let's say something on the pipeline: we think it is wrong. Was there . . . .

JONES: State can take credit for being right on the pipeline issue. For one thing, State has to consider the economic side as well as the whole range of bilateral and multilateral issues. We didn't just go in to the European Union and a lot of NATO countries with just one thing we wanted. We had whole baskets in every conceivable area affecting our security, our desires for this, our desires for that. Since you can't get everything, State always had a very balanced approach, and the various bureaus in the clearance process were very frank about it.

There was the time when we tried to stop the heavy-water shipment going through Paris to a "bad" country. The customs agent in Paris missed the shipment, despite the intelligence we provided, because he was looking for the French label for heavy water and not "heavy water." Then we had information that it would transship from Monrovia. The nonproliferators wanted to make a démarche to the Liberian government, headed by Sammy Doe, but were dissuaded by the African Affairs Bureau, who asked them if they really wanted Sammy Doe to shoot the plane down, as that was his way of doing things.

From INR, I went on to East-West trade at that point, but kept contact with my INR friends. I greatly enjoyed my three years in INR and was glad that I had extended the stay a year. I had to give up chemistry, and if I had to work for State, INR was definitely the place where I felt I could contribute the most and where I belonged. I also had dealt with intelligence as a physical sciences officer in ACDA.

Summing Up in INF and Abramowitz as INR Director

Q: What were you doing when Abramowitz came in? This was when?

JONES: OK, '80—to '82 I was OES; '82 to '85, it would have been around '85, I guess.

Q: OK, so this was still high Reagan period.

JONES: Yes. The actual political masters at the higher levels did not really have that much of an effect on us, except for Abramowitz.

Q: What were you getting from your colleagues on the effect of Abramowitz coming in? Was this a change?

JONES: Yes. He changed the basic role of INR. INR under Montgomery considered itself an intelligence service organization for all the bureaus, not just the assistant secretaries and the secretary of state. The focus was all on getting the secretary's attention, so much blood was shed in the writing of the morning briefing. In Hugh Montgomery's tenure, we were there to make sure that the working level got as much in-depth intelligence as was possible. In most cases, given the nature of the material, they would come to my desk and read the compartmented material or communications intelligence material.

Q: This being essentially the eavesdropping results.

JONES: Yes, and any other agency reports, because when you deal with things like export controls, you deal a lot with their debriefing of U.S. citizens who have gone to major conferences and so on. You had, more or less, a more complete picture. For example, we had a "nuclear winter" scare at the time. It took a lot of extra background to get a more accurate picture.

Under the Abramowitz regime, I understood that everyone got up practically at dawn so they could prepare something that would make the chief briefer, who was Abramowitz, look good with the secretary of state. That is fine. Every head of a new bureau likes to do that, but everything else was neglected. It was sad to see.

It was easier on the science side in INR, where issues were much clearer than when we were trying to determine the personal intentions of the head of the Greek government with base negotiations.

Q: That is one of the things that I have noted, that is sort of natural, that overseas—I was in Greece, for example. I was consul general, and to the station chief, I would say something like, "An American came in and said his cousin was beaten up by the police"—the police were beating up people a lot. The station chief would say, "Well, I talked to the chief of police there, and they said they weren't beating them up"—the problem being there is something if something comes out of intelligence, a lot of this you paid for in one way or another, and it sounds much more impressive than just the sort of thing you might read in the newspaper or hear in casual conversation. Something you haven't paid for, just out of the ordinary diplomatic reporting thing.

JONES: Yes.

Human Relations and Some of My Principles for FS Work

Q: I am sure in Washington it is also the same principle. We have our sources you know, this all sounds great.

JONES: I can quote Montgomery: "It is the source, the source, the source, stupid!" Basically the quality of the source, the capability of the source makes a big difference. And what I found in my twenty-five-year career at State is that I had certain advantages. You have to remember I was in the position of a dentist being put into practicing gynecology. I had an advantage by having learned to learn in my scientific career. You have a very logical structure that helps show you what you still need to know. Every problem is different. Problems don't care if you have a PhD in physics when the solution requires electrochemistry. So you look to all sources. The legalistic work at State on treaties, such as comparing texts, was easy to understand. Thanks to the University of Pennsylvania College for Women requirement that made female science majors take twice the number of humanities courses as in the College for Men, I had had about twelve humanities courses and had learned to write.

Writing is important in science, because you have to communicate the facts as precisely and accurately as possible; otherwise, someone following your directions could blow up the lab. So the focus in science writing is not the nuance but the facts. That stood me in good stead. The human relations skills were taught by my parents. As for human resources issues like sexual harassment, I don't remember a single instance where I witnessed or suffered inappropriate behavior. Oh, sorry, there was one young man who made the mistake of asking a very attractive female intern for a date in the middle of the main office. She did not work for him; she actually worked for me, so it was sort of a sideways pass. She asked him how old he was. He said, "Thirty-two." She said, "You are too old for me." He had to hide for a week. Otherwise, he and I shared an office and I found it very difficult to block out his attempts to get different women to spend the weekend on his boat with him. He would go through the little black book, and eventually it would go further and further down. Every once in a while, the conversation would penetrate my blocking efforts, but I was not terribly bothered by it. He was being a gentleman. He was trying to ask these women out, and these women were coming up with a million and one excuses.

Q: You make me feel very sorry for the gentleman.

JONES: He had his moments. He tried hard. Later he did find someone; he married happily. I think his idol, the woman he really wanted to get to know, was Princess Di, but she was not available because she was a married woman.

Most Foreign Service officers with whom I dealt had learned a certain amount of diplomacy and were generally tactful. Occasionally, though never in my offices, there were people that were known as "screamers." The feeling there is if you had a screamer, you also had a way to take one out. Because, basically, every Foreign Service officer is in the position of a kamikaze pilot. They may not be able to do much, but they can take out a battleship if it comes to that. The powers in command recognized that. We had all sorts of terms such as a "suicide 2," or someone at the end of their career, able to retire with a pension and unlikely to go any higher. They were now in a good position to pay back any mistreatment. The behavior I saw was all perfectly aboveboard.

CHAPTER 12

The Trials of East West Trade in Export Controls (1985-1987)

COCOM Again—and Agencies Differences of View

Q: OK, let's talk about some of the issues. This would be '80. After you left INR, you went to East-West....

JONES: Export controls, East-West. That is where I chaired a committee of warring agencies so bad that DOD subgroups would call me asking if I could disinvite other DOD people. We, they, were supposed to make specific decisions at to what to do with COCOM. I had to draw on some kung fu strategies. It occurred to me that at all the meetings, everyone had 11,000 initiatives and that it had been like this for years. Therefore, there must be a lot of initiatives that we had proposed earlier. I went back and read through every COCOM record I could find for the three years before I arrived. I found that almost everything they came up with we had already proposed and our COCOM partners had already agreed to implement. My predecessor Vic Comras was a genius. My major contribution was to suggest that instead of proposing things, we remind people of what they had agreed and see what the implementation was. This helped a lot, and made it possible for me to actually see my children grow up. It was easier because I agreed with the goals, which were winning the Cold War and keeping it "cold." Once people got over various testosterone attacks, we could get the work done, because the work had to be done.

Operations and "Chicken Herding" in East-West Trade

Q: What were the issues, I mean the initiatives, that were agreed to, and then were they ever effected?

JONES: Better implementation, better reporting, better control of import certification, delivery verification. Better procedures when it came to third countries.

Q: Well, on this, was it a matter that you all were working on it essentially trying to make a better bureaucratic system, as opposed to saying "We can't sell centrifuges to so and so" and this sort of thing?

JONES: That part was easy once we fixed the problems of the meeting. The meetings used to run hours. I only had one hour. I figured out ways to do it. It took some extra work. For every meeting, I wrote not only the agenda, but I wrote a full report of the meeting right afterward and sent it to everyone for clearance. Eventually, the only things they remembered were the minutes and the agenda. We had to have clearer lines of who was to do what. We were a working committee. We were not there making great policy. For example, we were making sure that the Cuba paper was fully cleared and ready for the delegation.

Q: Well, tell me though, on the personal level, here you are particularly with the DOD and a lady, and a lady of Asian background and all that, with your science. I would think people would say "Oh, my God" because you had babies to take care of. You had an agenda; you wanted to get it done. These meetings are designed for doing what we are doing here, talking away, and displaying ego. I am talking as a guy in a bureaucracy.

JONES: Oh, yes. Actually, surprisingly enough, I got a lot of support from a lot of DOD colonels who too had offices to go back to. When I started, I said that the purpose of the meetings is to get the work done. I wore two hats. With one hat, I am just the administrative person trying to get actual work out of the pipeline. I am not selling a State Department position. I am going to write notes, minutes. I call the meetings. I get conference rooms. If I have to speak up for my bureau, I am going to announce that I am now wearing hat number two, so they know exactly where I am coming from. I also recognized that all of them shared common goals. They were all patriotic Americans. They all wanted us to have the most secure export control system possible and the most efficient. None of them to the best of my knowledge wanted to see our industry, technological might, or technological lead disappear. So we started with that.

I even had DOD agree with my view that we wanted to send the strongest possible delegation. We wanted the A-team. We didn't want to look like asses.

One of their strategies was to pull back their clearance about ten minutes before the delegation was to leave. My response was simple: other people may have time to play these games, but if someone pulled their clearances, then we would start all over again. As DOD was usually the agency pushing the initiative, they quickly decided it wasn't worth losing the time. We had our moments. I was told later in private by one of the women lawyers that she knew I was going to be difficult to argue with when she saw me pull my pantyhose up to my armpits. I would go in girded for battle in the traditional sense. Science and technology training actually helps, as getting a whole lab team to do something isn't easy and provides much interagency usable practice

Chemistry and East-West Trade—Some Parallels

Q: Did you get any feel for the difference between the academic process in chemistry, let's say, and the academic process in English or international relations?

It was very much like the way you would plan synthesis of a new chemical. You had to get the ingredients. You had to figure out the costs. You had to get the people to do their part. Then you had to test it. So the science background did help. Science helps you move a little beyond the actual problem itself. In other words, you could just sit back and give yourself a little distance, and sometimes things come forward that you hadn't noticed before.

JONES: Oh, yes. I met my husband David in 1959 at Penn. He majored in international relations and went to graduate school at Penn. I met all his fellow graduate students, and thought at the time there were tremendous differences. The professors in chemistry generally didn't attack each other much. They were busy trying to get very lucrative consulting contracts. Their reputations came from whether they could place their graduate students after their PhDs. in prestigious universities or top companies. The head of the department was president of the American Chemical Society, and owned a yacht as a result of a patent. And the graduate students didn't compete against each other because, basically, we all had the same problems. The only way to get the PhD was to solve your problem. And since many heads are better than one, most graduate groups would meet and talk over everyone's work, and then people would come up with suggestions. There was less individual rivalry. I noticed that in questions.

When you go to a chemistry seminar, the questions are likely to be, "On slide three when I did that experiment, I got 5.2 instead of 5.4. Can you explain it?" But the questions were real questions, even if hostile: "I don't believe your explanation using the molecular orbital theory makes sense. I go by another theory." When I first went with David to a political science conference, I was in shock. The questions were longer than the speech. I mean the people come up, they gave you their views. They cited their authors. I kept saying, "What is he asking? What is he asking?" I couldn't find it.

Q: Did you notice in this military approach with the military people? Was there a difference between them and maybe your experience in State Department and CIA?

JONES: Yes, a certain amount. What I try to remember is that each of these agencies had a different mission. Individual offices had specific missions within the agencies. So in order to familiarize myself with the portfolio, I carefully looked up exactly where each group came from and tried to get a feel for what they did in general. They were willing to explain. It gave me a chance to see what kind of views they had. The Department of Defense military and civilian components had their own specific views and missions and needs. I don't know how any ambassador survives getting a whole group in a country team meeting to agree to one single thing, because to me it is like teaching chickens, ducks, geese, and maybe an ostrich or two how to tango together.

I was dealing with groups of people with different aims. Once I understood the aims, I did what I could to come up with some kind of a framework of enough mutual benefit to stand. You would have a company that wanted to export, but they wanted the government's blessing because they also had an interest in getting government contracts and so on. You had DOD that didn't want this company to go down the tubes, because they were a good and reliable supplier. You had State Department that didn't want a trade war with a trading partner. You had the military that certainly didn't want improved guns on the other side. So with all of these, you could work out something.

It's different today in dealing with terrorism issues, as the only solution the terrorist accepts is your annihilation. The scientific training helps in organizing the data and making sense of it. It helps you know where to start the chipping the block of marble.

I had limited overseas experience—Brussels, Montreal, and Ottawa. I was always pleasantly surprised at how good the people were, and occasionally saddened by what they did to themselves. At the State Department itself, my experience in assignments counseling, recruiting, and the board of examiners was good.

Morale was a very noticeable problem during my time as a counseling and assignments officer. There was tremendous pressure. A promotion was more than a promotion. It was more than more income. It was an affirmation almost of self-worth.

On Being a Science Officer

Q: I have found this. After a promotion I felt for a year or two a certain raising of the adrenalin or something like this, somebody loves me.

JONES: Yes, and for a science officer, we are in a very privileged position. At the time I was on active duty, we were considered a subcone of the economics cone, but as a subcone we only competed against each other. There were only twenty some science officers in the entire Foreign Service; therefore, all they had to do was match the number of positions available when it was your turn; you got promoted unless you had done something totally awful. There was a lot less direct competition.

We are not really doing science work at State; we were translators. We were bringing to bear our knowledge in areas where a certain amount of scientific knowledge was useful. But we were not doing scientific research. In their innocence, the National Academy of Sciences has often wanted to send science attachés abroad. They have very little understanding of the work a science officer actually does. There is no such thing as a scientist, *per se*—there are a biologists, chemists, genetic engineers, material science engineers, and so on. We have three daughters in three different fields of engineering.

So the vision of the actual work you do is often not very clear. As I mentioned earlier, when I first met a science counselor in Paris, Dr. Edgar L. Piret, I met a man who was really on the periphery of the embassy. He was thrilled at the idea of sniffers that could detect heroin labs. When you process heroin, you use acetic anhydride. The problem is when acetic anhydride reacts with water, it becomes acetic acid, which is vinegar. Name me a restaurant in the south of France that does not have the odor of vinegar around. And as a result, they were able to map every restaurant in the south of France. The only analogy I could think of was the "Annie Oakley" system they used in Vietnam. It was a way to pinpoint incoming mortar fire by triangulation with two sensors. While it worked very nicely in the desert in test firing, it was not equipped to handle all that battlefield chaos and noise and had a hysterical attack and broke down.

A political, political-military officer at an embassy has a very clear mandate. He knows to whom he is reporting at the Department of State. A science officer oversees no specific mandate—and certainly does not do circular reporting for science agencies—which are focused mostly on their own research missions. Even agencies with a lot of international ties and links tend to set up the links directly. As for scientific intelligence, experts in any field know much more about what their foreign counterparts are doing than any science officer could hope to know.

The key is which agency has the lead. The political-military people have their slice of nonproliferation policy, but when it comes to the actual nuclear power trade, let's say, it is not State. It is Ex-Im Bank, it is the Nuclear Regulatory Commission, it is the Department of Energy. At the same time, we have to have Foreign Service officers who are technically literate, because they represent the most technological country in the world. There is hardly anything that doesn't have a technological aspect to it. If you talk trade, let's talk broadband communications, standards, blue ray.

The Soviets and Biological Warfare

Q: Well, this is where you say the role is really—I have never heard it before—basically a translator, which is extremely important. To say what are the issues, and there as a scientist, you probably can pick up the issues, can't you?

JONES: Yes, they are very straightforward. The issues, when you look at the political side of it, almost always result in the effects of this technology.

I reviewed a book entitled *Biohazard*, by Ken Alibek, on biological warfare. It was chilling. It made clear that even while the Soviets were letting us visit their facilities and signing all sorts of agreements, they were also producing biological agents in quantity. This work continues as former Soviet Union scientists sell their skills worldwide. Every Foreign Service officer needs to have a basic understanding of technologies and science that can affect us all.

We should thank Colin Powell, whose major contribution to State is making sure that every desk had an Internet connection. There were officers who did not know how to use the Internet when it had become important. Even when I was in INR, this was in the dark ages. We had something about the open flow of information and widely available data bases.

High Speed Integrated Circuits and Designing Nuclear Weapons

No one has any control over the technical information flow. For example, when the Air Force was developing very-high-speed integrated circuits, they kept the program under very tight security. Then they decided to see what was out there and paid a graduate student to write a paper on what he thought was going on in the field of very-high-speed integrated circuits. He just read *Aviation Week* and whatever other open source he could find. Even without the Internet, he still found a lot and wrote up a little paper for which he was paid nicely, bought a new car, and disappeared into the distance. They had to classify the paper. Because he was an intelligent engineer who understood integrated circuits, he had come up with some real intelligence on the Air Force program by using open sources alone.

In a similar vein, the Department of Energy—when we were talking nuclear controls—wanted to have a better idea of what someone could do if they couldn't have access to anything special, but they knew what was already out there on our atom bomb. Remember there is a book by Samuel Glasstone and Philip Dolan, *The Effects of Nuclear Weapons*. The key was really knowing that it could be done, as we proved in Hiroshima and Nagasaki. So the Department of Energy hired a group of retired bomb hands who had worked in the initial bomb project when we knew so little that one man actually killed himself by moving beryllium shells too close together around a neutron source. They had a lot of fun. Their first conclusion was that all this stuff on shielding for hot boxes wasn't critical, all you needed were lead bricks. You may indeed have cancer in twenty years, but you'd have a working bomb. They had to classify the results of that paper, which read like a bomb recipe book.

David and I were able to give each other unique slants on things. You might say he was my political-military teacher and I was his technical backup.

Q: *Well, getting back to COCOM . . .*

JONES: COCOM, the Coordinating Committee. It is now the Wassenaar group.

Detecting Nuclear Submarines and the "Toshiba" Problem

Q: *Were you involved? I think there was a famous case—I want to say Toshiba.*

JONES: Toshiba, yes.

Q: *Now was that during your time?*

JONES: Yes.

Q: *Can you explain what it was and whatever piece of the action you might have had?*

JONES: OK, we try to detect nuclear missile submarines coming too close to our shores with something called a SOSUS [sound surveillance system] line, which are sonar detectors placed about 1,000 miles out into the bed of the Atlantic. Therefore, the aim of every submariner is to have the quietest possible submarine. Submarines make noise because their screws as they go through the water do something called cavitation: the motion of the screws causes little air bubbles to come out of the seawater and makes noise, but if you have a screw shaped a certain way, you cut the noise tremendously.

Q: *This is the angle of the blades and its configuration.*

JONES: Yes. And to do so you need a very sophisticated, precise, five-axis machine tool, I think it is about fifteen feet high and weighs a couple of tons. This is not something you carry out in your backpack while you are visiting the plant. We had information that one such machine tool made by Toshiba Machine Tools, a Toshiba subsidiary, had gotten to the Soviet Union. The Hill got very excited, and some congressmen even bought a couple of Toshiba VCRs to destroy on TV. There was talk of trade sanctions against the Japanese.

The complication, however, was that the U.S. Army depended on a lot of Toshiba parts and even had ordered Toshiba laptops. So we could not shoot off the left foot while we were busy trying to use the right foot. I was in East-West trade at the time and was handed a junior officer who was having career problems. He was very bright, very personable, but had had problems while working as a consular officer in Tijuana. This could be his chance. I talked to him. The first thing I noticed was everyone seemed to know he was having problems. The junior officers working in the other divisions made fun of him—almost schoolyard bullying.

People depend so much on their self-image for their confidence, but the minute you have someone bleeding in their "amour-propre," the wolves will gather. It is an immediate hierarchy. Unless you are an old bat like I was, already armored, it can be very difficult to recover your self-esteem once nicked by the efficiency report process. The other thing is that anytime anyone has troubles, no one looks at the system for flaws. Think how much money it costs to get a Foreign Service officer from zero to an effective junior officer. The system has spent money, so if there is any problem, the system has to look at itself for failures and not only at the failed junior officer.

He was intelligent; he was a lawyer. He understood the law. He worked very hard, and I did a daring thing: I turned over the whole Toshiba-Königsberg case and all the press releases and the write-ups to him, and he handled it flawlessly. He also helped greatly in drafting comments on proposed changes to the Export Administration Act. I also had to cope with the fact that as soon as people are down, they work harder to kick you. All the cables that he wrote got turned back. I thought this was odd, as they were totally *pro forma* cables. So I told him to write it but put my name on it. Every single one of those went through. Then I went to the boss who had rejected his cables and confessed that I had written them. After that he was better. I gave the junior officer an honest efficiency report, and it got him tenure. It also taught me how the system can destroy the unlucky ones, and the only defense when attacked is to fight back. Unfair criticism can destroy self esteem.

Q: I have always found the grievance process, you know, sometimes there are real grievance issues, but people who go through it invariably talk about their grievance. That immediately turns their colleagues off. It gets to be a distancing, and I wonder about this.

JONES: It's still a chance to hear the second side of the story.

The Italian Hughes Helicopter Diversion to North Korea

Q: Yeah. Was there any foreign connection with what you were doing, or were the foreigners you dealt with the Department of Defense or the Department of Commerce?

JONES: Oh, we had some fun. There was also the Hughes helicopter diversion by North Koreans.

Q: Good God!

JONES: The South Koreans absolutely went up a tree, because these are the same helicopters that they use for their military. So you had the nightmare image of a helicopter supposedly from their military bombing the presidential palace, let's say.

Q: The Blue Palace.

JONES: Yes, the Blue Palace. And they were very unhappy, and they said so. In fact, one of the Korean diplomats in Washington made so many démarches against the Italian embassy in town that he was barred from their embassy. So he would come to State to rant against the Italians. He just had to get it out of his system. We often called in foreign diplomats to get answers as to their company's involvement in the diversion. There was a DOD colleague called "Mad Dog" [Michael] Maloof—eventually his nickname got out. Once as I introduced him, an Italian diplomat said, "Oh, you are the famous MMMM . . . Michael Maloof." He was the same Italian diplomat who had a fit because we didn't call him in to one of our sessions where we were basically yelling at another country for violating this and that. But, we said, "You didn't do it." But he insisted on being invited anyway. I was told by the Italian desk that was the "Italian syndrome." Never leave them out.

Q: What happened as you saw this helicopter thing? It sounds pretty serious to me.

JONES: It was serious. I think Hughes paid a huge fine. Individuals who were co-opted, including senior military figures in Europe, provided the false trail that led to a diversion to North Korea. Eventually, the South Koreans calmed down and they tightened procedures. As a result, Hughes eventually lost a very lucrative satellite contract. But I was not in it enough to know exactly what happened.

I also dealt with Foreign Science Counselors a lot, especially in OES when I was there on nuclear issues, and again later when I did science and technology cooperation. When you are female, Asian, and middle-aged, you become harder to "read." I did find it was a help to have the PhD, a post-doc, and the science credentials. It is the same principle for instance, that allowed me to get salesmen and mechanics to treat me seriously if I had complaints about their gas chromatography instruments when I did research.

The rule is that if you constantly look for slights, you will certainly find them. The bottom line was always just getting the work done. I didn't have the time to brood over things. Injustice collectors never run short of material.

CHAPTER 13

Economics Training and a Cox Sabbatical (1987)

Q: After you left the last assignment we talked about, where did you go?

JONES: After the Office of S&T [Science and Technology] Cooperation in the Bureau of Oceans and International Environmental and Scientific Affairs, I think I went to economic training after East-West trade. We had already gotten an assignment to Pakistan, science for me, political-military for David. Ambassador Arnie Raphel knew David, wanted him, but we did not get medical clearance so the assignment was broken. Since my assignment was broken, the only place I could be put was in economic training, which fit because science officers were a subcone of economic officers. It was a break, and fun for me. I had never in my life had economics. The only economics I had was reading David's textbooks when I was desperate for reading material.

Q: Samuelson?

JONES: Oh, yes. No problem. After reading thermodynamics, Samuelson was like a novel.

Q: When did you move to economics?

JONES: Let me see. Was it '87 or was it '85? Yeah, it was probably '87.

The Econ Course: Pluses and (Many) Minuses (1987)

Q: How did you find the economics course?

JONES: I enjoyed it a great deal. It was very relaxing because the beginning of it was mathematics. I really enjoyed my fellow students. We were a relatively small class—a group of ostriches, chickens, beavers—which they were trying to get to dance to the same tune. The training was very classical. The problem was that without truly in-depth training, even though you can cram in the facts, you can't cram in the critical thinking. The other problem was that the mathematics was a bad fit for many economic problems. While you can teach people to do algebra and to solve calculus equations, unless they understand the underlying basis, they can misapply it.

Economics misapplies it regularly, but for the small range of changes they deal with, they can get away with it. But they can't get away with it whenever they deal with what you would call a shock, such as a depression, a war, or a boom. They assume that things like pricing and quantity are independent variables. They are not. An independent variable in mathematical terms means that a change in one will not change the other. They are different dimensions.

The econ training was also very heavily pro—free trade. By the end of the course, when we finally had speakers coming from the University of Chicago economics school to present a major non—free trade school of thinking, I was amazed to see the class arise as one in defense of free trade. They had been successfully indoctrinated. Admittedly, the arguments went back to Adam Smith and the concept of comparative advantage. All the comparative advantages from free trade depend on ten basic assumptions holding, such as perfect market, perfect competition, perfect information, and so on. Time is not included in economic analyses except at the most sophisticated university levels.

I was more interested in the models than in defending free trade. I did fine on the graduate record exam on economics at the end of the course and, theoretically, I could have gone into a graduate program and headed for a doctorate in economics. But I also knew the difference between being able to write about something and being able to do it.

I had another problem with the training, and that was State getting its economic officers through in-house training instead of bringing in real economists—there is no shortage of qualified candidates with economic backgrounds who also pass the Foreign Service test. To me, any good organization that is world class should be able to bring in the skills it needs. There is a great deal of lip service about taking in your generalists and giving them a spot of training here and a spot of training there, but sometimes you do need real expertise. The Foreign Service Institute economic training was good for familiarization, but not for producing real, working economists.

The only reason for having in-house economics training is to equip someone to do economic work at a small post, along with doing other work. So I wrote an article about the course for the *Foreign Service Journal*. I doubt the course director, Lisa Fox, will ever forgive me. Her critique of my performance was I held them to too scientific a standard. I kept saying I wasn't holding them to standards, I was trying to explain why their standards were inadequate. There is a difference.

Q: In a way, looking at this, you came from really quite a different background than most of the people there. But my impression, and you are talking with somebody who got a D minus in economics from a man who later became Eisenhower's head of the Office of the Budget. He was an instructor at my college at the time. It was a well-deserved D minus—it was almost a gift. I get the feeling that economics officers really don't need to know an awful lot of economics. I mean, as you were saying, if you really want economics to a certain point, it moves to a level that isn't the job of the person back in the field to really discover. The main thing an economic officer can do is get the feel for the statistics right as the information goes in, and be able to talk the talk a little to people who may be able to give the information.

JONES: I made the point in the article I wrote for the *Foreign Service Journal* that we were not being taught as adults. We were still being taught the way they teach college freshmen, so that you tended to get lost in irrelevant details. On mathematics, it would have done a lot more good to explain to people the basis behind calculus, which is that it is a way of computing change, change that follows a pattern, a sufficiently clear pattern that you can actually do a mathematical formula that relates one factor to another to predict change or project change. When they dealt with matrices, there was no explanation of the problem that the error range the total matrix is the sum of the error range of each element. So if you have a 1 percent error in each element, which is very little, and you have ten elements across, and ten elements down, that is 100 cells, plus or minus 100 percent range of error.

To me, the credit should go to the brilliant intuitive insights provided by economists on the complex behavior of human groups. The important thing is how it mixes political issues, population issues, demographics, and resource issues with human behavior. My special interest was still in the effect of technology and technological change.

Q: As you looked at this, was there an approach to economics of the various approaches that particularly seemed to you to make the best sense?

JONES: When it came to trade, you had to move beyond the basic trade paradigms. Free trade is wonderful. Free trade does not take into account the power of one group when they get tremendous market share because of innovative and new technology. Free trade does not deal well with technological advances. For example, to make the original videocassette recorder, the Japanese took U.S. technology, which was Ampex, which had a system that was $5,000, then they put approximately 125 engineers to work on it for five years—about the same amount of effort as we did for our air defense system. They ended up with a $300 item, which gave them a tremendous market share. By the time an item is cheap and everyone can make it, you can't hold market position. You have to go to the next level. Therefore, government policies that protect nascent industries or nascent technologies or have unfair trade barriers are almost all designed to give their own people the lead. The United States did it earlier in its history. We had plenty of non—free trade rules protecting our own domestic industries.

Some Personalities from the Economics Course

I shared a cubicle with John Butler, who was later killed in Grenada. I got to know him fairly well. He was engaged to be married. He used to refer to his fiancée as his "main squeeze." He was just a very decent and unfortunate man.

Q: What happened?

JONES: There were people sent in there to inspect a police station for corruption. Somehow he got shot to death. I think one of the policemen went berserk and shot several people to death, including John.

I also sat across from Howard Kravitz, who may be the world's greatest linguistic genius. He rebelled against middle-class liberal parents in Philadelphia by becoming a bricklayer. When this wasn't enough rebellion, as his parents strongly opposed the war in Vietnam, he joined the Special Forces. He didn't like all that army discipline stuff, but was he linguistically talented! He had four years in Vietnam, going from rice paddy to rice paddy. His Chinese was superior to mine by far, because he could read and write. He was married to a Taiwan Chinese. Once he got so excited talking to her on the phone and to one of his contractors at home—who was trying to put the dishwasher in backwards—that he started yelling at the contractor in Chinese. He later managed to pass the Japanese test at FSI [Foreign Service Institute] with a three, which meant ready to go to Yokohama for further training, which he didn't want to do, as he was still refinishing his house. So he did a first: he protested his passing grade, which he claimed was just pidgin Japanese he had "picked up." They gave up and put him back in class. I remember talking to a classmate and asking how he was doing. His comment was, "They never shut up. He and the instructor never shut up."

Q: Who was this?

JONES: Howard Kravitz. I think he is still in the service. He is wonderful. He is brilliant. I think he has several children now. When he went into the economic training, they had no children yet.

Understanding Promotion Panels

But I did want to cover one thing I forgot my stint on the FS-3 to FS-2 econ promotion board during my period in East-West trade. I actually wrote an article about the results of that. For once, I cleared the article with everyone on the board because I wrote it with a feeling that no one was doing anyone any favors by having a truly opaque system. In those days, we had about 2,000 files to read. We were not told the number of positions. We were just told to rank the people, and then the top number X would get promoted. We had all sorts of representatives from different cones on the panel. I particularly admired one, Michael Marine, who was a consular officer who did a lot of good. We had one member of the board, Tom Miller, who thought only political reporting was important and ignored anyone who didn't have a political officer's touch with language, and so disregarded major accomplishments by consular officers who deserved promotion. We had real battles on it.

For example, we had a consular officer who was well overdue for promotion. He got a special commendation for thinking outside of the box in the case of an American in a Latin American country who had been lost in the Andes. They had flyers, they put out rewards, and he quickly realized that they weren't getting any action at all. They couldn't afford to hire hundreds, maybe thousands, of people to search, so he printed up flyers that had pictures of a pile of gold coins for whomever located the missing man. The coins were worth much less than the rewards that were offered, but the pictures spoke to the villagers. Whole villages emptied out to search the area for him, and they found the guy and saved him. This, I thought, was really striking. Well, his self statement was truly a pedestrian list of declarative sentences. His native language might not have been English. Michael Marine said this was the type of person who wanted the next level of consular work. Tom focused almost entirely on the English style that he disliked. Michael won. We all voted with Michael.

At the time, we had something called a "rat file," which is a rating officer file. Occasionally, you would have an officer whose record would be fine, and then all of a sudden there would be terrible reports. The question was, was the officer that bad or did he run into a really strict rating officer? By being able to call for the rat file, there were several cases in which the bad reports were frankly neutralized. Alas, you had a certain number of rating officers in the Foreign Service who believed they were God's gift to the diplomatic world, and everyone else was inferior, and they wrote the efficiency reports that way.

So I wrote the article to help people understand the system. The self statement was also appropriately called the "suicide box." For example, one person who had a minor little nick that said occasionally he could use fewer words in his cables wrote an eight-page, single-spaced rebuttal. We had never seen anyone prove the rating officer right so spectacularly. There were other lessons I learned about bad reports, which I applied when I was on different review panels. As a visible minority female, I got to serve on a lot of review panels, and whenever there was a bad report, I learned to make sure that the reviewing officer statement on relations between the rating and the rated officer was honest. If he or she did not know them, they should say so because this kind of report invariably ended up before a grievance panel. Truth was very important. If two people cordially detested each other or worse, it could affect the fairness of the report.

Until I served on the promotion panel, I had had little interest in the Foreign Service as a culture or organization; my focus was on the work. I often found that Sun Tzu's *Art of War* applied nicely to Foreign Service bureaucratics.

Una Chapman Cox Sabbatical—a Special Gift to the Foreign Service (1988)

Q: Ok, well, back to the battle: What about '88 or so, where did you go from the economic course?

JONES: I got an Una Chapman Cox fellowship. I offered the selection committee two possible projects. One was to do a better statistical analysis on the lawsuit brought by the women officers to see whether they were really comparing like with like. Part of my doctorate was doing sophisticated nonlinear error analyses, and I was well aware of how easy it was to skew statistical results. The adage is, "If you torture the statistics, they will confess."

When I did recruiting, I also found that the best correlation seemed to be between large universities, international relations and economics majors, and pass rates. Since more men than women took the Foreign Service test and majored in these areas, it would be difficult to use the statistics honestly to prove bias against women. So I felt a real statistician could provide a better analysis. Either it would prove that the State Department had some kind of tremendous bias, or it would prove that there was not, but it was an honest way to get the facts. That they didn't want—and I was discouraged from pursuing that proposal.

I also suggested something on better understanding how technology became commercialized, crossing the "valley of death" between invention and market. Other countries are using national means to do it. Japan had its MITI, the Ministry of International Trade and Industry. The Europeans had every conceivable way they were trying to help their people over it. We were big talking about level playing fields, but we weren't able to level other people's playing fields. We ended up with more innovation from universities by allowing cooperative research and development agreements. I argued that economic or diplomatic work on this kind of global technological competition meant that Foreign Service officers needed a better understanding of the government's role in the innovation-commercialization cycle. That proposal they okayed.

I also did a project comparing how other countries' science counselors do their work [as opposed] to how we do ours. I profiled the ones in Washington versus what we were doing in their home countries—let's say, what the French were doing in Washington on science and technology and what we were doing in Paris. I did interviews, sort of like your oral history, and wrote them up. The systems were very different. For example, the French use theirs to cover seriously every area in depth. That means you would need eleven people for eleven different areas, while we had one science counselor and one junior officer in Paris. We did a lot of coordination, but had little lead in any area. When our energy people want to talk to the alternative energy people in France, they often did so directly. You can be sure that someone who has spent their lives working in a specific area knows everyone in the world who is working in it.

Recruiting for State: the Hunt for Visible Minorities

Q: You were mentioning doing some recruiting. Looking this over, one of the things that has struck me there is this tremendous emphasis, at least in rhetoric, on the diversity of the Foreign Service, which seems to boil down to getting, more particularly, black males, or African American males. You know, among other things you represent a Chinese, or an Asian, which falls into the diversity thing, but obviously this isn't your particular thing. I mean you bring up other things to it, but what about the Asian recruitment? Have you been kind of looking at this? Is the Foreign Service very appealing to the Asian community, because you think about the University of California at Berkeley which is practically completely Asian . . . .

JONES: Their engineering school graduation when I attended it to see my nephew get his degree in computer science was about fifty-five percent Asian.

Q: In your estimation, was the Foreign Service reaching out and getting a significant or a fair number of Asian Americans into it or not?

JONES: Asians were not considered a "problem" visible minority, and they are a very small percentage of the general population. Asians generally do well in education, income, and testing. So the Asians tended not to come in via the special minority target recruitments. They pass the written examination. I was a member of the Asian Pacific American Federal Employees Council when Cora Foley, a friend, headed APAFEC. The biggest thing was that we had wonderful luncheon meetings where people could gripe about how hard it was to be noticed by anyone, as we troubled no one. We were a "model minority."

Q: I was going to say the food should have been great.

JONES: Oh, it was, absolutely. She had a group of Filipina grandmothers who were tired of retirement and had a catering service. Every time we had Asian American week, they would have one reception and she would call in these women. They even catered one on the Hill, something that would normally cost $15 to $20 a head and they managed a legendary feed for about $5 a head. But yes, we had job fairs, we talked to young people, but there was a bias certainly among Chinese and probably among Koreans toward science and technological careers or medicine or law. It was back to the desire for a "steel rice bowl." To do well in your new society without political clout, without huge numbers, the only way was to use education. Asians were not in a position to provide the political structure that allowed Irish groups to move up in Boston.

There was no way they would let a Chinese be a policeman in a borough in New York in those days. But you can make it through medical school, and someone who needs stitches is not going to care what race you are, especially—if they are aware that you had gotten there by doing well.

I had no bias problems through high school because I had other Asians who had already fought and won these battles. A Chinese group won Nobel Prize dealing with the parity principle just after we arrived in the United States. After we arrived in 1950, I met a woman who was part of that group. She was a skinny little Chinese woman who said in her day you had to give up on marriage. Years later, she looked at all the men she could have married and decided she had made a better choice. It was physics or making dim sums by hand for the spouse's lunch.

The Damage from Affirmative Action

We did do one thing that showed something that I thought was much more important. We did a survey of the educational attainments of the civil and Foreign Service award winners and compared that with the educational attainments of blacks and Hispanics. The minority group members were the most surprised to find out that their educational attainments were actually higher. They had internalized the idea that they only got where they did because of affirmative action. There were more master's degrees, there was more extensive additional training, there were more law degrees. This was an image and a bias that had internalized itself in the minority group.

So I thought that was one of the things that showed the true harm that can be done from well-meaning helping hands. Once you are not dealing with things like patenting new polymers, being able to catch a football, or to win a race, things that are *provable*, people were denied a chance to have real confidence in their real accomplishments. No one can argue that Michael Jordan wasn't a good basketball player because he was given EEO [equal employment opportunity] treatment. You could see it, or you could see that Wilma Rudolph won. In fact, some of the most successful black officers went back and took the written exam just to prove they could do it. I think Ambassador Perkins understood that point, and that was why he insisted that everyone go through the written test. Everyone has a right to be disliked for himself alone.

Q: OK, you got out . . .

JONES: Econ training, the Una Chapman Cox fellowship.

Q: What did you do after this?

JONES: Oh, I wrote a fair number of papers on venture capital, on the effects of computers and information technology, and on the effects of university technology transfer agreements and cooperative research and development agreements, plus the big paper I did on science counselors.

I used the Una Chapman Cox funds to set up an effective home office: wire properly my basement with fully grounded plugs and doubled the amperage going in. I had a fax machine. I had separate phone lines. I did a spread sheet of the expenses and used a specific credit card so that there would be no misunderstanding. I know they don't require the reporting of expenses, but I just felt more comfortable that way.

It was a wonderful time. I think I published things, I think I even published an article called, "Thoughts of a Wandering Recruiter." I did a recruiting session at UCLA and funded a brochure for OES to explain its functions for their public affairs people. In fact, David had a Una Chapman Cox fellowship before I did, but, fortunately, it didn't count against me when they reviewed my proposals.

Q: I was going to say you and David seem to have the virus. You can't help yourself. You write articles all the time.

JONES: Well, he does. I sent you an example of what we do for the National Council for Advanced Manufacturing. I do all the research and the first draft, and he puts it into much nicer form. It was a great way to use my Foreign Service reporting cable training and the discipline that comes of meeting deadlines.

Q: Oh, absolutely.

JONES: I even used my Foreign Service training skills to edit my daughter's PhD dissertation, which was on calcium ion channel mechanisms. She got her MD and PhD in bioengineering from Hopkins. I thought the work was proof of the existence of God, as nothing that complex could happen just by chance. I had to read three textbooks and about fifty articles before I could understand what she was writing. In the end, I only fixed some punctuation.

CHAPTER 14

Back to OES and Technology Cooperation (1988-1990)

Q: Let's go back to science and technology cooperation.

Scope of International Agreements

JONES: It was basically one of the traditional science counselor, science-counselor-wannabe positions because the office dealt with science and technology cooperation agreements with the world. The State Department has prime lead in something called the "umbrella agreement," the agreement under which all the individual agreements—say, energy researchers, health researchers, with their counterparts—takes place. In most countries there were no problems negotiating an umbrella agreement until we decided that we needed to cover the intellectual property rights that might result from the cooperation. The intellectual property rights would be covered in an annex to the main agreement. It was long, legalistic, and covered every conceivable type of discovery and invention. There was a fair amount of opposition from the various scientists, as basic research almost never resulted in intellectual property. If a U.S. government entity were involved on the one end, the intellectual property belonged to the U.S. taxpayer and not the agency.

I could very easily understand the basic reasoning on protecting intellectual property rights. I had, after all, had a summer job at American Cyanamid examining Japanese patents and looking for usable loopholes. However, the real problems with intellectual property rights were things more related to outright theft, counterfeits, and so on. On those, USTR [Office of the U.S. Trade Representative] had the lead and worked very hard, but not too successfully, because the governments either colluded or they were unable to stop the violations. So science and technology agreements were an easy target for bureaucratic triumphs.

To give you an example of how this was received, we went to the South Koreans and said, "Here it is." They said, "What are you going to do to us if we don't sign on?" Well, we weren't going to do anything. We have a very open system, and they were already doing all the research and cooperation they wanted to do in the United States. Then they said, "Well, what is in it for us?" And there wasn't a special benefit to offer, either. At this point, they said "bye-bye, Charlie." In fact, I had charge of the Asia, India, and Japan science and technology agreements.

AAAS Fellows at State

Q: That is where the real action was anyway, wasn't it?

JONES: State was not in a strong position. While the scientists knew they could live perfectly well without State, we couldn't do without their support. I loved the office. My colleagues were wonderful. It was my first experience with AAAS fellows. The American Association for the Advancement of Science had fellows in the State Department to give them exposure to policymaking, international science, and technology. It was easier to teach them diplomacy than to teach a diplomat the science. It was very glamorous for them, and since I jet lagged horribly, I was the one supervisor who was willing to send my AAAS fellows out with delegations instead of going out myself. Instead, I served as the twenty-four-hour backstopping person.

I may also have been the only person who recommended against breaking up the office into divisions. It might have made me a division chief, but I thought that any organization where an office director and a deputy director could not manage nine people was in serious trouble. If they had to have three divisions to add three division chief positions, State was in sad shape.

Q: 1989.

JONES: One of them, in fact, we teased a lot because she decided on a bicycle trip in China to go with her China visit. Just at the time Tiananmen Square took place. The National Academy of Sciences and the U.S. science agencies worked closely with the Chinese science community to help any U.S. citizens visiting. There were a fairly large number of Chinese Americans there under cooperation agreements, and the soldiers firing on crowds weren't going to care if you they were U.S. citizens or fellow Chinese. Plus, we had people we couldn't find. The U.S. Geological Survey lost track of their people who had gone to remote areas. Thanks to tremendous efforts by the Chinese, we managed to locate one guy deep in the mountains. But he refused to leave his equipment, so that was that.

Also the U.S. universities and scientific communities immediately worked to make sure that the Chinese graduate students here were protected.

A Maze of Circular 175 Memos

I seemed to do endless circular 175 memos, which authorized agreement negotiations.

We held regular meetings with the Japanese. Their energy people and the Department of Energy had agreements, and they had annual meetings. The meetings generally were in Hawaii, to everyone's utter delight. They did meet once at the University of California, Irvine.

There was a Japanese way of doing things. Once for a subgroup meeting, they insisted on having the minutes agreed to before the meeting. Despite some head scratching, DOE agreed, assuming that then they could get a lot of off-the-record discussion done. Instead, the Japanese stuck to the script.

At this point, I dealt a fair amount with the Japanese embassy science and technology people. Their science counselor had gotten his doctorate at the University of Maryland. He was a friend of a friend who had persuaded him to accept lox as American sushi. He was very easy to deal with. The political types were very sensitive on their prerogatives. At one point, one complained that the State Department let the Department of Energy talk too much during the meeting, and that policy would give the Japanese energy people ideas.

The Korean science counselor and the Korean embassy economic counselor often feuded, so I would be in the position of getting a démarche in the morning by phone from one and having it withdrawn by the other in afternoon. It was by phone because the Korean embassy refused to let the science counselor use the chauffeured embassy car. He could not come by taxi, as that would be a loss of face.

There was a fair amount of discomfort on the part of the Japanese and Korean science counselors dealing with an older female science type. But it solved itself very easily once they established that I was a woman of mature years, a mother of three children, and somewhat akin to being a creature from Mars. I was sort of outside of their hierarchy. I knew the Japanese were much more comfortable with me when they stopped sitting at the edge of their chairs with their hands locked on their knees staring at more or less my right or left shoulder. My boss, Marty Prochnik, had been a Foreign Service officer and a geologist before he shifted to the civil service. He understood all about Foreign Service types.

He was also a physical fitness maniac, and you would see him running around the reflecting pool every lunch. He would go on regular little diets to keep himself fit, but when he went on the diet, he would absolutely have a yen for donuts. But instead of buying one donut, he would get two dozen donuts, bring them to the office. He ate two bites, and we expanded our waistlines. But that was just one of the fun assignments I had before I went on to be a Una Chapman Cox fellow.

Q: Did you feel that the State Department was able to deal with science matters fairly well? I am talking about just maybe passing them off to the Department of Energy and other things, or did the State Department try to intrude bureaucratically? How would you describe the State Department's role in science and technology?

JONES: Basically, we had a statutory role which was easy for my office because of the circular 175 process. All the agreements had to be done through the process managed by State. However, as far as acceptance of the agreements goes, we did not have a real role. We had no funding capabilities, for one thing.

Environmental issues were the responsibility of another OES office; other offices dealt with space, health, maritime, and biodiversity issues. Another office dealt with space and one dealt with, for instance, things—like at that point it would have been the Montreal protocol—that were negotiated through the office of environmental and scientific affairs. And one office that dealt with space cooperation.

It was hard for State to accept that in certain areas we just had nothing like the lead. In fact, the other agencies tended to see us as more or less the administrative handmaiden to get their things done. They did all the prime negotiations.

For instance, on AIDS research we had a Thai princess who was also a PhD microbiologist. She wanted to make sure that they got better data on HIV data, but everyone recognized that having NIH people running around the red-light districts taking blood samples was not a smart idea. So the role for the Centers for Disease Control and NIH was to train Thais to do the sample collection. Although there was no intellectual property involved in getting data on HIV incidence, it was very hard to persuade groups like USTR that we were not trying to do an end run and destroy the U.S. intellectual property structure.

We had another incident where the minister for science and technology for President Corazon Aquino's visit to the United States wanted to have a signing ceremony for an S&T cooperation agreement. They proposed an agreement with the Smithsonian, which was a short paragraph in which both sides agreed to cooperate to help humanity. The Smithsonian wears two hats, one government and one private. For the government agreement, we presented her with our intellectual property rights annex, at which she looked at us and said, "We have offered you free love. You are handing us a prenuptial agreement." So they said "bye-bye" and signed with the private side.

We also had a curious incident. NOAA was getting rid of its old radar.

Q: NOAA being...

JONES: National Oceanographic and Atmospheric Agency. They were scrapping old radars. We had a scientist in Indonesia working with Indonesian counterparts, and he said, "Hey, you want a radar? If you pay for the shipping, you can have it." They agreed. No one told either government. He wasn't even there to sign their agreement, but had a colleague sign it for him. The radars arrived and were seized as spy equipment by the Indonesian government. Finally, the State Department was brought back into the action, and State's legal people managed some dexterous language that somehow managed to paper over the earlier omissions.

We had a little letter from NOAA. They had spent almost a year sending up sounding rockets in New Zealand to measure the ozone hole over the Antarctic. It all worked very nicely until it occurred to someone to ponder, "Gee, we should have had an agreement." So they sent us a letter asking us to craft an agreement. The State Department legal people went absolutely up the wazoo, but they managed some kind of complicated language that covered it for eternity backward and forward.

Q: A question arises: you mentioned the Thai princess. I have heard stories that when you are dealing with Thai royalty, you have all sorts of problems. I am thinking protocol-wise. Was that a problem?

JONES: No, she was acting as a microbiologist. Basically, she just lent her name to the effort. We didn't even know how they funded their side. Her basic idea was that before they could try different kinds of treatment, behavior modification efforts to help the sex workers, they needed to know how bad the situation was.

Q: When the epidemic of the AIDS disaster really came in full force and full knowledge. How did that impact on you all?

JONES: There is actually a special office in OES that deals with the medical issues. Our office was only in the loop if they ran into trouble under an agreement.

Access was always a problem, as many countries consider their mineral resources to be national secrets. They were always concerned about what satellites could pick up.

Occasionally, there were major successes in cooperation. The Chinese and the United States cooperated in a huge study on the impact of folic acid on spina bifida. Pregnant women were told to take folic acid to cut down the incidence and compared with women who had taken a placebo. For this study, they needed a huge population base, and they needed huge controls. Now the Chinese are pretty much genetically uniform. So you could compare like to like.

U.S. researchers helped by taking the raw data they had and doing the full statistical analysis with our advanced computer systems. Very quickly it became clear that it cut the incidence of spina bifida tremendously. Since the folic acid doses were very low, it became policy around the world to have folic acid as a supplement in your breads.

In fact, there were a fair number of studies done in China on the effect of various carcinogens, where again they collected the data and we analyzed the data. For example, there is a kind of special dish popular in parts of China which requires a mold to be grown on some kind of pickled vegetable, *mei gan tsai*. The mold adds flavor, but it also greatly increases the incidence of throat, tongue, and mouth cancer.

Q: How did you find India, which in that period was still an enclosed area? It was not open to the outside. I am trying to think of the term—well, a closed market and all of that. How did you find India?

JONES: There were a lot of barriers. OK, I had a very bright young woman called Marilyn Pifer whose husband Steve Pifer later became an ambassador. She handled the very difficult negotiations on intellectual property rights.

We had problems with the Canadians for another reason entirely—they already took care of the issue directly by filing for intellectual property rights in the United States and Canada if they came up with something. And if we came up with something, we filed for the intellectual property rights in Canada and the United States. And if the research was such that there was nothing but basic research, which they wanted in the public domain, no one had to do anything. So they again felt it was very unnecessary.

Even countries which were not intellectual property rights problems still had issues because legal systems were different. For New Zealand, for instance, we had to have teleconferences for the lawyers

Q: So you didn't deal with the Indians?

JONES: Not so much directly. I supervised it, as I supervised Linda Staheli, who handled the Japanese cooperation. She was extraordinarily diplomatic, patient, and organized. For example, she arranged a softball game with the Japanese embassy. They played right in Arlington. One of the OES secretaries was in one of the DC softball teams, and she was a power player. As a result, OES ended up with a nice little trophy presented by the Japanese embassy.

Q: How about Taiwan?

JONES: We did not deal with Taiwan issues at all. We have such an open system that the horse was never in the barn. We were trying to build the barn.

CHAPTER 15

A Bit of French Training (1991-1992)

JONES: I went into French language training because the State Department had changed its rules. I had passed out of the language requirements with Chinese, but I achieved only a 3+ because I could not discuss nuclear armistice in Chinese, my Chinese vocabulary being more suited to "How do you want it stir fried?" I was practically illiterate, but by memorizing about 1,000 characters I made it to survival level. I had done all my consular work on my 2+ and 3+ in French. Now I had to get properly certified by FSI as having achieved at least a 3/3 in one language. So they gave me six months, after which I was to go to the Board of Examiners. I went into language training for real this time. It was interesting. I had learned French from the written side, so I could write it, but speaking it was a different story. They were very good in understanding the linguistics.

We had a wonderful instructor called Solomon Atalie, who was from one of the African countries and had had to learn French himself once, so he understood the process a little better than people who just spoke it well. I completely ruined the assignment schedule by making it to 3+, 3+ in three weeks. I still wonder if they tricked me. Talking to the instructors, I once made some kind of crack about taking it easy and really learning it well, as I had months and months and finally I could learn French properly. I could always flunk if they tested me too early. A few days later, they told me they wanted to give me a test session. People went through proto, not real, test sessions all the time, so I went through it. I did all the things they required. Then they asked some questions on Henry IV, and I had a lot of fun describing Henry IV and his bed-hopping habits and his disdain for too much bathing.

Q: I didn't know he bed hopped.

JONES: He had a lot of other interests in life, believe me, and his wife often objected strongly to the fact that he came in booted and spurred and unwashed from having been on the hunt and would head for her bedroom. She was someone who believed in perfume and personal hygiene. So I passed before the board of examiners [BEX] was ready for me. Fortunately, FSI was able to have me read and discuss enough books and such to keep me occupied till I began at BEX.

We had one missing link. Students were tested. They had paragraphs in French, and then they were supposed to translate it into English as well as discuss in French the common links between the paragraphs. I realized students never got a chance to practice what they were going to be tested on. Also, some people read slowly. I am a very fast reader. So I spent the weeks going through all the French magazines and newspapers pulling out little paragraphs and doing up a big book of possible test material that students could use for practice.

CHAPTER 16

Board of Examiners—Selecting the Next FSO Generation (1992)

The Examination Process

Q: I wonder, could you describe how the board of examiners as an examiner worked at the time you were doing it, and your impressions of both the system and the candidates?

JONES: OK, we will start with the structure. We went out in teams of six examiners. Given the results of the lawsuit and the need to make the examination gender and race neutral, only four people were active during the examination process, while the other two would only be brought into play for the people that passed. Those two were the only ones who had any idea of the records of the examinees. For the others, we graded the candidates' essays without seeing the candidates, and they were never the ones you were assigned to test in the morning portion. For the essay, they would pick a topic and write (without word processors or computers). This is probably totally changed by now [2007]. The idea was to see their argumentation. The topics were popular ones for the day, such as gun control, education, and so on. We would then grade it on a scale with a certain number of points for the grammar, the structure, the logic. Several examiners graded the same essay. If they could not agree, then a third examiner was told to read it, and they had to abide by the third examiner. Very rarely, we had fights over it, but we had several African American examiners whom we eventually nicknamed "the hanging judges three" because they were so strict on spelling errors. Others were much more relaxed about bad spelling because we figured that was something that was easy to fix, whereas the inability to write a complete sentence was more serious.

We only saw the whole group in the afternoon exercise, when we judged the group exercise.

Case Study Method

The morning oral portion was role playing. This included having the candidate execute a démarche and write a reporting cable, and asking how the candidates would react to some hypothetical situations which were designed to elicit the candidate's reasoning and decision abilities rather than to elicit a "right" answer. For example, the examiners would ask, "What would you do if you were the only consular officer at a post and there was a crazy American woman there having hysterics, and they were getting ready to close the airport and, and, and so on." To make it fair, all the candidates were given preparatory and explanatory material before they were tested. We provided the knowledge and we wanted to see how they would solve problems. People could pick their area.

Let's say you could pick trade. The trade issue that person could end up with could be a rice démarche. They would be given a piece of paper explaining that they were supposed to present a démarche to two foreign government officials, the minister of trade and the minister of agriculture, played by the examiners. They were given talking points—just a few to make it easy to remember. Afterward, they were supposed to write a short reporting cable, about 300 words. To be fair, we would try to keep our replies within two or three very clear points. And they were allowed to provide a recommendation or whatever comments they wanted to make to show their thinking. They were allowed to take notes, although it was generally much more impressive if they didn't. We had a big playbook for all the subjects.

Minority candidates had all passed the written examination, and their biggest obstacle was probably "the hanging judges three" who felt strongly that you weren't doing anyone a favor to bring in someone who wasn't competitive.

The afternoon exercise is a group exercise. The candidates are told in the morning briefing what the procedures are. They were given material and told their functions in the group country-team exercise, with each person being given a project with a specific pot of money. In the first round, they would make the best arguments they could for their assigned project. In the second round, they are told that only half the amount of money was available, so some projects would get cut. All six candidates, and there are six candidates, could win. I think the highest number we passed was five at one point in Chicago, because they showed they could work together to achieve the best result for the U.S. government. Allowing candidates to work together to pick the best project evened the playing field on the quality of the projects.

For example, when push came to shove, the candidate could back the person who had a much better project, let's say, to refine water for village X. Once you had that, you could then work out something, so that in the end all could present a viable financial plan that met U.S. country objectives. Candidates were warned not to lie.

In many ways, too much depended on the specific group dynamics. We had one group session in California where two extremely aggressive women lawyers took each other out. They were so difficult, so nasty, so unfair in their tactics that they were eliminated instantly. And a young man, who was wearing a suit that probably belonged to his grandfather, spent all his time trying to make sense of things, to negotiate, to make peace, and to get them to work together. He passed. The frightening thing is if we had only one of the lawyers, all of these traits wouldn't have shown, and she would have been in command, an instant leader, and would have passed.

Q: Well, the chemistry is there and it changes all the time, depending on the group.

JONES: This was the way it was when we traveled a lot. I lived out of a suitcase. I think I did San Francisco, Los Angeles, Dallas, and Chicago at different points. I think it was Los Angeles and Dallas that were back to back. Texas was a lot of fun. That was the only time we had nuclear war threatened on the rice démarche.

The Candidates—a Mixed Bag of Qualifications

Q: What was your impression of the people produced by the written exam, the people who appeared before you in general?

JONES: The ones we saw, men, women, all sorts of backgrounds, older, very young, very bright, generally well spoken, good oral skills. The written skills were much more of a problem. We had people who had gotten doctorates and master's degrees who were unable to write 500 words—though I think they could have written 50,000. There was one that was written so badly that we actually had an argument on what topic he had picked. We had some who showed a lack of logical thinking. In other words, they couldn't seem to go from point A to point B. They went from point A to point X and then back to point G without any way to track why. We didn't mind going in strange directions so long as the reasoning was good.

Critique of the Process

I thought they were very good. At the same time, as someone who had been in the service for a while and had known really top Foreign Service officers, I felt they were not as good at the kind of original thinking that I noticed in these top people. The test system seemed to be skewed to passing smooth-spoken, obedient, competent diplomats rather than original thinkers.

I knew David's peers who were doing arms control negotiations such as intermediate nuclear forces negotiations. They had to command a huge range of political-military knowledge as well as understand the technical underpinnings. No amount of treaty writing could change the fact that missiles exist, and subsonic missiles and cruise missiles with terrain confirmation capabilities could go a long way without detection. A submarine-launched nuclear missile would only give nineteen minutes of warning before hitting the continental United States. This required more original thinking, which the team had under Ambassador Mike Glitman. Even my highest-passing candidates didn't come up to this standard.

But this was only my personal experience, although I saw hundreds of candidates; others did see stellar candidates. Those who passed were all races, creeds, and ages. We did have one case of fraud, where there was a ringer. He had flunked an exam before and the person who came in under his name was recognized by the examiners. We had one who was crazy and who was so disruptive he ruined the chances of the other test takers. He was fully delusional, almost violent. He could have been violently aggressive, except that he was a little guy and there were some very large males and females in the room who would have subdued him in no time.

We had a crazy female at FSI once. She was incredibly argumentative and irrational during the group exercise. We decided she was also ready to nail the male examiners with a sexual harassment complaint at the exit interview, so another female examiner and I switched with the males assigned to her to defuse the situation.

In the exit interview, we would explain why a person didn't pass, and it took a lot of tact and compassion. This woman threw an absolute fit during the exit interview and finally managed to see the head of the board of examiners, borrowed $20 for a taxi, and was never seen again. Passing the written exam is no guarantee of sanity.

There were funny moments. We did a security oral examination where an attractive African American woman with a degree in accounting had applied to work at State. Somehow she ended up in the security oral. When we did the exam and asked her would she be willing to use a weapon in order to accomplish her mission to defend her target, she said, "What are you asking me that for? I just want to do some accounting." We knew there was a glitch, but had to continue with the test. So we asked her what she would do if someone handed her a package and ran away while she was on guard duty for a foreign minister. She said, "I would run like hell." We did make sure her application went to the right office.

CHAPTER 17

A Northern Exposure—Montreal, Canada

Q: Well, then after you finished this, where did you go?

JONES: OK, then we had the assignment to Canada, which in itself was quite a job because we are a tandem team. Our medical issues were past. Dave had long since resigned himself to having his career end because he had not been overseas for years and because he chose arms control as his specialty. It takes ten years to get the expertise to the level that you need, but it is considered a career dead end. He wanted to work with Mike Glitman, who had been his supervisor in Paris and whom he tremendously admired. Then the incredible happened. They succeeded in their negotiation of the intermediate nuclear forces treaty and the entire team was rewarded with promotions. David made it into the senior Foreign Service, which made us a true assignment nightmare.

Dave Wilson was our career development officer and also struggling with the final stages of cancer, which killed him. We were truly grateful for his efforts, and he came up with assignments to Canada—Montreal for me and political counselor in Ottawa for David. Though Canada is not considered a fast promotion assignment, as no one saw it as a very challenging assignment, David loved it. After our retirement in 1998, he continued writing about Canadian issues and has done at least 100 articles for the *Hill Times* and a dozen for McGill University's *Policy Options*. He and a retired Canadian Member of Parliament [David Kilgour] wrote a book, *Uneasy Neighbo(u)rs*, which was just released by John Wiley and Sons [September 2007].

Q: So you did Canada from when to when?

JONES: '92 to '96.

Q: OK, you were in Montreal and David was in Ottawa.

JONES: I was in Montreal for two years. When the science counselor retired early and the position opened in Ottawa just at the time my tour finished in Montreal, they did an inter-Canada transfer, which worked very well. In Montreal, I worked for Consul General Susan Wood as the deputy and main reporter in everything.

Q: Who?

JONES: Susan Wood. Roberta Susan Wood. I enjoyed it a great deal.

Canada after the Collapse of National Unity Efforts

Q: All right, let's take Montreal from 1992 to '94. How would you describe Montreal politically and economically vis-à-vis the rest of Canada?

JONES: It was truly two solitudes; that was one of them. This was at the peak of the discussion on sovereignty. The Meech Lake Accord on which Mulroney had staked his prime ministership had collapsed when one of the provinces said no. This gave a tremendous boost to the Quebec sovereigntists, who played the refusal of all provinces to agree to Meech as proof that the rest of Canada didn't want them.

The Canadian government then proposed something called the Charlottetown Accord, which also failed. I did all the political and economic reporting. I did a lot of "checking the box" items such as reading the Pequiste [Parti Québécois, or the separatist party] platform. Oddly enough, I also advised David, who was the political counselor in Ottawa, but my efficiency report was reviewed by the economic counselor

I made a great many friends, and I joined one of the last remaining North American salons in Montreal, run by David and Diana Nicholson, who held an open house every Wednesday night for discussion. So, for the price of one bottle of wine, I would get the kind of intelligent and in-depth discussion from prominent Montrealers that no amount of diplomatic entertaining would get. It was all off the record, and I kept it that way. They remain friends today, and we visit them every time we return to Canada. [As of December 2010, they celebrated their 1,500th consecutive Wednesday night salon.]

Quebec Separatists

My focus was on Quebec's position in Canada. There had already been an exodus of Anglophones from Quebec when René Lévesque, head of the Parti Québécois, had become premier. I was tremendously impressed by the civilized tone of the debate. While other countries had violent separation debates, for the Canadians it just meant longer discussions. I went to separatist rallies in which I was immediately spotted as what they thought was a Francophone Allophone and practically loved to death by various sovereignists who wanted me to feel welcome. I had more bad coffee offered to me, and thought my kidneys were sure to go. Some would even translate from the Quebec French into French French for me.

Q: *At that time, how did we view the* Québécois *separatist movement, and how serious was it for Canada? And I am looking at what this would mean for the United States—I am trying to capture this.*

JONES: Well, there was one thing that was particularly of interest. A man called Jean-François Lisée had written a book called *Eye of the Eagle*. He used freedom of information material on our writing on Canada during the period at which Réne Lévesque had been elected premier of Quebec. All the analyses in it were very high quality. The point, however, is that this high-quality work was produced by Americans who were not Canada hands. We don't have Canada hands. They were professional Foreign Service generalists who did standard political analyses. They called the results correctly. But while we were doing all these correct analyses, in Ontario, which after all had coexisted with Quebec throughout Canadian history, all the pundits, all the Canadian policy experts were wrong.

Economic Factors in the Separation Issue

The fact that they could be wrong meant that there was a tremendous divide. My point, when I talked to various businessmen, was that both Ottawa and Quebec had such a bad debt situation at the time. So, in case of separation, both would have to collude to reassure world financial markets. The United States tried to help in the 1995 referendum in Quebec and slightly modified our mantra (we preferred a strong, united Canada). Instead of gratitude for this, we had newspaper editorials (especially out west) suggesting that the United States butt out. U.S. businessmen assumed that if an independent Quebec wanted them, they would have to make it worthwhile.

Q: Had the ambassador said something that . . .

JONES: Later, yes. That was after I went to Ottawa.

Q: But that was the time. Were you there during the referendum?

JONES: No, I was already in Ottawa then. It was a curious situation. I was David's Quebec eye, basically. My biggest contribution was suggesting that the embassy pay attention to Lucien Bouchard, who was head of the then eight-member Bloc Québécois, and a nobody in Ottawa, although later he became premier of Quebec. I also urged him to contact journalists, some of whom were superb analysts; one of these, Chantal Hébert, remains a valued friend today.

Q: Let's go back to Montreal. How did we view the situation there at the time you were in Montreal? Did you see this as potentially ripping Canada apart?

JONES: No, our figures didn't indicate that, nor did U.S. debt rating agencies. They saw it as a chance to make money. Financial markets react ahead of the event, so when the event doesn't happen, there is a bounce back. Therefore there was a 25 to 50 basis point difference between Ontario and Quebec debt. The United States did not anticipate a "Cuba of the north." We were just seeing it as something the Canadians had to handle. We got the most complete picture by talking to all sides, as I did even at the beginning of my career in the Arms Control and Disarmament Agency. For example, when I had a project on strategic antisubmarine warfare, I talked not just to antisubmarine warfare people but to all the submarine hunters as well to get a more complete picture.

But the experts saw that even in the case of separation with protracted negotiations, at worst there would be an economic hit of a drop of three percentage points in GDP [gross domestic product] for a few years. The key was no violence. Quebec has all the resources you would need for a country. The Parti Québécois platform was very much a social democratic type of program, with some trade—and business-friendly aspects. Francophones are still 80-plus percent of the population, but they saw the Anglophones as a necessary asset, especially in the financial sector. For instance, once at a Nicholson Wednesday night soiree, someone asked, "Hey, how much do you manage?" I think the total for that evening among attendees was about $9 billion dollars.

Q: These were Anglophones basically.

JONES: Mostly Anglophones with some federalist Francophones. There has been serious intermarriage for years among all the groups.

Q: How did you find the intellectual community there?

JONES: *Barbarian Invasions* is a movie I would strongly recommend for anyone who wanted to get a feel of Quebec views.

The French Fact(or)

Q: Barbarian Invasions. Anyway, I had the feeling that there was quite a chattering class of French intellectuals who didn't seem to go anywhere. Was this important, and how did you fit into this?

JONES: Well, I chattered with them. The Anglophones had certain very specific interests and concerns. Both sides did much navel watching, *nombrilisme*. It is a smaller pond so people could make bigger waves.

We did meet the number two of the Parti Québécois at the time, Bernard Landry. [Later he became the head of the party and then premier]. He, in fact, invited David and me to one of his little yacht trips on Lake Louise. We had a chance to talk. He was a trilingual economics professor and also a dedicated sovereigntist. You could see that he felt that there is a potential destiny for Quebec as a country with very close ties to Canada, but only if the people were willing to make some sacrifices for a few years. Then they would forever be able to protect their own culture. Their culture is not French culture, by the way; it is a very distinct North American one with roots in 17th century Brittany, Normandy, and France. My feeling was that if they achieved independence, then France would step in—Canadian relations or no. But there was never any intimation that the Parti Québécois would support violence. Everyone had horrified by what had been done by the FLQ [Front de liberation du Québec] in the '80s and by Trudeau's imposition of martial law.

Q: This was a series of bombings.

JONES: They killed someone. They kidnapped two people and murdered one of them. Pierre Trudeau is not the popular icon in Quebec that he is in the rest of Canada. They saw his attempt to force all Canadians to make Quebecers feel at home all by becoming a bilingual country as not protecting their culture in Quebec. In fact, Quebec used a "notwithstanding" clause in the Canadian Constitution, the repatriation of which did not have the Quebec premier's agreement, so the repatriation was considered a betrayal and was called the "night of the long knives." Quebec and Ontario are two groups who have wonderful command of each other's dental nerves. They know exactly how to lift an eyebrow to give someone in Ontario heartburn. The same goes the other way.

Q: Did you get the feeling that this was Ottawa versus Quebec, and the western provinces were doing their thing, and it is a completely different world?

JONES: Except for the national energy plan, which was known as destroying the patrimony of the western provinces to give cheaper gas in Toronto. There were Quebecers who told me they had lived in British Columbia and there had been serious bias against them. One had been beaten up at a bar. So there were things the Canadians didn't particularly want to face. As an American, I will say that in Quebec I found less of the knee-jerk anti-Americanism.

Anti-Americanism in Ottawa School

Our daughter Margaret went to high school for three years in Ottawa, Lisgar Collegiate. She finished four years of their program in three years so and was able to graduate with her friends. [High school is five years in Ontario.] She faced a fair amount of anti-Americanism. She was a five-foot, two-inch, 100-pound Eurasian who certainly wasn't threatening. She said that in history class they made a big thing about the fact that we attacked Kingston, Ontario. Her comment to the teacher was that Canada was British North America then, and it was the War of 1812. We never went to war with Canada. They also sacked Washington, DC, so it could be considered even. She ran into this constantly. They would have biases on what they felt Americans were like.

For example, the school paper, *The Lisgarite*, had to go to the PTA for money; they needed about $250 Canadian dollars. She was editor of *The Lisgarite*. This was at the time of the 150th reunion. Alums were all over the halls, but *The Lisgarite* staff were told to only sell copies of their anniversary issue from their office, which was in a dark corner of the school basement. Margaret looked and she said, "This is dumb. All we have to do is walk to the alums." So they each grabbed a stack of papers, went through the school, and earned hundreds of "Loonies" (Canadian dollar nickname) in an hour. She was then reprimanded for acting un-Canadian. No matter how much things look alike, Canadians are different. Quebecers didn't seem to have this defensive anti-American attitude, as they were much more secure in their identity. They didn't have to trash us to feel more Canadian. My husband's book *Uneasy Neighbo(u)rs* made this point in detail.

Atlantic Provinces Have Their Own Attitudes

Q: Well, the anti-Americanism has always been generated essentially from Ontario, which was the residue of where the loyalists ended up, a certain amount of the loyalists ended up. We fought a little war around there in the War of 1812.

JONES: We went to Halifax. We went to New Brunswick. We went to Prince Edward Island. You could see an incredible number of little communities with plaques honoring the American loyalists as founders. But there was much less of an anti-American undertone in the Atlantic provinces. Again, I think they are very secure in their own identity. Identity security is the key. A Swede is a Swede. They don't have to trash Norwegians to feel like a Swede. Those that don't like Americans, don't like Americans for other reasons rather than to affirm their own identity.

CHAPTER 18

On to Ottawa—Two Years as Embassy Science Counselor (1994-1996)

Q: You moved to Ottawa and when you were there, did you find the view from Ottawa different, or were you sort of the Quebec watcher in the embassy?

JONES: No, I was now an economic officer, so my focus was much more on economic issues. Then it was all science and technology, on which we had enormous levels of contact. Canadians could bid for our government contracts, for U.S.-funded government grants, and did so with good success.

Scandal in National Institute of Health Grant

We did have a scandal that started in Quebec when a Quebec doctor who was part of the national cancer and bowel study faked his results. His lab made an error and turned in something to NIH [National Institutes of Health] that had false data. He was reporting on patients who had died as if they were alive, because he wanted to continue his access to Tamoxifen, which at the time was used to treat aggressive breast cancer. He felt the NIH guidelines were unfair, so he decided to get around them by lying about his patients, which probably killed a good number of his patients. Curiously enough, his name was Dr. Poisson ("fish" in French), and the project manager in the states was Dr. Fisher. The issue was that the NIH folks who came to investigate didn't bother to tell the embassy. The science counselor at that time, Tom Wajda, called me to tell me to tell them that without formal permission from the Canadian government, they couldn't take any information out. So we had to backtrack to find the NIH people. He was able to locate someone in the medical research council in Canada who had every reason to help, as we funded 15 percent of Canadian medical research purely through their success in getting NIH grants. Dr. Poisson was offended by the NIH protocol, which denied entry into the study for any woman who had cancerous tissue in both breasts, since that meant the cancer had spread and she needed more than Tamoxifen. He lied. They died.

Q: What happened on the investigation?

JONES: Well, first we had tons of lawyers come calling us, saying they would be happy to represent NIH when NIH sued. We talked to NIH, and they were thinking seriously of suing because it cost a lot of money to dig out the data the doctor had turned in out of the whole study's results. They were going to leave it to the Canadian authorities as to what else was to be done to the doctor. I was amazed that none of the patients or the families of the deceased patients sued. We explained to NIH that suing the hospital was probably not a good idea because they were already down to their last cent and had patients in the hallways. *Barbarian Invasions* did not exaggerate.

The Failures of Canadian "Universal" Health Care

Q: You had patients routinely sent to the United States for treatment and others, I don't know about the unions, but it appeared the hospital wasn't being used—this was in the movie, Barbarian Invasions—*the hospital wasn't being fully utilized, because the unions didn't want to work there.*

JONES: Well, they had all sorts of things. In order to cut costs, they let a whole lot of nurses retire early. There are only some ways to cut costs when you have a system that does not allow a private sector. The ideal of free universal health care with the government as the only paymaster sounds lovely. In actual fact, with limited resources and a cap on what doctors can earn, it means rationing. One of the Canadians who worked at the consulate general had coronary artery blockage. He was only sixty-seven years old. He was put on a waiting list. Six months later, he was still on the waiting list when he died of a massive coronary. We had a friend in the States who was diagnosed with a similar condition at the same time and he got his bypass surgery in twenty-four hours.

Q: Well, I went in to have a routine angioplasty about a year and a half ago. They stopped looking at me after about fifteen minutes and said, "Well, you are going to have to have a triple bypass, and we can either do it today or tomorrow." I had it tomorrow.

JONES: Yeah, and there is a reason for it.

Q: They said this is what is known as the widow-maker type of thing.

JONES: Yes. It is much easier. The doctors care a lot about their batting average or success rate and it's much easier and safer to do the surgery before the heart attack. You don't have the scar tissue. You don't have dead cardiac tissue. So they fix it, and your heart retreats back to what it was before you had the blockage.

The Boundary Waters Treaty/Commission and Environmental Controls

Dealing with the Canadians as science counselor was a lot of fun. I also had responsibility for the International Joint Commission, which was managing the Great Lakes under the U.S.—Canada Boundary Waters treaty.

Q: How did you feel about emission, exhaust, or something?

JONES: Oh, there are two different philosophies on environmental controls. We are extremely legalistic. We battle to the death over the actual levels, every group screaming and yelling, and finally we have a standard set. Then if you violate the standard, we really get you. EPA [Environmental Protection Agency] actually has the right to put a city that violates the air quality standards under some kind of draconian extra regulations. We fine companies incredible amounts of money when they violate it, and so on.

Perspectives on Polluting the St. Lawrence River

The Canadians are different. They set an extremely low standard that the environmental groups can only dream of achieving, but they don't enforce it. The standards are set by the federal government. The implementation is by the provincial government. For example, the St. Lawrence River is polluted despite being very fast and efficient at getting the pollutants out to sea. Their regulations say that a company that dumps in the municipal water supply, which then goes into the St. Lawrence, is not considered as dumping into the St. Lawrence. For example, let's say I make titanium oxide paint and create all sorts of nasty stuff. I dump it into the local town's water supply, sewage supply, and they dump it into the St. Lawrence. I am not covered. I have not dumped into the St. Lawrence River. A few times they have caught a titanium oxide plant dumping directly into the St. Lawrence River, and they fined them I think $10,000—not even a wrist slap.

Air quality depends often on which way the wind is blowing and who has more cars. We and they both have problems because they allow additives that we don't. I think MTBE (methyl tertiary butyl ether) is an additive they use because they think it makes the fuel burn better in the winter time. We see it as a bad additive, so it is banned on this side of the border. There are never-ending border issues.

Some Representative Bilateral Water Issues

There is the example of Devil's Lake, for instance, in North Dakota, which feeds into the Red River, which goes into Manitoba and eventually Lake Winnipeg, which supplies Winnipeg's drinking water. It also regularly floods. There is a long history of problems in trying to keep the floodwaters on the other side. They built a barrier, we tried to dynamite it. The lake waters have been rising since the 1940s, and the whole area has been flooding. The town of Devil's Lake used to be ten miles from the shores of Devil's Lake and right now is right on the shores of Devil's Lake. North Dakotans wanted to breach the lake to pour the extra water into the Red River. The Canadians said no, unless we pretreat the water so that it is potable. Plus, they worried about alien species introduction. Our people were beginning to make noises about dynamiting a breach anyway. Unsaid in all this is that the Canadians already have thoroughly polluted all the water going into Lake Winnipeg because of runoff from the farms. I believe that the argument will continue until a major drought, when both sides can fight on water allotment.

Water-level management is another issue, as the St. Lawrence Seaway requires the Great Lakes to provide enough water for ships to move. This occasionally means that the Thousand Islands area becomes the Five Hundred Islands.

I also worked with the Navy attaché by providing technical advice on the potential of CANDU (Canadian deuterium uranium) reactors to burn Soviet weapons' plutonium.

CHAPTER 19

Home Again: Washington and Mother State (1996-1998)

On Being a CAO for Seniors

Q: OK, we did Board of Examiners; how about senior personnel? What was your impression of that?

JONES: After we left Canada, I came back to counseling and assignments in the State Department doing a CAO's work. I planned to retire when David did, which was 1998. Before I retired, I worked as a counseling and assignments officer and learned much of what I should have known years earlier. Someday Dave and I hope to write a book on the inner workings of the Foreign Service. Both David and I have published articles on the Foreign Service over the years. One that I did was always rejected, although I thought it made some good points. My view was that the system is at fault for the abusive people in at embassies and at State. They deserve the dysfunctional supervisors they have because they never seriously reflected the truth in efficiency reports. I know of one case where the administrative counselor was pulled out of a post after a no-confidence cable from the ambassador. The ambassador wrote it because the entire section threatened to resign if she didn't leave. Yet the efficiency report on her said absolutely nothing about this. Good management means preventing abuses.

I thought the CAO assignment was very interesting. The whole system was set up for serious conflicts of interest, because if you were in personnel and you expected to go on for another assignment, a senior counseling officer was the only one who would be competing against his own or her own clients for positions.

In fact, when I came on board there had been a big whoop-de-do because a predecessor whose name I do not even know apparently told the bureau that someone they wanted was unavailable for a very nice position, I think in South Africa. Then he himself got it. Then the person found out from someone else in the bureau that he had been stabbed by his personnel officer.

I was comfortable doing it, first because they were abolishing the science cone. Second, I intended to retire when David did, so it was just a matter of timing for us. Third, you really had to be willing to fight hard for your clients. We had shoot-outs when two people wanted positions or three people wanted positions. It was a fairly senior position. It was up to the CAO to argue for the client. You made all the arguments based the client's efficiency reports, based on the career needs, and occasionally based on medical needs. This took an enormous amount of work. I think I won every one, but each one was a nightmare amount of work. If you had two clients who both wanted the job, you had to hand one of your clients off to another counseling officer.

Q: Here you are dealing with the science officers, is that right?

JONES: I handled science officers when I represented science and labor officers and also anyone with last names beginning from C to G. Then we also represented bureaus, so I had the consular affairs bureau and inter-American affairs, at the time, Latin America.

Q: Well, let's say there is a job open. It is a desirable job. You have the stable of people. So in a way, whom are you representing? You can't represent the stable, because they are all your clients, aren't they?

JONES: Well, the first thing you have is the bid list. So when your clients bid for any single position, you have a list of your clients C to G who wanted this particular position. I thought the fights would be over postings to Paris, London, and so on, but our shoot-outs were over things like Beirut, Hanoi, and Tananarive.

Then we had bureau shoot-outs rather than post shoot-outs. Several posts might want one person for a specific position. The system had its glitches. At one point, I had two people with the same last name ask me to check their personnel file. Both had just gotten promoted, and we found out that their files had been switched. They had gotten promoted on each other's records.

We had individual people who called in who were low ranked. One person mentioned that when he had taken this assignment, it had cost him his marriage, had estranged him from his children, so why didn't he get promoted? We had to explain that it was not a case of what you sacrificed on the altar that got your promotion.

We had others where there were last-minute emergencies. One had a son fall very seriously ill, so he had to come back to the States. There would be emergency openings, such as when someone was killed or died. In one case, it was a consul general position in China, and we all rushed to our client lists to find the right replacement.

The Office of the Secretary of State could often cause problems. Madeleine Albright's group was very closed; she had her favorites, and she had a senior woman who said absolutely the last word on everything, and occasionally this last word was to fire someone with no notice or explanation.

Q: Who was the senior woman?

JONES: I don't remember her name and was fortunate in never having to deal with her personally.

Q: Going back to the Albright group, you say that there was one of her inner circle who had control pretty much over at least vetoing certain senior assignments.

JONES: Oh, yes, they did. And not only that, the word was passed out. I did the D Committee. The D Committee is the committee that meets to determine who would be presented as possible ambassadors for Senate confirmation. The secretary of state has a representative or is present. The undersecretary for political affairs and the director general and the deputy secretary of state were members.

Once we got a list from the White House of posts which were open to Foreign Service ambassadors, each of the counseling officers would go through their lists and see who was a potential candidate. I would actually call people. The bureaus were asked if they had anyone they were specifically interested in for specific posts. The director general could also add any names he wished. So whenever my clients had ambassadorial ambitions, I always urged them to go to the bureaus and to meet with the director general. At some point in the process before they could actually be named, they had to be vetted. The vetting required determining whether you had security problems, EEO problems, and so on. A certain number did get eliminated for bad inspections, grievances, EEO problems, security problems, and so on. Now this means that someone with a questionable corridor reputation could be very easily eliminated. But anything could happen with corridor reputation.

I had one client come in who was really upset. The director general had told him he didn't have a chance with his sexual harassment record. He couldn't understand it, because he had no sexual harassment record. He practically had a coronary in my office—he turned bright purple, actually. But we checked further and found out that he had never served at the post in question. Well, it turns out that if you are director general and you meet lots of people, one large, fat white male looks a whole lot like another one. He had remembered it wrong. So the man was able to go back, clean up that, and eventually he did get an ambassadorship.

Appointment of Ambassadors

Q: What was your impression of the D Committee, of basically the caliber and the appointment of ambassadors? In gross terms, how did it work?

JONES: Who you know really helps. This is my opinion, because a fair number of the best posts went to people whom the White House just put down for specific posts. It was not selection by the D Committee. To all outward appearances, this is a professional Foreign Service officer who got the ambassadorship. They were either well and favorably known by someone in the White House, or they had worked at the NSC [National Security Council] and were just named to the position.

I thought there were an immense number of really brilliant people in the Foreign Service who were champions at tacking to make speed under the prevailing winds. I was shown how the "reinventing government" exercise resulted in a book of instructions that looked like a paperback. Of course, the annexes made a stack taller than I was.

The level of computerization was still pretty pathetic. It took Colin Powell to put the State Department into the Internet world. Our information management people were still shifting over from being communicators to being computer experts. So we were having difficulties there. In personnel, we ran into such difficulties with the bid system that we had to reenter the bid cables manually. We all worked—I think I worked an extra fifteen hours per week doing it. It was pathetic as far as management went.

Q: Well, speaking of management, did you notice a dearth of candidates to be ambassadors in the management field? I am not speaking about professional managers, but somebody who comes out of the NSC or something often has managed a half a secretary at most. Was this at all an issue?

JONES: Exactly. Well, it helps to have been a principal officer somewhere to be an ambassador. In many cases, it was the administrative officers who had the inside track for these positions. So in that respect they did well, but the State Department attitude to administration was a very odd one. We are not the army. We are not a perfect pyramid with generals on top. The administrative skills needed for the army are quite different, such as actually having to move eleven hundred trucks from this part of Iraq to another part of Iraq.

At the State Department, logistics are totally different. I thought of the contrast because at one time my brother was working on a U.S. air traffic control upgrade project. He managed seventy-five engineers who had to produce. They needed to produce software to allow airplanes to be mapped and located following the actual curvature of the earth. The purpose of the administrative officers was to support those who produced.

In the State Department, somehow the administrative cone ended up dominating the other cones. So management skills became the mantra; everyone sought multicone assignments to prove you cold manage, but no one asked, "Better management for what?" Only the consular area had it right. First, they had products and a consular report to track actual work. They had to produce. When things went badly, you had people waiting for three days squatting in front of the consulate. The pyramid structure worked. But in the other cones, efficiency reports eventually began sounding as if the only purpose for an assignment was to develop administrative skills rather than a higher level of diplomatic and analysis abilities.

EEO as a Problem

EEO things could be a real problem. I had one client who was never able to overcome it. He had been brought back after retirement because of his language skills to work with a UN group in the former Yugoslavia. There was a sexual harassment claim and the post ejected him, but they had completely neglected the due process rights and forgot that he reported to the desk, and they had no authority over him.

No one even knew the correct procedure for handling sexual harassment allegations. It turned out to be a woman who made a habit of such allegations and who stayed on and worked for him for six months until her contract ran out. At most, it seemed to be some jokes at a Christmas party. He had retained a lawyer to clear up his record when the record disappeared. When I left personnel, he was still desperately trying to clear his name.

Then we had an EEO problem in our own office, where a senior civil service African-American female professional felt that she was not given her due for her accomplishments, and that the white female who headed our office particularly disliked her and did all sorts of things to undercut her. I actually ended up making a deposition on it. Now neither one of the women was a personal friend. I was careful once it started not to have lunch or to have social contacts with either one, because it would taint what I said. I kept what I said to what I actually observed. The director of the office refused to deal with it.

There was a similar case in Canada when the Foreign Commercial Service officer in Ottawa abused the head of the commercial section in Montreal and a Foreign Service national. Alas, the DCM just sort of hid from the whole mess. Fortunately, the Department of Commerce bit the bullet, sent an inspector, and removed the offending Ottawa officer.

Q: Well, I am just thinking, if you have anything from your experiences, particularly if they pertain to actual cases, you can add that to this.

JONES: Oh, yes. In the science work, it was very straightforward. I did have one fun case. The head of the International Joint Commission who came to Ottawa—Tom Baldini—he had a very unique problem. The Clinton appointees to the International Joint Commission were all experienced environmental types, very collegial and competent. Two were women who were tops in tact and expertise. The Canadians also named some stellar people. One was a world-class whale scientist from Quebec. One was a very prominent Liberal Party—connected senior lawyer from British Columbia. They balanced geographically. One was an environmental activist from Ontario. Alas, the Canadian side went to war with each other, as the female head of the commission from Ontario was extremely sensitive as to her perks and refused to accept the other two as peers. But they were not people you could order about. So our people were unable to determine what the Canadian position was because they would hear one, and then they would hear the other, and then they would hear the third. Baldini was in a position of trying to deal with warring relatives. So he said he wanted us to know so we could at least let the Canadian Department of Foreign Affairs know. He didn't want to go directly to them, because that wasn't right in the chain of command. So I wrote it up and faxed it to my contact. I sent a fax that explained the discord problems carefully in neutral terms, and within minutes I had a phone call asking me to classify it. Someone listened, because eventually the difficult one left and her replacement had no problems. Apparently, the last straw was when she insisted on some ministerial privileges that weren't appropriate. I saw her in operation and found her to be very bright, very dedicated, and with no people sense.

A FOIA Finale

Q: Tell me more about the period after your two Canada assignments.

JONES: I came out and did the counseling in assignments, and at that point I knew that I would be retiring before the next full year was up. So I curtailed so that they could replace me with someone who would be there for two years. I think he then retired also. I went to the Freedom of Information Act (FOIA) office, where I figured I had a very nice parking orbit and spent the time improving my understanding of Boolean logic. I rewrote some of the regulations to cover the new "sensitive but unclassified" category. I thought the FOIA people were wonderfully hardworking and unappreciated. It also made it possible for the retirees who came back to work to have some financial benefits while the system benefited from their experience.

CHAPTER 20

Comments on the Foreign Service

Retirement Seminar/Career Transition and Retirees

JONES: We went to career transition, which was three months at the time, which basically focused on telling us things that we could do. The very happiest ones in career transition were senior secretaries who not only were happy to be retiring but knew that they had immense value on the market. Any time they felt like getting money for a new Mercedes, it was just a matter of "temping" for some exec until they had it. They had totally portable skills. Most of them had worked out where they wanted to go.

The hardest and most difficult cases were the ones who were being forced out for time in class. I always thought their years of expertise could still be used, and I believe that was the idea behind the American Foreign Service Association's Foreign Service Reserve Corps.

There are so many good people, who even if they never became ambassador still had much to contribute.

At the same time, it was useful to remind others that confirmation as an ambassador was not deification.

The *Foreign Service Journal* and Foreign Service Writers

When I went to the Una Chapman Cox fellowship, I wrote whatever I wanted to. That was when I discovered I could indeed write.

When I was in INR, I was on the *Foreign Service Journal* editorial board. It was very sad in a way to see huge numbers of submissions by retired Foreign Service officers who had done wonderfully interesting things. One man wrote about postwar Japan. This was a period when the Japanese labor movement was very red and caused a great deal of grief. There were riots in the streets, so we all read the article with great anticipation. Alas, most of the article was about how he learned to do a reporting cable, because he had a wonderful DCM who was his mentor. Others that we received all read like memoranda to the secretary.

Q: I know. This is one of the hardest things to get away from. Well, what role did you feel that the Foreign Service Journal—*you were working for them on the board from when to when?*

JONES: I am trying to remember. I was still in INR, so it would have been '80 to '83, probably '83, but it might have been a year or so later.

Q: Well, in the '80s. How did you see the role of the Foreign Service Journal?

JONES: I thought they were respectable. They wrote well. They were necessary in the sense that the Department of State magazine was becoming more and more of a house organ. Over the years, I think they dropped all the controversial things they used to do such as writing up different grievance actions.

The American Foreign Service Association.

As for the American Foreign Service Association, they are both a union and a professional organization. This meant some of conflict of interest because the head of AFSA is almost always a senior Foreign Service officer, which put him in the management column. If after a term as head of AFSA, he had any hopes of another ambassadorship, then burning all his bridges while head of AFSA was not a good idea. At the same time, they were very limited and could not negotiate like a labor union.

I grew up in a union town in Vineland, New Jersey, and I know how the unions operated. Foreign Service officers don't think of themselves as part of a union. They think of themselves as professionals. Even junior Foreign Service officers get management duties overseas. For all the complaints, the turnover rate for the Foreign Service is very low, so people must be pretty satisfied.

Foreign Service Elitism—and Science Officers

They acted more as if they were part of an elite group. The testing procedure acted as sort of a common bond, which was further strengthened by the A-100 classes. There was actually less gamesmanship than I expected. I saw some things which I thought were odd, in the sense that people were promoted so much by their individual performance that always you had people who felt undervalued. You also had people fighting for the credit occasionally.

I was very fortunate to have worked in technical areas where no one fought over credit. They didn't view denigrating someone else's work to boost their own standing as useful. But I could hear the screaming and yelling, for instance, in the office across the way when I was in science and technology cooperation. The office of environment was headed by a man who brooked absolutely no opposition to his environmental views, so you were either an apostate or you were a follower.

A colleague of mine who was a chemical engineer and was also a professional science officer at State actually dared question some of the assumptions and had his career almost destroyed. The head of the environmental office, Andy Sens, seemed to relish dominance—if it helped him look good. He could have matched any commissar under Stalin.

There was so little recourse for a Foreign Service officer, unless you wanted to torpedo the aircraft carrier kamikaze fashion.

Impressions of Secretaries of State

Q: I don't have much data on the Albright group. It seemed to be an enclosed group. It has not worn very well. The Baker group was closed, but they were really very good people.

JONES: Yes, they were closed, but their efforts were to help. The Madeleine Albright group was proof that a woman can be just as difficult and bad as a secretary of state as any man can be. They were very ideological. If you were a Foreign Service officer who said something that didn't fit with the prevailing belief at the time, you were fired. I got to memorize the sixteen-digit computer codes for places temporarily in the Freedom of Information Act [FOIA] and in the historian's office, because they were the only places that had positions listed at senior levels open to fast assignments. The Albright people had the view that you were against them until you crawled enough to prove that you are with them. I at one point read efficiency reports that she had written when she was the ambassador to the UN. They made clear that the greatest Foreign Service virtue to her was jumping higher and harder at her snap of the fingers. That is what they valued. There were certain people whom they were especially against and whose careers they destroyed.

Q: *Do you have any idea what may have prompted being against?*

JONES: I have no idea, but in my experience it is always the super ideological who are totally intolerant of any difference. Whether you are to the left or to the right, the intolerance is the same. I noted it when I wrote articles on global warming that ran counter to the prevailing worship of Al Gore and the insistence that the science had reached the level of proof.

I argued that there was no need to use the science as God's cattle prod to make people do the right thing. It just didn't track with the actual level of knowledge or modeling skill. In fact, there are things that could be agreed to as good actions whether you believed in global warming, in global cooling, in helping the poor of the world, or in improving energy security. Remember, they had a mini ice age in Europe without any contributions from us. There are dinosaur bones in the Antarctic; the dinosaurs died out without any help from us.

Some Closing Comments

There are horror stories, some about political appointees but others from our own ranks. For example, when Ambassador Enders died, I noticed that not a single obituary said he was a nice guy. The drivers used to tell horror stories about him and his wife, the "Contessa" Enders, years after they left. Then there was Ambassador MacArthur, whose wife was even worse than he was. She exacted total obedience from the junior wives. And State allowed these abuses.

Our society is rich in talent, something that I was reminded of when I was on an air force plane with the Science and Technology Intelligence Committee. There were eleven general officers on the plane, so I asked what would happen if we went down, would it cripple the Air Force. The answer was simple: eleven promotion parties.

The greatness of the U.S. Foreign Service is the incredible depth of the skills, abilities, dedication, and willingness to learn. For example, when the Russian staff quit en masse at the embassy in Moscow, our science counselor ended as the principal driver because he was the only one to figure out the street maps. It's the "can-do" spirit.

There are always going to be horror stories, as well as wonderful tales, involving the political as well as the nonpolitical ambassadors. I remember hearing tales about an ambassador's wife who refused to let embassy personnel use the residence bathrooms when they were working there after the Nicaragua earthquake. Others opened their homes to all who needed help.

In sum, I was glad that I was useful in the State Department. I kept my scientific professional standards, so if I had to give bad news, I gave it. If I had to stand behind what I said, I did. And if I was wrong, I was perfectly willing to have it stuffed up my nose. That is my kind of discipline. As for human relations, I was saddened to see a certain element of chickens pecking wounded chickens. My family had a poultry farm in Dorothy, New Jersey, and I saw other chickens peck any wounded chicken to death. There was something of that, maybe in the foreign service competitiveness. Nevertheless, it was a good time, and I truly benefited from it, as we paid for three daughters' tuitions out of current income. The center of my life remained my family, but work in the Foreign Service made the rest of it interesting as well.

PART II

THE BOY FROM SCRANTON

DAVID T. JONES

CHAPTER 21

Preludes—Growing Up and Getting Started with Life

Born and Raised in Scranton, Pennsylvania

Q: Let's begin at the beginning. Could you tell me when and where you were born and something about your family?

JONES: Okay. I was born on December 22, 1941, in Scranton, Pennsylvania. My parents were Scrantonians. My entire background in that regard was northeast Pennsylvania and the United States, dating to colonial times.

My father (William Taylor Jones) was an architect and an industrial designer. He graduated from the University of Pennsylvania in 1932. My mother (Martha Elizabeth Evans) was a dietician and a housewife. She graduated from Pratt Institute in New York City. I was educated in the public school system in Scranton, completing Scranton Central High School in 1959. I went to the University of Pennsylvania and graduated in 1963 with a degree in political science.

Q: I'll move you back a bit. Where did you go to grammar school?

JONES: I walked to grammar school. The school was the school that my mother and my uncle James Evans had attended: Alexander Hamilton #19 school in Scranton. The city of Scranton, in the era when I lived there, was a dying anthracite-coal town. It was a classic extraction industry scenario. For a century, coal companies and miners dug anthracite coal out of the Lackawanna Valley. When they had dug all the coal out of the Lackawanna Valley (and strip mined it as well), Scranton just shriveled up, like most natural resource towns. A town that had 140,000 people in the 1940s when I was born and during World War II steadily went downhill. Right now, they say that the principal industry in Scranton is social security. The population is about 80,000.

Q: What classes were most interesting to you?

JONES: I was interested in just about everything. I was, however, particularly interested in history. There wasn't a concept for me of "political science" or "international relations." These disciplines didn't exist in the Scranton school system. On the other hand, the very first issue that I remember being interested in that would qualify as an international relations subject was the Korean War. I was perhaps eight and a half when the war started in 1950. I followed it very closely in the Scranton daily newspapers and in *Time* magazine. One of my father's little stories about me was that during the Korean War, when I was about nine years old, somebody asked another adult, "Well, what do you think should be done about the war?" I piped up and said, "I like MacArthur's views on the subject!" All of a sudden, that ended the discussion of the Korean War, and it went on from there. I don't remember this exchange, but there were those that thought I was saying too much already.

Q: When you got to high school, did you concentrate in certain areas?

JONES: At that point, my major interests were science and chemistry. So many of us in that era were particularly focused on what was happening in those fields because of "sputnik" and what this meant for the Cold War and East-West struggles. One of the subjects that most interested me then was science. I was academically equally strong at that point in both sciences and in history and social studies. Actually, I graduated first in both the science and history curriculums at Central High School, which was the college preparatory high school for the Scranton area.

Q: Were you thinking about what you were going to get into?

JONES: Yes. My interests at that point were in science. That was the direction where I was heading academically and personally. This was what I was most interested in studying professionally at the time. At the same time, I read an enormous amount of history—Civil War history, World War II history, and a wide range of military history.

Q: Did service abroad strike you as being interesting at that time, or did that come later?

JONES: No, I wouldn't say I had any special interest in service abroad. Although my parents were really quite educated for their generation—at the university level—they were not "traveled." Neither one of them had been further outside the United States than to Canada. I did not have other relatives who had traveled widely, although this was also a very highly educated family, certainly for the day and the era. I didn't think "Let's go to Europe" or of traveling anywhere else. My personal horizons, really until I went to college, were pretty limited. I don't think I had traveled further south than to Washington, DC, by the time I was a senior in high school, or further north than a brief trip to Canada in the same period of time. I had been as far west as Pittsburgh. This is a pretty limited geographic circumference. I think of it as astonishingly restricted in comparison with the life that my children have led or, for that matter, the life that my wife has led. But academically, my interests were almost between pages of books. This was also not even a period when there was extensive television available—at least in my family, which didn't have television until I was about twelve years old.

Q: You were in high school from when to when?

JONES: I was in high school 1955 to 1959.

To follow up on the television point, my family came a little bit late to television. We didn't have a television set until 1954, somewhere around that date. I read; I was always somewhat dismissive of television except for a handful of shows.

Q: Milton Berle, of course.

JONES: I never saw Milton Berle. He doesn't register at all. I saw a little bit of Sid Caesar. I saw a little of *Your Hit Parade*. I did enjoy almost all of the episodes of *Victory at Sea*.

Q: *This was the U.S. Navy.*

JONES: Yes. Later there were follow-on programs featuring the U.S. Air Force. It was authentic footage, something that was very different. That tied in very tightly with my interest in military history. So I saw a fair amount of that material and did that kind of reading and viewing.

Q: *Did you get down to Gettysburg?*

JONES: Yes, and to Valley Forge. As a boy, I had studied the Gettysburg battle as part of my Civil War history reading. I may have seen some of the fortifications around the Philadelphia area. I also was very interested in the Kenneth Roberts' books, such as *Rabble in Arms* and *Oliver Wiswell*. *Oliver Wiswell* was very interesting for many different reasons.

Q: *For me, it was a seminal book because it was the first time I got the view . . . that is, this was written from the point of view of a loyalist. It was the first time I thought, "Gee, there is another side."*

JONES: There is another side. I had not thought about that. The first time that I had seen anything positive written about Benedict Arnold was in Roberts' *Arundel* and *Rabble in Arms*. On my trip to Canada with my father, we partially retraced the route taken by Arnold up the Kennebec River. We got to Quebec City. Our interests were often military history and historical subjects generally. My dad, when the family sat around the table, talked history.

Q: *While you were doing this, was McCarthy a topic? This really hit a lot of people.*

JONES: It was interesting. I probably—at least so far as the local newspaper accounts of what he was trying to do, and remember that I'm eight or nine years old—might have had some initial sympathy for him until my father made a point to me. He said, "Well, what McCarthy is saying is that he can stand around and belabor Bill Jones [my dad's name] and then beat him about the head and shoulders, and when I'm proved innocent, all McCarthy does is turn around and say, 'Oh, it was really his brother, Dave Jones [my uncle].'" That immediately gave me a visceral illustration of just how unfair, in little boy terms, McCarthy was being. That was a very pointed way to illustrate how McCarthy was actually directed.

Penn—A Legacy as I Follow Family Footsteps

Q: You went to the University of Pennsylvania from 1959 to 1963.

JONES: Yes. Then I stayed another year and got a master's, and came back and worked on a PhD.

Q: At the University of Pennsylvania, this was '59. Was it politically active or did you kind of go there, get your degree, and leave?

JONES: You recall that this was my father's school [class of 1932]. It was also my uncle's school, who had been there ten years earlier [class of 1922]. So, to a degree, I felt proud about going to the same university that my father and my uncle had attended. Initially, I was trying to be a chemist. I was seeking a bachelor's of science in chemistry. I found I just wasn't going to be a chemist. I just couldn't do the work. I might have found myself, if I had graduated, capable of being only a rather bad chemist.

I started reviewing what I was going to do if I was not going to be a chemist. I found, not too much to my surprise, that the other subject in which I had always been interested, history, was also available—and available with people and professors who were brilliant and able to elucidate their points in a manner in which no high school teacher had been able to do. At the same time, I looked at the circumstances and felt that being a history major was a dead end. I thought that history would lead you to be a history teacher or, as one of my fraternity brothers had done, to go out and sell soap for Procter and Gamble. So I entered political science instead. I found that this was a far better intellectual fit for me. I found a number of professors, including a former Foreign Service officer, John Melby, who were particularly inspiring.

Q: I interviewed him about two years before he died.

JONES: I made arrangements to try to see him while I was in Canada, but he died before I was able to get to see him. He was living near Guelph, Ontario, and it's just far enough from Ottawa that I was trying to arrange it while going to Toronto, but I just didn't make it. I had great respect for him and found him to be a fascinating man. At the same time, another professor at Penn, Robert Strausz-Hupé, was for me a seminal influence. Strausz-Hupé had in rigorous and structured form the inchoate political/international relations ideas that I was feeling when I was in my late teens and early twenties. His personal influence on me intellectually was quite substantial.

The university at the time had less of the anti-establishment feel that characterized Berkeley. I never was at Berkeley, certainly not at that time, but the University of Pennsylvania was a much more conservative environment. Whether it was more conservative partly because of the Wharton School influence or not, I'm not quite sure. But there was some ferment on campus directed against several professors and an institution that had done some military contracting. Nevertheless, there was not the kind of sympathy on the Penn campus for protesting or using marijuana or other actions of that nature.

Q: This also came a little later, didn't it?

JONES: A little later, but again, to a degree, I bracketed all of these time frames. I was at Penn from 1959 to 1964. Then I was in the military for a couple of years. I came back from 1966 to 1968, and then I was back for another year, from 1971 to 1972. One of the other influences that I also have to make clear is that I spent a lot of time in one way or another with the military. I elected to go into ROTC [Reserve Officers' Training Corps], which my father and a couple of his friends had suggested. They noted adroitly that it was much more pleasant to serve on active duty as an officer than as an enlisted man. And, looking at the circumstances associated with the draft during that era, no reasonable individual could bet that they were going to be able to avoid the draft. You looked at it, and the statistics were simply that as an able-bodied young man, you were likely to serve a couple of years in the military. My father had never served in the military, having been deferred as a married man with a child (me) immediately after Pearl Harbor, but he respected his colleagues who had served. The judgment, made reluctantly on my part rather than enthusiastically, was that I would be better off going through ROTC, taking a commission, and working at that level. The results over a lifetime were extremely positive.

Q: Which ROTC was this?

JONES: Army ROTC. I wouldn't have qualified for any other program as I wore glasses. The Navy at that juncture wouldn't accept anybody without 20/20 vision, and Penn did not have an Air Force ROTC program.

Q: What about Strausz-Hupé? He's still alive and apparently still rather busy. You were going up to interview him.

JONES: I saw him on Friday.

Q: He was ambassador how many times?

JONES: He was ambassador starting in about 1969 to Sri Lanka (then Ceylon) and, following that, to Belgium; then to Stockholm; then back to Brussels to head the U.S. Mission to NATO [North Atlantic Treaty Organization]. He was dismissed as a political appointee when Carter won in 1976. As a result, he left his first round of diplomatic assignments in roughly April 1977. But after Reagan was elected, he was brought back and served in Turkey for about eight years.

Q: We're talking about when you were a student. What were you getting from him? What was he teaching? Did he have an approach?

JONES: Yes, essentially he looked upon and evaluated international relations and foreign policy on the basis of national power and national interest. His basic international relations course went through the elements of power and national power and focused on discussing what was really national interest. He used his own textbook and also a textbook by Hans Morgenthau. They were both standard works. At the same time, he had released a book that, in my generation, influenced quite a number of people either directly or indirectly: *The Protracted Conflict*. This was a judgment that our efforts to deal with the Soviet Union were going to take a very long time, that it was going to be a struggle in time as well as in space, and that we had to gear ourselves for a confrontation that was going to last for a very extended period. People have translated that into saying either that Strausz-Hupé hated the Russians or was a Cold Warrior. There was shorthand commentary of that nature, which I personally think is incorrect. Strausz-Hupé had not the slightest interest in war. He just simply had a very high regard for freedom and independence, and he believed that these could best be preserved by a close association between the United States and Europe. These were the twin pillars of his own life. As a consequence, he worked much of his life to develop both of these areas and to link the United States and Europe as closely as possible.

Q: *What was his background?*

JONES: He was born in Austria. He was young enough to have missed the Great War. He came to the United States in his early twenties, along with another young man for whom I think he was a sort of half-guardian. He wrote all of this in an outstanding autobiography called *In My Time* [1965]. Then he spent a short period doing odd things like being a picture framer in the basement of Marshall Fields in Chicago. Next he moved slowly into investment banking and managed to make this career a success, I think in New York, but certainly in Philadelphia. About 1925, he married a woman who already had children. She was an heiress from a man who had very substantial railroad money. They bought a farm on the outskirts of Philadelphia, a home that he said he's owned for seventy years. It's an old farmhouse that's slowly been reconstructed over the decades.

Little by little, he became more engaged in teaching, instruction, and study at the University of Pennsylvania, where I think he got his doctorate about 1940. Then he became a lecturer there. He ran part of a strategic intelligence group at the University of Pennsylvania during the war. Again, as things slowly developed after the war and throughout the rest of his academic time at Penn, he became one of the major founders for the discipline of international relations. He provided a good deal of the intellectual structure for foreign affairs purposes for many of the American conservatives. In this regard, he had connections slowly but steadily increasing on the political side with people like Hugh Scott, who was a senator in Pennsylvania, and with Barry Goldwater, and then more and more with Reagan, for whom he provided commentary, briefing, and insight on foreign policy. While much of the American conservative establishment was business oriented and not terribly articulate in dealing with foreign policy other than "better dead than Red," Strausz-Hupé was far more intellectually supple than that limited maxim, and he developed theses and approaches that presented the conservative movement more intelligently.

Q: You were a sophomore during the 1960 Kennedy-Nixon campaign. This is one that engaged an awful lot of people of a generation, more or less your generation, regarding political service and so on. Did that hit you or your immediate group?

JONES: Certainly, I was interested in it personally. I would also say that Richard Nixon was one of my early heroes. I thought that he was smart, intelligent, and tough minded. If I could have voted in 1960, which I could not because I was not old enough (21 was the legal age to vote at that time), without any question, I would have voted for him. At the same time, I could also see the personal appeal of John Kennedy. He came through the Penn campus in a motorcade during the election period, and I went to see him. I was not the least bit interested in voting for him. Indeed, I thought he had all the flaws that were being bruited about at that time. But as he passed and waved to us, I found myself clapping and cheering in response. He did have a visceral effect on people. I will also say that his inaugural speech, which I always found interesting because he didn't have the Massachusetts accent that he did in many of his subsequent speeches—it was almost as if he had deliberately set aside his accent to make this speech—is definitely one of the great speeches of modern America.

Q: And the spirit that went with it. This was beyond politics. It energized a generation, including certainly a generation that came into the Foreign Service. This was pretty good stuff. Government service was a good thing. Going overseas, you might make sacrifices, but you were joining a worthy cause.

JONES: I was not stimulated in that way by John Kennedy. If anything, I guess I would say that I was much more engaged in finding ways to make sure that the Soviets did not win. This was not a question of going forth to do good. As a result, I sneered at the Peace Corps. I found the Peace Corps to be a trivial and essentially valueless operation. But my personal view was that under no circumstances could we yield to Soviet aggression, that if I had learned any lesson, I had learned the "no more Munichs" lesson. As a result, I was certainly led down the direction into full and total support for our intervention in Vietnam, which was a catastrophe. If I learned a lesson from history, I had learned one of the wrong lessons or a lesson that turned out wrong.

Q: Many of us had that. When you graduated in 1963, you served two years in the army?

JONES: It's a little more complicated than that. Although I graduated in 1963, I had also submatriculated into graduate school earning graduate credit for courses taken as an undergraduate, and I went immediately on to graduate school. In graduate school, I had even more exposure to people like John Melby; to Strausz-Hupé; to William Kintner, who later was ambassador to Thailand. I dealt with people within Strausz-Hupé's institute, the Foreign Policy Research Institute, in Philadelphia; and even perhaps more importantly at the time—and this is another major component of my life at that period—to Chinese studies.

Meeting and Marrying the Girl from Novasibirsk

The woman that I married I met on the very first day of classes at the University of Pennsylvania in 1959. She is Chinese-American and was born in the Soviet Union in Novosibirsk. Her father was a Chinese diplomat who had been in the Soviet Union between 1939 and 1949. Eventually they escaped. They left Russia in 1949, went to Sweden, spent a year in Sweden, and came to the United States in 1950. They lived in New Jersey before my wife came to the University of Pennsylvania in 1959. Incidentally, I met her though studies in chemistry.

My vignette in this regard is that I met her on the first day of classes—in calculus. I introduced myself as "Davy Jones, as in 'Davy Jones's Locker'." She had no trouble remembering me as "Davy Locker."

She continued in her studies and got a PhD in chemistry, but eventually left chemistry after doing research for a number of years and entered the Foreign Service in 1974. She retired in October last year. So the combination of subjects that I was studying in that period 1963-1964 was international relations and very much also Far Eastern studies.

Q: When did you get married?

JONES: I was married just a couple of months after I went into the military. I went into the military in July 1964 after completing my master's in May 1964. I then went through the standard infantry officer basic training, intelligence officer basic training, going to first to Fort Benning, Georgia (infantry training), and then to Fort Holabird, Maryland (intelligence training). I went to jump school at Benning. Right after jump school in December 1964, I was married.

Military Service—and a Korean Experience

Q: What were you doing in the military?

JONES: I was an intelligence officer. The major aspect of my two years of active military service was a fourteen-month tour of duty in Korea. At that juncture, I went almost directly from my honeymoon to Korea. I had made a decision that if I were interested in Asia after a tour in Korea, I would really be interested in Asia. So rather than looking for other assignments that could have kept me within the United States, I sought an assignment in Korea. I had been assigned to Fort Bragg. I actually arranged an assignment transfer with another officer who was assigned to Korea. He didn't want to go to Korea. People think, "Why would this man want to leave his new bride and go to Korea?" But I was very interested in the Far East at that point, and the two of us walked down to the Pentagon together. We were just interchangeable second lieutenants, and they interchanged us. This to me is an illustration of just how flexible the military can be, in contrast to the reputation that the military always has for being incredibly hidebound and inflexible.

But again, to give you an illustration of how things are curious in life, my college roommate in 1963-1964 also entered the military and also went to Fort Benning about a class in school behind me in the military. At that juncture, they were offering an opportunity to spend your two years on active duty as an intelligence officer with the CIA [Central Intelligence Agency]. I had taken the exam for the CIA while I was at the University of Pennsylvania and come to DC at CIA invitation, and been told, "Well, Mr. Jones, when you get out of the military, please call us." If I had been one class later in entering Benning instead of in the class in which I entered, almost undoubtedly I would have taken the same option that my colleague did, who spent a career at the CIA. At the end of two years of active duty military, having already spent two years at the CIA, I probably would never have left the Agency and not have taken up the Foreign Service option, which I also had.

Q: Tell me about Korea. You were there 1965-1966?

JONES: Yes.

Q: What was your initial impression of Korea? Where did you serve? What were you getting out of it?

JONES: This was my first experience of being out of the country. This was the first time that I had been further west than Chicago—I had been as far west as Chicago for a fraternity brother's wedding. I had never been to California. I was so ignorant of circumstances that when I saw the APO [Army Post Office] number with California on it, I thought I was going to spend time in California. I was quickly disabused of that conclusion. The only time I spent in California was to transit San Francisco, and I had time only to go out and be part of a tourist group and be driven to the Top of the Mark and through Chinatown and then back to the airport to get on the plane to fly to Korea.

For Korea, it was an illustration of how limited what you learn from books and pictures and film can be in contrast to what you learn about a society when you are on the ground. If you study the Far East at all, you learn about rice, rice culture, and how important rice is in the entire society. And you learn about irrigation and irrigation patterns. In China these are combined with flood control, all of the factors associated with that system of dams, canals, and so on. But when I was actually on the ground in Korea and saw my first water buffalo in a rice paddy, I suddenly had a quantum jump in understanding of the entire range of material that I had learned previously.

Korea in 1964-1965 was truly struggling. The war was obviously over with the 1954 armistice. The peace had been in effect for ten years, but it was still a very battered society. I don't know if you have been back since 1951 or 1952 or whether you had returned to Korea…

Q: I went back in 1976.

JONES: It was a society in which manpower and buffalo power were still far more important than mechanical power. One of my vivid images is of a man and his wife struggling to push a cart heavily loaded with charcoal burners, those cylindrical coal-impregnated pieces of fuel for briquettes, up a long hill in front of the Yongsan compound. They were really putting their backs into it. Another recollection for me was an oxcart passing in front of the Blue House—the equivalent of the White House—in downtown central Seoul. You saw bullet holes in any structure that was still standing. This was also a society, unfortunately, when the very best thing that could happen to a Korean woman was that she have a liaison of any sort with a Western male. You could go out and hire a woman for a dollar. It was really pathetic. It was demeaning. But it was accurate that virtually any Korean female from Miss Korea on down could be made available without a lot of effort. At the same time, the Korean males seemed to be rather indifferent to a good deal of it. The attitude was sort of "Well, men and soldiers require women." There wasn't some incredible proprietary pride that somehow they were being debased because the American soldiers that were there were handling large numbers of prostitutes.

I recall one piece in a Korean newspaper—and this was at the time we were beginning to shuffle our forces to go to Vietnam—that appeared to be an argument over whether Korea should participate in Vietnam. The bottom-line judgment was that it was much better that Korean divisions go to Vietnam than that the Americans pull a division out of Korea and send it to Vietnam. This also was a pretty straightforward approach on their part.

Although the society was as impoverished and battered as it was, there was to me an enormous sense of the energy and the effort and the commitment of the people to succeed. Everybody was studying—I mean everybody. The woman who was running the elevator had a book. The guy who was your lavatory attendant shining your shoes was studying. These were people that, if they could pull themselves up by their own bootstraps, would break their knees pulling before they would quit. It was just clear in that way that if they had the chance, if they were given the opportunity, there would be more. But, boy, you looked at it at that time and thought that this was a society that had a long way to go. There was so little that was actually available. There was only, in effect, one significant highway in the country, and that was headed toward the demilitarized zone, the MSR or "the main supply route." There was also a reasonable highway that went to Inchon. There was a rickety old railroad that went to Pusan. As a group of young intelligence officers, we all got together and took the train to Pusan. This was most of the travel experience that we were going to have.

As an intelligence officer at that time, I was studying the "order of battle" of the North Korean Army, that is, its strength, composition, and disposition of forces. It was North Korean forces that I was studying more than South Korean forces. You had a serious sense for how tough any fight would be. The North certainly appeared to be very well armed, very well organized. Their commitment appeared to be rock hard. They certainly seemed to be focused on "liberating" or conquering the South. They at that time still had excellent relations with both China and the Soviet Union. It was a difficult set of circumstances that the South was perceived to be facing.

Q: What was the feeling you were picking up as a junior officer about the ability of the South Korean army?

JONES: We thought it was a pretty good army. Certainly, we thought the ROK [Republic of Korea] forces were tough. We thought that they were a lot better army than they had been in 1950. We were also slowly moving the main U.S. military forces off the front line. At this point, the ROK forces were holding almost all of the Demilitarized Zone (DMZ). At the same time, I had a brief experience with the U.S. embassy there. I had passed the Foreign Service exam. At one juncture, I went downtown with another officer just to see what the embassy looked like. We went on the compound, and an American Foreign Service officer invited us to step in and chat; we had a pleasant conversation. I don't remember the man or anything about the conversation, but it was a positive experience. But at the same time, the Eighth Army G2 got a batch of documents that the embassy no longer wanted. They were excess or extra copies of various studies, intelligence studies. They were all secret documents, and they were sent to Eighth Army headquarters without any handling forms or restrictions. We thought that this was incredibly sloppy and unprofessional. We sat down and everybody filled out official pink handling forms and put them on these embassy documents that had been sent over to us. Our attitude was, "Gee whiz, how can these people be so insecure?"

We, in our excessive commitment to security consciousness, not only had the responsible person sign it but then somebody double-checked every signature. The poor guy (an enlisted man) who was responsible for many of the classified documents, was under great pressure. The phrase regarding classified material went, "Well, there are no friends when classified documents are concerned." The infinite control effort for what in retrospect, of course, was very trivial material gave us this attitude of "Gee whiz, how could these people at the embassy be so casual?"

Q: What was the word of wisdom that you were getting as an officer about the threat from the North, and how likely it was that they might attack and, if they did, what would happen?

JONES: We were stuck intellectually with the feeling that we were always prepared all the time, that, no, they weren't going to come tomorrow, but we had to be prepared for this possibility. There was also the feeling that it would be a hell of a fight, but that everybody was always confident enough to think that we would win. Nevertheless, there was the feeling that this would be one hell of a fight. The distance between the Demilitarized Zone and Seoul and the level of defenses were at that time nowhere near the level of ROK defenses that there are now. There was a lot of worry over whether the North Koreans had been able to build up with newer equipment. They recently had gotten significant inputs of weaponry from both China and the Soviet Union. It was a worrisome set of circumstances. In retrospect, we are concerned about once every other year about a threat from the North. This analysis has gone on now for close to forty years. But in 1964-65, it was only ten years ago that this fighting had ended. There were many people who had been there "when" and were back for one reason or another.

Probably my biggest project during this period was to work out with the ROK intelligence G2 at their general headquarters an "order of battle" for the North Korean military forces. This study involved assessing the strength, composition, and disposition of their forces, and determining a table of organization and equipment for all North Korean forces, from the top of their Ministry of National Defense all the way down to their rear-rank privates and their armament. To complete that project, I did something that, again in retrospect, I think most people would have considered me to have been rather foolish to attempt: I extended my tour of duty in Korea by a month to finish this job. I was actually asked by at least one senior officer whether undue pressure had been put on me to extend to do this job. I suspect people thought it was either so unusual that I would not rush home to my new bride, or they were wondering whether I had a Korean mistress on the side that made me reluctant to return home. But I will once again say that I simply wanted to finish that particular job. I felt that nobody would finish it if I did not complete it. I was about two-thirds of the way through it at that juncture. One of the things that pleases me in retrospect, and amuses me at the same time, was a letter that a couple of my ROK counterparts wrote to my wife saying that despite all of their "efforts to tempt your husband, Mrs. Jones, he was not temptable."

Q: Of course, as anybody who has served in the military knows, particularly in the earlier times in the Far East, temptation was everywhere.

JONES: Temptation cost a dollar. The women were personally attractive. This was not as if you were hauling somebody off a downtown Washington "red light" district or a group of "street walker" prostitutes. Again, to say the least, with a Chinese wife, I had no prejudice against Oriental women.

Q: What about information about an order of battle? I would think it would be very difficult to get good information. Where did it come from? What was your impression of what you were putting together?

JONES: In retrospect, the information and the product were probably limited. It was probably best on the lower levels of the North Korean force structure. What we had were a series of defectors, people who had crossed the line from the North and who surrendered to the South; they then went to interrogation camps that were on the outskirts of Seoul. They were debriefed extensively. People just simply worked their way through what they knew little by little and squeezed them and interrogated them. Actually, a book that you might be familiar with is called *P. S. Wilkinson* [by C. D. B. Bryan; 1965]; one part of this man's experience was being an intelligence officer in Korea and dealing with interrogation and interrogation camps for North Korean defectors. The information on certain levels was reasonably good, and we rationalized how much some of these people knew by saying: "Well, these people don't have a great deal to do. Occasionally, they move from unit to unit, and they sit down and talk with each other about everything they had done and everywhere they had been, and it fills up their time. The fact this or that individual knows a gigantic amount is a reflection of the fact that he moved around a little bit in Korea and did that."

What I did not know at the time was how much sensitive intelligence was also available, Although we had access to what was called then "Church Door," which was photo intelligence of the North, and that gave us a good deal of insight as to what was happening in a purely mechanical "digging in the ground" basis, we did not have the type of electronic intercept, at least at my level and in my capacity, that other officers in Korea did have. I remember one instance where a senior officer came to our office and asked me to document whether such and such was happening. I provided from the information that we had this type of material. He accepted it. Presumably, he thought it could be used to prove to people to whom you could not release the electronic intercept material that such and such had been happening. At the same time, a group of us young officers said, "Hey, there is a unit here that has been carried on the books for X years. We haven't heard of this unit in this many years. We think it should be dropped." They looked at us and said no. Again, in retrospect, it appears clear that they had some other form of confirmation that this unit was still operating, even though there had been no confirmation of it over the time we were assigned. Indeed, there was a unit about which we knew nothing on the 8th Army compound, which we called the "Green Door" unit based on a popular song in the 1950s ("What's Behind the Green Door"), which may have been an electronic intercept unit.

I would say that we had for the era and for the intelligence a pretty good picture of what was happening. Of course, it was intelligence in slow motion. A great deal of what was happening north of the border was virtually frozen into place and had been frozen in place for years and years and years. It was not like Vietnam, where I never did serve, when information that was twenty-four hours old might as well be a history text. At the same time, if you had information in Korea from defectors, it might be three, four, or five years old, but it was useful information because so little was changing and so little had changed.

Another Image of Asia—Japan

Q: You came back in 1964. What did you think of Asia?

JONES: My experience in Asia had been Korea on the south side. I made a trip of about a week on leave to Japan. Of course, that was like stepping from one world into another. It was a dramatic and very interesting turnabout. I saw some of the most engaging aspects of Japan, both in Tokyo and then—when I took what was the absolute innovation of the era, the "bullet train"—to Kyoto. I went to the shrine at Nara. I was fascinated by that, found it very interesting. Probably my major pleasure in Japan was being able to have a glass of whole milk. All the milk in Korea that was drinkable was reconstituted. That had its taste problems. Upon return from the Far East and from Asia, I was still extremely interested in the Far East, extremely interested in Asia, and I was pursuing my academic studies at that time in Far Eastern affairs, particularly Chinese politics, history, culture, and subjects of that nature.

Again, Penn

Q: You went back to the University of Pennsylvania.

JONES: Yes.

Q: How long were you there?

JONES: I was there from 1966 to 1968. I continued my graduate studies, working for a PhD. I took my PhD prelims and passed, and began preliminary academic research. I was focused on studying the People's Liberation Army and its evolution and progress. I continued also to study in other Far Eastern areas. I worked with Dr. Hilary Conroy on Japan and Japanese studies. I'm not sure whether John Melby was still there by then. I don't think he was. I believe I also had a course with Professor Alan Rickett, a specialist in modern China, although he started modern China somewhere back around the twelfth century. The last lecture of the second semester covered China from 1912 to the then present, which I thought was a little unfair. But when I came back, it was also a time when the Cultural Revolution was taking place in China. We were very interested in that. It was also, of course, the time when our commitment in Vietnam reached the tip point of us moving out rather than in after the catastrophe of the Tet offensive.

Q: What about your wife and her family? Were they still connected to China, interested and all that?

JONES: This was a very Americanized family in many ways. My father-in-law elected not to stay in the Chinese cocoon in New York. When they moved to southern New Jersey, he had a chicken farm near Vineland, New Jersey, for a number of years and then both he and his wife worked in a Kimble Glass factory. His wife eventually went back to school and got a nursing degree. They were effectively the only Asians in the Vineland area. My wife was the only Asian in her high school, and five years later her brother was the only Asian in the same high school. Both of them were the valedictorians of the high school.

They had a very tangential connection with China. There were relatives in Taiwan. My wife's grandmother was still in China. My father-in-law's stepmother and his stepbrothers and a sister were in China. But contact between anyone in China and anyone in the United States at that period, and really until 1972, was very indirect, very third hand, very "wrote to somebody somewhere else who would forward a message." Writing back was equally laborious. Finding out anything about what was happening to any of your relatives in this regard was very chancy and very sporadic.

The Slow Progress Toward the Foreign Service

Q: What about the Foreign Service? When did this cross your horizon, and how did you deal with it?

JONES: It crossed my horizon about my junior year in college. Partly it was stimulated by having met John Melby. It was, "Well, what will I do with myself? The Foreign Service sounds interesting." What did one do with a political science degree when you're studying international relations? Almost with a delightfully blasé spirit, I assumed a career in diplomacy might be interesting. How do you go about this? Well, you take this exam. Okay, I'll take the exam. What do you do? Well, you go down to the post office at Thirtieth Street and Market Street, go to this huge room that is full of people, and take the exam. Well, of course, you had to write in on time and get yourself registered and so on. But that was it. It was without any question the most difficult exam I have ever taken in my life. No question about it. One way or another, I left the exam sure that I had failed. There was just no way that I could have passed that exam. Instead, a couple of months later (I took it in the fall of 1962 after I had just entered my senior year), I got notice that I had passed. They gave me a stack of forms to fill out and material to write up, an autobiography to write, and told me to come to the UN [United Nations] Mission in New York to take the oral exam. That was in January 1963. I was a second semester senior.

I went to New York and had the classic exam of that era with me at the end of a T-shaped table with three examiners. They asked me questions. I answered questions.

Q: Do you recall any of the questions?

JONES: I think I remember being asked to name the countries that were then in the EU [European Union], which wasn't the EU at that point. I think I got them all. I also remember saying that the military was our first line of defense, which suggested that I hadn't read or at least not internalized the little pamphlet that said that diplomats are our first line of defense. I remember vaguely one of the hypotheticals, but I don't remember the specifics about the hypothetical question. Partly I don't remember it because I've spent time listening to and talking about hypotheticals in the current Board of Examiners, so I can't remember those that I was asked. The examiners asked a fair amount of personal background in history and what I had done and where I had come from. I think, if anything, they might have wondered whether I was too young to be passed. I had just turned twenty-one. I think it helped me that I made it clear to them that I was not interested in immediately entering the Foreign Service, that I had a master's degree that I wanted to get, and I had two years of military service that I had to perform. I was not going to be presenting myself at their doors until I was about twenty-four, which I think they thought was probably better than not. Oddly enough, somebody suggested that I might benefit from a public speaking class, which may have stuck in my head because I had never been considered to be insufficiently oral or lacking ability to project. I had had high school dramatics and I can still fill an auditorium with my voice unamplified. That was it so far as my recollection of it. Other than the tension of waiting outside the examination room for the "baby" to be born, although you didn't know whether the baby *was* going to be born. So I sat in the antechamber to the conference room waiting for them to come out and tell me whether I had passed. I also had the impression that one of the people who was giving the exam was not in the best of physical condition. I think he might have been using his Kaopectate or the equivalent of that. He didn't seem to be all that enthusiastic about the job at that juncture.

Q: Were you able to postpone it until you had finished graduate school?

JONES: At this point, you had a thirty-month "clock" that supposedly started from the day you had taken the very first written exam. The clock ran, but the clock also was suspended when you went into the military. So I kept track of my clock. But I didn't immediately want to enter the Foreign Service when I came back from Korea. I still had an academic focus that I wanted to complete. I did have a State Department experience in the summer of 1967. At that time, they were still giving paid internships. I applied for that internship. It was competitive within the university. It wasn't selected by the Department of State; it was selected within the university community. I remember that I was initially the alternate rather than the primary selectee. The primary selectee was bumped because he apparently was not physically qualified. He could never have physically been in the Foreign Service. He came to me and asked, in effect, why I thought I was qualified to have been the intern. I told him that I had already passed the exams. He went away mollified, if not satisfied, by the fact that I really was better qualified than he was to be an intern for that summer.

Q: What were you doing as an intern?

JONES: It was a bit of an off-putting experience. It wasn't the kind of experience that I would recommend for an intern. I was in IO/UNP [Bureau of International Organizational Affairs, Office of UN Political Affairs]. I spent a good deal of time trying to transcribe commentary that was coming in from the UN by speakerphone of UN committee action/debate during that period. I vaguely remember trying to rewrite parts of a manual. Admittedly, I also did have a two-week break. I had to go off and do two weeks of army reserve training. But the head of IO at the time was certainly very well qualified. There were other members in the office, people like Tom Carolyn and Rob Jones, who were personally interesting, competent, and thoughtful. I can't say that the experience itself was particularly stimulating either intellectually or professionally. I didn't feel that I was given much of a chance to do much of anything. I actually, before that intern experience, had heard a number of relatively negative comments about people who were associated with the Foreign Service. People were talking to people who would say, "Yes, I met that Foreign Service officer, and he was pretty unimpressive"; or "He just seemed to be interested in playing golf"; or "He was an arrogant, unpleasant son of a bitch, and I certainly wouldn't want to have anything to do with people like that." So I would say the most positive aspect of the internship in 1967 was that I met people with whom I had a degree of personal and intellectual respect. They did seem to be intelligent and personable individuals. As a result, I wasn't reluctant to enter the Foreign Service.

Those Initial Foreign Service Experiences and the 83rd A-100 Class

Q: When did you come in?

JONES: I came in in June of 1968.

Q: What about the PhD?

JONES: I didn't finish it. I went back in 1971-1972 to Penn and worked again on it for a year and finished about two-thirds of the dissertation, but then I just essentially ran out of time. I took a year's leave without pay after my first tour. I worked at it sporadically after that, but, frankly, I couldn't be the kind of Foreign Service officer I was trying to be and still finish the degree. So I have satisfied myself subsequently with a wide variety of writing. But as for the degree, I didn't finish it.

Q: Could you describe your entering Foreign Service class and your impressions of the people you came in with and your basic training?

JONES: It was an interesting class and an interesting range of people. It was still much more heavily male than not. It did, however, have the first substantial selection of African-American officers. I remember all of them. I've stayed in reasonably close touch with all of them who stayed with State, people like Chuck Baquet, Bob Perry, Greg Johnson, Aurelia

Brazeal, Hartford "Terry" Jennings, Leonardo Williams, and Ed Williams. I remember all of them pretty clearly. There were also a number of USIS [U.S. Information Service] officers who disappeared. Some of them I never saw again after I left the class, and I have no idea what happened to them. There were several very sharp officers who subsequently became ambassadors: John Glassman (his interests were a mix between the Soviet Union and Latin American affairs), David Halstead (who became an ambassador in an African post), and Joe Snider (a very smart officer who has just retired). Also there was a man who might have been as good as any of them, but he only stayed one tour and left for the Agency [CIA], spending a career with the Agency before retiring. (Incidentally, he was not in the Agency beforehand as a "plant" to get "cover.") He had an extended tour of duty with the Foreign Service, but he became distinctly disillusioned with the Foreign Service as a consequence of his first assignments and found the Agency much more attractive and to his liking; he spent his career there.

Q: What about Vietnam? Tet was January of '68.

JONES: The most important aspect about Vietnam was whether we would be assigned there, and who would be assigned there and who would not. The Vietnam experience for most young FSOs was defined by assignment to Combined Operations and Regional Development [CORDS]—our effort to win "hearts and minds" during the conflict. The CORDS people were very much a part of our commitment, certainly the State Department's commitment, in Vietnam. What it finally came down to was that every unmarried officer who had not had military experience was sent to Vietnam. That was not greeted with overwhelming enthusiasm. It was more of a "Gee whiz, I didn't really want to do this" than outright animosity to our commitment there or to the circumstances of the commitment. I don't think people realized how dangerous it was in real terms. The number of people that we lost in Vietnam was at that point unknown.

Despite my own personal interest in Asia and in Vietnam, I had been assigned to Paris. I asked my career development officer, "What would the circumstances be for changing the assignment to go to Vietnam?" In effect, it was going to be a longer tour in Vietnam than I was prepared to do after having just spent a year in Korea. I wasn't, in the end, willing to leave my wife again for what looked like a two-year tour unaccompanied in Vietnam. But my personal interest at that time in Vietnam was still to have the war won, to see the war won, and that it was a commitment well worth making and continuing.

I don't remember people in class being outspoken in their objections to Vietnam or critical about our key policymakers at the time (Dean Rusk, McGeorge Bundy, Robert McNamara). I didn't hear any criticism that I remember of them or of our Vietnam policy. You also have to recall that it was just at this juncture also that the Soviets seized Czechoslovakia and winterized the Prague Spring. I remember another Foreign Service officer, Tom Lauer, and I looked at each other and said, "Of course that's what they should do." For the two of us, it was completely predictable. It was exactly what the Soviets, acting as the kind of antagonists that we were confident they were, should do. They did it, and it wasn't any surprise to us at all. But if anything, that was a reinforcement of my personal views on the necessity to continue the protracted conflict (to borrow Strausz-Hupé's title again) in dealing with and handling a relationship with the Soviets.

CHAPTER 22

Every Young FSO Should Have a Tour in Paris

Q: Did you go to Paris then?

JONES: Yes, I did.

Q: From when to when were you in Paris?

JONES: The spring of 1969 to the summer of 1971. We arrived approximately in May 1969. We had just missed "les evenements" [the events], the uprising and the rioting that so characterized Paris in the spring of 1968. As students were rioting, they definitely would have had all the young political officers (actually, we were multifunctional in a way, but we weren't "coned," or designated for one particular specialty). We were doing everything at that time, doing reporting on political and economic issues as well as rotating through the embassy's consular and administrative offices. But they probably would not have objected had the young officers in the embassy been on the Rive Gauche just trying to get a sense of what was happening.

Q: What were you doing in between your assignment to Paris and your arrival there?

JONES: I didn't depart immediately as I had the full round of standard consular training, French training, and a short stint in the Department of

Commerce to accustom me to the econ/commercial position to which I had ostensibly been assigned. The training was effective albeit uninspired; consular training was still focused on learning the regulations in the Foreign Affairs Manual as "ConGen Rosslyn" which provided simulated "hands on" training in visa issuance and consular cases had not yet been invented. The language training was serious and effective; I am not naturally gifted for language, and I've said that learning a foreign language was like chipping stone with my tongue. But my French was sufficiently learned to be effective in Paris.

That's essentially what absorbed the period of time from the several months that we spent at FSI [Foreign Service Institute] to the time when I left for Paris. Fortunately, my wife and I went to Europe on the *SS United States*. It was very close to the end of that type of travel for diplomats; It was a wonderful opportunity.

Q: What was your wife doing during this time?

JONES: My wife had been doing a variety of career-oriented jobs. After she got her PhD, which was approximately in December 1966, she did research on tobacco with the Department of Agriculture in laboratories on the outskirts of Philadelphia at Radnor. Then, when we moved in the summer 1968 to Washington, she worked again for the Department of Agriculture doing research on dairy products. She published a variety of papers in journals and then left the Department of Agriculture to accompany me to Paris. She worked at the Department of Agriculture until about April 1969.

The Environment: Embassy and Paris

Q: What were you doing in Paris?

JONES: This was the first tour. This was a standard first tour, Foreign Service officer's exercise. It was my first experience in Europe—it was my first Foreign Service assignment, really. Everything before that, almost close to a year, had been a combination of language training, visa training, passport training, familiarization also at the Department of Commerce, since, ostensibly at least, I was appointed in Paris as a commercial officer. This was at a time when there was still a commercial section and an economic/commercial officer. There was still a commercial sector in the Department of State. When I arrived, I found actually to my great satisfaction and pleasure that I was not going to spend two years being an economic/commercial officer. I was and would be still far more interested in doing political work. What they did in Paris with first tour junior officers was, I understand, relatively standard in the larger posts: they put you on a rotation. Essentially, you spent six months in four different sections in the embassy. The first of my tours of six months each was in the economic section. I never did straight commercial work. There had been and there still is a commercial trade center in Paris; it is a big operation there for us. While I might have expected to go to it originally, I never went there. I just did straight internal analysis for economic affairs in Paris for six months.

Q: *You were in Paris from '69 to when?*

JONES: Roughly July 1971.

The French—and Their Challenges

Q: *What was France like at this time? This was a year after the events of '68. This was their trauma time. How did you find France, particularly Paris?*

JONES: I guess the truism is that every young man should spend some time in Paris and every old man should go back and regret that he didn't take more advantage of his time as a young man in Paris. I guess you have to put it in the context of who I was and what I didn't know. I was remarkably untraveled to be a Foreign Service officer in the terms of 1999. Maybe in the terms of 1969 I was more typical in that manner. But this was my first European experience. It was also my first experience with the French, for whom intellectually I really didn't care very much. This was the France that had thrown NATO out of the country, led by Charles de Gaulle.

This was a France for which many Americans didn't appreciate in the least with regard to its foreign policies. It was a France that seemed to be more interested in putting a stick in our eye than giving us a pat on the back for whatever we were doing. As I spent more time there, at least I began to appreciate the rationale for what the French were doing and why they had done it that way. Although I never cared for it, at least I could understand it a little better. Although it will probably seem curious, I was not initially particularly interested in going to France. It wasn't my choice of countries because of the points that I have just outlined. But as a country to be in at the time, it was very interesting for some of the points that you raised—and interesting also because it was the period in which de Gaulle, in effect, left power and arranged a rather grudging transition between him and his then loyal deputy, Mr. Pompidou. This left de Gaulle in a sort of semi-retreat, retirement, or exile, and nobody knew exactly what he would do, or when he would do something, or what pronouncement he would issue on the politics and the personalities of the day. As he was always ready and willing to write memoirs and more memoirs and announce in his Olympian tones what he thought was best for France, it did make things politically interesting, because you didn't know what would happen. There was this process of transition from which de Gaulle, having lost a totally trivial referendum on a topic that, frankly, I can't even remember—the point was that de Gaulle always couched these referendums as "Do what I want or I leave." This time, with a sigh, the French population decided on a tertiary issue that they had had enough. So he up and left. The politics of the period were still relatively calm, to the extent there was no rioting in the streets.

Q: There had been enough in May and June of '68.

JONES: Yes. That was before I got there. There were still tiny, slight, distant echoes of what had happened, but there was not a renewal of it. The French government had managed to break the alliance between labor and the students. They had done enough in the way of offerings and commentary to the students—they had given them certain changes in how the educational system was operating and promised more money and less crowding, and other things along those lines—and got the students off their backs. As a consequence, the students were never really able to restimulate anything on the level of the disruption and the popular unity between themselves and labor unions. Students riot every spring. Who cares? The students are rioting. As a result, the police will come out, set themselves up, and put themselves in a position where the students start focusing on them, and then they'll have a great riot. Some of the students will get tear gassed, and a few of them may get bopped on the head. A certain number of the CRS [Compagnies Républicaines de Sécurité, the French riot police] will have injuries that will be cited. That's springtime in Paris. But in 1968, it was the combination of the students and the labor unions that created much more havoc and upset and disruption in the city and elsewhere in France. But it had very substantially calmed in 1969.

The French Establishment

Q: Your first job was in the economic section. In an embassy like Paris, you're really down in the bowels of the economic section as a first tour officer. What were you seeing and what were you getting from your more senior colleagues about the French economy?

JONES: It might amuse you to note that I had the best office in my entire Foreign Service career when I was the most junior officer in Paris. I was sitting right above the ambassador's office looking out over the Place de la Concorde. Why did I have that office? Well, because the economic section wanted to preserve it as its turf, and they needed to put an officer in it, so they put me in it. I have a picture of me against the Place de la Concorde looking out over this astonishing, memorable, historic view. What I think we did at this point—and again, what you have is a young officer trying to get trained, and not so much in economics because I don't think they expected me ever to become an economist—was to begin to be a Foreign Service reporting officer and analyst. So a great deal of what I was doing was as close to the bottom rung of that level of the Foreign Service as you're likely to get: writing economic analyses from newspaper material to put into airgrams, not a telegram—dredge it out of the newspapers, make new translations—this kind of work. What I think we gathered and what I would say that I gathered was that the French economy was doing reasonably well. It was, however, a very traditional, government-run, centrally directed economy. The problems associated with it were not enormous problems. This was a sophisticated, high-tech society.

What I noticed as much as anything from that portion of it and from other times was how organized the French ruling establishment was, how carefully educated they were, how they had come up through great schools of one educational discipline or another where they all knew each other. If you read their bio sketches, they had all been educated at the same type of very high-level, very carefully trained, very professorial-type universities. They were all deeply enmeshed in the French way of doing things, in French culture, in French history, in the virtues of France, in every element—its language, its cooking, its wine, its cheeses . . . . You go right down the line.

Those people at the top were very, very, very "French." You either liked this or you didn't like this. There are still, almost thirty years later, very, very positive aspects of what I could say are the French and France at that time. For example, they were and still are receptive to the use of nuclear power, something that we have managed to destroy as a basic source of power in the United States. The French were very practical about its development, its application, and its utility for their society. If you want an organized and directed societal elite running society, that was certainly France at the end of the 1960s and the beginning of the 1970s.

The French and the "American Challenge"

Q: Was there still the "defi Americain" [American challenge]?

JONES: Yes, Jean-Jacques Servan-Schreiber.

Q: Had that started?

JONES: Yes.

Q: Could you explain what that was?

JONES: It essentially was a book by Jean-Jacques Servan-Schreiber, who argued that the American challenge, "le defi Americain," was a substantial challenge to Europe and France. The Americans were doing it better, and the French, the Europeans, were going to have to change their approach, their style, in virtually everything. It was not by any matter only political. It wasn't limited to economics. It was again, on top of almost everything else, cultural. The American cultural challenge was a worldwide challenge. You can shorthand it down to the "Coca Cola-ization" of the world, but Servan-Schreiber didn't take that approach. It was a positive view that America was making this challenge, and it was not an unworthy one. It was one in which the French in particular had to respond, because they considered themselves to have a powerful alternative culture or a culture that they considered definitely superior to English/American culture. As a result, it was a challenge that France would have to meet, and perhaps have to change to meet, effectively.

Q: In our embassy in Paris, did you find a certain division among the officers, not necessarily according to France, but those that were almost Francophiles and those that were almost Francophobes? Was there a fissure within the embassy?

JONES: No, I wouldn't say it was that clear a split. There certainly were Francophiles. There were people that adapted themselves more totally to French culture. These are the ones whose clothes were more French in style, who worked very hard to get more deeply into French culture, French cooking, and French wines and cheeses. In other words, they were trying to make themselves more effective interlocutors with the French by being closer to them as appreciators of their culture and their qualities. The other side of the group I don't think appreciated France any less, but they believed that they would be more effective Americans if they didn't try to become second-class French.

There was no way that an American diplomat could become as French as the French and still be an American diplomat. If you attempted that route, you would be criticized implicitly by the French for not being a particularly high-quality French person. If you, in effect, did the equivalent—if they came to dinner and you served them chili and beans—they couldn't argue with you that your choice of wine had been less than exquisite and your soufflé had fallen. All they could say was, "That's an American meal. Maybe I don't like it. Maybe I'd rather eat anything else if it was made in France," but they couldn't claim that you were a second-class Frenchman or lacking a quality for being a real Frenchman.

And, in honesty, it was a hell of a lot easier to be an authentic American than pseudo French.

In honesty, there is nobody, unless you have lived at the very top of French society, who can be as French as a Frenchman. I think you could also overstate this division. There were certainly no sets of arguments in the embassy over "You've gone native." The French wouldn't let you go native at this point. This was still, if not daggers drawn, a recognition that we were only a couple of years from the time in which de Gaulle and the French had expelled NATO from France. In effect, France had absented itself from the unified defense planning aspect of NATO, although France continued to sit, as it still does, on the North Atlantic Council and in council meetings at NATO. But it did make for tension. It made definitely for bad feelings. It left some residual problems for the U.S. military that were still being handled in France, as they had closed facilities and rushed off to Belgium with considerable speed and not as much planning as they would have preferred.

Some Local French Staff

Q: What were you doing after the economic work?

JONES: The next set of work assignments I went to was consular work. In this regard, I was relatively standard as a consular officer, although all I focused on or was focused on was citizenship services. I may be one of the rare Foreign Service officers who never issued a visa. Because of that, I don't have those endless visa stories for cocktail party banter.

Q: I would have thought in the consular section, particularly in citizens' services, you would have had a French national staff who really were doing most of the work. I would assume they were a very competent staff.

JONES: They were. They were good, professional, longtime staff. But for American citizenship services, you also had a fair group of American consular officers. The biggest issue was the replacement of passports—this was the biggest citizenship problem. Occasionally you had a death. Occasionally you had a certain number of people seeking welfare and support. You had individuals in the United States seeking missing children who were wandering around Europe somewhere, and they vaguely thought, "Well, they said they were going to be in Paris in August," or words to that effect. They would get worried on Friday evening in the United States and decide to telephone the Embassy in Paris—and a consular duty officer would get the telephone call at 2 a.m. asking if you could find "Mary." So you had circumstances of that nature. As a result, all of us as young consular officers met a fair number of Americans in circumstances that were difficult for them.

What I did at that time was meet my supervisor, one of the smart, tough, senior consular officers, a woman by the name of Mary Chiavarini. Mary was one of these people that had a very untraditional Foreign Service career. She was one of the very few Foreign Service officers without a college degree. She started as a secretary, was a technician of one sort or another, and then became an officer. Through dint of absolutely relentless search for perfection and consummate attention to detail, she got very close to the top of her profession and finished as the consul general in Palermo after her tour in Paris. I was impressed by her professionalism and her exceptionally good judgment on risks of various people, as well as her attention to detail and desire to see not a single error crop up anywhere.

That bothered more people than not. It didn't bother me. I was able to appreciate this. But there was at least one young Foreign Service officer whose career she totaled by the type of efficiency report that she wrote on him and who disliked her immensely, and undoubtedly continues to dislike her. But other than that, she taught me a combination of patience and even more attention to precision and detail than I had previously appreciated. There obviously were not many people like her. If I remember a story out of the consular section, it would be that I had been, if not duped, at least sympathetic to a young couple that came in with a lost passport story. They were certainly perfectly legitimate Americans. Mary insisted that they be issued a much more limited passport, a very short duration passport, rather than a full duration passport. Subsequently, they turned out to have been involved in narcotics of one sort or another and were arrested later in their relatively short time in France. I recognized that one of the problems of being a consular officer is eliminating your implicit trust in your fellow citizens. You might be more suspicious automatically of some foreigner who is trying to get a visa from you, as you have every reason to be, but I think it's a little harder to be axiomatically suspicious of your fellow citizens who are legitimately presenting information showing that they are citizens. That was a bit of education.

Q: Did you get involved in any Americans caught up in the French legal system, prisons, or other aspects?

JONES: A little bit, but not as much as some of my colleagues and friends. What you had at that time, and what you still have, is a lawyers' list, and we regularly referred people who had specific kinds of problems to this list of lawyers. I did go to one trial. This was also at the point when the Vietnam peace talks were under way in Paris. There was a completely separate delegation within the embassy that was handling the peace talks, although I knew a couple of people in our delegation. At the trial I attended, the young man was facing the standard drug charges. I got the results of that trial and reported. In this case, I reported them to Ambassador Phil Habib, who was acting as our head of the peace talks, and stood there while he talked to the mother of the young man back in the States and conveyed to her the sad story that her son was going to spend jail time. I remember him saying, "Well, unfortunately, they also managed to bring in the fact that he had had a previous problem, which made the French even less sympathetic than they might have been." The French are not terribly sympathetic in their legal system. There are a number of people who suggest that French law is not to give you a guide to conduct but to assess blame after the fact. That was more of their approach to their traffic laws, for example.

The Atmospherics of the Era—Demonstrations

Q: This was the time, 1969 to 1971, when all hell was breaking loose around the world because of our involvement in Vietnam. Did that manifest itself at all, other than the peace talks? Did you find it was an embassy almost under siege by the French? How was Vietnam playing at that time?

JONES: I think there was the sense that the war was winding down with the beginning of the talks. Johnson had elected not to run again, and there was the suggestion that we were on our way out, although very slowly, rather than continuing to prosecute the war at the level which we had, let alone build up to prosecute it with even more intensity. I certainly don't think there was a great deal of sympathy in France for the United States. There might have been a degree of grim amusement. They had been there, and we thought we could do it better. The fact that we were now lying flat on our face in the shit from which they had only barely and unpleasantly extracted themselves amused them, maybe amused them a great deal. But there was also perhaps a degree of "I told you so"-ism, or "If you had really wanted to do this job, why didn't you help us when we were asking for assistance," or "You were so arrogant as to tell us how to do the job and now you are in the process of screwing it up and getting screwed by it that we have already gone through."

Q: Were you having demonstrations?

JONES: Certainly nothing that thirty years later gives me a twinge. I'm sure there were demonstrations. The French are always demonstrating against something. Part of it is because their unions are intensely politicized. There was both a communist union and a socialist union at that juncture. The communists were significantly stronger as a political force in France at the end of the 1960s and the early 1970s than is the case today. You had regular one-day strikes by the CGT [Confederation Generale du Travail], the communist union. But because they were not well financed and they didn't have real "war chests," they couldn't go out and close things down for weeks and weeks at a time. Their tactic was the sectoral strike—public utility workers, transportation workers—one group or another that would come out and have marches down the Champs-Élysées. But so far as specific violence associated with it, I don't remember that level of violence. I remember confusion, certain periods of upset when the Metros were not working or the buses weren't working—you had problems like that. Then you would always have people asking, "Is this going to be a repeat of May of 1968?" It just wasn't so. I suspect that you could go to the newspapers and conclude that it was a much more volatile and dramatic period than I'm remembering it, but I'm not remembering a level of personal drama. I'm not remembering any riots against the embassy, windows broken, stones thrown, or having to withdraw people from some of our outlying buildings. We were spread all over the city in at least six different annexes where our people worked.

Wine Wars

I would say that there was a struggle on our part not to get our culture accepted but to have our culture get an opportunity to present itself more comprehensively. You had in the economic section, which I remember at the time, various fights over "appellation" of wines. We, in the past, had labeled our wines as "Burgundies" or "Bordeaux," or given them labels of that nature. The French were just simply saying, "You cannot possibly bring a wine to France that has that kind of label because it isn't from that region." We were, at that juncture, arguing with increasing pressure and some degree of success that our wines were winning international blind taste testing. As a result, slowly over the last thirty years, our winemakers have become sufficiently confident of themselves that they're able to say, "This is a Napa Valley red," and they're not trying to label it in the way that the French, quite correctly although definitely irritatingly, were saying, "If this says 'Bordeaux' on it, it must come from Bordeaux." I think we've gotten past that. One of the successes of the last generation has been that

American wines have sliced out a niche in markets around the world for a certain type of quality and effectiveness in taste.

More Rotation in Paris—
and the Political Section the Stars Fell Upon

Q: Where else did you serve in those two years?

JONES: They rotated us to each section. I spent a certain amount of time, maybe less than six months, in the administrative section. I did a certain number of studies for them of the nature designed to keep this young person busy and try to induce him into doing more work in administrative affairs. If anything, I was almost irritated because they gave me excessive praise for work that I thought was pretty trivial, or certainly excessive praise for work that I thought was exceptionally easy and shouldn't have been praised at the level that it was.

But the most important work that I did in Paris, and the most important work as a consequence for the rest of my Foreign Service career, was done in the political section.

Q: In this period, what were you doing?

JONES: What I was doing was very standard internal domestic political section work. Let me talk a little bit about the political section. This was to me the Foreign Service equivalent of the West Point "class the stars fell on." During this period, in the late 1960s and early 1970s, Robert Anderson was the political counselor. He went on to have at least a reasonably successful career as ambassador. Bob is dead now, unfortunately. Anderson was a very smart and very interesting man. As a person, you would not want Bob Anderson as your enemy. But as a friend, Anderson would be fascinating. He showed off in special ways, but he also showed off in ways that were sufficiently clever so that you took a lesson from it. Anderson once was, so the story goes, reproached by a member of the inspector general's staff for having given excessively high ratings to his political section members. Anderson turned around and figuratively tore a stripe off this guy. He said that he had spent his entire career getting to the point where he would be political counselor in Paris and be able to select a team of the very best Foreign Service officers that he could assemble, and now that he had indeed assembled such a staff, under no circumstances would he rate them less than exceptional. I could run down the list of these people, and I will do so just to tell you how incredibly successful these people were. They were at that time almost all FS-03s, which is the FS-01 equivalent today.

Q: About the equivalent to colonels.

JONES: Yes, they were all colonel equivalents. All of these became ambassadors: Patricia Byrne, who was running East Asian affairs; John Condon, who was the labor counselor; Robert Frowick, who was the French communist and communist affairs officer; Allen Holmes, who has just retired; and Mike Glitman. Allen was the head of internal political affairs in Paris; Mike handled political-military affairs. Then there was also Andy Steigman, who was handling African affairs. Steigman, although he left the Foreign Service and has been out of the Foreign Service for probably twenty years, was also himself very successful as an Africanist. Steigman was one of the very few people at the time who actually was so far out of step as to wear a beard. This was at a time when any serious professional was clean-shaven. Today, it's a generational change that people wear beards and they don't wear beards—and it is irrelevant. I've grown a beard three times in my life, and now I'm clean-shaven. But at that time, I would not have worn a beard as a serious Foreign Service officer, and Steigman was virtually unique in so doing.

Q: He is teaching diplomatic practice at Georgetown. He's written books on the Foreign Service. He's been sort of a professional's professional.

JONES: Indeed. I have not seen him in a long while, but I have a great deal of respect for him.

During the six to eight months that I was in the political section, I worked for both Holmes and Glitman. (The time was broken by going back to the consular section because the embassy brought all of the junior officers to the consular section to handle the summer rush and the summer flow of semi-catastrophes during July and August.) Each of them is an exceptional professional, and most of the rest of my career was designed around finding opportunities to work with one or another of them. Indeed, in the rest of my career, I worked for Holmes at least twice and for Glitman at least twice.

What I did as a political officer was, again, a very standard, young domestic political officer reporting style. I did biographic analyses and ran the biographic files. I did a certain amount of analysis from newspapers, reading material and making presentations on the basis of this analysis both for political-military affairs and internal domestic affairs. Both Glitman and Holmes appreciated my writing style and gave me a certain amount of leeway in this regard.

Ambassadors: Changing of the Guard from Shriver to Watson

Q: Who was our ambassador at this time?

JONES: When I first arrived our ambassador was Sergeant Shriver. Subsequently, it was Arthur Watson. Shriver was a Kennedy-connected operator. He was interesting and popular as ambassador in Paris both with the French and pretty much with the embassy. Shriver was interesting, articulate, vigorous, and dynamic; he did a lot of outreach events and was very interested in youth, which made younger Foreign Service officers interested in him and interesting for him. He was, however, also absolutely maddening in some of his habits. One was that he was always late. He absolutely drove people up the walls because he would not arrive on time for the events that he was scheduled to do.

There is one little anecdote where he was out on a provincial tour. It was a standard process: The ambassador would go to different sections of the country and have meetings and give speeches and receive little awards and taste wine and participate in activities of that nature. He arrived very, very late for something. He gave a remarkably extensive and profound apology of how deeply unhappy he was, how sorry he was that he had been late and delayed. Of course, the audience forgave him. The next night, however, he was also scheduled, and he was again incredibly late to his next dinner. He faced an audience and gave again an extended, detailed apology of how he had run late and done this and that, and so on. This time, they were considerably less forgiving because he had perhaps forgotten that it was the same audience. They weren't all that thrilled.

But as a dynamic presence in France and as a dynamic presence in the embassy, Shriver very much was that. On his Fourth of July holiday celebration, for example, instead of having a standard Fourth of July event, he put together a fête at which people were dressed in colonial costume and organized games for handicapped children, which was very much an interest of Eunice Shriver. The Special Olympics, which were still evolving, were initiated by them. It was refreshing. He was different in that manner. He was not the clichéd pinstriped ambassador. On the other hand, he arrived in Cardin suits, wearing Guccis, and looked every bit as elegant and expensive as any man possibly could.

One of the interesting projects that I had was associated with the arrival of the new ambassador, Arthur Watson. He was one of the scions of the IBM empire, son of the IBM founder and a very senior Republican businessman. In contrast to Ambassador Shriver, Mr. Watson was obsessively punctual. He would run meetings in which if you were late, you contributed a dollar to a general fund that went into some charitable organization. It meant that you were on time. Watson was very tough on his more senior officers, but also rather lenient and engaged with his younger, more junior officers. This was interesting also in a way. We had an amount of contact with him that was unusual for the time. He would pick up the telephone and call you directly, which, for somebody who was hierarchical in thinking as I already was, was surprising and even flattering. However, for his senior people, he was very demanding and very tough on them. That made them less happy.

But one of the projects that Watson was engaged in was an assessment of everything that was going on in France that had a U.S. government connection, whether it was being run efficiently and cost effectively. So, each one of a wide number of officers was sent out and required to do assessments on different aspects of the American presence in France. I examined the American Battlefield Monument Cemeteries throughout France. There was one that was far down in the south of France that I didn't get a chance to see. But otherwise I visited, as a result of this project, all of the battlefield cemeteries in northern France and also one in Luxembourg. I went out on a trip with my wife in my then new car. This was a very interesting interviewing, reporting, and information gathering process. At the same time, it gave me some additional insights into how the American presence in Europe is permanent. As a consequence of the report, I suggested that the cemetery operations could be run more efficiently. Essentially, they were something of a sinecure for a fair number of older, retired noncommissioned officers that were getting relatively good salaries for a rather low amount of work, and that many of the cemeteries were not particularly heavily visited even thirty years ago. Certainly, our World War I cemeteries were not. On the other hand, it also gave me an appreciation for the politics associated with this operation. You could give this kind of an assignment only to a naive, credulous junior officer who would actually go out and not have an appreciation for the sacred cow status of the American Battlefield Monuments Commission operations throughout the world and in the United States. So the embassy, and I in particular, got a blast back from Washington saying in effect, "This person doesn't know anything about what he's doing." By and large, that was the way it ended. Watson wasn't able to budge the Battlefield Monuments Commission to do anything. But it was an interesting experience for me personally to have had this opportunity.

The French, the D-Day Anniversary, and Their Attitudes

Q: The battlefields came into a certain amount of prominence not too long before when de Gaulle had removed NATO from French soil. Supposedly, the remark was, "Do you want us to remove our graves, too?"

JONES: Yes, there was that line, but it also was a throwaway line. The French just sort of shrugged it off. "You want us out of France? Shall we dig up our dead and take them home, too?" The twenty-fifth anniversary of D-Day was also at that time. That was 1969. There was a feeling that the French participation in the anniversary was very grudging, that it was not at a level that we would have appreciated. The French participation was "correct," but it was minimalistic rather than maximalistic.

I also participated in, at least as an observer and viewer, the July 14 Bastille Day marches and parades by the French. I was struck by the fact that these were the most militaristic parades that I had ever seen. My conclusion at the time was that it reflected the fact that France did not want to become a secondary military power, but it was forced to do so by geopolitical reality. In one of the parades, it was the first time that the Foreign Legion had participated in many years. They were back out there again. A comparable American parade would have had floats and cheerleaders and marching bands and the girl-for-the-day waving from a convertible. But this was a serious military parade that was marching right down the Champs-Élysées to the heart of Paris. That also gave me what I thought was a little insight into the French and the France of the day.

Q: Did you have any contact with French officialdom at a lower level? Was there an attempt made on either part to get the junior officers in the French foreign affairs bureaucracy and the American and other embassies together?

JONES: No. We were not used as junior officers at the level in which we are now forced to use junior officers. We were very correct in most of our dealings with the French. As a matter of fact, there was an extended period of time in which our diplomatic list was limited. We were supposed to be matched with the number of diplomats that the Russians were permitted to have in France. This meant that for a number of months I was not on the diplomatic list, and there was something of a scramble eventually to put me on the diplomatic list officially. I don't remember exactly when I was so placed, but as a third secretary, eventually, I was slowly squeezed onto the diplomatic list. It made for one interesting experience when I was sent to do a little representational swing in an area of France. All of the political section officers were being sent out to do short regional trips to both show the flag a little bit and to get some insight into what was happening locally. Although I barely remember the specific details, I went into northern France for a couple of days and had a couple of meetings. One of the meetings that I had was with a French provincial official who had hauled out the diplomatic list and was asking, in effect, "Mr. Jones, are you CIA?" although he was not putting it that way. He was trying to make it clear that since I wasn't on the diplomatic list, or at least not on the copy that they had, just who was I? It took me some degree of protestation, a relatively extensive effort to describe, to profess, that I was not otherwise connected, that I was a legitimate American diplomat and Foreign Service officer. After listening to me for a while, they were willing to accept this. Whether they believed it, I don't know. But at least they had had this young man squirming in front of them while they looked at this particular curious representation of American diplomatic life. I'm not exactly sure whether they viewed me as a toad or a poisonous insect, or whether they were just willing to say with a sigh, "All right, this American wants to listen to us. We'll give him the party line." That's what they did. They just talked to me about local circumstances of how things were operated, and how things developed, and the like. It was an interesting experience in that manner, giving me a chance to practice my French and have the chance to see another part of France.

Q: Here you are under Bob Anderson. Did you have the feeling that we were reporting on the internal politics out in the provinces, but that the real game was being played in Paris, and what was happening out in the provinces was interesting, but more a practice run rather than the real game?

JONES: I think you've hit it absolutely. If anything, most of the officers were very reluctant to waste any time doing one of these regional trips. They were ordered to do so by the ambassador, and they would do their one or so obligatory regional trip. But the action in France was then, as it has been historically, centrally directed. This is a society that is run out of Paris. People have pointed out that, at least at that time, almost every country that had had a city of one million had at least a second city of one million or more. But France was the exception. In France, there was only one city of a million inhabitants or more, and that was Paris. You could say that Paris was the center of everything. If the United States has an economic center in New York and a cultural center somewhere else and a political center in Washington, in France there was only one center for everything. It was Paris. You looked at the roads, and went out on the roads—and the roads all are marked in miles to Paris when you are looking in the direction of Paris. The center of operations, the center of whatever was happening, the center of our interest in France, was in Paris and what the French officials were doing.

As the political section was organized, it was divided regionally and functionally, and there were officers addressing specific regional interests, whether it was Africa or the Middle East or European communist affairs, or Russia, and so on. If it was labor or political-military issues, we had an officer following those approaches. We found the information in Paris. You weren't going to get anything that was useful in the way of information, other than the general political feelings or sociological sense, outside of Paris. You could get a certain amount of flavor. You might do it just to have an opportunity to go someplace else and get out of Paris for a while, but the conclusion was—and I believe accurately—that you would find all you really needed to know about what was happening in France from your connections in Paris.

Those were domestic political connections as well. French officeholders can hold office at multiple levels, not just on the national level. A member of parliament will be also a mayor. He may hold other ranks in between. So these deputies in the National Assembly would also be able to be local spokesmen at the same time. This is a very curious phenomenon. It must exist elsewhere in the world, but I haven't encountered it outside of Paris, where you have this nature of interconnection between local, provincial, and urban leadership and national leadership. Of course, France is not a federal state. France remains a very centrally directed country.

Parents Are We!

My wife and I—this moves into the social, cultural aspect of the French experience—now became first-time parents. We were parents of twins, which was a rather abrupt surprise. We had not anticipated twins. It was at a juncture in medical practice when we did not use X-rays. People had gotten to the point where they didn't want to use X-rays anymore on pregnant women for fear and concern for the children. But they had not developed sonograms or ultrasound effectively enough, and they weren't available, even at the American hospital in Neuilly. They did the standard, listen-to-the-heartbeats bit. My wife, who is not a very large woman and wasn't any larger then, was very, very pregnant, and she was identifiable from a hundred yards because they had never seen anyone quite so pregnant. We used to say that she was the most pregnant Chinese woman in Europe at the time. The doctor would say to her, "One baby, Mrs. Jones. A big baby, but only one baby." It wasn't until the children were about to be delivered that we realized that there were twins. They were born in October 1969.

Nevertheless, we tried as much as we could to travel within France. We traveled with them and sometimes without them as much as we could throughout France. We traveled to Belgium, into Germany. We hit various places as extensively as we could around Paris. We traveled to a degree to the south of France, however, we did not get as far south as Marseille. But elsewhere, we did what we could under the circumstances and appreciated the opportunity a great deal. This, too, reaffirmed one of the truisms when they say that there are two types of French: the French in Paris, the Parisian, and those outside of Paris. It wasn't a night-and-day exercise, but you came to realize that if you compared the Parisian with anybody, you compared them with New Yorkers. New Yorkers are unpleasant, hostile, irritating, and difficult. You can get into an argument with any cab driver. They have no interest in you except for whether or not they can extract something from you. Parisians, although not having exactly the same characteristics, had the same level of indifference to anyone who was not a native-born citizen of Paris. Outside of Paris, it was much less so. They disliked Parisians. That always gave you something to talk about. You also got a deeper sense for the history, the culture, and the society and just what France was in comparison to other places in Europe or the world.

Communism and the French

Q: How did we view the French Communist Party at that time?

JONES: We were very hostile to the French Communist Party. There was only one officer in the entire embassy, Bob Frowick, who was permitted to have any contact with the French communists. We did not deal with the French Communist Party in any official capacity, other than this very tangential and not terribly frequent degree of association by Frowick, who had reasonably good contacts with them. Of course, it was much to their interest to be as open or approachable or willing to meet the Americans as possible. But I can't recall specifically whether he met, even occasionally, with their most senior figures—Georges Marchais, for example.

Q: Wasn't the feeling that the French Communist Party was a tool of the Soviets, or was there a different dynamic?

JONES: Certainly this was the most subservient Communist Party in noncommunist Europe. There was no Eurocommunism at that point, certainly not reflected in France. This was a slavishly Moscow-oriented Communist Party. They made it a virtue. This was a very, very old line, very Moscow-directed, Moscow-accepting Communist Party. They had deep roots in French society from the Commune in the late nineteenth century. They certainly saw themselves as still potentially being able to gain power. They were running at better than 20 percent of the electorate, and it seemed to be an unbreakable 20 percent. They put deputies into the National Assembly. There were substantial portions of the country that were clearly communist controlled, notably a "red belt" outside of Paris and in the Parisian suburbs. I believe that we did not want to be in the position of giving the communists any suggestion that we had the slightest degree of sympathy toward their interests, and we certainly did not want to give the French government the slightest intimation that we had any sympathy with the communists. For that reason, it was made very clear to us as officers in the political section that only Bob Frowick would have liaison with the French communists. No one argued the case. There was an acceptance, more grudging than not, that we did have to know what the communists were doing. But there was no real interest in associating with them.

CHAPTER 23

An Interlude—Leave Without Pay and the Foreign Service Opens to Married Women

---

Q: You left there in 1971. Whither?

JONES: At that point, I left to go on leave without pay. I was still very interested in completing my PhD, which, in the end, I didn't finish. But I thought I would be able to write a dissertation in a year. I was also faced with what seemed to be a greater likelihood than not that I would be assigned to CORDS [Civil Operations and Rural Development Support] as my next position. As I have mentioned, we sent hundreds of our junior officers there over the duration of the Vietnam war. Although I was a wholehearted supporter of American participation in Vietnam, by 1971 it was clear that anyone who went there was a fool. There was nothing that was going to happen that was going to be positive, helpful, or useful to American interests—let alone to a personal career—to go there. It was with a degree of disgust on my part but also with a degree of recognition that I had no desire to separate myself from my wife and children, who were just a little over one year old, to go there. And I was interested in returning to the University of Pennsylvania. That's what I elected to do. I got a year's leave without pay and returned to my wife's hometown, Vineland, New Jersey. I also got a dormitory room at the University of Pennsylvania and spent much of about a year in working on my dissertation, writing chapters. This was roughly 1971-1972.

Q: What was your dissertation on?

JONES: It was focused on the role of the Chinese People's Liberation Army in the period of the Cultural Revolution. I was doing a number of analyses on the army, its development and its role leading up to the Cultural Revolution, as well as certain aspects of its operation during that period. I made reasonably good progress on it. I completed several chapters, and I still think that I had done most of my research for the chapters involved, but I ran out of time, or I ran out of energy, or I ran out of my ability to do two things at once. That pretty much finished the dissertation, although I continued to work on it sporadically for another year. But it, too, eventually became something that I couldn't do simultaneously with my jobs at the Department of State.

At this time, however, it also became clear that my wife could enter the Foreign Service. There was a change of the law and the interpretation of the law at roughly this juncture, approximately 1971-1972, when the U.S. government eliminated two things that had previously prohibited her from being a Foreign Service officer. One was that you had to have been a citizen for ten years before you could become a Foreign Service officer. My wife was naturalized in 1963. There had been no expectation that she would have a Foreign Service career before that. The more important prohibition was that a married woman could not be a Foreign Service officer. When you look at this restriction in the retrospective of thirty years, you wonder how in the name of heaven we persisted until 1971 with a prohibition against married women being Foreign Service officers. But we did.

Also at this time, the officer efficiency reports included comments on the spouse of the Foreign Service officer. Again, something which today people would look upon and say, "Why would you have something like that in the report?" But it was standard until the early 1970s. What it did, however, was stimulate my career development officer to look at the very positive observations that my political section supervisors had made about my wife and say, "David, this is exactly the kind of woman that ought to take the Foreign Service exam." That surprised us. We had never really thought of my wife having a Foreign Service career until then. Indeed, her family's diplomatic experience had been somewhat more negative. It had not been a life of luxury to live as a Chinese diplomat in the Soviet Union during World War II. There are all sorts of good stories that I'll let her tell if you wanted to hear them about her family history—privation more than privilege was the circumstance.

We began to move in that direction. When we moved to Washington after I had spent the year at the University of Pennsylvania and in Vineland, New Jersey, we began to work seriously on an application for the Foreign Service. While we were living in New Jersey and I was studying at Penn, our children got through the "terrible twos" and did things associated with that period of childhood. She taught mathematics at the high school from which she had graduated as valedictorian and had been selected to teach mathematics by the principal and the math teacher that had been there when she had been the valedictorian. Then the school board forced her to leave and, in effect, fired the only PhD they had in their school system, because she didn't have teaching credentials.

So she spent a little time during that year taking education courses at a local community college and doing her practice teaching. She became a credentialed educator so far as the State of New Jersey was concerned. That was one of the alternatives we were considering. She also could have gone back to research at the Department of Agriculture, where she had rights for rehiring. But in the early 1970s, it was not a lush market for chemical researchers. This was a "down" time for them, and they were not hiring, so that was not an option that she was going to pursue immediately. Another consequence of the year of leave without pay was that I had renewed my contacts with the Foreign Policy Research Institute with William Kintner at the University of Pennsylvania, but not with Strausz-Hupé because he was out of the country on diplomatic assignments at that time. I did a certain amount of research work for the Foreign Policy Research Institute while I was working on my dissertation as well.

Q: After your year of LWOP, your wife took the Foreign Service exam?

JONES: What happened was that we finished our year in Philadelphia and Vineland, New Jersey. We returned to Washington, and at that juncture I had an assignment with the Intelligence and Research Bureau [INR] as the Korean analyst. Also in the fall of 1972, my wife took the Foreign Service exam. Then some months later, roughly in the winter of 1973, she took the oral exam. A year later, she was brought in as a Foreign Service officer in January 1974. But between the fall of 1972 until the summer of 1974, I worked as the Korean analyst for INR.

CHAPTER 24

The Intelligence and Research Bureau—Wrestling with Koreans

Q: From 1972 to 1974, you were in INR. What was the role of INR with policy? Was there any policy that could be changed at this time?

JONES: Of course, that was part of the problem of INR, and it remains part of the problem for INR that it has very little policy effect. As a young officer—and I'll never say that I was a particularly bureaucratically savvy officer—I did not realize how little effect INR had. I was still more academically inclined than operationally directed. With the exception of two years in Paris, my career had been academic. I was still interested in a PhD. I still had some abstract theoretical thought of teaching at a university. I looked upon INR as the State Department's research arm, the State Department's academic element. If I got a particular aspect of understanding of the academics versus operations in government, it was the recognition, at this point, that academicians have a substantially limited knowledge of what was or has happened, and they are always substantially months, if not years, behind the reality of what is happening.

Nevertheless, it took me a while to realize that INR's influence on what is actually happening at policy levels is very, very limited. It's a function of the fact that the expertise and the immediate knowledge is usually on the desks. That is where senior policy levels are going to draw their recommendations, draw their most pertinent policy related papers. If you are a semiacademic, yes, you could write in INR. But the number of people in INR who, at that time, had very little knowledge of the areas in which they were operating and attempting to be—and claiming to be—experts was much higher than those who had had substantial or relatively recent experience in the field who were assigned to INR. The people with the expertise, who had gone back and forth to the country, were the officers on the desk.

Q: What was the situation in Korea?

ROK Leader Park Chung Hee and Action in Korea

JONES: This was the period during which Park Chung Hee moved to take full control of the government and the society again. There was an earlier time when there had been the expectation by some, perhaps the hope by others, that he would step down and allow, if not a restoration of democracy, perhaps more of a general switch of leadership. U.S. analysts and officials were hoping that this would be the beginning of a slow transition from direct or slightly indirect military rule into a functioning democracy in Korea. Phil Habib was the ambassador in Korea. Obviously, we were disappointed. It did not happen.

Q: One of the mind-sets that was around about Korea was that Park Chung Hee is a dictator, there should be more democracy, but at the same time, Park Chung Hee was doing a remarkable job economically in taking what used to be considered a basket case and turning it into a real dynamo of energy, and that the Koreans were often called the Irish of the Orient, the idea being that if they ever got a democracy, they would be basically rather weak and divided and it might give an opportunity for the North. Was that in play at all then?

JONES: I would say that the first part of your comment is accurate. There was serious discussion as to whether we should attempt to reverse Park's reaffirmation of power when he did so. Phil Habib was inclined to try to do more—apply more pressure, more direct and public U.S. pressure, rather than the degree of public dissatisfaction that we evinced—but we never suggested that we would withdraw or reduce our military presence or our military support at the degree and level that we did subsequently in Greece.

The sense also remained that the stakes were still so high in Korea and that the North was so potentially threatening or that the fear that there would be a renewal of the war was so intense (whether the North could win or not) that we would not risk reducing our support.

North Koreans and the Regular Fear of Resumed War

This was also a period in which we were concerned, as we had been regularly every few years, that the North Koreans were going to invade. This was also when we were struck by the surprise 1973 war in the Middle East. We extrapolated from the reality of the surprise attack by the Egyptians and others in the Middle East to the potential for a surprise attack in South Korea from the North. Here, at the time, the military balance was still one in which we were not at all convinced that the North would fail if it attacked the South. The North and South in military terms still seemed relatively closely balanced. The North also had a good deal of support both from China and Russia. It looked as if they were very effectively balancing the Chinese against the Russians for an increasing level of support to them from both. Pyongyang would ultimately play both its Beijing and its Moscow cards. At that time, Russia and China were in intense political conflict. This was still at that point in the Cold War where countries played off the United States and the Soviets against each other to find ways to get more support. In this case, the North Koreans played one communist country off against the other. Pyongyang was able to do that. Clever.

This was also a period in which Kim Dae-jung was kidnapped. The kidnapping came when we were unclear just to what degree the South Korean government was willing to interfere with its own citizenry. I'll admit that, at this juncture, I made a mistake. I was a poor judge of whether the South Koreans would have directly involved themselves in seizing Kim Dae-jung. I thought that some other group had done it rather than the operatives of the South Korean government. The North had done such kidnapping previously. Consequently, I thought the North Koreans had been involved in the kidnap and seizure of Kim Dae-jung. But it turned out otherwise.

Assessing North Korea and the Foreign Broadcast Information Service

Q: What sort of information were we getting out of North Korea? Was this part of your province?

JONES: Yes. Frankly, much of the information we were getting was lousy. Let's say it was extremely limited information. I spent a great deal of time reading the Foreign Broadcast Information Service transcripts to try to get some sort of insight as to what the North Korean leadership and society were doing and how they were operating. It was largely regarded as the most closed society in the world at that time. An alternative in secrecy might have been Albania. North Korea was certainly one of the most difficult areas on which to obtain any specific information at all. We had very, very rare reporting from neutrals, e.g., Swedes who might have visited the North. The information that we had would largely be regarded as sensitive intelligence—type information. I suspect it remains sensitive intelligence. But the best of our information was very limited information. It resulted in us creating constructs where we had to lean always toward the worst case. Most of the information that we obtained was military-oriented in one shape or form. This was the most collectible information. We simply had nothing other than what the North Koreans wanted to provide to us directly from their publications to determine what the society was doing.

The potential for war by miscalculation on the part of the North was another unknown. We had no idea what the North was thinking. Since we didn't know what they knew, and we knew we didn't know what they knew, that meant that they could be thinking of anything. Their rhetoric remained very aggressive, very confrontational, very much a stimulus to worst-case thinking. So there was the fear that if we implied that our commitment to South Korea was lessening, we would be in the position of duplicating the hideous mistake that we had made in 1950. If then, by miscalculation in this manner, we forced ourselves into Korean War reviticus [renewed], it really would be a catastrophe. It was not that we believed that we couldn't ultimately win that kind of a war. It was just that the costs involved in winning that type of a war would be significantly higher than we wanted to pay for the potential objective of pushing Park out (even if we could, and there was no assurance that we could) by upping the pressure on Park to force him to reverse his decision to retain power.

So, with the stakes as high as they were on the downside, as low as they were on the potential for success, and as unclear as to what the result would be if we did stimulate his departure, the conclusion was that we should make the better of a bad case.

Koreans Pushing the Economic Envelope

There was no question in my view that South Korea was steadily improving. This was one of the areas that interested me throughout my career and in which I've had a couple of Korean experiences. I still follow the society and the operations there tangentially, at least. This assignment was an occasion of relatively short remove from my first Korean experience, which was in 1965. Here I am, back in 1972, so I am still pretty close to it. In 1971-1972, I could tell from the statistics that Korea was really beginning to pull itself up by the bootstraps in a way that I earlier suggested was their personal and societal attitude in some of my earlier comments. The society and the economics were working. I did not have the opportunity to make a visit to Korea during 1971-1972. I regret this, but this was a period when they had no money to send INR officers to their regions for familiarization/orientation. But I could see that things were clearly getting better. Park had made certain decisions against the recommendations of international economists such as building a superhighway from Seoul to the south. Others had suggested that there were much more effective ways to spend his money than how he chose to spend it. But the combination of still very heavy U.S. economic and military assistance, plus Korean natural willingness to work extremely hard, to be entrepreneurial, and to defer consumption, resulted in spending a good twenty years in building a society that economically has been quite successful.

Park was one of the people that pushed, led, directed, and helped set up a society and an economy that, with all of its many flaws—which an economist could happily point out to you—nevertheless clearly was starting to move the South ahead of the North. There were people in the mid to late 1960s and the early 1970s that looked at North and South and said that the North had the better of the potential economies, the better share of the natural resources, the better proportion of the hydroelectric power. There was the belief that its population was going to give Pyongyang certain advantages while the South, which was primarily a rice-growing agricultural area that had been substantially destroyed and which had very limited natural resources, was going to have worse problems. What was it going to do with all of its people and its limited opportunities?

I don't remember spending any time on the South Korean domestic politics as it might have been in a post—Park Chung Hee government.

That was something that we just weren't reviewing, analyzing, or working on at all. What I seemed to do was to spend a great deal of time writing, rewriting, and rewriting again material in INR which seemed to combine the worst of academic writing with the most labyrinthine, convoluted, and infighting-directed aspects of the Department of State. You realize only in retrospect that INR is a place where they put young officers who don't know any better and old officers who don't have much of a future.

What I slowly got myself into doing was providing more support for the specific Korea desk officers and working with them, particularly a man by the name of Don Ranard. Don was a very smart, tough, old Korea hand.

Q: He had a very strong point of view opposed to Park Chung Hee.

JONES: Yes. Ranard ran the Korea desk when I was the Korea analyst for INR. He repeatedly called in South Korean representatives and told them in no uncertain terms that their activities with regard to Koreans living in the United States were unacceptable.

Ranard was very professional. He was supported by Wesley Kriebel, an officer who went on to work in UN affairs. I lost touch with Kriebel a long time ago, but he also had Korean experience, although he was doing more Korean economic work in his assignment on the desk.

Q: Ranard was objecting to the activities of what was known as the KCIA, the Korean CIA.

JONES: Correct. We were also very interested in the activities of Kim Chong-pil, who was the KCIA chief. who was a close American contact in Korea and who continued to give us a wide variety of insights as to what was happening, in his view, at least, in Korean society and Korean politics. We got a great deal of information that seemed to be sourced from very senior Korean officials. But beyond that, there isn't a great deal. We spent more time worried about and analyzing, to the extent that we could, what was happening in North Korea.

The China Factor—a New Dimension for the Republic of Korea

Q: Did we see the opening with China, which happened around this time, as changing the equation?

JONES: Only in retrospect and only to the extent that we began to wonder whether Chinese support for North Korea might be lessening a little bit. We wondered whether the Chinese were also perhaps putting a little bit of a rein on what Pyongyang was able to do. There was some suggestion that the South Koreans might be slowly beginning to open lines of contact with China that previously they had had no opportunity to do. We were keeping careful track of the countries with which North Korea and South Korea had diplomatic contact and diplomatic relationships, trying to push the South Korean case forward and detract from the North Korean case with countries in this competition. That was one of the ongoing projects that INR studied and handled on a month-to-month basis and on which I put out regular reports.

One of the topics that interested us was an opportunity for China and South Korea to reach some level of contact. There were the beginnings, at this point, of meetings, always in some third country, that suggested the start of indirect contact or at least a lessening of the ideologically driven axiomatic hostility by Beijing toward South Korea. The South kept tossing out lines of potential contact and implying that there were economic opportunities for China to deal with the South.

Of course, this development was tied to what type of relationship South Korea had with Taiwan, which was something that obviously would have been high on Beijing's agenda. If South Korea wanted a better relationship with Beijing, it would have to reduce its level of contact with Taiwan. I can't remember the status of it at that point, but this was one of these slowly evolving relationships.

. . . and Also the Japanese

We were also concerned about the degree of contact between South Korea and Japan. , We were deeply interested in how these relations were going to develop. The South Korean and Japanese relationship was very tense. South Korea had a combination of very realistic historical animosity toward and ongoing competition with Japan. Japanese continued semidisdain connected still with a "Well, we really should do something for them"—not quite noblesse oblige, but "Well, we really do have to do something for them. It's not so much we were wrong as that the Americans keep pushing us to do something." You had this type of a gritted teeth relationship between them where the South Koreans were always eager to take offense and play the blame game.

Q: There was also a little North Korean activity in Japan, which was used against…

JONES: The North Korean group of agents and supporters.

Q: I can't remember when Park's wife was assassinated, but I think the assassin had ties to this Japanese group, which didn't help matters.

JONES: I can't remember that tie, but Park's wife's assassin was certainly North Korean directed and sponsored. The North throughout this period continued to do the wildest, most idiosyncratic kinds of assaults on the South. If you had some paranoia about what was going to happen from the North, it was well-honed paranoia. Every so often, you found one of these huge underground tunnels that had crossed under the demilitarized zone. Later they blew up a substantial portion of the South Korean cabinet while they were in Burma. It was just astonishing action.

Q: It continues. They keep picking up these damned small submarines.

JONES: Yes. Every so often, there was something of that nature. The North had regular infiltrators that were caught. It was always a bloody, ferocious firefight during which the northern infiltrators seemed literally to be quite willing to die, and sought to kill everybody they possibly could before they died. You talk about fanaticism. If the fanatic is on your side, he's wonderful. He's tremendously courageous and outrageously brave, and you think he's the perfect soldier. If he's on the other side, he's obviously a crazy, ideology-driven, drug-hopped-up madman. Well, at the same time, if you look at it with some perspective, fanatics are also terribly courageous, and you have to wonder how the society is able to motivate them to this level of action. This was the type of person that was coming from the North and attacking the Republic of Korea. Although we didn't identify them as such, they were the first wave of what we would now call suicide terrorists.

Q: You left INR in 1974?

JONES: Yes.

CHAPTER 25

The NATO Desk and the Beginning of the Core of My Career

Q: Where did you go then?

JONES: I went to the area in which I spent much of the next dozen years or so of my life: the NATO desk and EUR/RPM [Bureau of European Affairs, Office of Regional Political and Military Affairs]. From there I went to assignments at NATO and back into EUR. It was all political-military-directed work, which I would say extended from that time until roughly 1992.

Q: You were in NATO affairs from 1974 to when?

JONES: Essentially straight NATO affairs from 1974 to 1980, first on the desk from early 1974 until the summer of 1976 and then a switch to U.S. Mission NATO in the summer of 1976.

Some Personalities: At US Mission NATO and in EUR/RPM

Q: Who was in your chain of command at that particular time?

JONES: The circumstances were such that at NATO we were transitioning from Don Rumsfeld, who was particularly dynamic as an ambassador. He later became SecDef [secretary of defense]. He was a very vigorous person who drove people at NATO very, very hard. He had a DCM [deputy chief of mission], Gene McAuliffe, at the Mission. The description of McAuliffe was that McAuliffe, if you were on a slave galley, would fight his way to the point where he was the man who had the drum so he could pick up the pace. Rumsfeld would scream. Instead of McAuliffe being a buffer, he was an amplifier.

Within RPM, there was Edward J. Streator, who was a consummate professional. He had Arva Floyd, who was also very good, as his deputy. Then within RPM, there was Bob Frowick, for whom I worked at first. In the nuclear planning aspect of RPM and on conventional force issues, there was Gerry Christianson, who subsequently left the Foreign Service and went to work on the Hill for Senator Pell; he also became and was for many years the staff head of the Senate Foreign Relations Committee for the majority. He was a very smart man also. Subsequently, Streator left to become DCM at NATO, a job for which he was exceptionally well suited. He was replaced as head of RPM by one of the very finest Foreign Service officers of this era, H. Allen Holmes. Floyd left as deputy and was replaced by another excellent officer, Gerry Helman, who eventually became an ambassador as well. So did Streator. So did Holmes. After Christianson left, another outstanding officer, John Hawes, came to head that particular section of RPM. Hawes was, in the latter part of his career, deeply involved in political-military work and became a senior deputy in the Political-Military Bureau. He was an absolutely outstanding officer, who after retirement, stayed as a dependent and traveled with his foreign service wife. The structure of the organization within RPM and with NATO had a very high-quality group of officers.

Committee on the Challenges of Modern Society: NATO's Kinder Face and CSCE

Q: Let's concentrate on 1974-1976. What was your job?

JONES: I won't quite say that it was a supernumerary desk position, but it was within a subpolitical section within the NATO desk, certainly for the first stretch of the tour. We were doing support work for the Political Committee at NATO. We were also doing work for the Committee on the Challenges of Modern Society [CCMS], which was an environmental and scientific NATO subcommittee, an effort to make NATO a little less military and show a kinder and friendlier face for NATO. Even at that time, there was some concern that NATO shouldn't be viewed as simply a straight military alliance. When I arrived, it was also the tag end of the Year of Europe and the CSCE [Commission on Security and Cooperation in Europe] declarations, the Helsinki-related declarations. These were in the final phases of being created. The man with whom I originally went to RPM to work, Robert Frowick, who is the man running the NATO summit right now, the fiftieth anniversary summit, was then a deputy director or section director within RPM. He had been the general drafter, creator, organizer, of many of the Year of Europe declarations and Helsinki-related declarations.

Q: I'm trying to pick up attitudes. Henry Kissinger was secretary of State. I would have thought people like yourself, working with NATO, would have viewed things like the Helsinki as fine, but it really was something of no real consequence that was mostly PR [public relations].

JONES: There was an element positing that the Russians were getting a better deal out of this than we were getting. One phrase from the time was, "The Russians have gotten their half loaf, and we're going to have to fight for ours." The point for the Russian half loaf was the guarantee of borders—that borders were not going to be changed other than by the most democratic means. It looked as if, under those circumstances, what we had done was to put a seal on the permanent division of Germany.

The side of the loaf for which we would have to fight, which was being presented as a touchy-feely kind of thing, was the openings that they were supposed to guarantee, the greater freedoms, greater access to publications, to information, theoretically greater flows of information and movement of populations. There were people who thought that it would never come to pass, that it just wasn't going to happen, that the Russians would stonewall us, and we would get nothing out of our side of the CSCE. What it proved very slowly, over about fifteen years and more, is that CSCE was far more successful than skeptics thought it was going to be at the time. The series of CSCE review conferences always seemed to be a fight uphill, but we were steadily able to put the then Soviets on the defensive in the way of humanitarianism, human rights, openness of populations, greater elements of discussion, exchanges of publications, and subjects of this nature. Most of the people who had as much or more of a military spin to their thinking as a political spin to it didn't think they were going to be all that successful.

The NATO Political Committee and the Nuclear Planning Group

Q: What was your particular bit of NATO?

JONES: At the beginning, it was a very small bite, not much more than a nibble to the extent of assisting in the preparation of instructions for people at NATO in one of the subcommittees, the Political Committee. It was not even a very senior NATO committee. And I also worked on the Committee on the Challenges of Modern Society, which again in retrospect actually was a subject for which people had more hopes. They saw it as something that was being kicked off, something that might be quite dynamic and dramatic in its prospects. It has continued, but as a very tertiary element of NATO, and I don't think it has ever developed anywhere near the level that they hoped it might in scientific and technological terms.

Q: In many ways, it's been superseded by more global organizations, hasn't it?

JONES: I guess so. There have been other efforts that have emphasized global outlooks and global aspects for environment. Perhaps it never got anywhere because it was never possible for it to do so. My wife will tell you that, at some point, the science that was presented in the way of projects to be done in CCMS was science that couldn't get funding anywhere else because it was pretty poor science. The projects that they would support, like an electric-powered vehicle, were also things that were being done in many other places probably more effectively. I was involved with this for perhaps six to nine months.

Then I moved to another section within RPM. That proved to be more interesting and more productive in many ways. This was dealing with the Nuclear Planning Group, the NPG, and a variety of political-military studies that were being done on the utility of nuclear weapons use under certain circumstances and the development of certain new types of nuclear weaponry, for example, enhanced radiation and reduced blast. They were almost abstract political-military concepts, at least at my midgrade level.

I see myself as more of a political-military technician working on these studies than anything else.

The Philosophy and Psychology of Nuclear Weapons

Q: I'd like to probe the feeling about nuclear weapons. To the layman, the concept of Europe and tactical nuclear weapons seems to be a complete oxymoron. How can something be tactical and be nuclear? How did you approach it, and as you went on this thing, did you change? How did you feel about what people were talking about?

JONES: That is a marvelously complex subject with all of the iterations that you suggest. How did I personally feel about it? I felt that the weapons could be used. I did not believe that the use of one nuclear weapon or even substantial numbers of nuclear weapons meant that there was, without any question, going to be world annihilation. I felt that nuclear weapons in Europe were absolutely necessary for us to be able to hold off the threat of a Soviet attack. There was a complex NATO European working group going on as to where and how a war could or might be fought and under what circumstances.

I remember the very first NATO nuclear-oriented meeting I attended. I was still ignorant about some of these attitudes and European views on nuclear weapons. At the same time, we were urging an increase in European conventional force capabilities. There was a 3 percent plan in which we were steadily pushing the Europeans to increase conventional capabilities across a wide spectrum of weaponry and capabilities. Only one element of this spectrum was improved nuclear weapons and improved nuclear capability. But the question that I raised, in effect, was, "Why are you Europeans so resistant to increasing conventional capabilities?" I will never forget a German response: "We have no interest in making Europe safe for conventional war." They had been there. They had done that. They wanted—or at least this group of Germans representing that government at that time—very clearly wanted it understood that there would be a nuclear war if there was a war. They did not want a situation in which they were going to be forced into an extended conventional slugging match with the Russians.

As a result, we had elaborate scenarios as to what would happen under which conventional circumstances. We did not believe that we would be able to hold for an extended period with conventional weapons. Then the question would come as to what type of a nuclear scenario you would use. I bought into this. In honesty, I still think it not only would have worked but did work. We did indeed convince the Russians that if there was going to be a war, it would end by being a nuclear war—we would not hesitate to use nuclear weapons. I don't think we would have hesitated. We would have thought hard, but we wouldn't have hesitated. We would rather have gone to nuclear weapons use than to have lost Europe as a result of a fight with the Soviets. We just weren't going to lose Europe. We had convinced ourselves and the Europeans that a loss of Europe to the Soviets would mean a very, very isolated America and eventually our defeat as well. That is, we would end by losing our own freedom and security if European freedom and security were lost. As we were not willing to expend the financing or the social commitment to build conventional forces to a level that we thought would stave off a Soviet attack, we depended as well on nuclear weapons to do so.

At the same time, there were doubters. There were a set of European doubters as well. This was a question of whether our use of nuclear weapons would result in heavier strikes by the Soviets. In that case, the argument was that we would only lose the war faster if we resorted to the use of tactical nuclear weapons within Europe. This was an argument that, happily, was never resolved by real testing. But it was an ongoing, persistent argument.

Q: Did you get involved at all with at least the fruits of these people in the Pentagon who were sitting around planning, "If we lose twenty million people and they lose twenty-five million people, we're coming out ahead," playing at the mega scale about nuclear exchanges?

JONES: No, I didn't see that type of study. I worked a little on certain hypothetical exchanges on a lower level and whether some of these scenarios would work to our benefit. In particular, there was one case, which came out positive for NATO. That was how we could use nuclear weapons to beat back a prospective amphibious assault by the Russians, which was a very clean study in all manner, shapes, and forms. It was clean because none of this weaponry landed, in effect, on NATO territory. It was all maritime. As a result, there was less of an expectation that the Soviets would respond with nuclear weapons or they would have fewer immediate massed NATO targets to respond in the same way.

In the same manner, just about this time, we began studying a variety of new, advanced nuclear technology in an effort to find ways to make our nuclear weapons more usable on a tactical basis. These were the enhanced radiation weapons or enhanced blast weapons and a variety of what they called "earth penetrator" weapons to use against a hardened facility's air base or underground command post, targets of this nature. But the effort to use what later became known as the neutron bomb was indeed conceived of as a very humane exercise on our part, an effort to deal with the problems of Soviet armored formations. Their armor was large enough and heavy enough with thick enough armor that we regarded our regular conventional weapons as prospectively not that effective. We were just beginning to talk about precision guided munitions, which were also very expensive. Our conventional antitank weaponry was not deemed to be that powerful or effective. The soldiers using it were regarded as vulnerable when trying to use it. Consequently, one of the questions that they turned to was, "How can we use nuclear weapons, our most powerful and effective weapons, against armor formations in a way that would be tactically effective and less damaging to the area in which they would be fighting?" We never moved away from a recognition that this was our own territory on which we were fighting. No one was ever thinking of carrying the attack to the other side.

Q: *Except for interdiction.*

JONES: Right. But there was no talk about taking an opportunity to unify Germany if they were foolish enough to attack us. It was always a recognition that we would be killing our friends, or at least people who were not particularly hostile to us. We never thought that Warsaw Pact allies were particularly hostile to the West or particularly combat effective. There was some concern about the likelihood that the Russians would push these people to the front of the assault and force us to waste our weaponry on inferior troops while they were more or less lurking behind Warsaw Pact formations. But the nuclear philosophy was also not a last-ditch philosophy. We were not going to put ourselves in a situation where we wouldn't choose nuclear weapons until we were at the point of defeat. That was also both an American concern and a European concern.

Thinking about the Soviets—Not Very Subtle

Q: During this 1974-76 period, we had a plan for the worst. How did we view the Soviet threat and the likelihood that the Soviets might do something, and why?

JONES: I'm not sure I was particularly introspective at that point. There was an ongoing, endless concern that the Russians were just one or two steps away from being able to exploit a failure on our part. This is only six years away from the time in which they crushed all resistance in Czechoslovakia. Soviet willingness to beat their own people into submission over and over again was very pointed. It was something which, for young officers or midlevel officers of my generation, had been the abiding foreign affairs reality, that Soviet influence was behind virtually all the problems that we could specifically identify around the world, and Europe remained the area in which we could lose the most, the most quickly, if we were not constantly on guard. This is why there were ongoing, endless concerns about the degree to which communists were active in France or in Italy. It's also just about pre-Eurocommunism. The question was whether the communists were going to be able to put a more cleverly adroit face on their nefarious actions.

The "All Volunteer" U.S. Army and Its Challenges

Q: During this time, were people you were with concerned about the American army because of the abrasion that Vietnam caused on its fighting power?

JONES: Yes. There was a recognition that the army was not what it had been. There was serious concern that the army had not managed to emerge from being blamed for losing the war that the civilians had actually lost in Vietnam. The retrospective problems of transitioning from a draftee army to an all-volunteer army, the questions as to whether an all-volunteer army would work, and whether it would be the right kind of army for what we wanted, were still in play. We were still struggling with drug-associated difficulties in the military, particularly in the army. I don't know how long it took for us to get to a point where we were more confident in the military capabilities of this new all-volunteer army. Perhaps by the end of the 1970s, the early 1980s, we were beginning to be more confident that the army had turned the corner and that the all-volunteer military was working. But in these early to mid 1970s, it was still an army that needed recovery time.

Individual officers that I met, individual midlevel field grade officers that I met, were all very capable people, but they were also very dubious about the all-volunteer army. They were afraid that what you were going to get was an army that no longer reflected America and, as a result of this development, the population wouldn't support it. They were also concerned that it was going to be a pretty stupid army. The people that they were going to get as recruits weren't going to be from any university background. They were also going to miss, they believed, the better class of ROTC graduate officers who were from better schools and had always provided also something of a leavening effect within the military.

There were those that were afraid that we would start moving toward a praetorian military, which might erode the concept of civilian authority over the military. You did not have, in effect, a draftee army that reflected the wide range of the population. There were people that remembered enough from the French experience in Algeria and wondered whether we would start moving in the direction of an army that was politicized in some ways and divorced from control in others because it was an all-volunteer military. These were midlevel major or lieutenant colonel officers who didn't really like what they were seeing in this all-volunteer army. Perhaps they (and I) didn't like it that much because we didn't know what could be done with it.

Q: It was a step into the unknown.

JONES: Well, in some respects it wasn't. Historically, we had not been a draftee military. We had been an all-volunteer military. But it was the first time we were trying to meet circumstances that saw global responsibility rather than fighting Indians or being only a defensive force, having only a few thousand people. There were many people that looked at the pre—World War II military, which was an all-volunteer military, and said, "This was not a very good military. This was a Chinese army military," recalling the phrase "You don't make good iron into nails and you don't make good men into soldiers." That was the kind of military that people recalled in *From Here to Eternity*, a "James Jones military." They thought that this design would be the type of all-volunteer military we would get. Well, we are very fortunate—it hasn't turned out that way. But in the early 1970s, people certainly weren't sure.

Internal NATO National Politics

—Portugal

Q: Within your circle, not at the higher regions, what was the thought process about members of NATO? For example, this was a very critical time with Portugal. Did that come into play at all?

JONES: That was a little bit before my time. But, yes, we were certainly worried about communists in government. Indeed, we set things up at NATO so that we had confidence in the Portuguese ambassador there. But we put real limits on what he could do and see, and we managed our way around the fear of communists in government in Portugal. At the same time, we began thinking of a Portuguese military modernization program. How can we strengthen their military? How can we make sure that their military remains involved in NATO military activities? Some of this was a long ongoing program that I'm not sure has ever ended. But it involved a variety of areas in which we tried to strengthen the Portuguese military, particularly the Portuguese navy. Maybe that was Azores related. There was a long, ongoing frigate construction program for the Portuguese navy. But the Portuguese army was also one about which people were concerned.

—France

Q: What about the French? They were sort of in and out. Would they be with us, ahead of us, behind us?

JONES: The French were always infuriating. If you asked for a description of the French at the time, you would feel in some ways that they ranged between irritating and infuriating. At the same time, there was recognition that—on a very quiet military-to-military basis—the Supreme Allied Commander, Europe [SACEUR] had been working out arrangements with the French military. SACEUR had always been an American. I can't remember when General Al Haig was there, but he was SACEUR at approximately that time. The fact that the French had military divisions in Germany for the defense of Germany gave us always the sense that they would fight in a clear Soviet attack on Germany, not because they loved the Germans, but because keeping the Russians further away from the French border would obviously be to French benefit.

There wasn't much fear that the French would make a separate deal with the Russians. That prospect was occasionally bruited about as a worst-case possibility. It was something that the Russians would try from time to time in their discussions of "no first use" aspects of nuclear weaponry. But the French never left the North Atlantic Council [NAC]. They were always represented at the next step below the NAC, the Senior Political Committee [SPC]. They were always represented there. They were also always represented on the Political Committee, which was again another step below the SPC. But they had stayed out of the military side of NATO and, as a consequence, they also stayed out of the nuclear planning aspect. We very deliberately always kept a seat in the Nuclear Planning Group (NPG) for the French. The French were never closed out of these meetings so far as us removing their nametag and options to attend. We also kept a seat for the French in the discussions on Mutual and Balanced Force Reductions (MBRF). They didn't participate, but we maintained a seat for them. These were for discussions of conventional forces and conventional force reductions. This is a subject in which I was substantially involved while I was at NATO later, although not in this first two-years-plus that I spent on the NATO desk.

—NATO "Neutrals"

Q: What about the smaller countries—Holland, Denmark, Belgium, Norway? They had rather substantial neutralist groups, or at least groups that had not as much a tendency to feel they were on the frontline. How were they?

JONES: First of all, these countries did not send their "neutralists" to NATO; nor were their governments neutralist or ambivalent about NATO. As you indicate, in the Netherlands, there was a neutralist element. Historically, the Dutch have been neutral at times in European conflict. I would say that the Belgians were not. The Belgians were strongly committed to NATO. The Nordic countries were involved but not engaged. NATO, working on consensus, as it does, in theory allows any single country to stop a NATO consensus. That could mean that the totally unarmed and indefensible

Icelandic community could stand up and say that they refused to go forward with a particular level of agreement or particular proposal. In fact, however, this just didn't happen. None of the Scandinavian countries—Denmark, Norway, Iceland—ever prevented a significant NATO action from going forward. You had intelligent questions from them, and you had an implicit recognition that their military contribution was likely to be marginal (certainly little from the Danes and nothing from the Icelanders). On the other hand, Norway, given its geographic position, had serious concerns about its own vulnerability and, as a result, the country was as strongly committed to NATO as it could be; there was also the expectation and the plans that NATO forces would be sent to Norway to help defend it in case of a Soviet attack. There were regular war games, and there was steady commitment of forces to the defense of Norway. Norway was a strong NATO player and not neutralistic. Nor were the Italians. Over a period of time, the Italians wanted to be considered a significant player in NATO on the level of Germany and the United Kingdom.

—Italy

The Italians, despite a significant Italian Communist Party, slowly but steadily became more committed to European security and more committed to supporting NATO. Their ability to do so financially was always in question. Their ability to make real improvements in their forces was never at the level that we would hope. But politically they were much stronger than we thought they might be. Particularly through the 1970s, this commitment on the part of the Italians grew steadily stronger, and our concerns and fears about what Eurocommunism might mean, and particularly Eurocommunism in Italy, turned out to be less pointed than we thought they might become. I'm not going to say that an absence of attention to the Eurocommunism phenomenon would have been justified, but we and the Italians, fortunately, were able to deflect the Communist Party in Italy.

—Greece and Turkey (the Never-ending Feud)

Q: How about Greece? Cyprus had been invaded. We had an arms embargo against Turkey. Greece seemed to be far more interested in confronting Turkey. Turkey to some extent was tied up in the Greek business. Particularly, American political support was not there. Did that cause disquiet with the group you were with?

JONES: This was always a problem. It was only later in my own career that I became more involved in Greek-Turkish issues. But it was, has been, and remains a problem within the NATO structure. It has been absolutely impossible to work out a relationship between Greece and Turkey over the last quarter of a center. Ever since the Turkish seizure of the northern part of Cyprus and the division of Cyprus, the relationship between Greece and Turkey has been very barbed. This has meant a constant effort within the NATO councils to work around the problems or not to raise specific issues within the Defense Planning Committee or the Defense Planning Questionnaire, the DPQ, in which various commitments of each country's military forces are itemized, examined, and reviewed.

The point is that neither the Greeks nor the Turks have ever agreed on how the Defense Planning Questionnaire should be resolved. We struggled with this problem year after year after year, specifically over whether the stationing of certain forces in certain areas was legitimate or not. Consequently, NATO was regularly dragged into what NATO considers not to be its argument. NATO's view is that this is a bilateral argument; why do they insist on fighting the bilateral argument in the NATO arena? The NATO arena is designed to fight the Soviets. Why do you insist on fighting each other within the NATO arena? As a result, it was very difficult not to find an area in which the Greeks or the Turks, on any given day, might decide to make this particular NATO forum-quorum a subject for their personal or national fight.

It became very tiresome, always having to manage the Greek-Turkish problem. For the most part, the NATO representatives from Greece and Turkey were not themselves personally hostile. You would see, well, all right, they have instructions from capitals to go out and pound on the table in this manner or some new representative at the Foreign Ministry has seen this as an opportunity to put one in the eye of the other. So then the rest of us, whether it was Americans, Brits, Germans, Belgians, or somebody else, would try to find some way to mediate it, or to get them to withdraw the point, or to agree to disagree and move past their specific bilateral problem to get on with the overall NATO issue for the day.

The Never Ending Threat

Q: I realize you were at a relatively junior level of this NATO thing. But when you were talking to colleagues, how did we see a conflict breaking out? What were some of the hot points?

JONES: There was always the potential for a problem in Berlin that would spin out of control. Berlin was such a potential hotspot. People now forget that we had a garrison out there that was totally isolated, hundreds of miles away from the rest of the force structure. It was, as a result, both totally vulnerable in some ways and absolutely indispensable in others. There was always the fear that, for one reason or another, the Russians might decide to seize Berlin, because Berlin would just become too much of an irritant or that they would decide to make a point for us against everything else on Berlin, and war could begin over Berlin.

There was certainly always the concern within the military that we were not strong enough to be able to handle a Soviet attack, combined with the fear that if we weren't strong enough, how long could we last, and why or how the war would start? It was another and different question, whether the war would start; we couldn't predict in this manner. Each time we ran regular NATO war games, so-called Wintex (the winter exercise) and Hilex (the high-level exercise), in which we created artificial scenarios, but the point of which was still that fighting would begin. These were procedural exercise drills, i.e., how we would respond, what was available in our "books" and war plans to react in certain ways, what démarches could be made, what organizational structures would be activated. Then there was a step-by-step procedure through "game" controllers providing information and responding to reactions by the various NATO committees and councils. These war games were played with seriousness. They were certainly played seriously at NATO. The ambassadors were engaged; every NATO mission was engaged, fully. It was not played by some small cell within the mission that was doing it with a yawn. It was played seriously by all the ambassadors and, most people believed, by very high-level foreign and defense officials in the ministries throughout Europe. To a certain extent, it was real. It was real to the extent that these were serious plans made by serious people to get your team ready for a worst case.

On the other side of the exercise, it was illustrative that we were demonstrating to the East, to the Warsaw Pact and to Moscow, that we were serious, that this was a seriously organized NATO response, that we were ready if they were ever so foolish, misguided, or mad to attack us. That's why we would run through an escalation scenario that ended with NATO use of nuclear weapons. Now, the NATO use of nuclear weapons at that point blurred regarding what would be done or how long it would be done, or how much NATO use of nuclear weapons would be engaged. But it was a clear illustration, although all of this was classified at the time and held secret, there was also an expectation that the Warsaw Pact, and the Soviets in particular, would know the broad outlines of what we were doing so there would be no misapprehension on their part that they could seize a portion of the West and hold it. There was the fear that they might be able to drive to the Rhine and stop, seizing West Germany. You looked at the distances and the logistics base, and it was a relatively short distance from the Soviet jumping-off points to the Rhine.

There was the common concern that our requirement for forward defense was not militarily sound. The political requirement to fight for every inch of German territory, when tactically it might have been far more efficient to withdraw a substantial distance, could make things tactically and strategically worse than might have been the case if we were able to do what would have been militarily wise, although politically impossible. We couldn't get to a point of saying, "Well, the very best thing to do with the Soviets and a Warsaw Pact attack would be to withdraw to a line of defense along the Rhine River." You could make that case and then try to shorten our lines. We were also having serious logistical problems. We no longer had straight logistical lines of communication through France. Our lines of communication and our lines of resupply were very awkward indeed. We might hypothesize on a best case that, in an instance of Soviet attack, the French would reopen their facilities and allow us to move supporting operations through France, but with no prior planning for this sanguine possibility, we couldn't depend on it. This meant that the political requirement to defend every inch of Germany, let alone by the Germans, who would have to defend every inch of Germany, could have made the circumstances for the defense of NATO perilous.

So far as the overall effort was concerned, I've gotten you in some respects down into the weeds. More generally, NATO was endlessly involved in senior ministerial councils. NATO's work *qua* work was incredibly laborious and astonishingly detailed, with endlessly long hours. At the same time, senior officials gave it enormous attention. You just knew all the time that NATO, that RPM, was one of the focal points of whatever was being done. This meant very, very long hours, weekend hours for the Department of State. The problem was accentuated by the time differences at NATO. With it being six hours ahead at NATO, if they worked until midnight at NATO and drafted telegrams and got them out, they would have arrived at the end of the official business day in Washington. Consequently, if Washington worked all day until midnight, it could send off instructions and they would be sitting at NATO when NATO opened for business at 6:00 a.m. So, by a madhouse type of effort within the department and at NATO, you could work twenty-four hours a day. You would have same time turnaround at a time when communications were certainly very good, but not the incredibly good communications that we now have. So there were people who said that "RPM" really meant "revolutions per minute" for the frenetic quality of our work.

CHAPTER 26

Moving from the Desk to the Field: US Mission NATO as NATO's Engine

Q: You left the NATO Desk in '76 and went where?

The U.S. Mission at NATO: Structure and Operations

JONES: I went to the U.S. Mission at NATO. My job in RPM was a combination of training ground and recruitment center for people at NATO. I had been back in the United States since 1971, and this was a good opportunity to go overseas. I was "well and favorably known" by the people at NATO. I had visited some of them. The DCM at NATO, Ed Streator, had been the head of RPM when I was working there. He made it clear to me that he was interested in bringing me to NATO under those circumstances.

Q: You were in Brussels from '76 to when?

JONES: Nineteen hundred eighty.

I should also step back, at least at one point, to note that it was at this juncture, the 1974 time frame, that my wife, Teresa, entered the Foreign Service. Her first tour was with the Arms Control and Disarmament Agency [ACDA]. She was endlessly helpful to me on the arms control side, bringing me up to speed on technical issues associated with arms control and disarmament points. There was a major ongoing effort to develop a comprehensive test ban, an issue that we in RPM followed somewhat tangentially. There were also the ongoing SALT [Strategic Arms Limitation Talks] discussions—again an issue that in RPM we followed tangentially, but we always needed to be aware of its progress because of prospective NATO angles. All of these efforts were subject to endless consultation with the allies. This was being done at every level. You could not consult with the allies too often. It became a ritual: what is it that we have done lately? Well, we have to consult with the allies. Is it on SALT? Is it on MBFR [Mutual and Balanced Force Reductions]? Is it on comprehensive test ban? Is it on nuclear nonproliferation? We were endlessly sending out teams of briefers and discussants on just about any topic under the sun. Midlevel officers were always preparing briefing papers, talking points, background material, et cetera. Teresa regularly gave me good insights on how things would work on a purely technical side for arms control issues.

Q: When you started out in '76, what aspect were you working on at NATO headquarters?

JONES: I was what they called the executive officer or "XO." It's a curious position. It's not the ambassador's staff assistant. It's closer to being the DCM's DCM, where you were the general controller for virtually all paper within the mission, while at the same time you were also giving support to the ambassador. I also had a couple of dossiers associated with the political section that fell under my special purview, and they were the nuclear dossiers. I was able to retain them and continue at NATO the work that I had been doing in RPM. That gave me substantive credentials with the political section as well as being the XO.

You have to let me spend a minute or so talking about the Mission. This was not an embassy. This was a giant political-military section. It was a ninety-person political-military section, of which the diplomats were only one portion. There was an entire floor of some of the most capable mid-rank military officers I have ever encountered. This was an exercise on their part of preparing for war, of preparing (with the feeling that the military had throughout this period) while knowing that they were going to have to fight outnumbered and win or there was no future for the West. Day after day, you got this reflection not necessarily from what they were saying or from the people out in the field, but they planned. When they ran their exercises, it was not always known whether this was for real or whether this was an exercise. Were the Russians going to come through the Fulda Gap? Were we going to be able to hold them? Was there any chance of holding them conventionally rather than having to go nuclear? Although we were morally, intellectually, and politically prepared to go nuclear, this was nothing that anyone desired.

There was always the fear that the Russians were ten feet tall. There was always the endless recollection of what their units were like, how tough their armored forces were, how much artillery they had, how capable they were in military terms. All the numbers were always recounted straight out, so it was obvious that their numbers were always much greater than ours, let alone adding in their Warsaw Pact forces. It was a source of constant tension in a way that recedes into the background like a dull headache that only becomes a migraine occasionally, but you always knew it was there if you spent a little bit of time thinking about why we were there. It was a regular worry.

The NATO organizational and bureaucratic mission, as an operation, was really driven by the United States. We were the locomotive that was hauling the entire apparatus all the time. As a result, our meeting schedules were amazingly intensive and frequently intrusive. The schedules were such that we had a major meeting every Thanksgiving Day. It was impossible to prepare for the ministerial meetings that were early in the month of December unless we had a wide range of preministerial meetings. That required for us, as Americans, to be meeting on Thanksgiving Day every single year—not all day long, fortunately, but every single Thanksgiving Day, we were running tough, infinitely detailed preparation meetings where every single word and phrase was struggled over and consulted upon, trying to get fifteen NATO nations to agree. It was a very, very detailed task requiring just endless patience, endless consultation, endless flexibility, and discussions with Washington, with key allies, with the NATO international staff, and good leadership and good fellowship.

The Carter Transition in 1977 and the Ouster of Strausz-Hupé

Q: The Carter administration came in early '77. You like everyone else were watching the campaign. How did you feel before the Carter administration came in? This was quite a difference between the Ford and the Nixon administrations and Kissinger. Here comes Carter.

JONES: This was my first change of administration in the Foreign Service. I had entered in 1968 just as the Nixon administration was about to arrive. Here it was, 1976. The juncture at which I arrived at NATO was also the point at which a new ambassador arrived, Robert Strausz-Hupé, who had just gotten the assignment that he had hoped for—sought throughout most of his life—and been extremely interested in obtaining. He had slid from Sri Lanka, then Ceylon, to Belgium. He had spent a couple of years in Belgium. Then he was bumped out of the ambassadorship in Belgium and went to Stockholm. His wife died while he was in Stockholm, and he arrived in NATO just a little bit ahead of the time when I arrived. I had known Strausz-Hupé previously as an undergraduate student at the University of Pennsylvania. I subsequently met him occasionally. I had been, because of that association, his control officer when he was preparing to go out to NATO, but had been getting briefings in Washington. Then I arrived at NATO at the same time he was breaking in at NATO.

Certainly, Strausz-Hupé and, as a result, the rest of the Mission, overtly and to the degree that I could sense personally, were quite satisfied with the Nixon-Ford administration. Although almost every Foreign Service officer is careful about expressing political views or associating themselves in any direct way with a political party, there was no active dissatisfaction that I recall with the Nixon-Ford administrations, and certainly a general willingness, if not enthusiasm, to continue with Ford as president through the rest of the decade. Strausz-Hupé obviously wanted that to happen. To the extent possible, he tried to work to make sure that he was viewed as an effective ambassador at NATO at this period.

Q: Following the political campaign, was there disquiet about where Carter and his administration would stand on NATO, or not?

JONES: A transition is always one in which you don't know what's going to happen. I suppose in strategic terms, yes, you know what's going to happen. Carter wasn't going to pull the United States out of NATO. But what would happen with the projects and the programs that were going forward, whether it was NATO modernization, nuclear modernization, and so on, or what our attitudes would be on specific individual issues, it's much harder to say. In retrospect, I don't think we thought that Ford was going to lose. You can get pretty divorced from reality, even with polls and information of that nature. We tended to expect that Ford was going to win and that Carter was not viewed as tremendously able. After all, he's this former governor from an end-of-the-world kind of state (Georgia). What was his background? Things like that. I won't say that we were shocked that he won, because you saw the polls, you saw the numbers, you saw that Carter was leading, you saw that Ford could lose. But I don't think we *really* thought that Ford was going to lose and that Carter was going to win. We thought that way just because it was, if anything, easier to continue with what we were doing with the leadership that we had and with the directions that we had. You always find that our allies are just as happy to continue with the current U.S. leadership, who are the devils they know rather than the angels they don't.

Q: *After Carter won the election and was setting up shop in '77, did you find that there was a lot of consultation, at least unofficially, with European allies coming to you all and saying, "Who the hell is this guy and what does it mean?"*

JONES: Yes, there were people visiting. There were people coming from Washington quickly to consult with the allies and to reassure the allies. We had then Vice President Mondale. We had people at this level very quickly coming to NATO in early 1977 to consult, which was really to reassure European allies and to say all the right things so that officials would actually hear the right things being said—not that they didn't expect us to say the right things. That was fine. This was part of the "get together with the Allies, tell them that they're all loved, that we'll continue to be reliable partners." This was how we were trying to work the process.

Since I hadn't gone through a transition before, it was new to me. It was an incumbent ambassador who was going to be replaced, a political ambassador who was going to be replaced, but didn't really want to go. So Strausz-Hupé was trying to demonstrate to Washington how bright his work was, how many fresh, clever ideas he and the mission had. We had a series of "big think" projects. They were thoughtful, intelligent, coherent pieces of work that Strausz-Hupé inspired the Mission officers to think about and write. Individual people worked on them. God only knows what they said. But I remember them in these general terms as being intelligent, thoughtful, coherent pieces of work in which Strausz-Hupé hoped to be allowed to stay on to begin to implement, perhaps for six months at least, to give him a full year at NATO.

It turned out pretty quickly, however, that he had wasted his time and energy, that they were not going to leave a senior post like NATO filled with what they considered to be a Cold War Republican hawk. Everyone, including Strausz-Hupé, who thought that he had a ghost of a chance of staying on under those circumstances, was woolgathering. He didn't. He was told, in effect, to vacate by the end of March 1977. He did, with some of the unnecessary ill grace associated with these kinds of departures.

I was much involved in his effort to write a final speech to the North Atlantic Council. This is a traditional farewell address in which they offer and give the ambassador a memento, an award, a plaque, a plate, an object of this nature. I was engaged in some of the drafting, but it was Strausz-Hupé's speech that he wrote and that he sent to Washington for clearance. Well, the people in the European Bureau were equally nervous about anything that was being said. They didn't know whether they were going to be replaced or how they would fit in with the new administration. They were very touchy over what Strausz-Hupé was saying or what they thought Strausz-Hupé was trying to say, with Strausz-Hupé arguing back, saying, "I wasn't trying to do this" or "What I'm saying is exactly what the new administration is in the process of saying." But it turned out to be one of those gritted-teeth exercises on both sides, where you had a man who was then about seventy-four and was trying to say what he expected would be almost his final statement. It was not that.

He finally did give a presentation, which in many respects was brilliant. He gave a speech that was close to an hour long, in which he made not a single verbal misstatement, not the tiniest little verbal slip or blip. It was a remarkable exercise in that manner of speaking. Most of us can't speak two minutes without an "ah" or an "eh" no matter how hard you work on your own speechmaking delivery. It was a presentation for which I remember the format and not the content. But the *tour de force* presentation that he gave was remarkable in its own way. The commentary that EUR had made on the speech, with a perspective of about twenty years (I reread it all last summer when I was working through Strausz-Hupé papers), was silly but it reflected the angst of transition. Nobody knows what's coming, and the more senior you are, the more worried you are about what's coming, because you're the ones under the gun, while people at midlevel come and go without comparable anxiety. For young major and lieutenant colonel equivalents, such as I was at the time, you know there are going to be changes. It was just a question of who your boss was going to be. You hoped that they would be decent guys rather than crazy guys.

The Hallmark of the Era: the Neutron Bomb and Nuclear Deterrence in Europe

Q: I would imagine that the neutron bomb, or enhanced radiation [ER] weapon, became a hallmark of the Carter administration. Could you talk about that? Explain what the issue was, particularly with regard to Helmut Schmidt and how we were seen at your level.

JONES: In many respects, this was something that I was involved in from the very beginning. I was involved in it to a degree on the Washington side. It was something in which I was engaged throughout my NATO career and one of the major strands of my entire Foreign Service career. It goes back to the question of nuclear weapons being one aspect of NATO's modernization program. It is part of the entire 3 percent real increase in budget and improvement of NATO's defensive capabilities.

One element of this effort was tactical nuclear force modernization, or TNF modernization. There was a full range of discussion about what was needed, how/why it was needed, where it should be based, and under what circumstances it was to be used. Part of the issue was based on the problem that we foresaw of using aircraft as the major delivery vehicle for nuclear weapons. These aircraft were vulnerable in certain ways. We had dual-capable aircraft, which theoretically delivered conventional weaponry during the conventional battle but were also being reserved for the potential of delivering nuclear weapons. There was a conceptual problem. You were going to use all of your aircraft to fight the war on the conventional basis. But you also had to assume you were going to be losing aircraft and losing ground during the conventional war. You had to reserve in your mind and plans a certain number of aircraft for the delivery of tactical nuclear weapons. What would happen at the juncture when the war itself was raging, and perhaps even in the balance, but you had drawn down your conventional aircraft, your dual-capable aircraft, to the point at which you only had enough left to deliver your nuclear strikes? Would you then have to pull all of those conventional aircraft out of the battle in order to prepare them for using nuclear weapons? At the same time, would such a move mean that the conventional war that was perhaps at a tipping point was now going to be lost, forcing you to go nuclear? At the same time, would the signal that you gave to the Soviet and Warsaw Pact forces (by withdrawing your aircraft from the conventional fight) mean that you were about to go nuclear? Would that preempt nuclear strikes on their part to avoid getting a nuclear hit from us? This was a very serious conceptual problem.

Nuclear Capable Missiles—a Discussion

At the same time, we were reluctant to go through the political and military upgrading of our tactical nuclear missile force in Europe. This was when the Soviets were beginning to deploy SS-20s. The deployment of Soviet SS-20s was viewed as an increasingly serious threat by the Europeans, particularly by the Germans. They were saying, "We have to have a response to this. We have to have an American response to balance the Soviet missiles." Otherwise, the Soviets might come to the conclusion that the Americans would be willing to sacrifice existing forces in Europe to preserve the United States from any nuclear strikes. Only if the United States deployed comparable nuclear weapons in Europe would we be able to threaten the Soviets appropriately with intermediate-range weaponry that would assure that, if a war started, there wouldn't be a "burnt space between two green spaces."

Well, our first response was essentially a political-military reaction rather than a political reaction. Our first reaction was that our existing strategic forces and nuclear forces in Europe were more than enough to counter the increase in Soviet intermediate-range nuclear weapons and their SS-20 deployments. We were hypothesizing at that point that the SS-20s might be just a replacement for their SS-4s and SS-5s, which were obsolete by that time for a number of technical reasons. They were much more vulnerable than the SS-20s would be. The SS-20s were mobile, the SS-20s had multiple warheads, the SS-20s were solid fueled or better fueled—all of these aspects made the SS-20s a clear modernization.

We sent a couple of high-powered briefing teams to NATO in the late summer of 1976 in an attempt to convince the Europeans that our strategic systems, our SSBNs, submarine-based ballistic missiles, which were nuclear submarines that were actually allocated to SACEUR, were sufficient NATO responses, committed, dedicated forces to counter the

SS-20s. We thought we had convinced them. We seriously thought that we had convinced them, until Helmut Schmidt spoke to the IISS in London in October 1977. With this speech, he forced us to conclude on a political level that the force deployment that we had, our current strategic forces, were not sufficient to respond to the new SS-20 deployment. So we then began discussions on both a military and a political level with the Europeans. What became the High-Level Group [HLG] and the Special Consultative Group [SCG] began to meet and work out the question of how we would respond.

Q: This was approximately when?

JONES: This is around 1977-78. After a great deal of effort and consultations with the Europeans, we had gotten their technical acceptance of these weapons. Whether they expected them to be used, I have no idea. But the credibility of NATO nuclear use was always regarded as one of the key elements of deterrence. I did not hear demurrals from my European colleagues and other NATO diplomats about the use of these weapons or necessarily other nuclear weapons. On nuclear weapons specifically, the only system about which they appeared to be unhappy was the atomic demolition munitions [ADM]. That concern devolved into a long argument about "prechambering" for specific areas and whether you would drill the holes ahead of time for the use of ADMs. There was reluctance to do this; it was more political than military reluctance. It would drive home to the guy in the neighborhood that the likelihood of using a nuclear weapon was right there. On the flip side, the Germans had developed special equipment that would allow the drilling of emplacement chambers for atomic demolition munitions on relatively short order.

But the technical decision that we could move ahead with enhanced radiation weapons was one that had been made. It had been endorsed. It had been approved at the various levels within NATO. My recollection is that it had been endorsed at a ministerial meeting by the acceptance of the report. The study having being done on these weapons and the general NATO approval meant, as a result, that the alliance regarded enhanced radiation weapons as part of its military capability.

European Attitudes, Nuclear Weapons Deployments, Carter's Inexplicable Decision Not to Deploy ER Weapons, and Consequent European/U.S. Attitudes

Q: I did an interview with Vlad Lehovich, who was in Bonn. He was saying that the neutron weapon was viewed with a certain suspicion by the left within Germany and other places because supposedly it destroyed people, not property. This sounded very capitalistic as opposed to communistic, where it's much better to destroy property and if people go, that's too bad. Helmut Schmidt, who was a socialist, had been reluctant for political reasons to endorse this. Jimmy Carter as our president was pressing him very hard all the time. Were you aware of this?

JONES: This was certainly an element of it. You had Schmidt and the socialists, for the first time in many years, in power in Germany. There was concern about the left side of the ruling party. No matter where you went in Europe, the left was hostile to nuclear weapons, was hostile to NATO, was hostile to the neutron bomb, or fostered the "ban the neutron bomb" exercise. Indeed, your recollection is correct that the communists said that the neutron bomb was the perfect capitalist weapon, that it killed people and preserved property. Our response was that the neutron bomb was the perfect communist weapon because it would kill capitalists and preserve the means of production. But that was a propaganda tit-for-tat exercise. There was a clear expectation that the Europeans were going to be on board. We had argued and persuaded them that they should accept these weapons, this philosophy, and this report. Yes, we had.

Lehovich's recollection is also perfectly clear that on the left in Germany and on the left everywhere, they were not enthusiastic about nuclear weapons. They were certainly not enthusiastic about nuclear weapons that looked as if they could be used. They were even less enthusiastic about nuclear weapons that looked as if they might be usable in their neighborhoods. There was a "not in my backyard" view of nuclear weapons. Although these people were no longer screaming "Better Red than Dead," we thought of them as exactly the same type of people that would find any excuse to surrender. Well, we were also in the situation where we couldn't force the allies to take these weapons. They had to invite us to make these deployments. This was orchestration, in that they knew that they had to ask; and they knew that if they asked, we would make the deployments.

Schmidt got far out on a limb when he endorsed the deployment. This is my sense, that there was indeed no question that Schmidt, who had to be the leader on this subject because the key deployment of nuclear weapons presumably would be in Germany, would agree whether or not there were ER weapons in other areas. The most likely storage facilities would be in Germany, so Schmidt had to make this endorsement. He did. Then Carter decided to rethink it all. His decision to rethink it was a type of decision that was completely inexplicable at the time. I had one ambassador for whom I later worked, Reg Bartholomew, who was in the NSC [National Security Council] at that point and was dealing with this issue. He said to me years later that he received an endless stream of phone calls, and he answered none of them. He said that somebody later came to him and said, "Yes, Reg, your lack of an answer was profound." We had no answer. There was no explanation. There was no defense for what the president had done. We got Helmut Schmidt out on a limb, and we sawed it off and left him standing in midair. There was no way in which you could figure this decision on Carter's part. It left one speechless. All we could do was say, "Well, we're rethinking it. It's delayed rather than stopped. We're reconfiguring." Try to make some sort of rational explanation out of what was going on in his mind. It was, "Well, what's the parallel? Paul on the road to Damascus? This Rose Garden decision?" This decision left us with no idea how it had happened.

At that point, there was the general appreciation that European confidence in Carter just disappeared. Officially, they met with him. Everyone was very straightforward. We were all together, one for all, all for one, but there was the feeling that Carter had lost essential trust or essential appreciation in his decision making. There was the conclusion that he was not reliable. For everything that followed after that—for example, what happened regarding his reactions to the Russian's invasion of Afghanistan or his reaction to the Iranian seizure of American hostages—the Europeans always said the right words. They could be bulldozed into doing things like not participating in the Olympics in Moscow, okay, but it was because they were going through the formalities with us; they had no other choice than to continue to play on our team. But the team captain was just not a reliable leader.

Q: How did this affect you all? Did you have the same feeling?

JONES: It was one of these situations where, when Carter was elected, I said, "What we really need is a successful president. We have had a series of terrible problems. We had Kennedy assassinated. We had Johnson destroyed in office. We had Nixon's Watergate. We had Ford, who was never considered presidential timber before he became president, almost a caretaker president. Whether you're in favor of Carter or you voted against him, what we really need is a successful presidency, whether it was four years or eight years.

I thought that Carter was a very bright man. I'm always in favor of people that know something about nuclear energy and thus would not have, I thought, an implicit fear or terror of nuclear energy. It was something for which I had serious hopes. As it was, his steady deterioration in the polls was, even with the foreign policy failures that I thought he had engaged himself in and been involved in, still puzzling. I couldn't understand why his standing in the national polls declined as much as they did. Some of it I could see. Well, we really did have much higher rates of inflation that anyone wanted. We had obvious national difficulties. But at the same time, I was saying to myself, "We don't have domestic upheaval in the way that we had when our cities were burning at the end of the 1960s. We don't have real depression, we have an economic recession. We aren't engaged in a foreign war overseas. We're just out of Vietnam. Why is this man so far down in the polls?"

NATO was in Brussels with an endless flow of visitors, and we had the ability to get just about anything in the media, which provided total information. I could see what was happening factually but not have a feel for it. On one visit, I came back to the United States as an Army reserve officer on a two-week active duty tour. I saw two of my friends who were liberal Democrats. I went through this litany and said, "Is he really a 26 percent president?" They said to me, "Dave, he's worse than that." Then they each gave me invidious little vignettes on the level of his scheduling play at the White House tennis court and rewriting dedications (badly) on memorial plaques. It left people with the sense that he was a good man and would have been great as your next-door neighbor or your Sunday school teacher, but as a president, he was flailing and just failing. This was the impression that seeped out slowly but steadily wherever you were.

The SALT II Treaty

Q: This must have been rather disquieting as you moved ahead with NATO. Was there a feeling that we weren't as strongly led a nation as we might be?

JONES: That's something of a leading question. The fact is that the Allies continued to play on our team because this was the only team in town and they didn't have any other choices. There were areas in which people were trying to push ahead. We thought we had brought the SALT II treaty to conclusion. This was deemed a great success. I was involved with at least moving documents back and forth to Vienna in the last days and bringing material back to NATO so we could have briefings to explain what was happening to the allies. The Allies were enthusiastic about the prospects for SALT II. They hoped to be able to move subsequently to a SALT III that was more tactically nuclear engaged or intermediate-range engaged rather than the strategic arms reductions, which SALT II was to be. We had hopes at least that MBFR was going to make some progress. We were regularly engaging the Russians with packages of proposals, even though this was seen as a very long-range slugging match in Vienna. These were exercises in which we were engaging the Warsaw Pact and trying to find ways in which to move beyond the confidence-building measures of CSCE into something that would be real conventional force reductions. There was a nuclear package in the MBFR proposal that was being worked, the so-called Option 3. But these were areas in which, at least on the political-military side, aspects of NATO strategy were being steadily worked out. It was an incredible, and incredibly busy, time.

The Soviets in Afghanistan—and Not in Poland

Q: How did the December 1979 Soviet invasion of Afghanistan hit us? Was this just an affirmation that it was really an aggressive force?

JONES: It was a real shock. NATO certainly didn't expect or predict that this was going to happen. We thought that Afghanistan was sufficiently enough a Soviet puppet that there was no need for them to do anything of this nature. We were more concerned that they were about to invade Poland and seize and overthrow the Polish government. After the Afghan invasion, we called emergency NATO meetings, pulled people together, and had intensive consultations. Then we issued sanctions and made denunciations, and took actions of that nature.

My feeling was that we thought the Russians would make short work of anything in Afghanistan, that it wouldn't be any serious problem for them. We never predicted that Afghanistan would become as politically destructive for them on any level of equivalence as Vietnam had been for us. If anyone had said, "Afghanistan will be Moscow's Vietnam," we would have laughed at them. Of course, it was never at that level of societal equivalence for them, but it became a brutally draining exercise. In some respects, we learned nothing from the Russian experience, just as they had learned nothing from our experience in Vietnam. In short, trying to pacify a nasty, well-armed, bloody-minded people is a hell of a fight. We didn't learn from the Soviet experience in Afghanistan when we tried to impose our will in Somalia. That Soviet element of it, that portion of it, had much less effect on NATO than any of the other combination of events then in play. The seizure of our people in Teheran, the fear that the Russians were going to invade Poland and do to the Poles what they had done to the Czechs—these were more immediately pertinent than what was happening in Afghanistan.

Q: The Poles at this point had been going through reform.

JONES: Yes. This was communism with a more human face. This was Jaruzelski in control, but seen as a more liberal Polish communist. There seemed to be some question about the Soviets' perception of the Poles as a reliable ally. There was some perception that they were worried that their lines of communications through Poland might be less secure under the type of Polish government that was evolving. The entire question was one of how much strength Solidarity was gaining and whether Walesa was going to be a destabilizing figure so far as communist rule in Poland was concerned. There were flat predictions from very competent U.S. intelligence analysts that the Russians were going to move, that there was just no question about Soviet action; it was just a matter of whether they moved today or tomorrow or next week or whenever. They just felt that the Russians were going to move on Poland.

Q: Was this accepted that if they did move, we would not intervene?

JONES: Yes. There would certainly be no military intervention. We would leap and scream politically, we would offer new sanctions of one sort or another, would take them to the UN, and would denounce them from pillar to post. We would make them look as black as we could around the world to make political points wherever there was somebody who was a doubter that the Soviets were the unmitigated nasty SOBs that we all knew them to be. That sounds pretty hard line, doesn't it? But there were no peaceniks at NATO.

The INF Issue Evolves from Nuclear Force Modernization—Background

Q: Was the feeling there by 1980, by the time you left, that America had pulled up its socks and its military was getting better, or was there concern about the capabilities of our military?

JONES: By the time I left NATO, there was no reason to know one way or another whether Carter was going to win and continue as president, nor were we out of the "America held hostage in Teheran" problem. We were just at the beginning stages of INF [intermediate-range nuclear forces] deployments, which was one of the issues with which I was much engaged for an extended period, leading to a 12 December 1979 combined ministerial decision.

Q: INF, what does that mean and what were you doing? This is the '76–'80 period.

European Angst

JONES: The INF issues were the intermediate-range nuclear force issues. They were a spin-off, an evolution, from theater nuclear force modernization topics, about which we have had some discussion. The entire exercise was designed to bring matching U.S. intermediate-range nuclear forces into Europe on a modernized basis to counter Soviet SS-20 deployments. There were long, convoluted, and extremely agonized over political sets of decisions in Europe throughout this entire period. The Europeans were probably even more nervous concerning it, considering the problems that they had had with the neutron bomb exercise, and it took them a long time to convince us that they were truly serious about the requirement for a U.S. counter to SS-20s. We had argued earlier that U.S. strategic forces and U.S. SACEUR-committed ballistic submarine missiles were sufficient to counter the modernized SS-20s. The Europeans, however, did not believe that and thought that it was indeed necessary to have a visible U.S. component on the ground, something that would not be able to fly or float away, something that was not an aircraft, not a submarine, but a visible commitment by the United States on the ground.

Special Group (SG) and High Level Group (HLG) Activity

The exercise then began throughout 1979 to work on a series of Special Group [SG] and High-Level Group [HLG] analyses of what would be a proper and sufficient counter to the Soviet SS-20s. The HLG effort was to examine what the hardware would be and what would be the appropriate mix of ground-launched cruise missiles [GLCMs] and Pershing IIs, which were a follow-on to the Pershing I deployed in Europe for many years, but with longer range and greater accuracy. After a great deal of discussion within the HLG and examination of various mixes of missiles, they came up with a combination of Pershings and GLCMs. GLCMs had TERCOM [terrain contour matching] guidance, which followed contours of the earth and allowed for much more precise targeting than had ever previously been the case.

European Logic and Concerns

Q: What were you doing?

JONES: I was an action officer at NATO doing a good deal of the support for the Special Group, the political side of this effort. In this case, it was our effort to locate substantial European basing countries, countries that would accept U.S. cruise missiles. The Germans did not wish to be the only European host for INF. They wanted another host that was actually on the European continent,—that is, a host that was not the United Kingdom. Consequently, we had an extended, ongoing persuasive diplomatic exercise with each of our European allies to determine who else would accept cruise missiles or Pershings.

Q: You're saying the Europeans said we should have something that's not going to fly or float away. At the same time, we were trying to persuade people to accept them.

JONES: Yes, that's a good point. The point essentially was the politicized concerns that we were getting from the European populations at the same time. The officials who were at senior levels in the European governments also wanted to make sure that it was being done in a way that their populations—or at least the left side of their political spectrum—could be forced into accepting them, rather than the deployments being viewed as something that the Americans forced on them. The Germans, while they were willing to do this, didn't want to be the only target in Europe and essentially "isolated" facing the Soviets. As a result, they would be an object for relentless Soviet pressure. We spent a good deal of time on this issue.

Fortunately, about in May 1979, the Italian government, which we had not expected to be forthcoming and receptive for a basing agreement because of the relatively strong presence of the Italian Communist Party, indicated to us that they would be willing to accept INF basing. With the Italian agreement, we were able to work harder on several other European allies to accept basing. We worked in particular for the Belgians and the Dutch to accept these systems. It was this type of process which also, then from the Dutch side, led to a second, parallel track. The first track would be the deployment track of the systems. But the second track would have to be, in the Dutch view (and this quickly became the general European view), a negotiating track, that is, we had to be able to offer to the Soviets a proposal that we would not deploy if they did certain things.

Creating a "Second Track" for an INF Decision

The primary requirement on our part was that the Soviets would have to withdraw, destroy, or severely limit their SS-20 missiles in some manner. This was not, by any matter, being spelled out at that juncture, but there was perceived a need to have a political negotiating track for the INF effort as well as a deployment track to counter the SS-20s on the ground. We also recognized that it would be easier to sell deployments to European populations if we deployed in the face of Soviet recalcitrance to negotiate meaningful agreement. The expectation was that the Soviets would not agree. I don't think anybody expected the Soviets to agree to anything. But for us to have a better and more effective political cover for our own deployments, the political track was regarded as vital.

The December 12th, 1979, Decision Meeting on INF Deployments

Q: Did you sense that this deployment was almost being forced on the Americans because of the SS-20s? Or were they saying, "I'm glad they did it because now we can put these things in?"

JONES: This was a curious ambivalence. Certainly at the beginning, in about 1976, we argued vigorously to the Europeans that we didn't need anything more to counter the Soviets. This was going to be an expensive exercise. Making these systems was not going to be cheap. At the same time, there were people within our own bureaucracy that wanted to deploy more effective modernized theater nuclear forces because of the problems that I explained a little bit earlier regarding what would happen if you used aircraft to provide your nuclear strikes. As a result, when these systems were being developed, there were certainly people in the United States that wanted to be able to deploy them, and deploy them fairly extensively, to give themselves, in their argument, a better ability to handle any conventional war that might evolve. At the same time, there were also people who saw these as better, more effective nuclear systems with far better guidance and accuracy. As a consequence, they viewed them as prospectively a lot more effective than the nuclear systems that we had in Europe at that time—old Pershing Is and only the aircraft that were able to deliver nuclear strikes at an intermediate range. As it evolved, it came to this more or less famous twelfth of December 1979 decision in which all of this effort was supposed to be brought together, and everybody was supposed to be agreed at that point and sign off on a deployment decision. This first group was the defense and foreign ministers meeting together at NATO for a Defense Planning Committee. It turned out to be perhaps the most chaotic meeting in which I was involved during my career. As it evolved, neither the Dutch nor the Belgians were finally agreed on their willingness to accept INF deployment.

Q: I assume before you had the meeting that they were supposed to be all on board.

JONES: Yes. Again, that was our expectation. We were having Special Group and High-Level Group meetings about once a month or once every other month as this evolved. Indeed, as far as I ever had the sense going into the meeting, we thought that it was ready to be endorsed.

Q: This meeting was in December 1979.

JONES: What happened at that meeting was that, without recalling the details precisely, both the Belgians and the Dutch were not as decided as we had believed them to be. There was enormous pressure put on them. Reg Bartholomew, who had become the head of the Special Group meeting, tells a story of how he had one of these senior foreign ministers in a corner and was pounding away at him, and somebody came up behind him and said, "Say, old chap, you really shouldn't be pushing him quite so hard. Let me." It was the British foreign minister, who wanted him to step to one side so he could hammer on the Dutch. This was a meeting that ran on and on and on. As a consequence, the special celebratory *vin d'honneur* planned for its end was never held.

For me, this date was particularly memorable because it was my fifteenth wedding anniversary. The very first thing in the morning, I got up early. I went to the store. I got chocolates, and then went to the airport to meet David Aaron; I met him at the airport at something like 7:00 a.m. in order to get back to this meeting. At the meeting itself, we then struggled for hours and hours and hours in this session. The meeting broke up sometime well past 8:30 p.m. in the evening with what they believed then to be agreement, and actually was sufficient agreement. Then I spent another two and a half hours or so writing my portions of reporting telegrams on this meeting, after which I liberated a bottle of champagne from this never-held *vin d'honneur*, took it home, and my wife and I had chocolates and champagne at 11:30 p.m. at night on our wedding anniversary.

But we did get enough of an agreement for it to go forward and to have it announced that we had an agreement for deployment. It was clearly designed to be one that would be held in conjunction with negotiating proposals that would be eventually created and eventually devised to work with the Soviets. That is how the INF agreement got started.

Starting to Implement the December 12 Decision—Refighting the Fights

From there on, for the rest of the time that I was at NATO until the summer of 1980, we worked on the evolution of the Special Group, which had then become the Special Consultative Group. We began and continued to design possible hypothetical proposals that could be made to the Soviets and how deployments would be arranged and in what timing sequences. We needed to determine our own deployments and how the agreed-upon new INF systems, the GLCMs and the Pershing IIs, would eventually be made. Likewise, we needed to agree on what countries would get them in what time frame, when they would arrive, what would arrive at different times, and which countries would be the first and the last to have deployments.

In each of these countries, there were deployment concerns. As years went by, the negotiations were very slow, and there were ruptures in the negotiations that were held eventually with the Soviets in Geneva; the negotiations were very complicated. There were efforts by the Soviets to come to some sort of an agreement to prevent U.S. deployments and, on the Allied side, to get parliamentary agreement in each one of the countries for the deployments. What you had on December 12, 1979, was a commitment to do so, but, as time passed, each of the countries involved had an election. These elections were fought at least partially on the fact of the existing commitment to accept INF deployments. Again, at each juncture, the Soviets and their sympathizers within the individual countries attempted to put enough pressure on the electorate or offer blandishments to effect a change of government, which would have reversed the NATO decision.

Q: It wasn't completely Soviets and their supporters, but also the indigenous socialist left-wing groups in Europe who just didn't like nuclear weapons.

JONES: I agree with you completely. These were members of the old left and members of the new left. When I said Soviet sympathizers, it means that to the extent that these people sympathized with the Soviets on this particular issue, I would say that they were Soviet sympathizers. Again, throughout this entire period, I was working simultaneously on some of these issues, both INF and the end of SALT II, which had concluded in early 1979. I provided a tiny little part of the drama by flying to Vienna to pick up the texts of the SALT II agreement and bringing them back to NATO for distribution. We needed to demonstrate the small degree to which they had anything to do with the Allies so that the Allies could see that the text of the agreements did not threaten their interests or NATO interests.

Q: Particularly seeing what the Soviets did in Afghanistan, did this change the equation about stiffening NATO, as far as accepting cruise missiles and Pershings and those sorts of things were concerned?

JONES: There was at least a momentary endorsement of the December 12 decision, which literally had been made only days earlier. The point was that over a period of time this stiffening softened and wore down. We had to refight the battle in every election campaign that was held in each of the prospective basing countries. At the same time, the Soviets had started in their discussions in Geneva to push for a variety of freezes and no deployments, which would leave them with very substantial numbers of SS-20s and us with nothing in the way of deployments. There were complicated proposals put forward that still would have left us with a handful of deployed INF systems, but we would not have equality with the Soviets—and that was also the bottom line on our proposals. Whether we built up to these ceilings or not, our agreements with the Soviets had to be based on equality in the way of deployments.

The "Mansfield Amendment" and Conventional Force Reductions

I also worked, and continued to work through 1980 when I departed, on MBFR (Mutual Balanced Force Reductions, that is, conventional force reductions) in Europe to match conceptually, at least, the nuclear reductions, about which we were steadily talking to the Soviets.

MBFR has now been lost from memory and is one of the failures of negotiating history. But for quite a number of years, it was a primary focus of our negotiations with the Soviets and, for that matter, with the Warsaw Pact as well. Since it dealt with conventional forces throughout Europe, we had a NATO—Warsaw Pact negotiation in Vienna. I vaguely remember it started in 1973. You can see that it had already been running for six years by the end of the 1970s. There also were elements of a nuclear package involved in these MBFR negotiations, a so-called Option 3, an option that would have withdrawn a certain number of nuclear weapons and reduced a certain number of aircraft and missile systems.

But, for me, for the most part, I was involved with the MBFR working group. This organization dealt more with technical studies that were being prepared for the negotiations for our side. Some of these negotiations lasted internally for more than a year. We worked on what was called the "Associated Measures Paper." That system and discussions of it within the Alliance ran for probably about a year and a half. I remember arranging a birthday party for the Associated Measures Paper at its one-year mark. The measures that were being discussed were those that were linked to what kind of an agreement you might have in the way of confidence building. They included notifications, types of inspection routines, what kind of inspections might be held, how they would be held.

We had another major study that was called a "Flank Security Paper." This was a special concern for the Nordics and of very special concern to the Turks, who were convinced for any number of reasons that, if the Soviets reached agreement on force reductions in central Europe, they would pull them back to threaten the northern and southern flanks. So the Turks and the Nordics, in particular, wanted codicils to any MBFR presentation that would guarantee that the Soviets did not simply reshuffle their forces and put them in positions that would create greater insecurity for Greece and Turkey, more prominently for Turkey, and, for Norway in particular, in the north.

Q: What was the attitude during this period? This was the Carter administration, which came in a little bit starry-eyed as far as thinking things could happen. At least this is my impression. Was there concern in NATO that the United States might not show sufficient will and be too interested in agreement?

JONES: Well, I've already gone through with you in some detail the associated elements of the neutron bomb fiasco. My feeling is that there was a spillover into extraordinary, convoluted, detailed discussions that literally went on for more than a year and a half on some of these papers and some of these studies. There was and had been for many years the feeling that MBFR's negotiations were really designed to prevent what were then called "Mansfield amendment reductions." Senator Mike Mansfield had, in effect, said, "If you don't reach agreement, we should withdraw forces." Partially to stave off the Mansfield amendment reductions, which would have been unilateral U.S. reductions, the United States and NATO started the MBFR negotiations to hold off congressional pressure to make unilateral force cuts.

Unilateral U.S. forces cuts would have been seen as an indication that we were losing a commitment to Europe, or stimulated Europeans not to build up their forces in response but to cut their forces as well. In theory, such reductions would have made all of Europe more vulnerable. On the one hand, Europe would be more vulnerable to a potential Soviet conventional attack; at the same time, force cuts might have made the prospect of a nuclear war in Europe more likely. If the Soviets had attempted a conventional attack, we would have been even less able to withstand a conventional attack, and we would have to respond with nuclear weapons sooner rather than later.

Admittedly there was also always the feeling that there was a good deal of a place-holding operation going on in Vienna to talk a great deal about these reductions without a true expectation that they would come to fruition. An analyst in INR named Robert Baraz, who since has died, used to think that we might find ourselves "out clevered" by the Russians by eventually presenting them with the proposal that we didn't expect would be accepted, but the Soviets would say, "Done." He used to put it this way: "If you stand in a shower bending over looking for the soap long enough, somebody is going to...." But that never happened with MBFR. MBFR, despite efforts by its U.S. negotiating leadership, which apparently took it more seriously than other people within the U.S. establishment, continued to flail vigorously during the late 1970s and 1980s.

Afghanistan and U.S. Hostages in Tehran—U.S. Attitudes

Q: We're talking about December 1979. Our embassy had been taken over in Iran. We were worried about that falling apart. And then there was the invasion of Afghanistan. I would have thought this would have stiffened the spine.

JONES: Well, we did immediately after the Soviet invasion of Afghanistan have a frenzy at NATO of senior people coming for consultations and a very high level of effort to determine what could be done and what we could do. This led to more sanctions being placed on the Soviets and an effort to take action to punish the Soviets. This was the stimulus to stop holding the 1980 Olympics. But in NATO, there was a sense of shock. We did not expect this type of action against Afghanistan. We believed that the Soviets had as much control over Afghanistan as they had any need or desire for; that we had been, in effect, pushed out of the competition in Afghanistan; and that we had lost the influence battle in Afghanistan to the Soviets. When the Soviets invaded, it was our sense that they would make rather short work of any Afghan resistance. We just didn't think that the Afghans would be able to hold up against them very long. Yes, there would be places in the Khyber Pass that nobody would be able to traverse in small military units or patrols, but, so far as actually controlling everything of Afghanistan that needed any controlling, the Soviets wouldn't have any trouble doing that.

At the same time, we were also extremely incensed about what had happened in Iran. Of course, as diplomats, we felt even more angry that these were our people who had been seized, were being held, and that nothing was going on to release them. We felt that nothing was being accomplished, that we were acting weak. I personally felt that we should make far stronger threats against Iran to force the return of our people under whatever circumstances were necessary to get them back. I felt that all we were doing in the long-delayed exercise over our captured hostage diplomats was to set up a circumstance where the same kind of incident would happen again, and again, and again. We were unable to respond effectively. Then when we attempted and failed in Desert One actually to accomplish something, it was even less happy an outcome.

A Personal Sidebar

Before I came to talk to you, I thought I was going to have more time to prepare for this than I did in reading my diaries for the era. I got my diary from 1977. What I remember from reading this material is that a lot of it is just strictly personal. Our third child was born at NATO. Our twins were about eight years old. There are events of that nature. But looking at it in retrospect, I see again the appalling hours which we worked, where regularly I was at the USNATO Mission until 9:00 p.m. and it was early when I left at 6:30 p.m. We worked every Saturday at least half a day. The relentless pace of this work was completely and totally exhausting.

I have to say that it was one of these situations where I was in my mid-thirties and by the end of the first year, I was beginning to think I was an old man. The only way I realized how totally exhausting the pace was came when I went to the States for two weeks for an Army reserve tour and worked from 8:00 a.m. until 5:00 p.m.—and found that I had incredible amounts of energy. I went out and saw my friends, and we went to dinners. I had all sorts of energy. I recognized then that it wasn't that I was getting old at thirty-five. It was that NATO was so all consuming, so totally exhausting, so completely engaging, that there was virtually nothing left of any of us at the end of a given working day. To have anything left over for family, for personal life, for much of anything except sleep was rarely possible.

CHAPTER 27

A New Area and a New Problem: Cyprus

Q: In the summer of 1980, where did you go?

JONES: I ended my assignment at NATO and went to the Cyprus desk. This was an assignment that had turned up almost at the last minute. I didn't get the assignment until May. There had been various other assignments that had looked as if they were possibilities or more like actualities, but they didn't turn out to be that way. It was probably the influence of Allen Holmes that got me the job as the Cyprus desk officer over an individual who would have been the initial choice of the Southern European office director. I became the Cyprus desk officer in the summer of 1980.

Q: You did that until when?

JONES: Until the summer of 1982. It was a standard two-year desk officer assignment.

Reviewing the Bidding: Greeks and Turks and Turks and Greeks

Q: This was one of the points of contention in the world at that time. What was the situation vis-à-vis Cyprus when you arrived there? I'm sure this had been off to one side and was one of those minor annoyances when you were in NATO.

JONES: Yes. This was a constant neuralgic problem at NATO. The Greeks and Turks simply could not come to an agreement on virtually anything, but, by and large, we were able to keep the problem confined. It started far, far back in history. You can start centuries ago, but you can really start in 1974.

Q: *July 14, 1974.*

JONES: Yes. The Turkish troops moved in to Northern Cyprus and occupied a very substantial portion of the country.

Q: *After a Greek effort to take over the island themselves.*

JONES: Correct, this effort was led by a very hard-line, right-wing leader, Nikos Sampson, who would have been supported by what was then also a Greek military dictatorship. During the same period, the island had been only very tenuously under control for many years. There had been decades of rioting, decades of Greek Cypriot pressure on Turkish Cypriots, who were a minority of the population. During the period from the late 1960s through the early 1970s, the Turkish Cypriots were pretty much pushed out of any political influence within the Cypriot government and very marginalized in Cypriot society. It was a period in which, I would say, the Greek Cypriots had overwhelming control of the island, its politics, its economy, and the society.

However, when the Greek Cypriot right-wing leader attempted what was a coup, the Turkish government landed troops to prevent it from happening, and you had a vast refugee flow, which now would be called ethnic cleansing. At the end of these exchanges of population, there were virtually no Greek Cypriots in the northern half of the island and no Turkish Cypriots in the southern part of the island. In 1980, this was still a relatively fresh circumstance. There had been a steady assortment of peace plan proposals of one sort or another designed to end this separation and generate a new government, create a new governing structure, secure the withdrawal of the Turkish military forces, and mend the breach between the Greek government and the Turkish government. These bilateral relations, while never particularly good, had gotten particularly bad since 1974, to the extent that it was impossible to reach agreement on topics such as the Defense Planning Questionnaire at NATO, which gives

NATO authorization for force deployments and the circumstances for each country's armed services.

You had endless arguments over where Greek and Turkish forces could legally be located. There were arguments over whether there would be any implicit recognition of these forces if they were included in a NATO document (with the Turks always claiming that their forces on such and such islands were NATO-committed, and the Greeks contending that these islands were not Turkish but Greek islands). It's been a situation that has never been resolved.

Peace Efforts: Seeking an Answer to the Cyprus Problem

Q: What was the feeling when you took it over? You hadn't been dealing with it before. From our point of view, okay, we had to make noises, particularly because of the Greek lobby and all, but essentially it was pretty much a done deal. The Turks were on this side to the north and the Greek Cypriots on that side. Efforts made to allow the two groups to get back together again were something you had to do politically, but it just wasn't going to happen at least in the near future. How did you feel about it?

JONES: I used to say years later that you had to change Cyprus desk officers at least every two years. Otherwise, you got to the situation where your officer had seen it all, knew that nothing would ever work, and refused to believe that anything could work. Therefore, you needed a new Cyprus desk officer every other year who would come in with a fresh view, new hope, new inspiration, and an effort to resolve the problem.

No, in 1980, there was still a feeling that something could be done, partly because at that juncture people looked at the Middle East and said, "Oh, my God, we will never, ever, ever be able to solve the Arab-Israeli problem. We just can't. The Arab-Israeli problem is impossible. Is there anything easier?" Then they looked at Cyprus and said, "That looks easy in comparison." Cyprus *is* an easy problem. It's something that any student in Political Science 101 could sit down and draw up an equitable, honest, fair, workable Cyprus agreement. The only problem is that it would have to be accepted by the Greek and Turkish Cypriots, neither one of whom would trust the other under any circumstances. They have just had too long, too hard, too difficult a communal relationship where the problems were so intense, the rioting was so frequent, the unease (certainly on the part of the Turkish Cypriots) so persistent that any kind of an agreement that could be sold to the Turkish Cypriots would have to have included guarantees and almost admissions of guilt on the part of the Greek Cypriots for their actions in previous years. This proved to be impossible for any Greek Cypriot government to accept.

When I say that we were hopeful about solving it, indeed we were hopeful. Two years earlier, we had made a relatively serious proposal, the details of which now escape me, but it had atmospherics—people thought it was a proposal that if the Cypriots, and these are the Cypriots talking about its merits, had been a little less doctrinaire, it would fall into the range of the possible. That's the way that people were still looking at the Cyprus problem. The then head of the Southern European Affairs Office (EUR/SE), Ed Dillery, had been the deputy chief of mission in Cyprus. He never left me with the impression that this was an impossible problem for which we were just going through the motions.

I, on the other hand, coming to this with absolutely no knowledge of it, said at the very beginning, "Well, we give so much in the way of military support to the Turks, we ought to be able to put real pressure on them." Ed was very polite to me in saying, in so many words, "Well, Dave, it's not quite that easy." I listened to him, but it took me some while to understand why it was not so easy. In effect, the Turks were people willing to cut off their nose to spite their faces, and we had larger equities in dealing with the Turks than Cyprus.

For example, how were we going to retain a Turkish bulwark in the Middle East in a very unpleasant neighborhood, and particularly maintain defense against the Soviets? Damaging the Turks economically, militarily, and consequently politically for the benefit of the Cypriots didn't seem to have a great deal of logic behind it. You might be making a major effort to sacrifice a whale in order to benefit a sardine. It didn't mean that people were not interested in benefiting the sardine. Nor was it just something about which ambitious people who looked at the Cyprus problem said, "Well, there is a Nobel Peace Prize for the person who can solve it." In comparison with the Middle East, it was a lot more solvable a problem because the logic of it looked so clear. You really ought to be able to construct a bicameral legislature with guaranteed seats and guaranteed this and that, with a continued United Nations presence, and with a good deal of economic assistance to each side to buy an agreement. This was what the USG [U.S. government] and other officials were attempting to do. This is what I was involved in for about two years.

One level of this effort was an exercise stimulated by the British with us and through the United Nations. We had the British come to us and say, "We think there is a window of opportunity this year." This was in late 1980; the judgment was based on who happened to be in power at which time. They said that they, the British, would not hesitate to put a lot of pressure on the Cypriots to come to some sort of agreement if we, the Americans, would put a comparable amount of pressure on Ankara to tell the Turkish Cypriots that they had to agree.

UN Special Representative Hugo Gobbi

At that point, there was a newly appointed special representative of the UN secretary general for Cyprus. He was a former Argentine foreign minister, Hugo Gobbi. This man was indeed vigorous, energetic, intelligent, and dynamic. He started shuttling back and forth to Cyprus to offer various proposals under various circumstances, efforts to create patterns of land management that would result in reductions of occupied territory. Proposals included the amount of ground that the Turkish Cypriots and Turkish forces had seized and perhaps bringing Famagusta, a captured city that was an absolutely magnificent potential tourist spot, back into service. This also was at a time when the hotels that had been abandoned still had the possibility of being rehabilitated, being brought back into economic life relatively quickly. It had only been six years since they had been abandoned. While they had been damaged and there had been deterioration, the feeling was that there was an incentive of hundreds of millions of dollars in property that could be brought back into use. The thought was that perhaps the Greek Cypriots would be willing to make certain concessions to the Turkish Cypriots if the first thing that they did was withdraw from this particular city, which wasn't really being used. It was abandoned and was cordoned off with barbed wire, guards, and the rest of a security infrastructure around it. Gobbi went back and forth and was incredibly vigorous and innovative. We thought he was quite credible. We discussed his efforts with one of the leading political appointee figures in the UN, Brian Urquhart. We were talking enthusiastically about the prospects for what Gobbi was trying to do. I'll never forget his line: "Yes, I, too, think Gobbi can walk on water, but I wish he would start at the shallow end."

The Advent of the Special Cyprus Coordinator, Reg Bartholomew

What happened is that after a more than substantial amount of effort on the part of Gobbi and indications of progress and then indications of less progress, it just kept going in circles without a great deal of anything happening. We then had a change of administrations. With the change of administration at the end of 1980, beginning of 1981, Al Haig was appointed as secretary of state. You also had Larry Eagleburger, who then became undersecretary for political affairs. Eagleburger had a long professional association with Reg Bartholomew, who was his deputy or his colleague at the Department of Defense [DOD] and elsewhere in different positions within the Department of State and at the NSC. At the end of 1980, with the termination of the Carter administration, Bartholomew was removed from being director of the PM Bureau [Bureau of Political-Military Affairs] and, as a result, also from being head of the NATO SCG. He was replaced. But the question then was what they were going to do with Bartholomew? Ultimately, he was retrieved from studying German, where he had been sitting in the Foreign Service Institute, waiting to do something. Eagleburger had gone forth looking, ostensibly on Haig's behalf, for a "very special person" to be the Cyprus negotiator. Various names had floated up and been batted down. Finally, Bartholomew's name came to the fore. Bartholomew was nominated as the special Cyprus representative.

This was an interesting appointment. I then became Bartholomew's support person for this entire exercise. I remember telling Bartholomew that I was not all of PM, that I was not even all of EUR/SE, but I was all he had. Bartholomew proved able to perform very adroitly in this position against the expectations of almost everyone who saw him get the job. Bartholomew had no background in the area, and his reputation had been one of an individual who always tried to get an agreement, pushed extremely hard to get agreements, and was extremely active in so doing. As a result, we expected that he would create trouble rather than resolve trouble. But instead, Bartholomew appreciated the limits of the possible and recognized that the special Cyprus representative was indeed more of a place-holding exercise to respond to Greek-American and Cypriot-American concerns, and he would do his best to find out what could be done and do that whenever possible. But he did not try to generate negotiations, agreement for its own sake, or just to generate dust in order to say that he was in command of the whirlwind. What he did for a period of approximately a year was to travel regularly to the United Nations, travel to London, travel to Cyprus, and talk to the senior people on all sides, attempting to find out whether there was any leeway for serious negotiations, and whether there were any prospects for arrangements that would fall into an acceptable category.

Raul Denktash and Why Not to Make a Deal

I went along on all of these meetings, saw a number of these people, and came to the conclusion that there was simply too intense a level of suspicion. The Turkish Cypriots were led by Raul Denktash, who was their "president" and was probably the smartest person in the group. He realized that the Turkish Cypriot community was significantly weaker than the Greek Cypriot community in virtually every way—socially, politically, and economically—and an integrated Cyprus would mean that within a relatively short period Cyprus would be completely dominated by the Greek Cypriots. He thus always found ways, reasons, and rationales to make sure that progress was as limited as it could be.

The Greek Cypriots would have had to make a deal to which no one could say no. That is, they would have had to make a tremendous offer, an offer that was so obviously so generously designed to heal the differences, that they might have been able to reach across Denktash to the rest of the Turkish Cypriot population to prompt acceptance of such an agreement. The Greek Cypriots weren't willing to make that kind of an offer, at least partially because they continued to hold the moral high ground. Their country was the one that had been invaded. It was the Turks who were the occupying force. It was the Greek Cypriots who continued to have all levels of international recognition. It was they who could take the issue to the United Nations on a year-to-year basis and get a resolution denouncing Turkey and Turkish action. It was they who were prospering economically and they who would have to make the admissions of guilt or error and give up substantial elements of their own power and authority to get an agreement that would reunite Cyprus. In my view, they never thought it was worthwhile. It was far more pleasant to be able to belabor the terrible Turks than it was to make the hard compromises that would have been necessary to reach agreement.

Greek Cypriots: Clerides and Kyprianou

Q: What about Clerides, who was the other Siamese twin? Denktash and Clerides had been dancing around forever on that small island.

JONES: At the time, Clerides was in opposition. It was Kyprianou who was in power. None of these people ever die or go away. They are all still there. Kyprianou, Clerides, Rolandis, and Denktash have been the major figures in Cyprus politics for about thirty-five years.

Q: They all went to high school together or something like that.

JONES: There is the intimation that they all know each other perhaps too well. The only one of the Cypriot leaders who was prominent in the 1960s who had died was Archbishop Makarios. But all the rest of them continue now, older and older, to play exactly the same kind of games with one another. They used to say about Kyprianou that he could only have one toilet facility in his home because if he had two, he would have terrible accidents because he was never able to make a decision.

Kyprianou at the time was also apparently having a variety of mental-*cum*-physical problems. As a consequence, no one found him particularly reliable as an interlocutor. They just didn't think that they would be able to get agreement out of Kyprianou. You were also at the point where Andreas Papandreou was about to return to power in Greece. Consequently, again, it was harder and harder to reach agreement or any expectation that there would be agreement between the Greeks and Turks that would make it possible to come to an overall agreement on Cyprus.

Congressional Interest in Cyprus— An Illustration of U.S. Domestic Politics

Q: How did you find Congress? I went to a meeting one time of American Greek Cypriots. They had the usual run of congressmen and senators of Greek ancestry talking about "twenty-five years of Turkish tyranny on Cyprus." That was the title of the thing. They seemed to be completely oblivious to the fact of what precipitated this whole thing. That was the attempt to take over the whole island. How did you find dealing with Congress? Was this just a burden?

JONES: Congress was certainly part of the equation. I have said a number of times that if there were as many Turkish Americans in the United States as there are Greek Americans in the United States, we would probably have a more balanced policy on Greek-Turkish-Cypriot relations. But as a consequence of the Turkish occupation of northern Cyprus, you had a situation in Congress that initially had led to the embargo on arms to Turkey. This was a serious problem that was resolved only very slowly over a number of years, when we found that we simply couldn't influence the Turks, and we were not only damaging our relations with the Turks but making it easier for the Soviets to gain traction in Turkey.

One of the projects with which I was involved was yet another sop to Congress. Every sixty days, the Department of State had to prepare a report on Cyprus. Every sixty days, your Cyprus desk officer ground out a report addressing what issues had come up and how we were working to resolve this problem. Ultimately, it became pretty formulaic. But, nevertheless, this was something that in its inception, which was close to the time when I was on the desk, was being addressed reasonably seriously as a report that we had promised to Congress and were producing.

Student Scholarship Programs

We were also still giving economic assistance to Cyprus, for which, in all reasonable terms of what was required for a country's development, it had no need at all. It was a relatively nominal sum; I remember about $15 million. It was nickels and dimes, but first it was supposed to be directed to relief for the refugees. But when you went and saw the level at which the "refugees" were living at the end of six years, they weren't living badly at all. These were not people who were in tents or suffering any substantial privation. Finally, they moved to create a scholarship fund that was designed and it may still be continuing—I'm not sure—to use the money that was involved in this funding (or perhaps it was half of it)—to generate a scholarship fund that would bring Cypriots to study in the United States.

Q: Anything for Turkish students?

JONES: This was Cypriot students at large. I assume that there was at least the option that Turkish Cypriot students could apply. I think there were some who did. I don't think it was run through the U.S. government. I remember it being run through something like the Fulbright Commission on Cyprus, an organization of this nature.

The Missing—Politics and Personal Anguish

Another problem with which I was involved was missing persons. During 1974 and during the Turkish occupation of the North, a number of people disappeared. One of these was a young American Cypriot who had disappeared. We spent a great deal of time pressing for information on these individuals. To address the problem of missing persons, they also slowly created a set of intercommunal talks between Greek and Turkish Cypriots. This, too, was about as convoluted and disputational as you can imagine over matters such as which lists would be exchanged under what circumstances, what information would be provided about people, and how you would talk about the cases. There were Turkish Cypriots as well as Greek Cypriots who were missing, which required balance in the discussions.

Q: By that time, I assume that everyone was assuming that these people were all dead.

JONES: Let's say everyone who didn't have a vested personal interest in it or a political reason to keep the issue alive assumed they were dead. The leader of the Turkish Cypriots had declared all of the missing Turkish Cypriots to be dead, in order, he said, that the families could get on with their lives. But for the Greek Cypriots, it was a different case. The fact that there were missing persons always generated reports in the same way that our Vietnam POWs [prisoners of war] and Missing in Action have generated reports for the last twenty-five years. The Greek Cypriots would find or hear some intimation of somebody who was being held in a Turkish prison—never in Turkish Cyprus. There would be reports that they were holding some poor Greek Cypriot. As a consequence, you had regular reports—I won't say "orchestrated" because it's unfair to say that someone's grief is orchestrated—but I might suggest that individuals whose husbands, fathers, sons, or brothers were missing were exploited by propaganda in Greek Cyprus. The point, of course, was to keep the issue of Turkish barbarity and excess, and the image of the "terrible Turk," as alive as it possibly could be.

At that point, you could hypothesize, at the six—or seven-year mark, vaguely that one or two of the younger people might still be alive. You couldn't automatically discount the fact that, well, here is a report. The report recounts that somebody said, or somebody heard, or somebody saw, or somebody listened to an individual who said they were somebody of that nation. So, among other issues, we talked to the Turkish Cypriots about this problem, particularly about the American Greek Cypriots. We were told bluntly that Denktash personally had gone looking to try to resolve some of these specific issues. He was told, and told us, that there wasn't going to be any answer, no answer that would be satisfactory to us. In effect, implicitly, he told us that they were indeed all dead. But this did not mean that you were not going to have these extended discussions and intercommunal talks.

Of course, the next spinoff would be, "Well, if they're dead, if you think they're dead, or if you believe they're dead, where are they? We want the bodies back." Then, of course, where would the bodies be and under what circumstances would they have died? Would this provide additional opportunity to charge the Turks with atrocities of one sort or another? For that matter, there were people who just threw up their hands in confusion. They said that some of these people undoubtedly were killed during the coup, Greek Cypriots and Turkish Cypriots. They didn't know what happened to them. Were they killed? Were they buried secretly somewhere? Was somebody particularly outrageous or obnoxious and killed for that reason? Did they haul them away from their northern Cyprus homes, push them into a ravine, and shoot them full of holes? It's certainly possible. What you're talking about was significantly fewer than one hundred people. I remember twenty-five to seventy-five. It didn't mean that the individual tragedy wasn't as vital as if it were 775 or 75,000. Nevertheless, in absolute terms, the numbers of missing people were really pretty low. But that didn't mean that the intensity of the discussion was not very, very high.

Turkish Military Coup

Q: Was the Turkish military arms embargo still on when you were there?

JONES: The arms embargo had been lifted by Carter. At this point, you also had the Turkish military coup in October 1980. At that juncture, where there had been tremendous societal upset, rioting, terrorism, and great turmoil within Turkey, the military moved to throw out the civilian government and impose order, which they did quite effectively. We as a government had no real objection to this action. I think we made a few *pro forma* statements about the role of democracy and the need to have free elections and comments of that nature. But neither the Carter government at the time nor the subsequent Haig—secretary of state—Reagan government had any real problem with the fact that the Turkish government had moved in this manner to secure order. There was always the concern that a destabilized Turkey could go communist.

CHAPTER 28

Preserving Our Bases in Greece—Once More with Bartholomew

Q: After two years of doing this and you've run out of every option you could think of with these implacable antagonists, what did you do?

JONES: I moved on with Bartholomew. He became the Greek base negotiator. The issues involved regarding our bases in Greece were based on a long-standing agreement with the Greeks for our defense and economic cooperation. This was an agreement that was virtually not able to be cancelled. It was tied to Greek participation in NATO and it was, as a consequence, an agreement that was very satisfactory for the United States. We did not care whether it was changed or not. But with a Papandreou government, there was a fresh impetus on the part of the Greeks to force a new agreement with us. At the same time, prior to Papandreou's victory, there had been regular efforts on our part with previous Greek governments to have a revised DECA [defense and economic cooperation agreement]. But the pre-Papandreou government, a conservative government . . .

Greek President Karamanlis

Q: Karamanlis?

JONES: Karamanlis was the president at the time. They were never able to decide whether the revised status of forces agreement(SOFA) and the defense economic cooperation agreement(DECA) with the United States were supposed to be new agreements or were supposed to be a device to win reelection for them—in other words, a mechanism that would show that they had gotten the better of the Americans. This had to be a deal to show they had gotten tremendous benefit from the Americans. That they had gotten a deal that would balance off the perception that the Americans favored Turks over Greeks and, therefore, would justify the reelection of the conservative government in Greece. Consequently, there was an extended set of negotiations around 1980 led by the ambassador on the spot, Robert McCloskey, with a support team essentially led out of the embassy. This support team struggled heroically with the Greeks for months and months and eventually failed. The effort failed.

The Base Negotiations and Their Issues

Q: Greek base negotiations—we've talked about the background. Can you talk about what were the issues? What were the particular points that you had to deal with in 1982, and how did you and Bartholomew operate?

JONES: We had had this long-standing relationship with the Greeks with a basing agreement which, very much in our interests, was tied to the duration of Greek participation within NATO. There was no terminal date for the U.S.-Greek base negotiations agreement. That meant that when we had had previous rounds of negotiations and discussions, if they failed, it was no skin off our teeth. The status quo continued unless the Greeks chose to interrupt their relationship with NATO. Obviously, that action wasn't in their interest, because NATO was viewed by the Greeks as one of their shields against the Turks. They were by and large hung up on how they could get a better agreement with us without having to damage their relationship within NATO.

The previous conservative governments had looked at the base negotiations and their long-standing agreement with the United States as also a domestic political problem with Papandreou and his socialists, PASOK [Panhellenic Socialist Movement]. They were involved in constant criticism of the Greek government and the United States regarding these bases, and the government for maintaining the relationship.

Why PASOK?

What happened was that the Greek conservatives were always at sixes and sevens as to how they would come to any new arrangement with the United States. For an extended stretch of time, they tried to find an agreement, and there was a set of negotiations in 1980 that ultimately failed. With these negotiations, the conservatives were trying to find a defense support and assistance package that would be large enough for them to say to the population, "Well, we won the negotiations, and now you should reelect us." But they were never able to find a package that they considered large and secure enough for them to say that they had won the negotiations and be able to take it to the population and into an election. As a consequence, when they finally were forced by the parliamentary term limits to hold the elections, they lost.

Bartholomew and the Base Negotiations: A Tour de Force

So here we had PASOK and the socialists in power. That was not perceived or expected to be a lot of fun. Papandreou was even more pointedly hostile to us at that juncture than he was in later years, reflecting his belief that the United States had connived with the colonels to oust the previous Greek government and had particularly been hostile to him while he was in opposition. But, nevertheless, there was renewed pressure for a new set of Greek base negotiations. This led to a requirement for a lead negotiator. Bartholomew, who had been the Special Cyprus Coordinator, was tagged to be the Greek base negotiator. This was no special accolade or special privilege for Bartholomew. In effect, he was given a set of negotiations that were expected to fail. First of all, we didn't think we would be able to come to a successful arrangement with PASOK or to an agreement that the Greek socialists would let us have; and second, we didn't give a damn whether they failed or not. If they failed or didn't come to an agreement, the status quo simply continued.

But Bartholomew went about the preparations for it in a very sophisticated way. For this I accord him a great deal of respect. What he did was to start at the very beginning. He pulled out all of the documentation and material that we had available on the previous round and went through these inch-by-inch and line-by-line. He then went and co-opted, or at least neutralized, prospective Defense Department and Joint Chiefs of Staff concerns. He worked very carefully on this approach, making it clear at all levels that the State Department wasn't going to negotiate away their bases, which was their implicit thought. DOD/JCS suspected that any time you put State Department officials in a room with foreigners, the State Department will give away the store and just do anything to get an agreement. Well, Bartholomew was probably better placed than many people to counter this attitude because he had spent time at Defense. He had headed the Political-Military Bureau. He had some very substantial senior-level support in the State Department, specifically Larry Eagleburger, who at that time was the under secretary for political affairs and who was backing Bartholomew from that position. Bartholomew met with all of the concerned agencies. In this case, it was the NSA [National Security Agency], the Joint Chiefs of Staff, and the DOD, to discuss in very substantial detail what they wanted and how they wanted to go about it. One of the little litanies that he constantly reiterated was, "We want to know what you want because you're going to have to live with this agreement." This preparation and this transition period took much of the fall of 1982.

Switching Special Cyprus Coordinators: Chris Chapman Takes Over.

Simultaneously, Bartholomew was transitioning from being the Special Cyprus Coordinator, where I was his support person, and transitioning into being the Greek base negotiator. There were a number of trips to New York to wind up his activities as Special Cyprus Coordinator and hand off these responsibilities to Chris Chapman, who previously had been the DCM in Paris and was almost assassinated while there. Chapman's terminal assignment at the department was as the Special Cyprus Coordinator.

I continued to transition from being the Cyprus desk officer while helping Bartholomew get ready for this Greek base exercise.

There were interesting administrative elements to it. It showed another side to Bartholomew, one that was particularly interested in pomp and ceremony. Instead of just grabbing a room and a desk and a secretary and starting away on it, he spent a substantial amount of time getting special quarters arranged for him, for example, carpeting and furniture were requisitioned that reflected in his position his status as the U.S.-Greek base negotiator. The hypothesis for this approach was that he anticipated perhaps having rounds with the Greeks in Washington for these negotiations or meeting senior Greek authorities in these offices. This was the rationale behind it. He also worked vigorously to assure that he had a very extensive and full travel budget and a large representational budget. He really worked much harder than I've seen other Foreign Service officers work to secure these perks, although I'm sure it's not unique. But he worked very hard on the amenities and the trappings that he perceived were appropriate for this particular assignment. Actually, it was the first time that Bartholomew ranked as an ambassador, even though this was a special ambassadorship. But this was the first time that he had the personal rank of ambassador. He had seen all of these privileges associated with the rank, and he wanted to be very sure that he had them all.

I won't say that he went down an itemized checklist, but he certainly must have had a mental checklist on how this was to be done. I, working as his executive officer, spent a fair amount of time with the executive office (EX) in EUR to get it done. What was interesting also was that they gave it to him. That result was, as much as anything, an illustration that Bartholomew really did have seventh-floor backing at a level that I wasn't able to appreciate as simply a midlevel officer. He had authority to fly business class or first class on his flights to Europe. He had authority to use military air. The latter wasn't very hard to secure, but the first class or business class travel was relatively unique almost twenty years ago.

Our Bases in Greece: An Individual Assessment

The preparations in Washington included a great deal of detailed review of the previous set of negotiations and obtaining some sense for what was still available in forms of military assistance that could be packaged and offered to the Greek government. It was also a period when we looked at each of the bases; we reviewed each base, as we needed to know in more detail what each did and how each functioned.

There were four bases. Two were within the Athens vicinity proper. One was Hellenikon, which was the military half of the Athens civilian airfield. Essentially, it would be as if the British government had half of National Airport. A second was a naval communications in the suburbs called

Nea Makri, which also had a variety of special communications elements attached to, subordinated to, and incorporated within the facility. Then there were two facilities on Crete. One was a gigantic facility at Heraklion. The other was a combined U.S. and NATO facility at Suda Bay. The facility at Heraklion, since it's now been dismantled, can be identified openly as a very sophisticated and extremely useful electronic intercept site. The facility at Suda Bay was a combined facility with NATO, but it had a variety of important supplies prepositioned there. It is a very good harbor and an excellent overall naval facility.

Proper Prior Preparation Prevents . . .

We started our first round of negotiations leaving Washington on October 20, 1982. Demonstrating just how sharp Bartholomew was on this topic, instead of going to Athens directly, he went to the major military commands in Europe. We had started in Washington having seen senior people within the DOD. He met with Frank Carlucci, who was then Deputy Secretary of Defense. He met with Richard Perle and talked to him extensively. He talked to senior people within the Joint Chiefs of Staff. I believe that he spoke to General Lincoln, who was head of NSA at that time. The NSA was our intelligence intercept and decoding facility. Each one of these organizations pretty much designated a senior, trusted point of contact for Bartholomew: with John Monroe at NSA; Jim Hinds, an army colonel in the DOD; and Dwight Beech, an Army lieutenant colonel on the Joint Chiefs of Staff who was also an Army expert on Greek issues, a foreign area officer. Beech had had previous assignments in Athens, and was a Greek language officer as well as being the representative from the Joint Chiefs of Staff on our team. Beech was also a substantive expert on Greece and Greeks, while none of the rest of us had had any specific experience with Greece *per se*, although Bartholomew and I had worked on Cyprus, and you can't work on Cyprus without working on Greece and Turkey.

The preparation effort was extensive. We went first to Frankfurt. At that point, we were at USEUCOM [U.S. European Command] and had discussions with their senior generals. General Patch was the head of that command. Bartholomew reviewed all our objectives for reaching an agreement with the Greeks, but not an agreement that was unsatisfactory to the defense operations. We then flew back to London and had an extended session with the chief of U.S. Naval Forces Europe. After that, we flew once again to Germany, had more discussions within Germany, and finally flew on to Athens.

The Negotiations: A Unique Approach

At the end of October (October 27), we had what turned out to be really the only full formal negotiation opening with the Greek negotiating team. Here again, to preface the way the negotiations developed, there was a very distinct decision on Bartholomew's part to hold a different kind of negotiation. Instead of having full negotiating teams with spinoffs for subgroups, Bartholomew elected to do it alone. He had the DCM in our Athens embassy, Alan Berlind, along with him partially as his note taker and partially as his expert on Greece. But for the many, many meetings that followed this one, which were held with the Greek Deputy Foreign Minister Yanis Kapsis, Bartholomew pursued the approaches to the discussions himself.

That approach led to a number of bureaucratic pullings and haulings, particularly within the embassy in Athens. Here, too, Bartholomew elected an approach that I can only describe as different. He set up the DECA team as specifically separate from and literally gated off from the rest of the embassy. We were within the embassy, but we were within a suite of rooms that had been vacated for our purposes, with a locked gate barring entry to all except those of us who had the combination for it. While there was one member of the embassy staff, the political-military officer, Peter Collins, who was part of our group, the rest of the embassy was assiduously excluded. It was a unique circumstance where they were not permitted to see our traffic or read our incoming or outgoing messages. We did not brief anybody other than the DCM and the ambassador; and Ambassador Monteagle Stearns pretty much held himself apart from these negotiations.

Stearns, I think, believed that these negotiations would fail and that they would turn to him again to pick up the pieces since the previous ambassador had failed. Stearns wanted to keep clean hands regarding this exercise, where they would let Bartholomew do his thing until it didn't work out, and then Stearns and the embassy would be able to put up their hand and say, "Your special negotiator from Washington came and did his thing and it didn't work. What that demonstrates is that the resident ambassador should be the negotiator for these kinds of negotiations."

Concepts for Base Negotiations

This also illustrates one of the underlying questions of how to manage one of these special negotiations: Do you do it with the embassy team, which is expected to be expert, coherent, and well plugged-in, but perhaps too close to the government, having other fish to fry, with the government having other points of leverage that can be applied to them implicitly if not explicitly? Or do you do it with a special team from Washington that has nothing to win or lose except the negotiations, but presumably lacks the substantive expertise on the intricacies of the country involved?

In this case, it was the Greeks, their history, the issues in play, and perhaps such a team wouldn't be supple enough to recognize ploys being presented by the other side, or perhaps not able or interested in making the implicit or explicit trade-offs with other issues that might be in play in the bilateral relationship. That was one of the issues that U.S. foreign policy faced during the early 1980s, when the USG was doing base negotiations. Indeed, there was an assortment of such negotiations that played out in different ways.

We had them in Greece first, then subsequently under Bartholomew as ambassador in Spain. We had them in Spain, where he reversed his own position and decided that "where you sit is where you stand," and actually he had a hell of a difficult time as the negotiator for the Spanish base agreement while simultaneously being the U.S. ambassador. There are people who feel that he lost this time. You had another one for the Azores in which, in effect, we did send something of a special team to negotiate in the Azores. But, what we came down to was asking ourselves what seemed to be best on each one of the agreements. This also was true of the Turkish base negotiating effort. We had a different approach. It worked differently for each issue; on each base negotiation, there were different sets of tensions. In this instance, by sending the special team from Washington, we had created what was, if not a first, at least a first in dealing with the Greeks. We had had one fully failed negotiating round previously, and there had been earlier, abortive efforts to reach agreements with the Greeks, which simply didn't work out. But this effort by Bartholomew, in this manner, was designed to try something new.

But What Did PASOK Want?

Q: What was the reading when you got there on Papandreou and PASOK? What did they really want?

JONES: This became one of the ongoing exercises in speculation and analysis. We certainly knew that PASOK was hardly friendly to the United States. PASOK and Papandreou were continuing to be cozy with the Libyans at a time when we certainly were far more hostile to Qaddafi and the Libyans than the Greeks were acting. It was the Greeks who were more pointedly difficult with the Turks than we thought necessary, at a juncture when we thought perhaps there were chances to reach agreements to lessen tensions with the Turks. But this objective was not on the Greek agenda. This was true bilaterally with the Turks, trilaterally through Cyprus, and multilaterally in NATO, as well as directly bilaterally with the United States. As a consequence, there were things that Papandreou wanted from the United States, benefits such as a presidential invitation to visit, that he never got.

But what did they want as an agreement? We thought that they wanted at least some of the bases eliminated. That would be their great victory, that they would remove specific bases from Greece. One of the most obvious was Hellenikon. It was a flashpoint at all times for demonstrations. The Greek Communist Party, which stood even further to the left than PASOK, stimulated demonstrations. There were endless labor fights associated with specific individuals and specific elements of the union that operated on Hellenikon. It was a highly visible U.S. presence in a country that wasn't terribly thrilled with us. That led to constant tension—tension that PASOK was quite happy to exacerbate on a regular basis. If they could make us uncomfortable in Hellenikon, if they could push us into a position where we would conclude that we were better off doing what we were doing in Hellenikon someplace else, we could have been manipulated and nudged into giving up our position in Hellenikon. This possibility was also in play because we also flew major important missions out of Hellenikon that were a fairly obvious kind of flight.

Q: But wasn't the other shoe that we kept saying, "Okay, we understand your problem with us and we're not that happy with you. We have our friends the

Turks over here who will probably do better by us." *Anything that we do for the Turks is a negative, as far as any Greek government is concerned.*

JONES: You're right, and this was one of our counterstatements. Bartholomew would regularly say, "We don't stay where we're not wanted. We assume that this agreement is beneficial to you," and note the various things that we were doing bilaterally and multilaterally in the way of military support and assistance. Nevertheless, trying to use the Turks against the Greeks has its downsides as well. My aphorism is "The more you deal with the Greeks, the more you like the Turks. The more you deal with the Turks, the better the Greeks look." For all of their intensity in being difficult, we also could remember that, at the end of the road, we tended to get what we wanted from the Greeks in the way of port calls or military aircraft overflights. We would be under constant challenge, repeated argument, and there would be a constant irritation associated with these requests. There would be constant arguments and difficulties about it. But in the end, we tended to get what we were specifically seeking.

It was just that getting there was not half the fun. On the other hand, we always had the feeling that the Turks were sort of like us—the bluff, hardy type. But trying to get a Turk to change his mind when he had said "no" was impossible. If you added up the entire column, the Turks really didn't give us as much as we might have thought we were getting from them. We just assumed that we had a better relationship with the Turks because they didn't yell and scream and throw hissy fits all the time. They just said "no" and didn't go much further beyond that. The Greeks made a great deal of commotion over the entire exercise, leaving us completely exhausted, worn out, and unhappy—and hardly noticing that we had gotten pretty much what we had wanted when we went into these discussions.

I think PASOK in the end wanted and needed something that looked like a victory for them. Otherwise, there was no way that they could rationalize having come to terms with us. We were, after all, their *bête noire*. We represented what they had so criticized the conservatives for in dealing with us. They had to have some strong rationale of their own for reaching an agreement with us at all. Thus, this negotiation actually was the long, slow process of discovering what they wanted, what were their bottom lines, and how they fit into what we could agree to as an acceptable arrangement for ourselves.

USG Negotiating Tactics and Approaches: Round by Round

One of the tactics that the Department of Defense always resisted was a prioritizing of what their most important base was and what their most important activities within these bases were. They were convinced that if they gave any priorities, we would immediately lop off the bottom line and say, "How fortunate you are that we saved your top three." We never got the DOD to prioritize its activities, at least during the process of our negotiations. Perhaps we could have made judgments of our own, but we weren't doing that. We were trying instead to develop a full appreciation within ourselves as a team for exactly what we were doing in support for the Greek government. We needed to know what agreements were extant with the Greek government, what could be developed in the way of military assistance and support, and what could be done in the way of special economic cooperation so that it wasn't just a defense cooperation agreement; it would be a defense and economic cooperation agreement. We could provide what would be viewed as more and more general support for PASOK to come to an agreement with us.

In that first round, which ran until November 16, we went out, after the initial meeting with the Greeks on a formal team-by-team basis, to each one of the bases. We flew to each one of them separately, and we had extensive discussions with the people on the sites in Heraklion, Suda Bay, Nea Makri, and Hellenikon and got a very good sense of what they were doing, how they were doing it, why it was important; we then appreciated issues of this nature.

Again, this was all preparation for Bartholomew. The bottom line would be that Bartholomew was astonishingly well prepared. He was, instead of being the neophyte negotiator in Greece who was going to be chopped up by this canny old journalist expert in Greece, Yannis Kapsis, far better prepared than Kapsis. Kapsis took this effort casually, in the way that "Well, we always assume that as citizens of our country, we know our country and its problems and issues." While that's certainly true in a way, it may not be true on very specific subelements and a very specific set of issues. Bartholomew, by the combination of the prior preparation for readings of the previous material and endless work on the negotiation while he was in Athens—and to this degree his support team gets some credit—mastered, internalized, and used extensively a briefing book that at the end was probably about three inches thick. While Kapsis used to refer to it jestingly as "Bartholomew's brains," it was a reflection of Bartholomew's personal preparation and his ability when given one problem, no matter how complex and how difficult, to master it so comprehensively that there truly would have been no one in the world who was better prepared or more able to work at that problem.

For the first round of negotiations, we only had three people on the U.S. team. They were Bartholomew, Lieutenant Colonel Beech, and myself. This round lasted until well into November. We came back and immediately went into the same type of round-robin discussions and review that had characterized the exercise prior to going to Athens. Bartholomew briefed the Joint Chiefs of Staff in the "tank" about how the negotiations had evolved. We started again a series of working group studies on how the negotiations were developing. When we went back the next time, which was the second round between December 6 and 21, we had a military expert from the Defense Department, Colonel Jim Hinds, accompanying us. The negotiations settled into a pattern where Bartholomew would go out—oftentimes at what would be relatively late in the evening in U.S. terms—after what would be the end of the normal Greek/U.S. working day, and spend many hours in discussion with Kapsis. Bartholomew was usually accompanied by Alan Berlind. But Bartholomew would then come back, and we would debrief. We used the secure facility, the "bubble," within the embassy constantly, which is basically a plastic room within a room.

We continued to work on some portions of our exercise, such as what form this agreement would take; we had a draft agreement on which we were working. We had various preambles that were evolving, and we worked on them and slowly began moving toward an exchange of text and discussions of this nature. All of this activity was gamed out. One of the things that particularly interested us was clandestine reporting on what was happening within the Greek government and how they were viewing the base negotiations. We worked very closely with many people within the embassy to try to get the best judgments that we could on what the Greek government was thinking and how it was thinking these thoughts. Indeed, there was one instance where a senior official in the Greek government was reported as saying to another senior official in the Greek government,

"Well, suppose we ask them to leave and they won't?" The reflection somehow was that, if we were anywhere near as powerful as the Greeks and PASOK believed we were, we wouldn't have had any problems at all.

But in retrospect, this sort of struggle on their part to understand what they could secure from us, as much as our effort to understand what they were willing to settle for and what they really wanted out of the agreement, might be interesting in diplomatic historical terms and senses. How does a relatively new socialist government work its way through a relationship with a country that is both overwhelmingly powerful, immensely potentially valuable to it as a counter to its hereditary enemy, and yet not at all in sympathy with its personal ideological objectives? How does this work? PASOK had a circle to square. Our strength in the overall historical aspects, the fact that we did have a theoretical, if not real, Turkish counter to put forward, and our ultimate indifference as to whether we got an agreement or not, were very substantial strengths.

At the beginning of 1983, we were still involved in the base negotiations with Bartholomew as the negotiator and a relatively small team of people as our negotiating backup group. What happened between the early part of 1983 and mid-July was that we went back and forth to Greece four more times, each one of which was about a three to five-week segment of time except the very last point when we went back for about four days in mid-July to wrap it up. It remained a very contentious process. Bartholomew continued to meet virtually alone with the Deputy Foreign Minister, Yannis Kapsis. These sessions would often begin very late in the evening for Americans, which put the pressure on us, but which was not so intellectually and physically different for the Greeks. You would start after what we would consider a working day to be over and sometimes continue well into the evening. The discussions between Bartholomew and Kapsis would then run for hours, sometimes many hours.

We continued to negotiate almost on a basis of implied hostility rather than in any format that would reflect the fact that we were both NATO allies. For example, we never socialized with the Greek negotiators. The money that had been allocated for representational activity was never used. The contacts, although they were ostensibly friendly and social and Bartholomew met with Kapsis, were really just very tough, very difficult negotiations.

Q: Even when we negotiated with the Soviets, there usually was a time when everybody would break and go off in little groups and have snacks, tea, or vodka and kind of work around the edges. Was this on purpose on the Greek side, on our side, mutually?

JONES: You're certainly right in how we dealt with the Russians in the INF negotiations in which I was involved. We always had a certain amount of social engagement, and that was one of the areas in which people floated ideas unofficially—but always officially in reality—and tried to get some indication regarding their thinking. But this was, in my view, much more a decision on the part of the Greeks not to socialize with us. We had programmed a good deal of representational money that we could have used if they had been more interested in reciprocal parties and socializing and activities of that nature.

I also have to say that by the time we got to mid-June, we thought the whole thing had fallen apart. At the end of our sixth round, we didn't think we were going to be able to come to closure. We had exchanged texts and, at a point where we thought we had just about wrapped it up, the Greeks came in with a very extensively revised new text, which was completely unexpected and largely unacceptable. So with a substantial amount of regret, we packed up and went home.

In the intervening four weeks before we went back in mid-July, there was an effort (in part directed by the department and by Ambassador Stearns) to get the Greeks to think more realistically about elements of the proposal and the negotiations that they had been pushing. Stearns had kept himself pretty far out of the negotiations. That was partly out of irritation that he had not been given the responsibility to do the negotiations. It was partly also an effective tactic of having that guy from Washington be the "bad cop," while he was the very knowledgeable and extraordinarily congenial Monteagle Stearns, who would be able to serve if necessary as the "good cop."

In effect, what happened was that there was some additional compromise on each side of the Atlantic. One of the issues that had been worked over most extensively was the question of the duration of this agreement. We reached a term of agreement, which was for five years. What we had done in the process was largely strip the agreement down to address less in the way of defense support and status of forces. It was much closer to being a bare bones agreement, a much shorter agreement, than previous extensive aspects and extensive agreements on base negotiations. The result was an agreement in which technically we gave the Greeks very little of what we thought we might have to yield. Indeed, Bartholomew had constructed a labyrinth of "withholds" that we would not give the Greeks unless we were pressed or in return for some aspect of negotiating more attractive language here and a concession there. In the end, he had held onto almost all of these. In theory, the Greeks could have gotten a significantly better agreement for themselves, but they did not.

At the same time, we believed that the Greeks did get the kind of agreement that ultimately they wanted, which was one with a time limit associated with it instead of the open-ended agreement that had previously been the case. But as none of the individual bases were affected, that was also sufficiently satisfactory to us. When we went back to Greece, there was the standard flurry of emotional intensity with a good deal of back and forth in the way of telephone calls within the department to people in the United States, within the Greek government, and also a session with Papandreou which wound up some of these elements of aspects of criminal jurisdiction. For example, who would have what authority over American military servicemen who were in Greece? As there had been a couple of incidents involving Americans, and the Greeks handled them in ways that certainly dismayed the U.S. military forces there, we were standing very hard on the continued existence of the current status of forces agreement, which gave us authority over our own people rather than the Greek government having authority over them.

Even after the negotiations officially concluded, there was one additional stretch of problems with the DECA agreement, which, as one might imagine, was based around both the duration of the agreement and the translation of the English into Greek. Bartholomew, although he is very linguistically talented and was learning Greek as he went along, wasn't interested in Greek writing, which is completely different from the spoken language. There needed to be an official translation that was accepted by both sides. We got hung up on the word for "terminating" the agreement. In Greek, the original translation implied that the agreement terminated at the end of five years. In the English translation, it was "may be terminated" or "is terminable." We didn't want a situation where we had agreed that the agreement just flatly ended at the conclusion of five years. There had to be a more open-ended aspect for negotiation allowing, indeed, requiring the Greeks to take an action to terminate it. So, after a good deal of struggle back and forth, which didn't get completed until early September 1983, we did come up with language that implied that there could be negotiations afterward, and the DECA certainly did not terminate automatically at the end of five years. There still had to be specific action by the Greek government to bring the agreement to an end. As a result, there were still other series of base negotiations, and each of the countries with which we were negotiating immediately grabbed the Greek model to see what they could get from it in the form of additional benefits.

Some Personal Touches

The only light aspect of the negotiations was that, for part of one round, several of us were able to bring our wives to Athens. Although they didn't socialize with the Greeks either, it was slightly easier, because between October and July, about nine months of work, we were out of the country close to half the time, which was not unbearable but, nevertheless, almost all of us had young children or other requirements at home. Being able to bring our wives there once, and that was the case for me and also for Bartholomew, made things just a little easier. It gave the wives a little better sense of what we were doing and what we were enduring, because our negotiations went on despite the fact that they were there. They were perhaps touring or enjoying activities of that nature during the day, and then we would socialize in the evening with wives. But with the Greeks, we didn't socialize at all. Frankly, I have no recollections of any of the individual Greeks involved in their team operations or their support. It's possible that I only met them at the very first introductory meeting.

We had a certain amount of fun during this period as well. One of the touches of humor was associated with Bartholomew having broken his commitment to stop smoking. This was at a time when everybody smoked everywhere, and this was particularly true in Greece, where Greeks smoked even more heavily than Americans. But Bartholomew would be in the bubble and he would have his cigarettes, but he would not be able to find matches. As a consequence, the team, even the nonsmokers among them, started carrying matches and, when Bartholomew started patting himself for matches, we would start tossing books of matches at him. We ended also at a party back in Washington in which my wife had drawn a large cartoon figure that was actually a European caricature of the American Western hero. This Western cowboy hero was "Lucky Luke." Lucky Luke was so fast on the draw that he could outshoot his shadow. We had Bartholomew as Lucky Luke, the gun slinger. Kapsis was the shadow who was full of holes. All around him were stapled and pasted books of matches and it just simply said, "For our matchless negotiator." That was a cute denouement to the exercise.

Security as a Subset of Our Problems

JONES: We spent a good deal of time in the "bubble" reviewing developments and plans. We were concerned about security as one subelement of our problems. We were concerned about security in two directions. First, we sought protection against terrorism within Athens, because the November 17 movement, which remains extant, was certainly very active at that time and, every so often, about once a year or once every other year, a U.S. government official was killed. As a consequence, we were somewhat aware to very aware of this type of problem. We had a Greek bodyguard and an official escort when we traveled.

Second, we had secured rooms within the Hilton Hotel. We always used the same rooms. We had them swept periodically for potential electronic eavesdropping. We had one instance, which was never explained, in which someone was seen in Bartholomew's room. We were never able to determine who this individual was, what he was doing there, or anything associated with that event, which left people a bit nervous.

There was, at least for me, a curious combination of tension, pressure, and semiholiday associated with many of the experiences and times there. So we could understand Greece better, we toured. We went to a number of the famous sites—the Oracle at Delphi, Mykonos, Crete, and elsewhere within the country from time to time, trying to get a sense of the country historically. We all read deeply on Greece, but yet the curious hours that we were keeping, the night and day exercises in which we were at the embassy early in the morning, late at night, on weekends, on U.S. holidays, and the tensions associated with operating in an area that we considered—if not as hostile as the Soviet Union, potentially dangerous in ways that not even the Soviet Union could match—were unique.

Q: You don't worry about assassinations in the Soviet Union.

JONES: You didn't worry about being assassinated or killed by accident in the Soviet Union. If anyone had been killed in the Soviet Union, you would assume that it was deliberate. But the November 17 assassins were and have remained very mysterious. Their ability to strike without being able to be tracked down has been one of the enduring mysteries of Greek domestic terrorism. I personally felt that our driver wasn't a terribly smart driver in security terms. He persistently drove down the most crowded street and made a left turn to our hotel, which hung us up for an extended period making that turn. It made me continually feel that a man on a motorcycle zipping up a side street and turning while we were there could fill our unarmored vehicle full of holes in seconds and continue zipping up what was the main street in Athens and away into the distance without being caught at all. For that reason, I often walked back from the embassy rather than take the automobile.

Addressing the Greek Media and Avoiding Its Traps

One of the other issues that we faced immediately, which was one of the reasons for preventing the rest of the embassy from having virtually any access to us and to the negotiating information, was the thoroughly unprofessional, in Western terms, Greek press. The previous negotiations had been plagued with rumors, leaks, misinterpretations, and misinformation, to which the embassy and the Greek and U.S. governments had to respond to in some manner. When literally nobody in the U.S. embassy spoke to the press in any manner, shape, or form, and nobody in the embassy except the ambassador, DCM, and one individual in the political-military section had any access to our material, we closed down all information that could be attributed to the U.S. government by the Greek press. It didn't matter to us whether the Greeks made all sorts of statements that were incorrect. If accurate information was in the Greek press, then it had to have come from the Greek government, and we could task them for having leaked and ask why they were leaking this material.

As a matter of fact, to give you an illustration of how inaccurate the Greek press could be, they reported the instance in which we flew to Naples to talk to Admiral Crowe, then head of CINCSOUTH [commander in chief, Allied Forces Southern Europe], who later became our ambassador to the United Kingdom. We spoke to him and came back on the same day. The Greek press had us going to Naples on the wrong day in the wrong type of aircraft to meet with the wrong person and returning at the wrong time. There was simply nothing that was in the Greek press that could be trusted. We did, however, to keep witting of what was going on in the Greek press, have an individual from USIS, a Greek national, come to us on a daily basis and report what the Greek press was saying about the negotiations. We simply listened, heard him out, and said nothing.

U.S.-Greek Relations as Reflected in the Congress

Q: You mentioned security and leaks. There are two major lobbies in the United States in foreign affairs. The Israeli lobby is renowned. Anything that comes out of our embassy in Tel Aviv is said to appear on congressmen's desks faster than they can get to the secretary of state. The Greek lobby is very big. Were you concerned about reporting back to Washington and friends of Greece in Congress particularly, or not?

JONES: I don't really feel that this was a specific problem at that time, partly because the Greek government then was not the Greek government that was most loved within Congress or even within a lot of the Greek-American community. What they would have wanted was an agreement that benefited Greece and, to the extent possible, disadvantaged Turkey and aided Cyprus. But it was also a low-key negotiation because so little was expected of it. This was a type of negotiation that we anticipated would fail rather than succeed, and it didn't matter to us whether it succeeded.

If we had a question relating to the Hill, it was going to be how we would present any agreement that we reached. Would this be a treaty or would it be an executive agreement? In the end, we certainly thought that we were better off with an executive agreement. Trying to get a treaty through Congress was even harder twenty years ago when we had had even less a record of success than we have had in the late 1980s and early 1990s with a certain number of the arms control agreements and general international agreements, which have been presented successfully to Congress as treaties.

But it had been very difficult to get anything other than a generalized base agreement in an executive agreement form through Congress. That was what we finally elected to do.

Some Final Thoughts on Greece and Our Bilateral Relations

Q: I'd like to go back to the feeling at the time. There must have been the feeling both with the military and with State that, "okay, but we've got to figure out how to get the hell out of Greece. Greece just isn't that friendly a place anymore." This old brothers-in-arms business was almost dead by then.

JONES: I wouldn't say so at all. This was certainly not the case for anybody in the military. Every single one of them wanted to maintain every base. We did not want to leave. We wanted to be able to stay doing the things that we were doing, particularly at Hellenikon, Nea Makri, and Heraklion. All of those were facilities from which, at that point, we couldn't do what we were doing there in the way of intelligence collection by anything other than extremely expensive alternatives. Now we have satellites that are doing most of our SIGINT [signals intelligence] and ELINT [electronic intelligence] work, but in 1982 and as far as we could tell into the future, that just wasn't going to be the case. Hellenikon was a very useful transit point when we were headed into the Middle East; it was very useful for our entire military airlift. Nea Makri was regarded as one of our primary relay stations for all varieties of diplomatic communications. It really wasn't anything that we wanted to get rid of. Suda Bay also was not only regarded as an extremely useful NATO base for the Mediterranean, but also it was an area where we had positioned a certain amount of war materiel. Although it was the smallest of our bases, we didn't want to give up any of this.

Q: Was there the feeling at any point that the Greeks might just say "Get out"?

JONES: Again, that was conceivable. At that juncture, before this DECA, we had an agreement that tied our bases to Greek participation in the NATO agreement itself. So the Greeks really could not leave, as in throwing us out, without also leaving NATO. NATO was regarded by them as something of a shield against the Turks. They had a variety of complex problems as well. Also, NATO was a mechanism in which not only could they shield themselves against the Turks, but also they could belabor the Turks and give Ankara a good deal of difficulty by getting assistance from NATO and working in great cooperation with NATO. Of course, NATO requires consensus and, if the Greeks were there to prevent consensus, the Turks couldn't get certain things multilaterally that they would if the Greeks had suddenly and totally withdrawn from NATO and evicted U.S. bases.

Also, there was certainly a problem for Papandreou because you still had a situation among Greek conservatives, who believed that the American presence was a shield against communism. If the Americans, who had saved the Greeks from communism, were suddenly evicted by this substantially left-of-center government, there were people within the Greek government who thought that action could stimulate still another coup, despite the fact that the Greek military was hardly in good condition or in good favor with the Greek population. I mentioned too that there was this question that we understood was circulated at an intimate, high-level meeting of PASOK activists where one of them said something like, "Well, suppose we told the Americans to leave but they wouldn't?" To us, even at the time, we couldn't believe that they could believe that if we were directed to depart, we wouldn't depart. Bartholomew, as part of his negotiating presentation, was saying, "Our assumption is that these bases are as useful to you as they are to us, and we don't stay where we're not wanted," which was a useful negotiating ploy, but it was also the truth. As Bartholomew tended to say, it had the Kissingerian virtue of being not only a useful presentational point but also the truth.

So, no, we didn't want to leave. If we had been told that we would close down these bases or we had to close this base, we would have done so. We took our bases out of France, and we certainly didn't want to leave France in the mid-1960s either. Probably we wanted to leave France even less than we wanted to leave Greece. But we did. All of our bases in Greece were of substantial military utility at the time. As time has passed, the activities that they were doing became less necessary and less useful. My understanding is we have closed almost all of them, if not all of them, by now.

CHAPTER 29

Interlude—A (Temporary) Child of the Hill as a Pearson Fellow

---

Q: When did you have your farewell party and get on to something else?

JONES: I wrapped up my work in this in the middle of July 1983. At that point, I had already been assigned as a Pearson fellow for a year on the Hill.

We got to a point where I was effectively finished with the negotiations; I had been nominated and given a Pearson fellowship on the Hill. These are congressional fellowships that send Foreign Service officers—then about ten of us annually—to offices in the House and in the Senate. The program has been in effect now for more than twenty years. I don't know how useful it is for each side. We seem to go to our friends and never to our enemies. Our enemies at the same time are never interested in having us. It becomes a self-reinforcing cycle in which certain congressmen and senators seem to have an "in" on getting a Pearson or a congressional fellow each year.

Actually, I had an interesting preliminary experience in this process. Although I had bid for a Pearson, I was not by any manner sure that the base negotiations were going to be finished in a way and at a time that would allow me to take it up. As a consequence, although I was bidding on other assignments within the department, I accepted the Pearson because if I had accepted an assignment in EUR or on another desk or in PM and then wasn't able to take it, there would be a lot of hard feelings. I certainly didn't want to leave the negotiations until they were completed one way or another. But taking a congressional fellowship, which was simply a benefit—you could always find another person willing to go to the Hill at the last minute—was something that wouldn't give me problems and was also an interesting assignment to take.

But in the process, you see the list of congressmen and senators on the Hill. There is also a list of those who have said that they would be interested in having a State Department officer for a year, as well as those who had already had them in the past and were still interested in having yet another. I went to Teddy Kennedy's office to see what might be arranged there. Here, I put my cards on the table right off. I said, "I'm a conservative Republican, but I'd still be interested in working in this office." There was this long silence as the man who was in charge of getting people for Kennedy's staff thought about that for a moment and then asked, "Why?" I said: "Well, wherever Kennedy is, there is going to be action. He is one of the major figures in American politics and is an interesting and dynamic figure. Under those circumstances, I would be interested in working for him. But I thought that you ought to know at least that my personal political preferences are other than his personal political preferences. But I don't think that would prevent me from doing a good, professional, technical job for him under whatever circumstances. Nevertheless, I wanted him to know what my circumstances were politically." Well, he said, "Thank you, but no thank you."

A Pearson with Senator Hart (D-Colorado)

I went looking elsewhere. I ended by interviewing once more with a senator who at that time was virtually unknown. This was Gary Hart, a Democrat from Colorado. Hart was interesting to me because he appeared to be particularly devoted to something that was of personal concern: military reform. He had a cerebral, intelligent reputation. At the same time, he also had what was then a tertiary-level presidential campaign in the works. What I thought would happen was that he would very quickly find himself ending his presidential campaign, but I would have had at least a minor insight into what was happening in a presidential campaign by one figure. Then I would have what would be a standard Senate-related experience because he was on the Armed Services Committee, and I thought that I would find out a good deal of the inner workings of the Senate in American foreign policy and in American domestic policy. As it turned out, I had an extended experience in a presidential campaign.

Contribution to Hart's Policies

Q: So you ended up with Gary Hart. Can you talk about your year there, '83-'84?

JONES: What I was for the Hart staff was the person with real professional expertise in foreign affairs. Hart did not have anybody on his staff, certainly not at the beginning of autumn and through the early part of winter in 1983-84, who had real background and expertise on arms control or on any number of foreign affairs and foreign policy issues. Hart was very busy in this regard; he was busy campaigning. During this period, I cranked out endless memos, comments, short briefing papers, official statements on virtually every aspect of the arms control issues of the day, issues like build-down or the MX missile [missile experimental] or the anti-satellite program. It just went on and on because he had idiosyncratic desires and needed to separate himself both from other Democrats and from the Reagan administration. I began work on a very extensive white paper on foreign policy for him. There were others drafting it, but I was the coordinator for this general topic and worked on it for several months at least.

Hart's Personality and Style

Hart was a very distant person. In contrast to almost all politicians that I have met subsequently or have heard of, he operated at a very distinct remove from his staff. Other than a small coterie of people with whom he had an intimate, personal, long-standing relationship, he was not "political." He did not spend any time with his office staff. For many of the people who join any political personality's staff, whether it's a campaign staff or an office staff, it's to get a sense for what a particular politician is like. This is a major disappointment for many people. I, at least, had the pleasant initial experience within a couple of weeks after the time I had gotten to the office. There was a retreat seminar where we stayed overnight, had discussions, and listened to Hart. I thought that was an indicator of the manner in which the office and Hart would work. I said something to that effect to somebody else in the office, and they said that was the first time they had seen Hart in six months. Indeed, that turned out to be pretty much the case throughout the entire time that I was there. He did not talk to members of the office staff individually. He didn't do the standard office walk-through that you expect whether the boss is an ambassador or running a small business. As a result, he dealt with paper. We pushed paper forward to him. He acted on it.

What happened, of course, if you remember the history of the time, is that the Gary Hart phenomenon against Mondale became a remarkable illustration of how somebody could rise out of nowhere or rise out of an unexpectedly low status, one in which he ended by winning the New Hampshire primary. Then he went on and had a number of other victories in some of the early primaries in Maine, in Massachusetts, in Florida, in Rhode Island, in Connecticut, while at the same time Mondale was also piling up points.

But it wasn't obvious, one way or another, that Mondale was going to win the nomination. Hart, while still an outsider, was nevertheless generating a degree of excitement. What was interesting to me was the degree to which everybody came looking for information about Hart. As I was the person dealing with foreign affairs at that point on his staff, a number of people from embassies and from elsewhere suddenly developed a great love for me personally. Oh, they couldn't wait to get to meet me. Oh, how interested they were in me. It was one of those circumstances where those people that come to see you and profess interest in your ideas and your comments are not the slightest bit interested in you personally. They're interested in you because you are the U.S. government in situ in the country in which you happen to be located. Or in this instance because, boy, they didn't have the slightest idea what Gary Hart was like or what his foreign policy positions were or anything like that. All they could do was grab the nearest warm body that they could locate, which in this case was Dave Jones. They would try to pump me for whatever they could extract. That was an interesting, intellectual social experience.

Q: Were you getting guidance, or was this David Jones sitting there looking at the ceiling and saying, "Well, I think this should be Hart's foreign policy," and, therefore, writing papers and they disappeared and you didn't know what was coming out?

JONES: You got a certain amount of staff guidance and you had a certain amount of previously written Hart material, that is, previous positions that he had taken in response to constituent letters that had been designed and cleared. You had issues that you were asked to expand upon, develop, and you might get a sketchy set of comments on them. But then what happened to the work was often puzzling. You would perform the work, or you would get a draft statement done, or you would provide input to a speech, or you would comment on material that others had produced. After that, you went on to the next problem of the minute, not even the problem of the day. You would simply get these disparate requests.

Or as you suggested, the other side of it is, you saw a problem coming, or you saw an issue emerging, or you saw something in which it looked obvious that there was going to have to be a position by the senator or the "candidate" and did something to respond. Again, in theory, a candidate is supposed to keep his campaign separate from his office. This is a legal requirement as to how one spends money. The senator's staff was supposed to be doing work that was associated with the senator rather than with the candidate. Of course, that line didn't just blur. That line was trampled upon other than in the most obvious ways. He did not specifically assign people who were being paid by the federal government to go out and campaign for him in New Jersey or anything like that. But at the same time, certainly people in the office staff were encouraged to take leave that would be unpaid or marginally paid in comparison to what they were getting in the office, and go out and campaign for him as loyal employees of Gary Hart. Now, it didn't go over that well for some of the people on the Senate staff, partly because Hart had developed no personal affections among them. Indeed, at the very end, there was a major request that people spend their weekend campaigning for Hart in New Jersey. *Nobody* responded. I thought that that was an interesting illustration of the lack of loyalty that he inspired. Because of my position and Hatch Act rules at the time, I had nothing to do with his campaign and did not go out to any of the specific campaigning events. There were times when, as the foreign affairs adviser or a member of his foreign affairs support team, I would go to a speech that he was giving in public that was also obviously campaign oriented, but, nevertheless, it was something that I felt that I could go to without any questions being raised about why I was there.

Jerusalem Issue Defines My Relationship in the Office

In the end, however, I got into a very specific controversy that complicated my personal position there. This was the question of what position Hart would take on Jerusalem. While this is an absolutely classic position which has turned up for years and years and years in political platform planks and documents of that nature where the candidate would say, "Jerusalem should be the capital of Israel," or "I will act to make Jerusalem the capital of Israel," I argued to the contrary. I contended that Hart should not take this type of position, that it was the wrong position to take, that it was diplomatically incorrect, that it was in contradistinction to our commitment to various UN resolutions, and that he would be much better off not taking this kind of position. Well, essentially, the Israeli lobby pretzeled him. Arguing for this approach was a very unpopular position to take within the staff. Although I initially got agreement that he shouldn't take that position, he ended by taking it.

Q: Particularly when the New York primary was coming up.

JONES: The New York primary. I was told at the time—and I have no way to refute it or confirm it—that American Jews supplied 50 percent of the "soft" money [unregulated contributions to political parties] that was directed to candidates. This was the money that was not "hard" money, that is, money that was specifically committed, annotated, and regulated by the Federal Election Commission. That observation was given to me as the rationale for the reason that he took the position that he did on Jerusalem. It was an interesting factoid. At that point also, and obviously because Hart was being seen as a more realistic candidate, he got more people with a foreign affairs background on his staff directed toward him. More people joined this staff. My personal role became much, much less. So, while it happened in midwinter that they began adding more foreign affairs staff, by April or May, it was pretty clear that I didn't have any significant role in foreign affairs on the staff. I became much less interested in the job.

There was also a constant shakeup within both the Hart senatorial office and the campaign as they struggled to find some way to transmute lead into gold. The person that I had a close relationship with professionally and intellectually, his legislative assistant, his "LA," Kent Hughes, who subsequently did a good deal of work both in Democratic politics and in the current administration in the Department of Commerce as an assistant secretary for international commerce, was fired. He was fired. Other people came in to try to help manage Hart. There were two of them who at one point had a discussion, the upshot of which was one saying to the other, "I'll keep him focused if you prevent him from being such an unpleasant person." The second said, "Oh, you have the easy job." The first responded, "Well, I chose what I wanted to do. You're responsible for the other side of it." In the end, when I left, Hart was as much of an enigma as when I entered.

Feminism and Females as a Force on the Hill—and for Hart

Q: People make somebody into what they think they want him to be. I think we're going through this phenomenon with George W. Bush as a candidate. Hart had that rugged look. Later, he was sunk by sex. But I would have thought that even at an early stage, he would have had an awful lot of young female groupies around who would see a handsome man. He seemed exciting. Politics is like musk and it attracted. You would have found this going on in the office. I'm not talking about real sex, but about people, women particularly, who wanted to just get close to the presence.

JONES: I think you could say that generally about the Hill. One of the phenomena that I observed during the year on the Hill was that the young women there are at a high level of attractiveness. They were significantly more attractive as women than the young men were attractive as men. It was just true. The fact that this was also specifically true within Hart's office wasn't surprising. At the same time, like a number of men in politics at that juncture, he was gaining credit with those who were then barely being called "feminists" for putting women in substantial positions within his office. He had several women, at least one of whom was not particularly attractive, doing serious work for him within his office. At the same time, his press secretary and a couple of his press people were quite attractive women. He also had minority groups within his office. He had a range of significant women providing input for him.

Now, whether he was specifically involved with any of these women, I don't have any idea. That was a problem almost four years later. What you could tell was that his wife was not a happy woman. His wife was not a secure woman. There was one instance when we went to his home as a staff group because he was participating in a debate, and we were there to watch it on television as part of an office activity. His wife just was totally insecure. I might normally have looked at her as the equivalent of "Mrs. Ambassador," whom I would have expected to have met us graciously and, in effect, directed us to this, that, and the other, where refreshments were all laid out, everything set. Instead of being in the obvious position of head of the household since she was the senator's wife and the hostess for our group, however, Mrs. Hart just seemed to be very worried, very tense, and very willing to be secondary to virtually anybody else who wanted to take a prominent position in this group activity. At the end, I felt vaguely embarrassed for her, vaguely concerned that she wasn't being treated fairly, or she didn't allow herself to take the position that was hers by definition. It was a curious operation and a curious exercise.

My conclusion for all of this congressional experience was that I was a child of the executive rather than a child of the Hill. I ended later by writing an extensive article that was published in the *Foreign Service Journal* about State Department congressional relations and topics of that nature, which I thought was a useful piece of prose.

Pearson Fellows and Relations with State

Q: While you were there, did you get involved in answering inquiries from the State Department and that sort of thing? Was there much in the way of interplay between Hart's office and the State Department?

JONES: Certainly not in the manner of the State Department directly asking me to do anything or asking me to provide any specific information about what Hart was doing. There was a good deal of exchange in the other direction, where, since I was constantly being asked for information on obscure areas for which I had no knowledge, I would call a desk officer or somebody and ask for instant expertise, enough information so that I could provide some sort of intelligent comment or commentary. For instance, Soviet leader Andropov "dropped off" (died) in the midst of my year with Hart. He was the Soviet leader at that time. Chernenko was brought forward. I provided brief sketch information, which certainly didn't come totally out of my own head. On the other hand, a great deal of the arms control material was information on which I did have personal background and knowledge from NATO. Consequently, I was able to argue for positions that were probably closer to those of the administration or at least those of standard U.S. arms control positions, whatever administration it was, than the more liberal and discursive sets of ideas that were always bubbling up out of the left of center.

When I ended my experience with the Hill, I had been told earlier in the year that I was going to be the Greek desk officer. To the extent possible while I was on the Hill, I tried to do all the studying that I could about U.S.-Greek relations, Greek congressional relations, and people who were on the Hill who had interest in Greece. I tried very much to get ready for the assignment in this manner. I also had the good fortune to be promoted, which was again clearly a reflection of the work I had done on the Greek DECA and the Greek base negotiations more than anything else. You could say that Reg Bartholomew got me promoted, or his success dragged along the people that had been associated with him on his team.

I left work on the Hill by the early part of June. I elected not to have, for example, any connection with the Democratic nominating convention. If I had waved my hand vigorously, I might have been able to go to the Democratic National Convention, although it was clear that Hart was going to lose. It might have been something worth the effort to go there. In retrospect, it might have been a useful experience, but I was tired of Hart, tired of the Hill, and eager to get started on Greece, so I passed up that opportunity. After some vacation, I went from the Hill to the Greek desk in early July 1984.

CHAPTER 30

A Year with the Greeks

Q: You were on the Greek desk from early July 1984 until when?

JONES: Only for a little more than a year. I left the Greek desk at the very end of July and started in the PM Bureau at the beginning of August 1985.

More Papandreou

Q: What were the issues on the Greek desk when you arrived?

JONES: The issues were still Papandreou-related issues, trying to build and continue a relationship with a government that we considered to be implicitly hostile, if not actively hostile. There just seemed to be nothing that Papandreou did or would do that was not an irritant to a conservative U.S. administration. Papandreou continued to play footsie with the Libyans, continued to make overtures to the Russians, and was invariably obstructive in any relationship with the Turks. So far as his relationship with us was concerned, we just had an absolutely constant, unending set of irritants associated primarily with our military activities.

—Our Battered Bilateral Relations

Q: Did you find yourself on the Greek desk being in the European Bureau but representing "unruly barbarians"? In other words, did the upper command of EUR really care much about Greek relations?

JONES: The upper level of EUR was simply forced to deal with Greek issues. Greece had been part of EUR for about a decade by then, so it was well out of NEA [Bureau of Near Eastern Affairs]. Greece was always considered the more "European" element of the three countries. Greece was causing problems with Turkey, with which we had many irons in the fire; was generating difficulties within NATO, which was even more important; was developing relations with the Russians, which was a vital concern; and was engaging with the Hill in domestic politics to make sure that it got at least its fair share of defense assistance and security. This combination witches' brew made our bilateral relationship politically potent. The senior levels of EUR were involved, and certainly one deputy assistant secretary was devoted full-time to Southern Europe (SE) affairs, although the Southern European office itself was not huge by any means. Greece-Turkey-Cyprus issues—Greek issues particularly, and Papandreou because of his special personality—got a great deal of U.S. attention.

—**Greek Terrorism**

One additional concern that we encountered in Greece was the problem of terrorism. In late spring 1985, we concluded that Greek terrorism was enough of a problem and the Athens International Airport was sufficiently insecure that we issued a tourist advisory regarding travel to Greece and going through the Athens International Airport. Well, under those circumstances, this action just drove the Greek government and Greek Americans absolutely up a tree. What we had done was just shoot a bullet through the Greek tourism industry.

Nevertheless, we certainly clearly believed that security at the Athens International Airport was very poor. Our decision was a reflection of the shocking terrorist incident in Rome's airport. Well, what happened, after a great deal of thrashing by the Greek government, was a virtual total Greek cave-in on this topic and commitments to upgrade security at Athens International Airport. We backed away from our tourist advisory. But it was also a reflection of how poorly we thought of Greece and the Greeks at that time. I won't say that we gave them an awful lot of notice on the tourist advisory. There had been warnings. There had been concerns. There had been indications of our problems with security at Athens International Airport. But at the same time, we were quite happy to throw down this gauntlet and tell them that they were very weak on terrorism. It also reflected the problem that we had never gotten any real responses to our efforts to get them to make serious commitments to hunt down the November 17 terrorists, who every year or so would kill an American official. But it was, as much as anything, illustrative of the poor nature of our relationship with the Papandreou PASOK government at the time this tourist advisory was issued.

Q: At that point, was preserving our military relationship about the only thing we really cared about with Greece?

JONES: On reflection, I can't say yes, but I would also say that the sets of issues associated with the military concerns were the overwhelming set of issues with which I dealt while I was on the desk. These really did run through an almost endless litany of aspects associated with our bases and other military issues. We were trying to develop a new status of forces agreement, a SOFA. We were talking about defense industrial cooperation, another major set of concerns. We had a wide variety of questions associated with military procurement for Greece of surplus U.S. military equipment, such as whether they were F-5s or F-4s. We had begun to get into the problem of being able to develop an F-16 purchase for the Greeks. I spent, along with PM and the DOD, a good portion of the year working on this issue. General Dynamics wanted to be able to develop a sale of F-16s to the Greeks.

Nuclear Powered Warships and other Nuclear Problems

We had constant problems related to nuclear issues, for example, with nuclear-powered warships, whether they would be able to visit Greece and under what circumstances. We had a number of nuclear storage sites in Greece. We had a very extended set of internal discussions about how we should handle these storage sites and systems. We discussed whether we should continue to hold nuclear weapons in Greece, whether we should remove any of the obsolete nuclear weapons that we had in Greece and reposition them someplace else, or have them destroyed. A number of these weapons were there for what seemed to be political rather than military reasons since the systems to which the weapons would be mated were no longer in Greece. But taking the weapons out might have been translated (into Greek—and Turkish) as sending a political signal that we didn't think the Greeks were trustworthy. So we went around and around in this dog-chasing-its-tail circle style.

Q: Even in my time, there was a concern about the safeguarding of nuclear weapons on Greek soil. This is not a stable country.

JONES: Well, this was another element of the discussion. One side of it would say, "Well, you can only secure them by getting rid of them." The other side would say, "Well, we can certainly secure them better by upgrading the facilities by doing this, that, and the other." One side would say, "That's expensive and unnecessary. The systems themselves aren't necessary any longer. We should withdraw them." Then the other side would return to say, "But the political concern of withdrawing them and perhaps not withdrawing them from Turkey would suggest that we don't trust this government, which would make things worse than leaving them there." We didn't make the judgment that they were really insecure, that they were potentially subject to destruction or to terrorist seizure—we never felt that they were anywhere near that level of insecurity. Nevertheless, there was always the technical possibility that things might not be as secure as we would desire them to be. So we had this semiconstant subtheme.

Greek Domestic Politics and Elections

We also had several significant political events during the year that I was there. Papandreou in effect refused to support the continuation of President Karamanlis as president. That Papandreou decision was a surprise to us, although Karamanlis was a very distinguished conservative politician obviously not personally sympathetic to Papandreou. We believed, however, that he and Papandreou had reached a *modus vivendi* in which Papandreou was provided a certain amount of shelter on the right by keeping this very respected figure in this very senior position. Conservatives felt that as long as Karamanlis was president, he might be able to prevent excesses on the part of Papandreou that otherwise would be a real problem for conservatives in Greece. As a consequence, we thought that Papandreou would retain him or at least not argue against him as president. Instead, to our surprise, Papandreou and PASOK said that they would not support Karamanlis' continuation as president. Karamanlis then said he wouldn't run for president. The point was that the presidency in Greece at that time was decided by parliamentary vote rather than a popular vote. If Karamanlis did not have PASOK support, he wouldn't be able to be president. He wouldn't campaign for it because he felt it was beneath his dignity as a former prime minister. He was, himself, a man of a revered, respected position, a man who had, if not created modern Greece, led Greece back from the period in which the colonels had been running the country, and he had refused to cooperate with the colonels when they seized power earlier in the 1960s. But we were wrong.

Then again, as a bit of a surprise, the Greeks moved to hold elections roughly in May 1985. There were people within the embassy that believed that the conservatives would win. Indeed, the ambassador wrote a telegram predicting that the conservatives, the New Democrats, would win. We were puzzled about that. The rest of the embassy sent a telegram predicting that PASOK would continue in power. We thought that perhaps the ambassador didn't really believe that the conservatives would win, but felt such a prediction was what Washington wanted to hear. He may have believed that Washington wanted to take counsel of this hopeful possibility rather than what most of the rest of us regarded as the more realistic expectation that, whether we liked him or not, Papandreou was sufficiently popular and the conservatives still sufficiently unpopular that he would win again. And he did. Papandreou did win again.

A Personal Sidebar and the EUR/SE Office Director

I guess I had the classic desk experience at that point. The election was on a Sunday. By midafternoon, the election results were in. I went to the Greek embassy information office and picked up their official statement. Then I went to the department to write a memo for the secretary in this regard. So, you have me in an early evening at the department. I sat down and composed a one-page memo to the secretary telling him the results of the Greek election. Then the office director came in and spent four and a half hours rewriting and retweaking and retwiddling this one-page memorandum until, as a consequence, I didn't leave at least until midnight. That was an illustration of the manner in which the office director, Bill Rope, operated.

Rope had had no experience at all with Southern Europe (EUR/SE) before coming to be the office director. He had been a China hand and was very controversial in that capacity. He was an intelligent, dynamic, and exceptionally difficult, controversial, irritating, and vindictive individual. I'm pleased and delighted that he never became an ambassador. He did as much as he could to become an ambassador, but he also managed to have the knack for infuriating his superiors as well as alienating his subordinates. Despite a high level of both intelligence and industry, he certainly never got where he wanted to get in the Foreign Service.

Day-to-Day on the Desk

This was an illustration of the work that I was doing. It was, for the era, a classic desk officer's work. I had one subordinate on the desk. For the life of me, it's almost hard for me to remember what he was doing, except, as I told him, "You will do everything I don't want to do." It was not that there wasn't a lot of that to do, but it was more the economic and social aspects of U.S.-Greek bilateral relations. I handled all of the political, political-military issues. This went through an extended day-by-day struggle with all agencies and within the department on virtually every minute element of our political-military relationship, trying to get the bases agreement to work effectively, trying to deal with labor problems on our bases, and so on. There were specific, very left-wing labor elements whose interest in their jobs was secondary to their interest in creating labor difficulties for us. I don't think there was any way in which we could have handled some of these people, but our inability to meet their demands gave them a constant cachet with the left-wing Greek press.

Q: While you were on the Greek desk, did Cyprus rear its ugly head?

JONES: Cyprus was a standard set of problems and concerns, but I can't say that there was anything special going on at that point. At the very end of my time on the Greek desk, I was working on an interagency group paper for how our relationship with Greece should be handled. I worked on that and was the primary drafting officer on that issue for most of a month. To give you an illustration of the intensity with which we were working on it, I came into the office on the Fourth of July and worked for ten hours on it, from 8:15 A.M. until 6:15 P.M. before going to watch the fire works on the Mall with my family. But I was the primary drafting officer for this exercise of an interagency review of U.S.-Greek Relations. To be absolutely frank, I have no idea what happened to it after I left. On the Fifth of July I reported to my new assignment in PM.

—Greek Area Handbook

Another project with which I was involved was a secondary, but still time-consuming, effort to rewrite the Greek area handbook that the American University was doing as part of its endless series of area handbooks. The Greek handbook was much in need of updating. As a result, all of the draft chapters came to the desk for revision. I don't know how many hours I spent on that.

What I have from my memory is a virtually totally exhausting experience that only on rare occasion ended at what was the official close of business [COB]. The norm ran an hour, two hours, three hours after COB and almost invariably included work for an extended period on Saturday. While this was the norm in the mid-1980s, it's become even worse now, as I gather from my discussions with colleagues on desks.

CHAPTER 31

Deputy for Theater Military Policy— My PM Experience Begins

By early January 1985, I had been asked to be the deputy director of the office for Theater Military Policy [TMP] in the PM Bureau. I was approached by officials within PM regarding the position. It became clear that I was also the candidate of the negotiator for the prospective treaty on intermediate-range nuclear forces, Ambassador Mike Glitman. And there were other people who were joining PM at that point that I respected professionally. One of the deputy assistant secretaries was John Hawes. Ultimately, the PM Assistant Secretary, Allen Holmes, also supported me for the job.

All were quite happy to support me for this position which was personally gratifying. The new office director of TMP was a particularly intelligent and vibrant woman with Civil Service background, Jenonne Walker. Although she had also had CIA background and a certain amount of diplomatic experience, she was not a career Foreign Service officer. I was assigned essentially to be the deputy for nuclear issues and particularly for intermediate-range nuclear forces negotiations and their concerns. As a consequence, I, in effect, broke the standard two-year Greek desk assignment in order to take this position, which was of considerably greater interest to me personally.

Q: You did political-military work from when to when?

JONES: From the summer of 1985 throughout much of the rest of my career—certainly from that summer through the end of 1987, when the INF treaty was completed, and then for much of 1988, during which the treaty was approved by the Senate. From the summer of 1985 to the summer of 1987, I was the deputy in the Theater Military Policy Office (TMP) in the Bureau of Political-Military Affairs. Then I had a sabbatical year, a fellowship, and went from there to be technically assigned to PM but operating out of the office of the Chief of Staff of the Army and the Secretary of the Army. I spent a little more than two years as the Chief's foreign affairs adviser before my final real Foreign Service assignment in Canada between 1992 and 1996.

The Political-Military Affairs Bureau— Organization and Personalities

Q: Let's talk about that: 1985 to 1987.

JONES: PM at that time was a big bureau. It still had a director; it didn't have an assistant secretary at that point. While I was there, the director became an assistant secretary, and PM's real power became recognized with the legality of having an assistant secretary as the head of the operation. Within PM—in my view at least—there were two substantial flagship offices. One was dealing with strategic nuclear policy, (SNP). That office dealt with the START [Strategic Arms Reduction Treaty] negotiations, the residue from SALT, the SDI [Strategic Defense Initiative], and questions of ABM [antiballistic missile] concerns, issues of that nature.

The office for which I was the deputy director was the TMP. It was headed at that point by a brand new director, Jenonne Walker, who was and has been and remains something of a controversial personality. As mentioned earlier, she had a CIA background and origin. Then she was lateraled into the Foreign Service. She operated at one stretch of time essentially on CSCE and OSCE [Organization for Security and Co-operation in Europe] issues. She was assigned to Stockholm. But she was always something of a stormy petrel in Foreign Service terms. She remained, and was in this instance, a GS rating [civil service[in what was oftentimes a major Foreign Service position. She was also regarded as more liberal than the normal tone of officials dealing with arms control. She was in constant arguments with officials elsewhere in government. It really didn't matter where in government—whether in DOD, at NSC—or whether they were other people within the Department of State. She was in a struggle of such nature many, many times. On the other hand, she was an exceptionally bright and very hardworking official. She is the type of woman who was willing to stay ten extra hours on the one-tenth chance that she could get a word or two changed on a draft or a set of instructions. This was simply the type of approach that she took on the work with which she was dealing. The work that she was then doing was certainly 98 percent of her life. She expected commensurate commitment from the people who were working for her. I had the good fortune, in some respects, of living close to the State Department. No matter how brutal the hours I was working, I could pick up the telephone and my wife would be at the C Street entrance at State before I finished turning off my Wang computer, closing safes, and getting to the C Street entrance. In other words, I could get my wife to the front door of State in about seven minutes, and then I would be home seven minutes later. But for those people who were not as interested in, dedicated to, or willing to work those hours, Jenonne was more difficult on them and just generally harsher in her personal regard for them.

TMP's Responsibilities and My Work Load

TMP as an office covered a gigantic range of arms control issues. Theater Military Policy started with the most obvious, the INF negotiations, but it also had PM responsibility for MBFR, for other conventional aspects of arms control. We were also dealing with the chemical weapon [CW] treaty in draft. We were also dealing with remnants of the BW, or biological weapons, aspects. We dealt with the Conference on Disarmament, which was connected with the UN and annually had large numbers of papers and documents to clear.

Ostensibly, TMP was designed to have two deputies for its office, but throughout the two years that I was there, I was de facto the only deputy. We had two different officers that came for very brief periods of time, a couple of weeks or a month, but then for a variety of reasons—one retired and the other had another position he thought was going to be more useful for him professionally—they left. That was a disadvantage in the fact that it gave me a great deal of extra work. Instead of splitting the work so that I was dealing with INF issues and the other deputy was dealing with all other conventional forces issues, I dealt with all of the issues, although Jenonne, whose expertise was greater on conventional forces issues, tended to deal more with them on specific matters. On the other hand, it was an enormous professional advantage for me to have this incredible range of material with which to deal and to be able to handle it and to demonstrate that I was able to handle it throughout the two years that I was there.

Nevertheless, on an overall basis, reviewing my diaries, I found that once again I was working absolutely appalling hours. In retrospect, you can only say that you can work these hours if you're young enough and energetic enough—or perhaps foolish enough—to start work in the vicinity of 8:00 a.m. or earlier every morning and then work about twelve hours and do this day after day after day. There was one period of time I noted in my diary that I had gone home once with my carpool during the course of a month. My carpool left at 5:30 p.m., which was a half hour after the State Department's official close of business. This was the norm—6:30, 7:00, 7:30, 8:00, and well past 8:00 p.m.

Q: As I interview my Foreign Service colleagues, some talk about the tremendous hours. In retrospect, was considerably more accomplished by working twelve rather than eight hours?

JONES: I can't say. I never worked eight hours. That's sort of a flip response. But in a serious way, the question wasn't whether you were accomplishing more but whether you were expending every effort to accomplish that which could be accomplished. There was an enormous amount of interagency struggle. This reflected a combination of true ambivalence on the part of the more conservatively oriented officials both at the NSC and in some places in the Pentagon, in DOD, versus in the Joint Chiefs of Staff. But it also was a reflection of the enormous complexity of almost all of the issues with which we were dealing and the ability of very bright people, all of us, dealing with these issues. We looked into them more and more deeply and, with each level of examination, found a greater complexity that needed exploration and resolution of individual issues.

—A Day in the Life of . . .

Q: What would you do? You're working long hours dealing with nuclear matters. But what were you doing?

JONES: I will try to put together some of this activity for a day. For example, what you had during the course of a normal day is, you would start with communications and discussion with Geneva, which had ongoing discussions and negotiations with the Russians on INF virtually every day. If they were not meeting formally, they were meeting informally. You would have a telephone conversation with them to give you some of the insights that had happened during the course of the day. During that period, immediately after that, you would sit down and write a note addressing this conversation to the people in the front office to inform them as specifically and clearly as you could. During the course of the early morning, you might also have gotten a question or several questions from the press office, to be dealt with immediately and cleared throughout the government within a matter of a couple of hours or less, to handle the questions and the answers that were going to be set up for the noon briefing. I almost failed to mention, but in passing, we might have six inches or more of telegrams that would have come in from around the world dealing with all of the arms control—and NATO-related issues that I mentioned at the beginning of this discussion. To the best of your ability throughout the course of a day, the evening, or the weekend, you should be trying to learn and deal with exactly what you have there. You would be involved in the process of creating guidance for each of the delegations that were out there or people who were going out on delegations.

We had regular visits by foreign embassy representatives who would come in for consultation; they wanted to know what our views were on a recent initiative on a particular type of weapons system or how it was going to be handled—German Pershings, nuclear-warheaded GLCMs, conventional warhead GLCMs, and so on. If you had a meeting with these particular foreign representatives and the head of the PM Bureau, you would write a reporting cable on that exchange. Oftentimes, toward the end of the day, you would sit down and write an official-informal telegram, an "OI," to the Geneva delegation to inform them what the specific developments were on INF during the course of the day or the last couple of days.

At the same time, as the TMP deputy, sometimes when I was sitting in for the office director—Jenonne would occasionally be away for a few days, for a week, on her vacations or special projects—I would be managing and reviewing the work of everybody else. Sometimes it would be dealing with odds and ends—type of issues, such as how one handled the U.S. nuclear weapons that were stored in Greece or how the problem of "poison [yellow] rain" as a Cold War problem in Southeast Asia would be discussed and managed.

We were in the process, at different times, of addressing questions as to whether chemical weapons were being used in Southeast Asia. We had a U.S. Army chemical officer who was assigned to our staff. He worked such CW issues extensively, exploring how to determine whether CWs were being used, and we had a variety of operations in connection with the Thai government to try to obtain samples and review possible exposures by individuals who had been sickened in one way or another by this "yellow rain."

Q: Did Iraq come up then? Had Saddam Hussein started his chemical warfare?

JONES: Iraq doesn't impinge on my mind at this juncture. It was much more a question of whether Soviets or Soviet-connected individuals were using CWs in one manner or another.

Q: Libya?

JONES: No. It's possible that Libya came up, but the TMP's focus was almost invariably on Europe.

Working the Special Consultative Group

On an everyday basis, we might be involved with the preparations for people who were coming back from Geneva to have briefings and discussions in Washington. We were engaged in creating and designing briefing books for the Special Consultative Group [SCG] at NATO. The SCG was headed by the United States and chaired by the head of the PM Bureau. The SCG was designed to go to Brussels, to NATO, and discuss with the allies exactly what was happening on a virtually monthly basis—although sometimes it seemed more frequent than that. In preparation for this or in preparation for any of our own major initiatives in arms control, we would have interagency meetings. These interagency meetings were to discuss what the other side had done and why it had done it, and what our assessment and analysis of this would be and what our judgment of it would be. A paper would be drafted that would be put to the secretary, or perhaps even to the president, and would take hours and hours of discussion on a line-by-line basis. During the course of this period under discussion, we also created, analyzed, reviewed, critiqued, and, finally in Geneva in early 1987, presented a draft INF treaty. Again, this activity was something that both lawyers and political elements examined with intense concern. This was material that we would be dealing with over a great deal of time and with a great deal of effort.

National Security and the Philosophy of Arms Control

Q: Listening to you talk—and I've interviewed people like Jonathan Dean, and others—the explosion of the nuclear weapons at Hiroshima and Nagasaki, fifty years later the fallout seems to be of bureaucracies all over the world staying very long hours with lawyers and everybody else involved and talking about this. They seem to have created a terrible challenge to bureaucracies of how to deal with it. The point is, they haven't been used since then.

JONES: I think you've made the point that for all of the arms controllers, no matter how conservative or how liberal they might have been in their personal philosophies, the point wasn't just that they not be used but that your own security as a nation be maintained regardless of what level of armament you had. It is *not* the objective of arms control to eliminate weapons. It is to enhance security. You can argue very effectively that a disarmed world could be a very insecure world, while a very heavily armed world could indeed be a rather secure world, if people recognized that the consequences of using weapons are greater and more invidious than the consequences of not using them. Instead, you decide to pursue your national objectives without using the weaponry that may be available to you. One of our taglines was "enhanced security at a lower level of armament." If that outcome could be obtained by negotiation, such indeed would be the effective objective. But the negotiations were not ends in themselves;

we had to be willing to walk away without agreement if no agreement was better for our national interest. There were people—you mentioned Jock Dean—who believed that Dean was caught up in the belief that obtaining the agreement was more important than enhancing security. Dean was criticized for having such an attitude.

The INF negotiations, the negotiations with which I was most familiar and most devoted to, always had that particular Sylla facing us on one side. The Charybdis was total failure and not getting anything out of the negotiations. Of course, at the same time, we not only had to be prepared to walk away from the negotiations at any juncture, but the Soviets had to recognize that we were so prepared. They had to realize that our objective was to improve security and, in the INF portion of it, to improve not just U.S. security but European security generally and, eventually, as our negotiations proceeded, to improve security worldwide by the elimination of this particular class of weaponry.

The Soviet Union, Gorbachev, and the INF Negotiations

Q: Did the fact that you were now in the middle of the Gorbachev reforms in the Soviet Union quicken the pace?

JONES: I think there is no question about that. Gorbachev's Soviets made agreement possible. Before then, we were not simply going through the motions, because the motions were incredibly intense. But the likelihood of and the prospect for an INF agreement that would be acceptable to the United States and its allies was much lower. We had certain set desiderata that only the Gorbachev Soviets were willing to meet. Until Gorbachev presented a series of proposals that met our most intense concerns, it didn't look as if we were going to be able to get an agreement. What we would be doing would be continuing to negotiate, pushing forward one set of ideas that would be unacceptable to them, with them reciprocating with another set of ideas that would prove unacceptable to us. But Gorbachev did slowly present a series of proposals that allowed a number of areas for agreement.

There were several major elements in the INF agreement that Gorbachev presented that made a treaty possible. One of those was that we would not include the nuclear weapons held by the French and the British in the agreement between the United States and the Soviet Union. Ostensibly, you can make a good case that they should have been included, but we managed successfully to argue, and the Soviets were ultimately willing to accept, that those weapons were to be excluded. After a great deal of back and forth as to whether there should be a residual number of INF systems permitted, but not in certain areas in Europe, we were able to move this issue to what they called a "global zero," that is, no intermediate-range nuclear weapons. We also moved this agreement to include a number of shorter-range nuclear systems, which wiped out another subclass of nuclear weapons that would have been very difficult to verify. Slowly, over a period of time, we got Soviet agreement to types of inspection and verification procedures that had not previously been acceptable to them, but the absence of which would have made it extremely difficult, if not impossible, to get a treaty first agreed by the Department of Defense and then ultimately through the Senate. But, yes, your bottom line has to be that the change in Soviet regimes associated with Gorbachev's judgment as to what the Soviet economy could stand, how the most effective approach by the Soviets to attract Western European support would be designed, and what image Gorbachev wanted to present opened the path to agreement. Perestroika and a general opening of the Soviet Union was the image that he wanted to present of the Soviet Union, and that approach was what generated these changes.

Q: How did you feel about the Soviet Geneva INF negotiating team during this '85-'87 period? What was your impression?

JONES: At that point, I hadn't met them personally. The reflection that we got back from the delegation was that they were competent, able, but not particularly innovative or creative. They were indeed directed by, and run by, what they were being told to do on instructions from Moscow. If they changed a position, we would know about the change in position. There was not a great deal of subtle nuance presented in any of these instances. When the Russians made a change, it was usually a change that was reflected in a high-level, highly visible, well-publicized speech.

USG Internecine Bureaucratics: ACDA, DOD, JCS, NSC

Q: Here you are, in PM, dealing with this. What is the Arms Control and Disarmament Agency [ACDA] doing?

JONES: ACDA was obviously one of the major actors in the entire process. They had overall administrative control of the delegation. They also provided the basic structure and logistic support for the arms control negotiations, not just INF but the other arms control negotiations. They were also the officials who officially chaired the interagency group, which meant that they provided the first drafts of instructions. Their lawyer was the person who was a primary drafter of the INF draft treaty. ACDA, in many respects, was the lead agency within the arms control procedure, but in some respects, it was sort of like being the proprietor of a hotel with a bunch of unruly guests, none of whom could be evicted and each one of whom had a veto over who went out the door in the morning.

Q: Wasn't there any effort at any point to take this away from political-military and put it in arms control or dismantle the arms control agency? It seems like a duplication.

JONES: You're a long way away from any ability to dismember the Arms Control and Disarmament Agency, which had a specific congressional resolution creating and sustaining it. What you did have within the Department of State was questions as to who would be the lead actor within State. The argument was always between the EUR Bureau and particularly the NATO desk as to how much authority it had over these issues versus the Political-Military Bureau, saying, in effect, "These are arms control issues. They aren't local geographic issues. As a consequence, we have the lead."

We were very fortunate during this era that some of the battles that had been fought between PM and EUR over this and other issues when people like Rick Burt or Reg Bartholomew were head of PM and people like Larry Eagleburger headed EUR were over and gone. This was an instance when you could have said that there was something of an era of good feeling, when Roz Ridgway was the head of EUR and Allen Holmes was the head of PM. Each of them was rational; whether they did so deliberately, or implicitly, I don't know, but there was nowhere near the level of disagreement between the two of them that there had been between their many, many predecessors and successors for that matter. But Holmes was clearly given the lead on these issues with the recognition that, so far as going to Brussels was concerned, we were playing our game in EUR's ballpark. Of course, whenever we went there, we were supported by the NATO staff and backed up by US Mission NATO personnel.

Q: During this time, how about with the Pentagon? You had officers from the Department of Defense on the staff. But during this '85-'87 period, was there a noticeable difference between the thrust of the Department of State and the Department of Defense?

JONES: As always, I suspect this is a little bit more a question of nuance than a question of radically differing approaches. Within the Department of Defense, it was generally perceived that the Joint Chiefs of Staff were not innately hostile to arms control. Without my being able to remember or name specific individuals within the Joint Chiefs of Staff, they were not ideologically opposed to arms control. Their concern was a professional exercise in enhancing the security of the U.S. government.

There have always been a fair number of military officers who think that the use of nuclear weapons is unlikely and, at the same time, the requirements to secure them, to protect them, and to train with them detracted from the opportunity and ability to train for what they considered to be more likely: use of conventional weapons. Essentially, tactical nuclear weapons ate up manpower and resources in the requirement to secure and protect them. Even setting aside the ideological question of whether nuclear weapons were so terrible and horrible that, if they were used, it would mean the end of the world and the annihilation of everybody involved, the uniformed military oftentimes did not have visceral ideological commitment to nuclear weapons. This position was regardless of the fact that the weapons systems that we were talking about eliminating in INF were indeed the newest, brightest, just-arrived weapons: Pershing IIs and GLCMs, in particular.

On the other side, there were people within the Department of Defense—the most obvious name being Richard Perle—whose commitment to any type of arms control that was not very much to the national advantage of the United States was pretty limited. Perle's ability, because he again without question at that era was one of the most intelligent, active, able, and well-connected officials in government, was well known. Perle was simply able to get things done, or more prominently, not get things done or prevent them from happening. He had people working for him on issues such as Doug Feith and Frank Gaffney, both of whom have continued through the present to appear from time to time in newspapers and out of think tanks of a conservative nature like the Cato Institute or the Heritage Foundation. These two men were also extremely bright, and very able, and had some basic questions that continually had to be raised. Because they were intelligent and able enough to raise these questions, they constantly had to be addressed.

Q: How about the NSC? The '85-'87 period was one of considerable turmoil in the NSC because of the Iran-Contra affair and a rapid changeover. Was there a general thrust coming from the NSC?

JONES: There was one particularly able Army officer there, Donald Mahley. There was also another colonel, who later became a general, Bob Lenhard; he has since died. Mahley was one with whom we dealt frequently. Then there was another official, Sven Kramer, who was a civilian on the NSC staff dealing with INF and nuclear issues generally. In my view, he was uninterested in nuclear agreement and more interested in finding ways simply to spin out the negotiations. Topics such as Iran-Contra were certainly items of which we were aware, but they were not INF directed. I can't measure any effect that this activity might have had on elements of the NSC staff that were dealing with arms control, whether that was CW, BW, MBFR, INF, or any of these issues. But there were times, in retrospect, it was clear that it was never clear. When you're digging the ditch, it's sometimes unclear whether you're going in a circle or heading straight forward, you're just focused on throwing dirt out of the ditch. There were certainly times when our ditch was being dug in a circle and many, many circles within themselves.

There clearly were officials in the NSC who were distinctly dubious about any arms control that was not very, very much to the U.S. advantage. Instead of resolving the issues, they weren't resolved. The issues were then kicked back for more analysis, more assessment, more review, more study, and more discussion. This, I guess I would say, was a difference within the Department of Defense, to begin, and it was reflected within the Department of State. The problem was how to get to an agreement that was to the advantage of the United States and to the advantage of NATO and our other allies, but not so much to the disadvantage of the Soviets that they would find it unacceptable and just reject it out of hand. We did not have, in my view, at any point on the U.S. INF negotiation team, negotiators who were not willing to walk away and let the whole process collapse. Up until the day before the treaty was signed, the delegation was willing to end the negotiations without an agreement.

The delegation was led by exceptional people. Ambassador Mike Glitman is probably the best Foreign Service officer of his generation. He certainly was the best in my experience in the Foreign Service. Glitman's overall ability was unparalleled, and his ability to move this particular set of negotiations further was unique. He worked exceptionally hard with extraordinarily good effect to bring it to completion. While, of course, every negotiator is limited by the flexibility given to him and the ability of others to respond to flexibility and good ideas on the other side of the table, his ability to move the process forward and do his very best with the material that was given to him and create bricks, when there sometimes appeared to be neither straw nor clay, was quite remarkable.

Pie in the Sky: World Without Nuclear Weapons

One of the oddities that also happened during this period was a reflection of some of the discussions that Reagan and Gorbachev had had in Geneva about the total elimination of nuclear weapons. PM and other offices at State went through an interesting exercise in determining what a nonnuclear world might look like in the way of armaments, and how one would try to create a security system for the United States without nuclear weapons. Most of us went through this process somewhat tongue-in-check, but, nevertheless, it was one of the more intellectually interesting exercises during the period. We had a couple of younger Foreign Service officers who were assigned to TMP—two men, Tom Reich and Bruce Pickering—who did some interesting blue-sky drafting that turned into a respectable paper for something that would be the equivalent of the Martians landing on Earth, but nevertheless it was an interesting thing for them to do.

Again, to step back, we had a very good office of professional people in TMP, a mix of several military officers who were assigned as exchange officers often dealing with special issues such as nuclear-powered warships, chemical weapons, and CW issues generally. These officers—Stan Richie, Stan Weeks, and Dave Lambert—were also intelligent, active officers, usually on the lieutenant colonel to colonel level, and went on professionally from there. We also had a number of very bright midlevel officers, several of whom worked on INF—Doug Kinney; Ron Bartek, who had come over from CIA and then became a civil service employee at State; and Mark Mohr. Both Mark and Ron spent extended periods in Geneva working in support of the delegation.

Then we had almost a separate subgroup of people that worked on CW treaty issues—BW issues, conventional forces issues. This was also the period in which MBFR was brought to a conclusion. MBFR evolved into a new effort to create a Conventional Armed Forces in Europe Agreement, a CFE, and it was decided to use CFE as the acronym. When the thought of having a "Conventional Armed Forces in Europe Agreement," with the acronym "CAFÉ was advanced, it was dropped because such an abbreviation might be considered a little flip by the media and not entirely serious. So we transformed MBFR, which had definitely run out its time, into CFE. Ambassador Blackwill, for reasons that I probably knew at the time but have now forgotten, desired to close down MBFR as a negotiating exercise; he felt, accurately, that it had come to no successful conclusion in the many years in which it had run. Indeed, there were quite a number of people that buried a career or at least a substantial portion of their career in a commitment to a conventional forces agreement in Europe, which never worked out at all. The MBFR treaty process had been started—some people thought to fend off the Mansfield amendment requirement for reductions of forces in Europe, which would have been done unilaterally—and slowly evolved over the years into this endless process which Congress eventually began to regard as simply an exercise to prevent the Mansfield amendment from coming into effect. There was a degree of reality to that conclusion, but there was also a degree of feeling that we were having a great deal of difficulty coming to any sort of agreement with the Soviets and, in this instance, the Warsaw Pact as well, over what acceptable conventional force levels would be.

If you've spoken to Ambassador Dean in any detail, he could give you material by the pound regarding how this was done. Dean's reporting was often viewed with considerable suspicion because he had a tendency to provide a twenty-page reporting cable on a two-hour meeting and bury somewhere on the seventeenth page an important, vital suggested change that people would occasionally miss. Because it was put in there in the manner in which it was, people felt that he exploited this reporting tactic inappropriately. If not quite telling tales out of school, I'm giving an impression that I'm sure Ambassador Dean would dispute vigorously, if not violently. But that was the impression that he left. Indeed, it was almost a requirement to provide a summary as a consequence of his reporting style. Initially, early in the negotiations when he was in charge of them in Vienna, there were no summaries on these twenty-page reporting telegrams, which made them even more of a challenge to read.

CHAPTER 32

End Game for the Geneva INF Negotiating Team and Senate Ratification

Q: Political-military affairs in '87—how had things progressed by that time?

JONES: Well, here, what I will tell you about is a series of transitions for me. Until the summer of 1987, originally I was assigned—actually in the late fall of 1986—to go to Islamabad, where I was going to be the political-military officer for Arnie Raphel. Ambassador Raphel and I had hit if off very well, and I was expecting and planning to take up my assignment in the summer of 1987 after having received this assignment in the fall of 1986. But roughly in April, I encountered family medical problems, and we simply could not go to Islamabad. So I was faced with the question of what do I do and how do I get it done? For a number of months, we worked to find, create, and put me into a position on the INF delegation. This was an assignment that took quite a long period of time to do because… I'm not sure why. The creation of the position was opposed by ACDA. Me going to it was opposed by another group at one juncture. But, finally, it was possible. I was assigned to it in July1987.

What eventuated from there was the question of how I got to Geneva and what work I would do with the INF negotiations for the theoretical year to which I was paneled into this position. Throughout the entire negotiating period, we were sending out one officer per round to support the INF delegation. We would send one officer from TMP to give assistance in drafting and recording and work of that nature. But the position that was created for me was to be Ambassador Glitman's special assistant. For several months, I stayed within the Department of State working as Glitman's liaison officer on the spot within the department; I gathered information for him, engaged in the process of drafting and writing, and I represented him and the delegation in the meetings that were then being held in Washington. So, for several months, I continued simultaneously to support the INF negotiations within TMP and support the delegation in Geneva from my position in Washington. Ultimately, I went to Geneva in September 1987. That period turned out to be the most intensive two months of the negotiating process, during which we brought the negotiations to completion. But before then, I felt that it had been a very successful two years in TMP. I got a Superior Honor Award from it and learned an enormous amount.

Q: Nineteen hundred eighty-seven to 1989 in Geneva: What were you doing?

JONES: It's a little less than 1987-1989, but what I'll discuss now is my experience with the INF negotiation at the end of the year, 1987, and the work that was done with the treaty ratification until the end of May 1988. To review: In the late summer of 1987, I was trying to find out what I was going to do next in the Foreign Service. I had been unable to work out an assignment. The assignment that I had to Pakistan was canceled because of family medical reasons. As a result, I stayed on in the department. At that point, the most obvious suggestion was that I continue to work with Ambassador Glitman on INF, which had been the major topic on which I had worked as the deputy in the TMP office in PM. In any event, for a couple of months as a result of that set of circumstances, I was Glitman's main coordinator in Washington on INF issues. Then, starting in late September, I moved to the U.S. delegation for the INF in Geneva. We were now very much under the gun. The president had announced on September 18 that INF as a treaty had been agreed in principle. On September 20, Glitman supposedly was told by the secretary of state that they wanted the treaty done by October 20, which made it potentially a very exciting month. It didn't turn out that way, but that was the initial impetus that we were given in late September. I arrived in Geneva on September 21. Glitman had been coming from a different part of Europe. We met in Paris and went into Geneva together.

The entire structure for negotiating these nuclear arms control agreements was quite complicated. INF was only one of three elements being negotiated. The other two elements with separate negotiations going on in Geneva were strategic arms, or START, and Star Wars, or SDI [Strategic Defense Initiative]. Over this entire structure, there was a senior negotiator, subsequently the counselor in the department, Max Kampelman, a very senior and very longtime expert professional in various arms control general negotiating frameworks. He had a vested interest in how this entire process was running. It became clear over the months and over a couple of years that the only negotiation that was going to be completed in the near term was an INF agreement. However, at the beginning of the process, there was at least some thought that the three negotiations would move forward in tandem, and there would be one magnificent, overall, incredibly large agreement covering all aspects of nuclear armament. With considerable adroitness, the INF negotiators moved into a separate track policy in which each negotiation was able to move ahead at the speed that was appropriate for it and that the negotiating traffic could bear. But that original concept still meant that there was an overall ostensible framework, one portion of which has never been completed. Still, this framework theoretically existed for many years, and they operated within the framework of how we were going about the negotiations.

U.S. Delegation Structure and Personalities

I settled into a curious role of being the major reporting and drafting officer for the delegation for the next two and a half months. This arrangement had me working also with the State Department representative at INF, a senior Foreign Service officer, Leo Reddy.

The exercise in Geneva was a very complicated, multifaceted, interagency exercise on the U.S. side and then dealing with the Soviets on the other side. Within the delegation, we had representatives from each of the agencies—ACDA, OSD [office of the secretary of defense], JCS, and the State Department. At the same time at the head of the delegation, there were actually two ambassadors, Mike Glitman and John Woodworth, a representative from OSD [Office of the Secretary of Defense] who was tied personally to senior people in OSD, or at least ostensibly he was responsible to them. Woodworth had been a longtime career DOD civilian with a great deal of experience at NATO, where I first met him in the late 1970s, and then in various arms control capacities within the Department of Defense. He was and still is a very knowledgeable individual on arms control, and he remains a personal friend as well. But you can see what a dual-hatted, two-ambassador situation and a multiagency operation can create in complexity. There was also a CIA representative initially.

Each of the agency representatives was also responsible to their home agencies and communicated by "official-informal" telegrams and "secure voice," as well as arguing their cases in Washington and in Geneva. Each side that thought itself a loser in one set of arguments would then carry their argument either to their special representatives in Geneva or send their arguments back to their agencies in Washington so the arguments could be reviewed and renewed again.

Some Rituals within the Delegation and with the Soviets

To handle our discussions, we worked many hours and almost every day in the bubble, the secure facility within almost every embassy. These discussions would last hours and hours on many points. Then you would deal with the Soviets. People dealt with the Soviets on multiple levels. You had a substantial number of two-on-two negotiations in which Glitman and Woodworth would meet with their Soviet counterparts, Obukof and Medvedev. You would have those meetings. Then you would have more complete groups of the INF delegations on steering groups. These often met twice a day. We alternated; we would meet in the U.S. delegation, or we would go down the hill to where the Soviets were located. It was always amusing as to how we would meet one another. It was as ritualized and formalistic as a May Day parade, as the Russians would be standing in rank-order line, and we would get out of our vehicles and walk through their rank-order line shaking hands as we went through this exercise. When they came up the hill to see us, we would do exactly the same thing, and there would be a yell throughout the delegation just before the time of their arrival, "The Russians are coming!" mocking the movie title. We would rush into line knowing that holes would be left in the line for the people who were still hurrying to make it to their spot. There were times when the Russians were virtually coming through the door and our people were hustling into position in order to shake hands and say, "Good morning" or "Good afternoon" or "Isn't it a beautiful rainy day today?" Then you would go into the conferences and discuss. The discussions were almost without exception led only by the senior officials.

Later, as the negotiations became even more intense and the work became more focused on specific items, we broke into groups that handled each of the specific treaty protocols, one for verification and inspection, another for "elimination," or the destruction of the INF system. There were other delegation members who were working on the exchanges of data, which were highly statistical and highly intelligence related. Overall, there were people who were working on the Treaty format and the associated legal language.

Attitudes and Concerns During the INF End Game

Q: Hanging over this whole thing, was there the feeling that the Soviet prime minister, Gorbachev, and the American president, Reagan, had been getting together? They wanted this, and you guys had better come up with something?

JONES: Well, clearly, we had this impetus when the president announced that the treaty was finished. It had to be worked out. But at the same time, there was an almost curious acceptance by the delegation that we would sink the ship rather than have a bad treaty. There was not a single dove in this delegation. That didn't just mean that there was only a question of how fully plumed the hawks were. Any dove would have been eaten alive at the first bubble meeting. It simply wasn't that way. We, perhaps by being willing to sink the whole treaty at the end regardless of how much we desired to get it, to complete it, were even more focused on resolving the issues. We were absolutely convinced that we were still better off to have no agreement than to have a bad agreement or to have an agreement that was a good agreement in technical terms but that couldn't be ratified.

Q: Were you getting any feel for your counterparts in the Soviet delegation, what they were working under?

JONES: In retrospect, my feeling is that they had an impetus to complete the treaty, but by no means did that entail being particularly cooperative. It was much more, "Here is a problem, Americans. How are you going to solve it?" Certainly, this was true on the technical end, "Here is a problem,

Americans. You think this is so important. We're willing to take it another way. You find a way to solve it that won't bother us."

Q: In other words, the onus kept being thrown into the American lap?

JONES: Certainly, that is the way we felt. You get yourself into a curious hothouse environment of enormous intensity and great pressure from all directions in this effort to complete it. At the same time, there were people in Washington within the OSD who did not care if it ever was completed. There were at least one or two people within the NSC who didn't care if it was ever completed. Toward the very end of this negotiating session, a representative in OSD, Frank Gaffney, who is still prominent in conservative circles and writes a column in the *Washington Times* about once a week, resigned because he was informed that he was not going to be promoted to Richard Perle's former position as the assistant secretary for international security affairs. This individual was, in effect, the primary person within the OSD dealing with arms control issues. Gaffney resigned and said that we should slow down the INF process rather than push it forward.

There also was a representative within his office dealing with inspection, who was so ritualistically difficult that the difficulty could only be considered, in my view, obstructionism rather than principled concern that the very last conceivable possibility for verification had not been explored. Yes, you did have a great impetus to get the job done, but you had some very serious conservative objections. They turned out to be objections that could be overcome, but they were overcome by a combination of great care during the negotiating process and the political impetus to move forward. There was also a degree of cooperation by the Soviets that previously would not have been anticipated; it required a degree of openness on their part, which I think they found almost personally disconcerting, such as the degree to which information on intelligence holdings and specific elaboration of numbers and statistics of different missiles and their locations had to be provided to the Americans. There was one Russian military officer who said, "We don't even give this to our Foreign Ministry officials." Now they were forced to publish it in a data exchange. Each portion of these exchanges was clearly very painful for them. It was indeed as if they were making sacrifices, which in a more open society such as ours was information that wasn't being hidden. We had very little to hide, and they had, in the past, a great deal to hide. That is what made some of our problems particularly intense.

—Intelligence Concerns: Where Are the Missing Missiles?

Our intelligence judgments and projections as to how many missiles they had of the types being limited were based on projections as to how many could be pushed out of a factory given certain production-type runs. As a result, we had a high range and a low range. The Russian data figures came in much closer to our low-end projection, which generated a conservative storm of criticism saying, "Where are all these missing missiles? There is a hidden SS-20 force somewhere. We have to be able to find it." Then they would hypothesize a kind of anywhere, anytime, everywhere, all-the-time inspection in the Soviet Union, which was impossible. These hypothetical inspection regimes were deliberately conceived and presented not to find the ostensibly missing SS-20 missiles but to make sure that the treaty couldn't be completed, because their level of trust in the Soviet Union was so low under any circumstances that their position was that any agreement was worse than no agreement.

Q: Also, looking at production figures played to… We always assumed that the Soviets were more efficient than common sense would have told us they were from observing how they built other things, that factories were doing an extremely efficient job of producing missiles when they probably were not.

JONES: I'm not sure how the production projections were made, but if you think that they're going to run three shifts a day and push out missiles 365 days a year, and that their major focus is to produce this missile rather than another one, then, at each level, you push the theoretical figures up. If you take other projections, you put the numbers further down. However, in the end, we would have been happier if they had come in a little closer to the midpoint in our estimates. What it did was to make it harder for us to say where those missiles that we didn't find might have been, and we had to find additional mechanisms to prevent the possibility that these theoretical missiles existed. We had to tie down and prevent any flight testing. We had to tie down and prevent any training in these systems. We had to tie down the movement of systems in and out of their major SS-20 production facility, which was also producing other missiles, so we had to find devices and mechanisms that would allow us to inspect for SS-20s while not catching technical or intelligence information on their other missiles that were being produced at the same time. This required a lot of creative thinking and creative drafting. Then we had to find a facility on our part that would allow the Soviets an equal facility to inspect. We weren't producing that system anymore, but they still had to have something to inspect. We found a facility. We were able to find a method to inspect their facility that proved acceptable.

Grinding Onward—Team Spirit

The work that I was doing there turned out to be an incredibly intensive drafting experience. Since I went to almost every steering group meeting and was debriefed by Mike on almost every one of his two-on-two sessions, plus doing the basic drafting requests for guidance from Washington on outstanding issues, plus doing end-of-week roundups on where things stood in the negotiations each week, plus writing official-informal telegrams to the PM Bureau and other people at State to keep them up to speed on what was happening, I never worked harder in my life for a more extended period of time than those months in Geneva. At the end, I counted up that I had worked thirty-three consecutive days. Our normal workday at the beginning of this process in September was twelve hours. At the end, it was at least fourteen. By no matter of means will I say that I worked harder than most. The amount of work that I was doing was on the high end of the group, but there were many people who were working even longer hours and harder and, of course, with much more responsibility than I had specifically. I tried to be creative in the manner in which I did my drafting for guidance.

Q: Your piece of the action was to go around and draft for the different components? The technicians were working and then you would draft?

JONES: We would have the meetings and exchanges with the Soviets. I became very close to the person who would give the immediate account of what was most prominently happening in a special steering group meeting. We would determine what were the most immediate responses that were occurring in the two-on-two meetings, or what fresh guidance was needed, or what the status of old guidance or existing material was, and what we were going to have to accomplish during this period. That was the kind of work that I did.

Q: Was your feeling at the time that while you were all willing to go down with the ship if you had to, were the military members and the State Department members, were you a team or were you going in different directions?

JONES: The delegation in Geneva was a team. That's a reflection of the guidance and energy of Mike Glitman. In the end, he managed to persuade and co-opt the agency representatives who were there, persuade them that what we were trying to do and the manner in which we were trying to do it was correct, and that there was nobody who had the slightest intention of selling us short by a millimeter. As a consequence over a longer period of time, the OSD ambassador, John Woodward, suffered professionally by not being more obstructive or more difficult or more of a mouthpiece directly for his OSD principals. Instead, he stood on his principles and continued to push for the obtainable treaty. The group in Geneva was a very substantial team in that manner and worked to sustain its coherence very effectively.

—The Famous Photo: The Delegation in Exile

At the same time, my illustration of our willingness to accept a failure was the delegation photograph that was taken late in November. This photograph was a ritualistic exercise in that the Russians would come to our delegation—perhaps in other years we had gone to the Russian delegation—and we would take joint delegation photographs of everyone who was there on this round of the negotiations. This time, we were in an absolute panic. We were struggling to try to complete this exercise. We had just sat down and taken our formal photograph, and we were about to leap up and go away and back to our work when the executive secretary of the delegation, an Army lieutenant colonel, Jeff Ankley, said, "Stop. Wait a minute." He went to the side and opened a box and out of the box he pulled a series of bags that had eyeholes on them labeled "INF Delegation." Every single one of us was given a bag to put over our heads. This was to be the photograph of the "Delegation in Exile" if we failed. A number of us still have these bags—and I have mine framed and mounted as part of an INF memorabilia "shadow box" package. It is a juxtaposition of the delegation that succeeded and the delegation that failed. We were in hysterics as a result of the photograph session, but it reflected the reality that days before the agreement was supposed to be completed, we were willing to take the ship down if it didn't meet our needs and was to our satisfaction.

Throughout the process, we also had people coming to Geneva to solve problems or to buck us up in one way or another. We had senior people from the State Department and from Washington come at a couple of different junctures during these final days and final month to put additional impetus behind some of the specific issues.

However, the three-headed negotiating format also led Kampelman to come back to Geneva approximately November 16 to deal with his senior counterpart on the Soviet side, Vorontsov. In effect, waiting for him to turn up delayed progress on core issues in the treaty for somewhere between ten days and two weeks, although people continued to struggle forward with more specific elements of it. Then, finally, on November 23 and 24, Secretary of State Shultz came to Geneva along with some senior people within the department both in the European Bureau (Charlie Thomas) and the assistant secretary from the Political-Military Bureau (Allen Holmes). Again they attempted to push forward some of the more specific problem issues and to generate more attention on the individual protocols that were being negotiated to try to solve problems of elimination and areas of that nature.

Probably by the end of November—specifically on November 24—when the Soviets provided technical information in an official exchange of data, that move indicated that they really were committed to completing the agreement also.

This final willingness of the Soviets on November 24 to provide intelligence/data information would have made it very difficult for them then to have walked away from a treaty. The amount of information that they provided, which had not previously been provided, assuming that it was accurate information, was a level of commitment on their part that would have been considered a serious loss, a serious breach of Soviet security, if nothing had resulted from the exchange of information. Without us realizing that point as clearly as we should have at the time, in retrospect, it would have been very difficult for them not to have completed the agreement having made this data exchange. This is why the data exchange was delayed as long as it was. They had information about us that we didn't have about them. We had provided information that was virtually public knowledge, almost down to the last millimeter of length of our systems. What they knew about us was perhaps 95 percent or more of the information. What we knew about them was maybe 50 percent. In the end, until they provided the information, we really didn't know how many systems they had. Then, of course, we got into the extended fight to prove the number that they had provided for their systems was accurate.

Q: *When you say a "system," what do you mean?*

JONES: What I meant was a missile that fell into the requirements of the INF treaty, the 500 to 5,000 kilometer range, that it was ground launched, either a ballistic missile or a GLCM, and that it was a weapons-carrying vehicle.

The last week of November and the first week of December 1987 became an even more intense effort to get the treaty language right, to complete the legal elements of it, and to have a legally acceptable treaty that would be signed. By then it had been announced that this treaty was going to be signed between Gorbachev and Reagan on December 7. It didn't turn out to be December 7 because there were other people who said, "Do you know what December 7 is?" But there were, indeed, people whose sense of history was so minimal that signing the first significant arms control agreement with the Russians on Pearl Harbor Day was something that had slipped by them. You wonder still if there are people with a sense of history that feeble, but there are people who just missed that point.

In any event, the treaty objective signing time was then to be on December 8. But this day delay didn't make it any easier. There is always a benefit to a forcing event, but all it does is ratchet up the pain rather than make it easier. People work longer hours and become more and more tired. Some years later, I saw a psychological study that said that when you're sleep deprived, it doesn't mean that you can't continue to work. You can indeed continue to work using various stimulants, whether they're simply coffee or whether they're anything more powerful than that. But what you lose is flexibility. You lose intellectual adroitness, a suppleness, a facility, a way to find an answer-path around a problem other than just continuing to hammer your head directly at the problem. Unfortunately, the brute force approach of trying to resolve the problem was what we often were forced to use. "Do you want this agreement or not?" "All right, then this language, or this comma, or this word would have to be the ones that are agreed."

Wordsmithing the Russian Language

Some of these exercises ended in very arcane studies of the Russian language versus the English language and the translation of each. One of these words in the final document resulted from an exchange between one of our senior negotiators and the senior Soviet negotiator. The senior Soviet negotiator seized upon what was considered an infelicitous U.S. term, but because it was delivered at such a senior level, it could not really be gainsaid. It then became our effort to find a Russian phrase and translation that would not damage us or harm the manner in which the treaty could be interpreted either by the Russians or by the U.S. Senate. As a consequence, our very adroit Russian translator spent a good deal of time with dictionaries and ultimately did locate a word that was sterile, old, but accurate Russian, and it was the term for our English word that we insisted upon. The Russians, of course, didn't like it because it deprived them of the flexibility that they had seen and seized upon. But, in the end, it was the very last word in the treaty that was agreed. We left it at that.

Signing Ceremony in the Delegation and Getting Home

The process itself had generated a level of exhaustion that left some of the people on our side virtually prostrate. At the end, we had one of these significantly memorable exercises where at midnight on December 6, entering December 7, we had a treaty signing, initialing essentially, ceremony between the head of the Soviet delegation and Mike Glitman. We all gathered around this event, which was held in the U.S. mission. We had glasses of champagne. We had tears from pure exhaustion. It was the first time that I had seen people cry from happiness. The combination was striking. We were just standing there, and all of a sudden there were just a whole group of people, including myself, with tears streaming down our faces. It had taken so long and it had been such an incredible effort to get it to this point, which was as close to being the last minute as you conceivably could have.

We went from there to a very different type of exercise. You would think people who were going to fly to the United States would fly by civilian airlines, the Americans on our airlines, the Soviets on their airlines. But instead, because we could see that we were going to need every minute and we just simply were not going to be able to depend on commercial air, we got a military aircraft to fly us to Washington. We took the senior Soviets along with us, which was even more unique. We not only took the senior Soviets along, we took their word processor, which was about the size of a small refrigerator. In the "refrigerator," buried in the core, was their copy of the text. Along with it came a little Russian secretary who had apparently typed every single word of every single aspect of their draft. We, at the same time, had it on what is now an absolutely archaic and totally antiquated disk. We took one disk with us, which had our copy of the treaty in electronic form along with paper copies. On the off chance that the plane didn't make it, we FedExed copies of the disk to Washington at the same time.

During the process of this exercise, we had a C-141, which if you've never flown in a 141 is like flying inside a vacuum cleaner—it is just incredibly noisy. It is designed to carry cargo and paratroopers. It's not designed to bring little old ladies politely from Los Angeles to Hawaii. Some of us fell asleep, and we would wake up and eat a second bad lunch from the military rations that we had with us. During this process, we also had additional levels of initialing ceremony. The exercise was required since two of the protocols had not been completed, that is, not officially initialed by the negotiators. While we had initialed the main text and the elimination protocol in Geneva at midnight, we had not initialed the exchange of data memo of understanding or the inspection protocol. So these were initialed with the Russians sitting on one side of a table in the front of the plane and Mike sitting on the other end of it. They would pass the papers from one to the next and we (Mike) initialed them.

To show you the creativity of the executive secretary, Lieutenant Colonel Jeff Ankley, sometime early in the fall had purchased fifty to seventy-five ballpoint pens and made sure that each and every one of them worked by "starting" them to assure the ink would flow properly. During the course of the original initialing at midnight, Mike sat with a pen. He would initial a page and then put the pen into a box, pick up another pen, initial it, and put that pen into the box. These pens were distributed that evening to the individual members of the delegation. As the initialing went forward on the plane, we went up and handed Mike the pens that we had been given; he would use them to once again initial one of the protocols and give the pen back to us. That was a creative exercise. It was very exhilarating, very exhausting. We arrived on the seventh of December. The treaty was signed on the eighth.

The people who went to the treaty signing were almost entirely those stationed in Washington. The people who had done the work in Geneva got to see it on television at a party that we held separately at a Marriott hotel, put on for us by a corporation that had contributed to fund the celebration. We saw this happen, and we heard Ronald Reagan say, "Trust but verify," which was the core of the agreement. From there, we started on the exercise to ratify the treaty.

CHAPTER 33

Obtaining Senate Treaty Ratification— Not Half the Fun

We had to believe that the easy part of the entire experience was ahead of us. Having done all this work for so many years, having put so much effort into the completion of the treaty, with the president and Gorbachev having signed it in such a high level and highly visible ceremony, we thought it would have a relatively smooth and straightforward path to Senate ratification. That turned out to be wrong. It was not as hard to get it ratified as it had been to get it negotiated, but it proved to be far more difficult than anybody had expected.

Trying to Educate the Senate in Advance for the Treaty

Q: Ever since the League of Nations treaty was rejected by the Senate, it's been an article of faith that you want to get some Senate representation on major treaties in at the beginning, at the takeoff as well as the landing. Had there been any such effort to keep informed or to keep the Senate knowing what was going on?

JONES: Yes. There are people who ignore history, such as proposing Treaty signature on the seventh versus the eighth of December. But these were not the people who were in the overall review of how the treaty was being negotiated. What we had for many years was a Senate oversight group, which was invited to come regularly to Geneva and look in on, discuss, and meet with the negotiators on both sides. For quite a number of years, we had this process and this designated group of senators from both parties. It was supposed to consist of a relatively small group of senators who were going to be in the Senate, likely for a long time, had an interest in arms control, and were not going to be constantly rotating because it did require a degree of expertise. As a consequence, also their staff people were engaged. The structure was there.

Unfortunately, it didn't work as well in practice as the structure should have in theory. What happened was, over a period of time, the entire negotiating process on arms control had gone very slowly. It was not really obvious until close to the end that we were likely to get an INF treaty. A certain number of people in the Senate, if the vote isn't on an issue that is going to take place tomorrow or it's not a constituency-sensitive problem, don't pay a great deal of attention to a subject. The material associated with the treaty was complex, arcane, detailed, and lengthy—it was not something that an individual normally sat down and cuddled up with for light reading.

At one point, to illustrate to you that there were also slippages on the Senate side, we had a batch of questions directed to us from Senator Byrd's staff and office reflecting a treaty text that didn't exist anymore. It was old. Somehow they had never gotten him the updated, complete, final treaty text. But, no, we were aware of the need to get this Treaty through the Senate. We were particularly aware also of the need for a Republican administration to get it through a Democratic Senate in an election year. Yes, this was a very popular treaty. It was endorsed by everyone from the Veterans of Foreign Wars to the League of Peace. It was widely popular throughout the country. It was wildly popular with our European allies, all of whom wanted it. It got to the point where Kissinger, who wasn't enthusiastic about the treaty, said that it should be approved because not approving it would be more damaging to NATO than approving it would be, which is the "damming with faint praise" that Kissinger is often prone to do.

Domestic Political Tensions in Play

Nevertheless, there was this definite inherent tension between the executive and the legislative branches. The Senate had just returned to Democratic hands after six years in which they had not had controlled it. They had just resumed control of the Senate in 1986. This circumstance meant that they were not going to be taken lightly. It became one of those instances where it's difficult to endorse something that you know the Republicans want to use to run on in the next election without saying, "Gee whiz, the Republicans did such a great job. Isn't this wonderful? President Reagan's enormous expenditures of defense money have paid off with an INF treaty." At the same time, how do you turn down something that is very, very popular, and essentially something that the Democrats had always wanted: more arms control? The people who wanted it least were the conservative Republicans. Why do we as liberal Democrats, they asked themselves, give something to this handful of conservative Republicans by being so obstructive that we then look as if we are just being deliberately destructive and political?

The administration, after a very heavy initial dose of publicity associated with the signing, did not go out as it had in SALT I, SALT II, and attempt with a group of people whom we used to call the "SALT sellers" to beat up any opposition and to sell the merits of the treaty throughout the country. Essentially, they felt that the treaty was selling itself. Indeed, it *was*, and it remained extremely popular throughout the entire process. The question became how to get it through all of the various hoops and over all of the hurdles that were being put in front of it. It became the view of the people that had negotiated it and were trying to get it through the Senate that the Democrats couldn't really oppose it. Instead, they wanted to give it enough nicks and scars and damage to show that "we Democrats are smarter than you Republicans were," and "while this treaty is not fatally flawed, it's definitely not anywhere near as good as we'd like it to be. We're going to have to fix it up." Therefore, the exercise was getting it through the ratification process without having to accept reservations or amendments that would have been damaging, made it impossible for the Soviets to ratify it, or force us back into negotiations with the Soviets in a way that would protract the exercise even further. These were the problems. They became in the end at times almost as intensive and extensive to deal with as the original negotiations in Geneva.

USG Organization for the Ratification Process

Q: What was your role in this work?

JONES: My role was defined in the structure in which the operation was put together. Ostensibly, there was overall leadership out of the White House and an effort through the NSC to orchestrate extremely carefully all of the testimony and all of the responses to questions that were posed so that no one would be saying anything that would be contradicted by anybody else. Under that regime, each of the individual agencies, particularly DOD and JCS and to a degree also the CIA and, particularly, the Department of State and the Arms Control and Disarmament Agency, had individual working groups that were set up for INF ratification.

The State Department had an INF ratification task force that was headed by the previous State Department representative in Geneva, Leo Reddy, and I was the deputy for that task force. Ambassador Glitman was positioned separately as a general resource for the entire interagency community. He ended by testifying to more committees on more issues than anybody else. Although we were devoted obviously primarily to the Senate, we also did briefings for the House.

This structure within the Department of State had me as the deputy for this task force. There were other people from within the Department of State, the European Bureau, the Political-Military Bureau, and, in particular, the Intelligence and Research Bureau, who were designated as representatives on the task force. We were to do everything that we could to provide testimony, speeches, backup information, and analysis; among other responsibilities, we also undertook what turned out to be the longest, most complicated, most difficult process: answering the questions that were posed by individual senators and official staff members. We had package after package of questions brought to us.

Questions, Questions, Questions

Ultimately, we had more than 1,000 questions that came to us in packages, which were designed not just to ask questions about the treaty, but to ask questions about virtually everything else that had the slightest connection with arms control and administration foreign policy. Because the administration was under the gun to answer these questions, we had to devise appropriate responses in one manner, shape, or form.

As the questions came in packages, we also had made a decision that we would not return the questions as they were answered individually but return them as packages. Unfortunately, in almost every package, there was at least one problem question, a question perhaps on which the administration would be divided and for which complicated answers—or ways to avoid an answer—had to be created. We were faced with this ongoing problem.

I was the orchestrator of these questions. Going back through my diary, all I can say is that for weeks and months we pushed this package forward, were answering questions on that package, or we handled another. The most complicated, labyrinthine, and extensive questions were asked by Senator Helms.

Senator Jesse Helms and His Ritualistic Rejection

Q: Jesse Helms of North Carolina, an archconservative.

JONES: Whether "arch" or not, he was definitely a strong, direct, and committed conservative who believed that the treaty was wrong. He had some able staff members who created sometimes puerile but oftentimes difficult and intensely complicated questions, which needed to be answered one by one by one. Then, having answered the questions, they had to be cleared legally. They had to be cleared with every other agency that had an input on this topic. This was also the case for the questions directed to the senior officials testifying on the treaty. You started with testimony. After the testimony, sometimes coincidental with it and sometimes before it, you had questions. The questions had to be answered in one way or another.

Suffering under Sofaer

We had another problem, though. This is the problem of what was called the "Abraham Sofaer Doctrine." Sofaer was the legal advisor to the Department of State at the time. He devised this doctrine in association with the Anti-Ballistic Missile [ABM] Treaty. What he said was that the administration could make judgments or adjustments to the text of the treaty based on the classified record that we had held, whether or not that classified record had been shared with the Senate and whether or not that classified record was perhaps at variance with what the administration had said to the Senate officially in testimony. Well, there was then, as there is today, an intense ongoing debate as to what we should do in relationship to the ABM Treaty, "Star Wars," or issues of that nature. The Democratic

Senate was certainly not going to let the Republican administration get away with a treaty, a brand spanking new, shiny treaty such as the INF treaty, without making their points on the lack of validity, in their view, of the Sofaer Doctrine. So they demanded that the official record be presented to them. The official record then became a subject for intense negotiation as to what exactly composed the official record. Finally, it was determined that it was all of the formal presentations that we made and all of the specific direct accounts of the meetings themselves, but not our requests for guidance or our backchannel official-informal telegrams. But reconstructing the official record itself became a major exercise on our part for an extended period.

What I had done in Geneva was the quick, extended summaries of these individual meetings and the steering group meetings that were being held in the negotiating sessions. There were also, however, semiverbatim records of these negotiations and discussions that had not been completed simply because they were very long, and the people who were doing them in some instances were very much engaged in doing other things. For example, the detailed accounts of the two-on-two meetings between Glitman and his counterparts were to be done by the translator-interpreters who had been taking notes as they accompanied the principals. But they, for many other reasons, had not produced these full texts. So full texts had to be produced, and it had to be negotiated as to what exactly was being given to the Senate, who would have access to the documents, and under what circumstances they could be read. No copies of them were to be made. Details of this nature had to be resolved. Eventually, we set up something like five cubic feet of documentation to be held in a room in which senators or very specifically designated Senate staff were permitted to go and read. In the end, virtually nobody looked at them. Certainly, nobody spent any extended period of time on them. It was simply another exercise in political accountability rather than technical accountability of the negotiations.

Senate Testimony and Treaty Analysis—
the Nunn Objections

But we did have a very extended set of discussions regarding the treaty. The intelligence committee testimony was almost all classified. We had testimony before the Senate Armed Forces Committee and then before the Senate Foreign Relations Committee. While the foreign relations committee, headed by Senator Pell, was willing and indeed eager to get the treaty through, the armed services committee was less enthusiastic or more skeptical and more focused on generating questions and creating a more intense analysis of the treaty. This process was headed by Senator Nunn. While Senator Nunn had and retains a well-deserved reputation for intelligence and concern for defense issues, he can also get himself and has gotten himself, into situations where one wonders why he is taking the position that he is. Aside from the INF treaty, I'll never quite understand why Senator Nunn decided to oppose U.S. participation in the Gulf War to the degree that he did. But he did. I think politically and historically, he suffered for it.

—The "Double Negative."

Likewise, I am profoundly skeptical of his technical reasons for finding ostensible fault with the INF treaty, but he came up with two objections. One was what was called the "double-negative problem." This related to a relatively obscure portion of the treaty, which stemmed from the fact that the Soviets used the first stage of their SS-20 in their SS-25s as well. So, while they were banned from producing this particular stage of the SS-20, they did not want to be caught in a situation where we would prohibit them from producing the SS-25 as well. But at the same time, neither could we permit an unlimited exception that they could simply produce endless stages for a missile that really could be intended for the SS-20 as well. What we did was to devise a relatively complicated exception saying that a missile stage section that was outwardly similar but not interchangeable with another missile was permitted on a one-time basis. We could do it as well. We could produce one stage of the Pershing II if we wished to for another missile, so long as it was not directly interchangeable with a Pershing II. Senator Nunn chose to see that as a "double negative," which he argued would allow them to produce a stage that was outwardly, in effect, interchangeable with the SS-20. Our answer as the negotiators was that, no, it wouldn't; something that was identical and interchangeable with an SS-20 stage would be an SS-20 stage and, therefore, banned. That was one portion of the senator's argument.

—"Futuristics"

Then there was another issue that generated protracted discussion. It was called the "futuristic debate." This was an exercise in what conceivably could be done with future systems that might fall into the range that the INF systems included. We got ourselves wrapped terribly around the axles regarding whether there were "black," compartmented systems about which people were not cognizant, whether you had some sort of Star Wars "phaser" weapon in development that conceivably could be mounted on a ground-launched cruise missile. We then began arguing over what a weapon was and what it wasn't. A problem for us there was that if you managed to create some sort of an exception for a ground-launched cruise missile that wasn't carrying a warhead but theoretically might at some future time carry something that could be regarded as a weapon, you left yourself totally open for the Soviets to do the same thing. The problem was that there was simply no way to distinguish between a ground-launched cruise missile carrying a conventional warhead or some future system and a ground-launched cruise missile that was carrying a nuclear warhead. So we banned them all. But in this argument over what future weapons would be, we got ourselves into a situation where we exchanged letters between Shultz and Shevardnadze, but the exchange didn't satisfy the Senate. It satisfied the people that weren't looking for invidious misunderstanding, but it didn't satisfy the most lawyerly of lawyers.

The team including Shultz went back to Geneva on May 13. I wasn't with this group. Shultz left the meeting and announced that agreement had been reached and everything was fine; then the negotiators, Glitman and his Soviet counterpart, spent ten hours at night negotiating on a paragraph, the contents of which I have not the slightest recollection, except that in some way it was an effort to nail down finally, completely, and absolutely that ground-launched cruise missiles would not be involved in any future weapons. Of course, what we have done is to use ALCMs [air-launched cruise missiles] and SLCMs [sea-launched cruise missiles] to handle any of these futuristic-type weapons or to handle the navigational-type radar, the observation-type systems that will surveil the battlefield. The fact that we set them aside for ground-launched cruise missiles and prohibited them really hasn't restricted us in the slightest.

Q: While you were having these questions, were you doing any checking with your Soviet colleagues to make sure you weren't getting out of bounds?

JONES: I would tend to say no, except on a couple of very specific areas. There were some extremely technical points on which we had to make almost tiny wording changes. Although we had all read the treaty itself, the text of the treaty, literally one hundred times, we found there were tiny little grammatical difficulties. In some cases, they were periods or a word or things that were missing, and we had to send a corrigendum (correction document) on these. We did have exchanges with the Soviets to try to fix some of these points on "futures" and on the "double negative" to resolve the issues that had been generated by the Senate Armed Services Committee. But regarding the thousand questions—plus, we didn't go back to the Soviets.

Forcing the Ratification Action to a Conclusion

But the process, something that people had blithely imagined was going to be finished sometime in March after a Christmas break, allowing people to relax a bit and organize themselves for a quick run through the entire treaty and a rapid ratification, just started to drag. The more it started to drag, the more people worried that something was going to go wrong, something would foul it up; somehow the obstacles that were being put forward, created artificially, in our view, were going to lead people to a sense of exhaustion. We feared a conclusion of "well, no, we aren't going to be able to get it done; maybe we had better defer it until after the election."

The president and the executive branch created another impetus in that regard, which was that they were going to go to Moscow, have a summit. At the summit, they were going to sign the treaty officially and formally, and exchange ratification instruments. This schedule created what was an artificial deadline, but which became the forcing event to push people out of the committees, out of the committee discussion, end the endless rainstorm of questions, and actually move us to official debate within the Senate. We knew that if we could get the treaty to the floor, there wasn't any question that it would be able to be done. In a test vote earlier, there had been something like a ninety-one to six vote on it. That had made it clear that it wasn't going to be a problem—if we could get it there to have it voted upon.

The last week in May, we moved our operation from the State Department to the Senate. Again, we over prepared. We created huge briefing books for both individual senators and for the leaders in this debate. We wrote floor speeches for people whom we assumed would be sympathetic. Most of them were never used. We created answers to every question. We created responses for every amendment that we believed might be presented, trying to beat back even the most ostensible motherhood-type of amendments such as, "You will adhere to all previous treaties as well as to this treaty" or "We think that this treaty should be done in conjunction with conventional forces reductions." All of these prospective amendments sounded good, but would either make it almost impossible to get the Soviets to agree to it or would tie the hands of the administration in further negotiations. Well, this was possible finally. We sat in the Senate and listened to a lot of people make sometimes a little better educated presentations than others did, but for the most part, they spoke for the record. In the end, we did indeed finish it as predicted: the vote was ninety-three to six. That obviously reflected overwhelming satisfaction by everybody. But we had, of course, Jesse Helms able to vote against it. Among others, one of the more puzzling people that voted against it was Fritz Hollings. He is supposed to be so ostensibly noble, and one of the people that pursued Nixon throughout his career. I have never quite understood why Hollings elected to vote against the treaty. Helms I could understand. He just simply opposed the treaty and opposed anything to do with the Soviets.

Wrapping It Up and Winding It Down—
INF Aftermath and Assessment

Q: What was the feeling subsequently? Was it postpartum blues?

JONES: I think there is always a degree of that. I remember noting the fact that there was a sadness in a way that this incredibly long effort had finally come to an end, even though it was the successful end that we had all sought. We did do a little after-action work, to the extent of meeting with people in the Senate, staffers, and people within the department to try to determine what lessons we should learn from this experience. We thought such lessons were going to be applied perhaps fairly quickly to a START treaty, which again people believed was much closer to being completed than it turned out to be, and much more complicated.

START almost had to start over again after the 1988 election. But we did a series of what I think were useful, even thoughtful, analyses of what it meant to deal with the Senate under these circumstances, why we had had problems associated with this exercise, and what might be done to do it better.

Q: Did you have any feeling that proponents of missiles—cruise missiles and land-based intermediate-range missiles—within the military, within the Pentagon, were there any people that you had the feeling were going around, behind you, whispering to people, in particular the Senate staff, trying to sabotage this? There is always a camp of people—maybe they build the missiles or they've been trained in the missiles, and they want to keep these things.

JONES: I would say less so than might be imagined, particularly not within the uniformed and military services. There were certain people—Richard Perle and Frank Gaffney, in particular, within the OSD—who believed that (and this was certainly true with the concept of a conventionally armed cruise missile) this particular type of system on a ground-launched basis had a great potential. What has happened is, they have been proved right in the potential of accuracy from this type of missile. But we have used it from air platforms and sea platforms instead—and not nuclear. But we have now the incredible, precision-guided munitions that are able to land within a square meter. If those had been retained on a ground-launched missile, presumably they would be just as effective as the air—and sea-launched systems. It just turned out that it was impossible to make any distinction between the nuclear armed and the conventionally armed cruise missiles. They simply were identical. You could not tell the difference. You could stand there and verify that this was a conventional cruise missile and have your hand on it. You left the base, people would pull out a nuclear warhead from a bunker, and it would be a nuclear-armed cruise missile instantly. It was simply that easy to make an exchange.

But within the uniformed services, they believed what in the end many of us believed: the entire INF treaty was a very important, but very limited, first step in an arms control regime with the Soviet Union. The INF systems were very important for the Europeans, far more than they were for us. It was at best a secondary system so far as what the United States was using for its military and political security. For the Europeans, it had a far higher basis of importance. What we managed to do was to eliminate, not just for the Europeans but for a number of our Asian allies, what was perceived as a specifically threatening system designed against them. Nobody bothered to argue or discuss the fact that strategic systems can always "shoot short." People elected to view this reality with a degree of psychological blindness that can be amusing but is nevertheless real: they thought, "If these systems aren't designed specifically to hit us, we won't be hit." Therefore, the

Europeans saw the INF systems as designed to threaten them specifically. As a result, we first created the counter with our deployments and then finally began the effort to eliminate them all, which was very satisfying to the Europeans.

Q: In many ways, the deployment of an SS-20 and our counter were really political moves anyway.

JONES: Yes, they were. They were not militarily useless. They had very specific military rationales for their deployments, particularly enhanced accuracy and survivability. But the stimulus for them was certainly political. As a result, in the end, they were argued for and against on a political basis; in many instances, they were viewed as a major political counter, and played in a very political way within Europe, and then also by the Soviets, in saying, "Well, look, this is part of our overall European homeland. Look at what we have done with you Europeans to demonstrate genuinely our desire for peace." So there were political, psychological, and propaganda advantages to their elimination, just as there had been political advantages to their initial deployment.

But to step back, I will once again emphasize that I don't think the uniformed military services were objecting, certainly not in any significant way that I ever encountered, to the INF Treaty. They did buy into it. Perhaps some of them bought into it in the same way that senior military figures will indeed accept civilian control and resign if they object. If the most senior people in your civilian establishment say, "This is what we should be doing, Admiral So and So," they will say, "Yes, sir." We can believe when we disagree personally with what our major political leadership is doing that it isn't a smart idea, and we would appreciate a little more military objection to our political leadership decisions, but in the end, no. You really have to have military services that support the executive's decision, or resign.

CHAPTER 34

Another Interlude—
An Una Chapman Cox Sabbatical

Q: This takes us up to when?

JONES: To the end of May 1988.

Q: Then what happened?

JONES: I had been faced during the winter of 1988 and the early spring with what I was going to do next. At the same time, we were working until 7:00 p.m. or 8:00 p.m. at night, most nights, on this treaty ratification process, which was far harder and longer than I ever conceived it would be. I still had to look for something in the form of a foreign service assignment to do next. It turned out that, in at least once instance, I wasn't fast enough to put my desires and interests forward. As a result, in that position, the people who would have supported me, and said they would have supported me, said, "Unfortunately, we are now officially committed to Mr. X rather than to Mr. Jones."

As a result, it turned out in the end that the personnel system came to me and said (this was supposed to have been in one of their discussion circles): "Maybe Dave Jones doesn't want another twelve-hours-a-day job. Maybe if we offered him this (which turned out to be the Una Chapman Cox sabbatical fellowship), it would be what would be most appropriate for him at this time." At that point, I knew nothing about the Cox fellowships. I had the vaguest recollection that it was something that a few people each year got a year off to do. My personnel supervisor said, "Well, why don't you write down briefly what you would want to do for a year off if you did this?" I sat down in front of my Wang [computer] and I wrote a one-page statement about some of the things I might be interested in doing in a year off. I gave it to my wife, who gave it to the personnel assistant with me saying, "Is this along the lines of what I should write if I'm to apply for this?" They took it and said, "Yes, we'll award you the fellowship if you want it." That was one of the only things I've ever done in one draft. It certainly was the only thing that I had done for years and years in one draft. But they awarded me the Una Chapman Cox fellowship for the year, to begin in August 1988 and run for a year until the fall of 1989. I believe that they had awarded the fellowships earlier to the couple of people that were going to receive them, but one of the recipients, for whatever reason, had declined. These goodies normally don't end up at the very end of the assignment process, just sort of floating out there. They are assigned early deliberately to get them done. But it turned out that one of them was available. I looked like a candidate who might benefit from it, and I did it.

The Cox Legend and How the Sabbatical Operates

The fellowships are really fascinating in their own way. They come with at least a little perceived associated history. The legend goes that this lady, Una Chapman Cox, had been traveling at one point in India or some other end-of-the-world country and encountered some sort of difficulty, whereupon your ever present, brilliant consular officer had waved his magic wand over it and made the problem go away. Ms. Chapman Cox, who lived in Texas and had at least some oil, real estate, and/or cattle wealth, was so delighted, pleased, and amazed that any official American was there to exercise this assistance for a mere American citizen while traveling that she put out a substantial sum of money in her will, the interest from which was to be used for the benefit of the Foreign Service.

The organization exists and has existed for quite a number of years. There is a foundation in Washington, usually headed by a retired quite senior Foreign Service officer, normally of former ambassador level, who works on various projects associated with the advancement and development of American support for the U.S. Foreign Service. It's not a widely known organization. It doesn't seem to get a great deal of publicity. It has been involved in activities over the years, such as helping to finance a TV program that ran on public broadcasting about what several different Foreign Service officers did at one point in their career. But what it did that most benefited me—and ultimately benefited my wife, who also subsequently qualified for a Cox fellowship—was to fund at that period two and sometimes three Foreign Service officers for a sabbatical year. At the same time, the department continued to pay us our salaries while the Cox Foundation came up with $25,000, which we were permitted to use pretty much as we desired. The manner in which these funds were to be directed were to support our sabbatical year, whether this was travel, office space, office equipment, research materials, books, manuscripts, hiring somebody to do some research work for you, activities of this nature. There were some limits. For example, you were not supposed to buy an automobile, travel across the country, and then sell the automobile to your satisfaction. Nevertheless, the desire on the part of the Cox Foundation was to find people who would be able to use this opportunity for a combination of intellectual enhancement and general stimulation. It was not supposed to be used to go back to college and get another university degree.

But while the Cox officials did not care at all what you did with it, the department preferred to see something a little more structured. Different Cox winners over the years have worked on various manuscripts, done certain research projects, or involved themselves in community activities, and some have done very little or maybe even nothing. But, nevertheless, because there is really no onus so far as the Cox Foundation is concerned with what you have done with the money and what you haven't done, it is a free year.

What Did David Do?

Q: What was your project?

JONES: Well, I had a variety of what I would say were multiple projects. I had seen many people in my life start off with the equivalent of "Let's finish my PhD thesis" or "Let's write a book" and get themselves deeply into their project but find that at the end of a year they were maybe 60 percent finished, had a stack of paper and research notes, but that was all that they had. I honestly wanted to accomplish something. My concern, having spent about twenty years in the Foreign Service, was that I was no longer sure I could write as anything other than a bureaucrat. I wanted to know whether I was still capable at all of writing anything that somebody else would be willing to publish, that somebody else would judge better than, "Gee, that was an outstanding memo to the Secretary." So, I conceived of a variety of different topics that had been irritating me or nudging at me for years.

One of them was a pure amusement exercise. For years, I had come through the entrance to State at C Street, looked at the names on the memorial plaque, and read what had happened to this or that named but forgotten person. Particularly, these were the plaques on the left hand side, the west side, of the entrance. These were people that had existed and died far before anyone had been in the Foreign Service, as far as I was concerned. What I wanted to do was to find out a little bit about them, to do some research on them, to find out who these people were, what they were like, why they were there, when they happened to die, and if necessary what caused their death. I started a project along those lines. I did a series of sketches and studies that eventually were published in *State* magazine on people like Thomas Nast. I had seen Nast listed there and mused, "Gee, I'm sure that's not the guy who was involved with the political cartooning, the enigmatic donkey, the Grand Old Party elephant, the guy who flayed the corrupt regime in New York, Boss Tweed."

Q: Cartoons got him identified in Portugal or something like that.

JONES: There was this consul by the name of Thomas Nast who had died in Guayaquil, Ecuador, of yellow fever. It turned out that it *was* that Thomas Nast. At the end of his career, when he had been on his uppers in semi-poverty, he was given this consulship in Guayaquil. He spent about a month there before he got caught up by yellow fever and died.

Another man who interested me, partly because of the INF Treaty work and other experiences, was Madden Summers. He was listed as having died of exhaustion in Saint Petersburg in 1917. As somebody who had spent a lot of time exhausted, I wondered just what Summers had done that had qualified him for death by exhaustion. There was indeed enough material to find that Summers had been, in effect, chargé for the entire time during which we were struggling with the transition between the various temporary and provisional Russian governments and the Bolshevik government. There was a great deal of perfectly understandable and very modern interagency backbiting and intraembassy backbiting for which Summers, who ultimately became also the senior Western representative in St. Petersburg at the time, was trying to care for all simultaneously. These responsibilities included the movement of people to safe havens and the coordination of other consulates that were opening. Ultimately he lost the struggle with his own personnel, who were at sixes and sevens with him, and the department. He proved that the adage that hard work never killed anybody was wrong. He really did die of exhaustion.

Q: Were you doing a series of these things?

JONES: Yes, including one for which I had six to ten shorter vignettes about people for whom I simply didn't have the information for a long article. I did an article on the memorial plaques and the origin of the plaques themselves. Essentially, these were warm-up pieces for some significantly more major work.

Then I worked with Leo Reddy, who had also not been particularly well rewarded for his work as the INF State representative. He went to CSIS [Center for Strategic and International Studies] for a year. But the two of us combined on an extended monograph on "burden sharing" as a concept, and whether this was the right issue to be talking about so far as our relationship with the Europeans was concerned. I did a good deal of research and writing and combined with Leo to produce this as a monograph that was published by CSIS in their series. Then I worked on an article that was titled, "How to Negotiate with Gorbachev's Team," which was a study of the endgame in Geneva. I put that together and published it in *Orbis* [summer 1989, 33: 357-374], which is a foreign affairs magazine run by the Foreign Policy Research Institute in Philadelphia. I then wrote an article on the prospects for a chemical weapons treaty, which was one of the things that I was familiar with because I had worked on elements of it as the deputy office director in the TMP in PM. I worked on that issue and published an article on the subject in the *Washington Quarterly* ["Eliminating Chemical Weapons: Less than Meets the Eye," spring 1989, 12: 83-92].

Throughout this time, I also started for the first time to write fairly extensively for the *Foreign Service Journal*. I felt that this was perhaps a time in which I could try to give something back to the Foreign Service in the way of writing, argument, and analysis of foreign service-related issues. I wrote one article about the State Department relations with Congress, spinning off of the fellowship that I had had earlier and spent on the Hill for a year. I evolved the article from that congressional experience. I wrote a couple of pieces that were INF related that I put into the *Foreign Service Journal*. One was a set of vignettes, little stories, out of the treaty experience. Another was a question of what the INF treaty would mean for NATO and how it would develop. I wrote an article on political ambassadorships, what I thought they meant for the Foreign Service, and how that process was developed; the *Journal* published that piece also.

Travels with Cox

I did some traveling, which took me in two directions. These were two major trips, one to Europe and the other to the Far East, where I had not been in more than twenty years, really almost twenty-five years. The focus on this area travel was what did the INF Treaty mean to Asians? What would it mean to the Far East? In that extent, I started by going to a conference in Hawaii. From there, I flew to Japan and had discussions in Japan with Japanese officials. I flew from there to Korea and was in Korea for the first time since I had left in 1965. I gathered a sense of what had happened and developed in Korea in twenty years. The embassy had arranged discussions for me with officials, particularly arms controllers, within the Korean community. I was then able to go to China, made contacts through the embassy there, and saw people within the Chinese government to talk to them about their views of the INF treaty and what it would mean. (I had followed the same approach in Japan.) Finally, I went to Taiwan and talked to representatives from our facility, the American Institute, and to officials in the Taiwan government. It was also very beneficial. At the same time, I included more than a little touring, and was able to see things that I had never seen before or had not seen in many years; I had a delightful time. It was useful, and I produced an article that was published by *Asian Survey* as a consequence of those meetings and discussions.

Q: It sounds like Cox got quite a bit of money out of this one.

JONES: Well, I got a lot from it, but I also wanted to be very sure that I couldn't be charged with having done nothing. The other process I followed was to keep very meticulous financial records, and I produced a steady stream of almost monthly reports to the supervisor, Joe Montville, who was overseeing this project within the Foreign Service Institute's hierarchy. He was the person who was managing the entire exercise.

An INF Manuscript

Then, after having said I wasn't going to write a book, I won't say I started to write a book, but what I started to do was to assemble the material that could theoretically have been a book. Some of the process was to get INF colleagues of mine to write chapters of what might be a book associated with the specific areas in which they had worked. Geoff Levitt, a man who had been our chief lawyer provided material. Roger Harrison, a State Department official who had worked as a Washington insider and a subsequent ambassador, wrote an item for this proto manuscript. He was our ambassador in Jordan during the Gulf War. During the INF period, he was one of the deputy assistant secretaries in PM. Another colleague, who was pretty much in charge of working Through the Elimination Protocol, Ronald Bartek, provided a chapter. He is now a private citizen contractor and a consultant in the Washington area. I did a great deal of writing on this project also in an effort to assemble a text that possibly could be published in some manner, shape, or form. One of the biggest elements of it was a detailed analysis of the "Senate and the INF Ratification Process," which I ultimately published as a monograph from the Army War College.

Q: The Cox fellowship ended when?

JONES: In the fall of 1989.

Q: That puts you at the wrong part of the assignment cycle.

Battling Over the Next Foreign Service Assignment

JONES: Yes and no. Of course, I was bidding during the summer and the Cox sabbatical was something that could be shortened a little bit or spun out a little bit. Again, it was one of these situations where I got an assignment that I very much wanted, beat down the bureau, but had to have my assignment directed into the position that I wanted. The bureau appealed and went to the under secretary for political affairs, who reversed my assignment.

The director general had endorsed my assignment. The European Bureau sought to overturn the decision of the director general who put me in that particular position—for which I was eminently qualified—not that the person who didn't get the position was unqualified, but at the time, I was more qualified than the person who got the position. But I was not the choice of the European Bureau. The head of the bureau at that time, the assistant secretary, wanted this individual who was a close personal associate from a previous assignment. So the European Bureau appealed to then Under Secretary for Political Affairs Larry Eagleburger, who endorsed the European Bureau's position. I would have been the deputy in EUR/RPM, a position for which I was certainly qualified. I had six years of NATO experience, the experience on the INF negotiations, various awards that I had won in association with the Treaty, and had just been promoted into the Senior Foreign Service while I was on the Una Chapman Cox sabbatical.

CHAPTER 35

Foreign Affairs Advisor (POLAD) for the Army

Q: What happened?

JONES: There was a good deal of back and forth as to what would be the next best thing for me to do. I elected to take the position of the foreign affairs adviser for the Chief of Staff of the Army and the Secretary of the Army, an assignment in Washington in an area in which I had a good deal of personal and professional expertise. I took that assignment in the fall of 1989 and held it until the summer of 1992.

POLADS: Who and What They Are and Where to Find Them

Q: How did you get the job and what was it? What were you doing?

JONES: This position was a POLAD [political adviser]. Over the years, it has had a lot of different names, depending on for whom you were working—foreign affairs adviser was the final label for me. But it is a role that goes back to World War II, when Bob Murphy was a diplomat assigned to the most senior levels of American military command to provide diplomatic and foreign policy advice. The number of POLADs has varied over the years. Essentially, we have sent one senior ranking Foreign Service officer to each of the commanders in chief (CINCs) around the world. At the same time, there has been a POLAD assigned to the Coast Guard and to the Chief of Staff of the Army at the Pentagon.

Q: You were with whom?

JONES: I was with two Army chiefs. The first was General Carl Vuono, from the time I arrived in the late fall of 1989 until June 1991. Then he was succeeded by General Gordon Sullivan, who was chief for another three years.

Q: There was not one assigned to the navy?

JONES: No.

Q: Was there any particular reason for that?

JONES: No. Some of these assignments were traditional. Some of them were officers assigned to CINCs. There has been one assigned to SHAPE [Supreme Headquarters Allied Powers Europe], SACEUR. There has been one at Norfolk for an extended period.

Q: One down in Naples, too.

JONES: The one at Naples has ended. They may have taken the one away that was assigned in the United Kingdom. There was a POLAD assigned to one of our senior commanders there. At one time, there was also a POLAD with the senior military commander in Stuttgart. There has been one assigned off and on at NORAD [North American Aerospace Defense Command], sometimes yes, sometimes no. And there has been one assigned to CENTCOM [U.S. Central Command]. That process has expanded and contracted in the numbers of people assigned. But for an extended period at least, for quite a number of years prior to the time when I took the job, the position as POLAD to the Chief of Staff of the Army and the Secretary of the Army was held by George Barbis. I think he had the job for about eight years. He enjoyed it immensely and got along with a series of chiefs whom he tended to have met when they were more junior commanders, although still general officers, and pursued that relationship quite effectively when they became chief.

On Being a POLAD

Q: Let's move to the 1989-1992 period. What was your job?

JONES: The POLAD's job is very flexible. You're assigned to give the senior commander, your boss and solely your boss—you don't report to anybody else—your advice. Specifically, the Chief of Staff of the Army is your sole rating and reviewing officer, and that is the person who writes your efficiency report. You have a direct pipeline to your commander. But again, this circumstance is very individualistic. It will depend upon your personal and professional relationship with the man. It may change when the commander is replaced. People cycle through all of these jobs very quickly. If you have a two-year or a three-year assignment in a POLAD position, the odds are that you're going to deal with at least two commanders. My specific job was to provide foreign affairs advice and counsel to the Chief of Staff of the Army and the Secretary of the Army. The effort evolved in many ways from that point.

The Army has been one of the elements that has been primary in my own life. I spent two years on active duty and then I remained as an army reservist, ending with a total of twenty-eight years of army service. So I was very interested in the Army. That was one of the aspects of my life that led me first to consider and then to accept an offer to be a POLAD—that, plus the fact that I had a previous personal and professional relationship with one of the key staff officers for the Chief of Staff of the Army, a man who ran an in-house think tank and hot-potato-handling group for the Chief of Staff of the Army, the Chief's Analysis and Initiatives Group [CAIG]. Because this officer knew me and approached me at a time when I was interested in a follow-on assignment from my Cox sabbatical session, I became interested in it as a possibility, and that's where I ended working.

The Chief of Staff of the Army is not a commander in the way that the CINCs at CINCPAC [commander in chief, Pacific Command] or CINCSOUTH or SACEUR are commanders. As a result, he is a support person, a very senior support person and one of the members of the Joint Chiefs of Staff—but he is not a commander and has no combat forces subordinate to him. As a result, his emphasis and interests are organizational, logistical, personnel related, focused on the development of what the army will look like in the future, and, to a degree, more of its foreign relations with other armies. At that time, he was the only Washington-based chief who had a POLAD. It was easier for me to remain closely in touch with what was happening at the Department of State and elsewhere within government than it is for the POLADs who are assigned hither and yon, a long way from Washington. They are a long way from having any relationship with the Department of State, and, consequently, often feel out of what is happening.

I keep circling around what I was doing, because so much of it was coordination, organization, counsel, and advice. On a day-to-day basis, I could be at the State Department for several hours. I arranged to attend the Political-Military Bureau's regular staff meetings, which is something that the previous POLAD couldn't do. For some reason, he had decided that he wouldn't be given this access and had not asked successive directors of political-military affairs. I said, "Well, nothing ventured, nothing gained." I asked Dick Clarke, the then assistant secretary for PM, if I could sit in on his standard staff meetings. All of the POLADs are technically controlled by the PM Bureau. And he agreed. So, a couple of times a week on a scheduled basis, I would be at the Department of State both making it clear to PM what the Army was doing and what the Army was interested in around the world and on a political-military basis. At the same time, I would gather information that would be of interest to the army, particularly in arms control issues. Then, on a regular basis, I would go to individual desks in State offices and bureaus, particularly if there was an issue of Army interest in a particular country or a trip that the Chief was planning to take or a trip from which he had just returned. I would obtain material, organize briefings, provide debriefings, and do other tasks of that nature. At the same time, the Chief of Staff of the Army was the host for a virtually endless stream of counterpart visits.

The chiefs of staff of various armies around the world would come to Washington for insight, comment, and discussions, and then travel around the United States for visits with and exposure to American military units and particular types of equipment; these included areas or units that they may have asked to see or equipment they might want to acquire. There were also equipment and techniques to which we wished to expose them. These schedules would usually begin in Washington with sessions with the Chief and senior army officers; then they would go to the field. I was involved in the organization, planning, scheduling, and preparation for these meetings.

—A Hypothetical Visit by a Foreign Army Chief

Q: Let's just take a random example. Let's say the chief of staff of the Brazilian army is coming. What would you do?

JONES: Once again, you will not be surprised that the Army really prepares for these events. If the chief of staff of the Brazilian army is coming, it's because he has been scheduled to come—a year and a half or more in advance. The schedule for which visits the Chief of Staff of the Army will receive and which trips he will make is designed at least a year ahead of time by a detailed set of proposals, each one of which is justified, rationalized, and reviewed for utility. Probably several months ahead of time, there would be the beginnings of a preparation with an action officer on the Army staff—who might be a foreign affairs officer, and usually the foreign affairs officer for the particular country or the particular area—assigned for this particular visit. This action officer would then begin to design a Washington schedule and build a set of briefing papers, talking points, and discussion areas. This is a process that I would coordinate with this action officer. I would be giving him diplomatic guidance, insight into the area, especially if I happened to know more about the area than others.

Q: Let's say Brazil, and this is not your area. Would you call the desk?

JONES: Absolutely. I would call the desk. I would go to the desk and talk with them, pick up papers and material that might not be available to the Army staff, although the Army staff also got the huge array of normal reporting traffic that our embassies produce. But if there was something that was more esoteric, something in which the Department of State had a special interest—perhaps we were going to be engaged in selling M1 tanks to Brazil, or something of that nature—I would talk to the desk to arrange for this discussion. It could very well also be a situation in which this meeting was very esoteric, and very complicated. It was very important for us to have a positive effect on the Brazilian chief of staff of the army. We might call in or request briefings by senior U.S. officials or citizens, including perhaps the American ambassador to Brazil if that official happened to be in town during the visit. We would arrange for him to come to the Pentagon and talk to the Chief of Staff of the Army. Or if that was not the case, the office director with one of the key desk officers might come to talk to the Chief.

From there, you would develop a "book." The person in charge of all counterpart visits is the DAS—the abbreviation stands not for the deputy assistant secretary but for the Director of the Army Staff. In my case, in this instance, it was a very intelligent, very able three-star lieutenant general, Don Parker. Parker had an introductory little axiom: "You only have one chance to make a first impression," which meant that he really wanted these events to go right without being tremendously overbearing about it. He was a large, happy bear of a man who every so often, but not without cause, would show you why bears have large teeth and not every bear is going to be happy all the time. He could administer a most professional chewing out. Happily, I was never at the chewing-biting end.

Parker would run through the preparations for the visit, and these invariably started with an arrival ceremony, a full welcoming ceremony at Fort Myer with an honor guard, a pass through and official words, and a return to the Pentagon for a formal call on the Chief of Staff of the Army. From there, the Chief would host a lunch or, if he didn't host it, someone senior on his staff would host it. Then they would go to a roundtable in which all of the issues that had previously been agreed for discussion would be chewed over. Both sides would be making presentations. They would tell us about their interests, concerns, how their army was operating, what it needed, and what its problems were. We would give a combination of wide, general overall briefings about what our army was doing, where it was going, and subjects along this line. You then usually ended the day with a dinner at Quarters One, the residence of the Chief of Staff of the Army on the Fort Myer base.

All of this was performed with great professionalism. As part of the preparation in between the reviews given by the DAS, there would be an IPR, an in-progress review. The Chief would be briefed by the members of the Army staff connected with the meeting, and he would provide any further guidance on his objectives for the visit.

Here again was an illustration of some of the basic standard operating differences between the Army and the Department of State, that is, who briefed the Chief of Staff of the Army. Who briefed the Chief of Staff of the Army, the most senior military man in the army? Usually a major or a lieutenant colonel briefed him, after having had his briefing and his presentation reviewed by two or three echelons of other senior military officers. But it was the major or the lieutenant colonel—the action officer or the foreign affairs officer—who was, in effect, in charge of the briefing. None of these briefings were the type of standard Department of State oral briefing where you sit down and chat with your boss. They were very structured, very organized, flip-chart briefings that themselves were as orchestrated as the computerization available in the early 1990s permitted. Every action officer was an expert in making slides and charts for briefing books—again, something that is either an amazing phenomena for somebody at that level or totally useless, depending on your views and attitudes toward this process. But it was a very structured environment. Everybody had an assigned, specific seat. Almost at every instance, when you approached the office of the Chief of Staff of the Army or one of the standard briefings, you would look at the seating plan. Outside the office, one of the aides to the Chief would have this seating plan available. If you were looking for yourself, you could point to where you were headed and go off in that direction. That's either astonishingly over-structured or a refutation of the totally casual Department of State approach, where often the only person who knows where they're sitting is the host, and everybody else comes in and sort of scrambles around. If you're the note taker, you're trying to get close enough to hear what's actually being said. The military plans for all of these little time-wasting inefficiencies by creating a structure into which each round/square peg is properly placed.

Some Substantive Issues

Q: During this period, you got in when the Bush administration came in. Several issues: One was Panama. Another was Somalia. The change in relations with the Soviet Union with the end of the Soviet bloc. Yugoslavia. Then the cooling of relations with China. The Gulf War. There may be others. Panama came first.

—Panama

JONES: Let's talk about Panama a little. It occurred at just about the time I arrived. I came in November. I went to a major meeting called the Conference of American Armies in Guatemala with the Chief and the departing POLAD. I want to talk about that group (CAA) a little bit more subsequently. But then the exercise in Panama came off on December 20. I had been on the job only about two weeks at that point. What can

I say about Panama? I never visited it. The Chief of Staff of the Army went there at one point to see troops, but I did not go along on that trip. The question about Panama was why you had to find something for every military service to do? This was so organized a participation by every single service that it almost was a bit amusing. At the same time, the military, and the army in particular, made a tremendous effort to be exceedingly careful about civilian casualties. It didn't always turn out that way. There were charges that a lot of people were killed who were civilians. But there was definitely a great effort on the part of the army to avoid civilian casualties and to avoid damaging monuments or structures that they thought were or would be very prominent symbols for the Panamanian people. There was one statue in Panama City that they identified as particularly important to Panamanians and paid a great deal of attention to avoid hitting it.

This was an operation run by General Max Thurman. Thurman was the man who invented the Army slogan "Be all you can be." Thurman died relatively soon after the Panama operation of Hodgkin's disease, of lymphatic cancer. But during the time he was there, he was in command of SOUTHCOM [U.S. Southern Command], and he was the overall commander of the force that moved into Panama. The Army was pleased at the way it operated. They were pleased with the effectiveness of the manner in which they had operated tactically and pleased with their equipment. They looked upon this experience as a far better operation than Grenada had been, let alone other exercises like the long commitment in Lebanon in which our forces had gotten themselves blown up. This effort was regarded as reflecting a very high level of professionalism.

Q: I've interviewed somebody who noted that our POLAD to SOUTHCOM wasn't around at the time. There were two things that were maybe minor, but at the same time I thought that a POLAD might have done something about. One was that our embassy was kind of left open. There weren't troops around just to make sure nobody went after the embassy. But the other one that had a terrible effect in public relations was when Noriega took refuge in the Papal Nuncio's palace; the troops surrounded it with boom boxes and bombarded it with raucous music. A POLAD would have said, "Hey, cut it out, fellows." It sounded cute, but it just seemed that there wasn't a little hand there working on touches.

JONES: Well, I have to admit I don't know anything about that. I recall that the boom box exercise didn't last very long. Noriega eventually elected to leave after a great deal of pressure on the Papal Nuncio to expel him. At least we were smart enough not to go marching into the Papal Nuncio's quarters and haul him out by his heels. Whether that was the result of diplomatic advice or just good judgment on the part of the military, I don't know. I will add the point right here that, at general officer and senior staff and Washington senior staff level, you really didn't have any klutzes. You had a remarkable assortment of very intelligent, very capable people. One of my wife's observations was—and I will agree on this—that it was a lot easier to see why a man was a general officer than why a man was an ambassador. That wasn't because of the "fruit salad" ribbons and decorations that they might have been wearing. The number of colonels that I encountered who certainly were far above the presumptive capability of a colonel, both in their personal effectiveness and the authority that they held, was quite remarkable. My role as a POLAD wasn't to constantly say, "Oh, you stupid idiots, how could you have done something like that?" It was much more an addition of a final brush stroke or a secondary level detail or a suggestion that "you might be interested in this approach or this approach as well." This was really not a question where you would have had to have a senior diplomat throwing himself in front of the leading combat platoon saying, "Don't go into the Papal Nuncio's quarters."

What the circumstances were around the U.S. embassy, I simply don't know. I don't know how fast we got people there. I don't know what level of warning was delivered to the embassy. I don't know whether the embassy people were advised to evacuate. This was something that you could see coming once Noriega declared war on the United States. There was an amazing degree of shin kicking on his part until we picked him up by the scruff of his neck and tossed him into the dustbin of history. What I would say again is that the military was very pleased with its performance overall. They were pleased with the way they had operated out of Panama. They were pleased at the degree of control they exercised over their violence. They were certainly well satisfied with the manner in which their equipment operated. And it gave the Army a level of satisfaction in their new capabilities in the 1990s that had been dissipating, and it certainly was not the feeling that they had after the Grenada operation.

—The Fall of the Berlin Wall and the Slow-Motion Disintegration of the USSR

Q: Let's look at the fall of the Berlin Wall, the dramatic changes at the end of 1989 and Eastern Europe. This was the war that the army was preparing for—on the plains of Europe. All of a sudden, with that in '89 and thanks to Gorbachev, that ended. Did the army have another mission? Were they hauling out Plan B now that you no longer had to worry about the Poles, the Czechs, the Hungarians?

JONES: It was slower motion than you express. People were waiting for other shoes to drop before there was an expectation that radical change was going to be required. There was in August 1990 the attempted coup against Gorbachev, which was reversed and overturned. At that point, people began to believe that there was going to be the opportunity for serious change within the Soviet Union and with the Russian military. They did begin outreach planning for work with the Russians. There was a visit by the Chief of Staff of the Army to Russia that was on again and off again. Finally, he did go. There were plans for and proposals for visits by Russian military officers to the United States in a fairly extensive program run out of a major U.S. university to expose them to some elements and views of democracy, political aspects of this nature. There were plans and programs to reconvert a major U.S. military school in Oberammergau for dealing with Russians into a more general school for Russians and Americans. All of these were ideas that were being explored. There was a clear recognition that no one wanted to play "triumphalism" games.

—Conventional Forces in Europe

One of the points that I dealt with a great deal for more than two years were the details and developments of the Conventional Forces in Europe (CFE) agreement. This was a spinoff of the mutual balanced force reductions. It was an exceptionally complicated set of negotiations for the reduction of military equipment and access to these areas to watch the destruction of it, the inspection of the items being destroyed, distribution of equipment being reduced or transferred, how it could be reorganized, where it was going to be sent and stored, or given to other countries. This was a significant interest for the Army, although the Army wasn't a player. The Army could play only through the Joint Chiefs of Staff, who were the representatives on these negotiations. But because of the Army's interest, this was something that I followed for them, and I got repeated briefings and wrote quite a variety of analytical memos and notes keeping the Chief of Staff of the Army and the Army staff aware of what was happening in the negotiations, and aware of what the Department of State was thinking. In that degree, this reflected what we were doing, planning, and thinking.

—Reforger

One of the projects in which I was engaged very early in 1990 was what was called "Reforger." Reforger was an annual exercise that brought U.S. forces to Europe in ostensible response to a Warsaw Pact military buildup and possible invasion. So, each year, we would exercise our plans, bringing substantial numbers of U.S. forces from the States, some to move into prepositioned material—what they called POMCUS sites [prepositioned overseas material configured in unit sets]—to have them join in a possible response to an invasion. Well, these exercises and others of similar ilk went on constantly and continued to go on. During my time with the Chief of Staff of the Army, I was in Europe several times with the Chief. Almost every time, he went to bases and units in Germany, saw what they were doing and how they were doing it, and discussed with the commander of Seventh Army (who most of this period was General Saint) exactly what was being done and how the exercises were developing. But these were clearly going to be scaled-down exercises. The last big Reforger had been run, and the staff recognized that they were now going to have to do a much wider variety of command post exercises and map exercises. The day in which you would run massive numbers of troops through German potato patches was done. You simply had reached a point where the German civilian population would no longer be receptive to seeing their forces, let alone foreign forces, doing substantial damage every year to farms, fields, and infrastructure, even though they were paid on the spot for any damage. There were damage assessors accompanying the troops. Somebody crossed your potato field instead of going on another piece of terrain, and there would be somebody there to assess the damage and pay on the spot. But it was a psychological change that people could sense was coming. As a result, they were making plans to respond to this type of problem. We could see that there were going to be force reductions associated with the Conventional Forces in Europe agreement. This would be something that simply was going to happen.

—Burden-sharing

Another area in which I became involved—this was a subject that had interested me for a number of years—was "burden sharing." This is, how do you persuade the allies to do more while we're doing less? There was an ambassador for burden sharing in the Department of State, H. Allen Holmes, who had been the assistant secretary in PM and eventually ended his career as an assistant secretary for a number of years at the Department of Defense. I've always regarded Allen as one of the princes of his generation in the Foreign Service and have the highest regard for him. But during this burden-sharing ambassador period, he was being given a place-holder job at State because they didn't want to dismiss him. He spent a couple of years working around the margins of major activity with this role. One of the things that he did that didn't involve me was going around the world to do what he said was the equivalent of "rattling a tin cup" during the 1991 Gulf War and getting contributions of all types. But in the capacity in which I dealt with him, he had as his key military action officer a young lieutenant colonel who had come from the CAIG. So I was involved again with that officer. What I did was to carry water for both sides on burden-sharing issues, making sure that Holmes had access to our senior military commanders, the Deputy Chief of Staff for Operations, the Vice Chief of Staff, and the Chief of Staff of the Army. There were people of comparable rank on the Army staff who would go to State and talk with Holmes about the wide assortment of burden-sharing problems and issues—what we needed, what we were most interested in, getting what we were interested in, and securing a relationship with the Germans, in particular. There were projects that we were seeking to have them support. Even if we no longer wanted to support them, we still wanted to maintain the capability, and we wanted to know what would be the best tactics to use in making these approaches. Holmes and the Army staff would use an occasional intermediary on this work on burden-sharing issues, and the further we moved into an almost post—Cold War period, the more this was of interest to the Army.

The Changing Army

Q: Did you see a change in the army? One of the big things in the army that everybody talked about—I remember this back in the mid-1950s when I was a vice consul in Frankfurt—was the Red Army coming through the Fulda Gap. That was in a concise way how we looked at the threat. Obviously, the Red Army was not going to come through the Fulda Gap since the events of '89. Was there a dramatic shift in forward thinking about, okay, what are we going to use our army for in Europe?

JONES: Again, I suspect that more of this thinking happened later than we might project, or at least later than I remember it happening. Within six months of Panama, we were into the fighting in the Gulf. The Gulf aftermath probably absorbed a year. At that point, of course, you had an enormous amount of change, shifting of units, forces, and force concentrations, and great satisfaction from the success of it.

But to get back to Europe, for this period, we could see that militaries were being reduced. We visited just about every one of the national military commands and their senior military army officers. We visited at different points during this two-year period with the British at least twice, with the French, with the Italians, with the Germans twice, with the Belgians and the Dutch. In effect, we hit all of these senior European allies. At each level, they told us clearly, and we recognized, that their force levels were being reduced and their armies were going to be restructured. Some of them were moving closer to an all-volunteer force or a substantially greater number of volunteers, and we heard that they were running into budget plan problems. All the way along the line, this developing future was clearly what we saw. We knew that there were going to be problems maintaining force levels.

We anticipated that as a result our own force levels would fall. The army was always concerned about its strength and what level of strength it could maintain. The army did think into the future to the extent that the senior officers insisted that they would not create or not fall into the trap of becoming a "hollow army." This was one of their major themes. Another major theme was that readiness was absolutely essential. This was a key phrase delivered by Carl Vuono at his retirement parade and speech where he delivered in the strongest possible way the maxim, "Never compromise with readiness." This position meant that they were willing to take reduced force levels if the operational tempo for the troops that remained was high and the forces were properly equipped.

The army was at the same time steadily examining alternatives for the weaponry that it was going to need and the concurrent support material. They had concluded that there was not going to be a new tank in the out years, that there simply wasn't going to be anything other than the Abrams and the Abrams variants that they had. No one was going to design a completely new tank. They were quite satisfied with the Bradley fighting vehicle, which was also a replacement for previous armored personnel carriers. They were pleased with their multiple rocket launcher, which was just being deployed. Their focus had become more directed at the logistical support vehicles that would be necessary to keep up with and maintain the extremely rapid-moving combat force that they now had. So, there was indeed a certain amount of planning and emphasis on how one prepares this army of the future, what one does with it, and how they do it.

Examples of Senior Officer Excellence

The Chief of Staff of the Army in the early 1990s was in the process of revising operational texts personally, giving them an amazing degree of attention. The equivalent would be if we had the Secretary of State working on a FAM [Foreign Affairs Manual]. But the Chief of Staff of the Army was working on the basic operations manual for the army. It wasn't that he was writing it, but he was engaged with the detail.

To step back, as an aside, I was constantly struck by the ability of these very senior officers to pay enormous attention to detail without getting lost in it. They truly were able to get down to the quality of the material for the Army green shirt while at the same time being able to handle and be equally comfortable with wide strategic policy development affecting the Army. On the other hand, they were very Army-centric. One of the things that I also noted was that in the Army Operations Center during the Gulf War, which met every single morning very early in the morning, 7:15 a.m. to 7:30 a.m., they would talk, giving an overview of circumstances. It was, however, interestingly characterized and would be on the lines of, "Yes, we have our legs—they happen to be the marines. We have some eyes—the air force. We have a left arm—the navy. But the most important thing is our strong right arm." Then they would spend 95 percent of their time discussing Army issues associated with the gigantic level of detail and complexity necessary to move and prepare the Army for the operations in the Gulf. These people were able to handle detail in great detail, but also were able to move to the most complex and abstract levels of strategy.

I also used to say that if there was an Army officer who was concerned with the concept of a 400 ship navy, or the Marine Corps Osprey helicopter, or the Air Force's plans for an advanced generation fighter, he wasn't doing his job—which was to focus on Army concerns.

The Gulf War: Saddam Hussein and the Kuwait Invasion

Q: Let's talk about your role and your observations of the events of August 1990. When Saddam Hussein moved on August 1 into Kuwait, where were you? What was the reaction within the military? What started to happen?

JONES: It was very interesting. Just before that time, we had had a briefing from planners at CENTCOM.

Q: This was General Schwarzkopf.

JONES: Well, it was his planning officers, but not Schwarzkopf personally. They talked about the threat in that area. It was almost an abstract circumstance at that point. They talked about how hard it would be to get to the region to defend it. Indeed, they didn't think we could get there in time. Certainly the prospect of trying to defend Saudi Arabia against an Iraqi attack was seen as so daunting as to be virtually impossible. We were concerned that we would be defeated if we arrived in the time frame that we could program. The first troops we could get there were airborne troops, and some officers said they wouldn't have been a speed bump on the road against Iraqi armor. Then after that, you were talking about perhaps forces from other countries and our Twenty-fourth Mechanized Infantry Division, which was the first available heavy force. But on top of that, and subsequently, we had an intelligence briefing by the Deputy Chief of Staff for Intelligence of the army staff. He came and the Army Vice Chief of Staff received the briefing. As somebody who had been an intelligence officer, I could see that they were going through the various warning indicators. Somebody asked him, in effect, "Well, how much warning time would we have if Saddam moved against Kuwait?" He said, "We have been warned." In other words, we wouldn't have anything much more than "well, we hear the tank engines have turned on now," and that would be about the level of warning that was available. We had all the warning that we could have. It was a time in which, if anything, the United States was being counseled by the Saudis and the Kuwaitis *not* to take abrupt and precipitous action. Who had more to lose than the Kuwaitis?

Q: And they were telling us to butt out, almost.

JONES: Yes. They were telling us: "We can take care of this. We have handled this before. Don't do something provocative that Saddam could seize upon as an excuse. We've had this type of contretemps before with him. We think that it's manageable. So don't send highly visible naval forces to ride up and down the Persian Gulf. Just wait it out. We can deal with this." Well, there were no people that had more to lose than the Kuwaitis, and they were literally caught asleep. All you can say is that they were Pearl Harbored, so to speak.

At that juncture, you could say that militarily we weren't surprised. The classic problem of intelligence is measuring capabilities and intentions. You knew all about their capabilities, and you knew nothing about their intentions. We're always taught as intelligence officers to measure only their capabilities and respond to their capabilities. If you know their intentions today, you may not know them tomorrow. They may not know them today, so how can you measure or assess their intentions? In the end, that differentiation becomes impossible. You have to take what you believe their intentions are into account. But the military planners are forced to deal with capabilities and capabilities alone.

Q: Let's talk about where you were and how we responded.

JONES: What I was dealing with at that point was that the president's decision to intervene showed that he had larger testicles than I did. I just was afraid from the briefings and information that I had had that we wouldn't be able to do the job. Essentially that without an incredible effort on our part, we wouldn't be able to get to Saudi Arabia in time to prevent an Iraqi invasion, if Saddam elected to continue to move south into Saudi Arabia. But it didn't happen that way.

Q: We're talking about capabilities. Looking back on it, how well do you think we had the Iraqi military pegged?

JONES: We were very well organized to move materiel and equipment. This is something that the army does very, very well. Year after year after year, they send people to Command and General Staff School at Leavenworth. Year after year after year, they develop plans to move units of all dimensions, sizes, shapes, and backgrounds, with appropriate supporting materiel there. This is not an *ad hoc* exercise. That was one of the most impressive parts of what I saw work. No one was making it up as they went along. They had plans and they had capabilities, and they matched plans and capabilities to take the actions that they did. But the decision to exercise those capabilities against the prospective problems was a political decision. It was made at the presidential level.

Q: What were the briefings saying? What were the capabilities of the Iraqi army that you were seeing before?

JONES: The capability of the Iraqi army, in retrospect, seems to have been much overstated. We were very concerned about the casualties that we expected to face. I made one note at the turn of November or so saying, "The Iraqi defenses were regarded as terribly tough" and that we wouldn't be able to breach them in a straight-on attack. This was certainly the decision approximately at Thanksgiving. This was a complicated military decision.

Q: By Thanksgiving, we had already committed ourselves to put defensive troops in.

JONES: Yes. We had made the decision in early August to move troops there, and we had been in the process of moving troops in massive numbers. But there was an added level of decision making after Thanksgiving. It became complicated, because at that point people were saying, "Well, we have enough forces there to defend Saudi Arabia." But that wasn't the objective. The national objective was to liberate Kuwait: "This will not stand."—as President Bush emphasized. So how did you go about doing this? How long could we keep our troops there? This environment was regarded as a complex political and social-cultural atmosphere in which to operate. After a certain period of time, we were going to have to rotate forces. We were beginning to think of which forces, which divisions, would be rotated and changed. Or could we actually directly invade Kuwait and expel the Iraqis?

Army Attitudes about Desert Shield/Desert Storm and Its Tactics

I did not make this trip, but there was a trip by the Chief of Staff of the Army and some of his key support people; they looked at the plans presented by Schwarzkopf, which were for a direct frontal assault on the Iraqi positions. They deemed them inadequate. They thought they were unimaginative and that they could very well be ineffective, certainly with the troop strength that we had there. At that point, we made a decision to start moving troops from Germany. This move, in its own way, was sort of startling for me. What it did was emphasize our conclusion that the possibility of a war in Europe was virtually nonexistent. We took two divisions out of Germany, as well as more divisions from the United States. At that point, it became clear that we were going to attack. We could not maintain the level of troops in Saudi Arabia that we had moved there indefinitely with no force rotation. We didn't have sufficient forces left to rotate them, and we weren't just going to let our troops sit in the desert forever. It became clear that we were going to attack. But, if anything, by no means was there a lot of enthusiasm on the Army staff for a full-scale war.

—Colin Powell

Q: The chairman of the Joint Chiefs of Staff was Colin Powell at this point. He made it very clear that he didn't want to do this. Did you feel that he was in sync? Were the army commander and Powell both in general accord?

JONES: From what we can tell from books written later, it did indeed appear that Powell was not enthusiastic about a war. This seems to have been reflected in his very initial advice in August about which I was just recently reminded by some newspaper columns. Powell was more inclined to let the situation in Kuwait stand and simply make sure that we saved Saudi Arabia. The military—and this is standard for generals on the Army staff—was hoping that a solution could be obtained diplomatically. It's a silly truism to offer, but it's still very true that it's the military that does all the dying. This observation is even more true at the senior Army level, since the young military personnel that were out there were often their sons and daughters. In the military at senior levels, you will often find that you have a general officer who has a son or a daughter who is a captain or a major in a combat unit. This was certainly true for the Army staff. You cannot help but realize this circumstance. They would mention it in a seemingly casual way: "Yes, my son is out there as a captain with the such-and-such recon Squadron," or, "My daughter is a captain with a Patriot missile battalion," or something along this line of casual (but not really casual) comment. Carl Vuono, the chief of staff, had two sons, both of whom were in Desert Shield at that time. Don Parker, the director of the army staff whom I mentioned earlier had at least one child who was engaged in this way. So their desire for blood-curdling, hand-to-hand combat exercise was zero. There were no war lovers on the Army staff. That's the reality I'm trying to project and explain.

Q: *We have an interview with Gordon Brown, who was POLAD to Schwarzkopf. What was your role?*

JONES: My role was a coordinative, informational role in many instances I was trying to get people who knew something about the Arabs to talk with us and discuss the situation with the Chief of Staff of the Army. I was obtaining information and views at the Department of State regarding their thinking and perspectives and making sure that the Army staff knew this thinking. I was writing briefing memos and commentary on what I saw as the circumstances evolving for the Chief of Staff of the Army and senior staff people. I cannot say, since this was not a combat-commander operation for the Chief, that I knew of subjects such as war plans. I didn't know war plans. I knew that we were certainly also thinking about things like how to end a victorious war. There was a full section of Army planners doing this kind of thinking—what next afterward? Things like, what will we do with our forces when the war is over? How will we get them back? How will they be distributed? Where will they return? What equipment do we want to leave where and under what circumstances? But a certain amount of this planning was being done in the dark because we didn't know what was going to happen.

—Norman Schwarzkopf

Q: *During the war, one of the disquieting things is the way the war ended. Schwarzkopf was told to arrange a cease-fire, and he wasn't given many instructions. When you talk about how to end a victorious war, it sounds like some people sitting down with some rather concrete ideas of what to do. How did this translate itself to Schwarzkopf?*

JONES: Schwarzkopf was an individual planner. He got instructions through the Chairman of the Joint Chiefs rather than the Army staff. The Chief of Staff of the Army was a support and supply chain for them. What did the CINC on the ground need, and what was the best way to get it to him? I mentioned the visit of the Chief and Army staff to the Gulf and their review of or their observation of his plans; their response was that they were not good plans, were not subjects that were thought out with Schwarzkopf so much as they were their private observations that this was not a good plan. This straight attack was not going to be a very productive approach.

An enormous amount of what engaged the Chief of Staff of the Army and the army staff was the most detailed of minutia, problems such as how to more effectively protect the rotor blades on helicopters because they were eroding more quickly by desert dust. There was a full program to wrap the rotors in a protective covering. Or how would you move a major water purification unit from storage to the theater of operations. You would have constant reviews at the daily briefings in the Army Operations Center of the available equipment, what percentage of it was online/operational, what was needed in the way of spare parts, what was in the pipeline, how it was being delivered, and what the capacity of various ships were.

Q: I want to go back to your role. How did you find the State Department during this time of crisis and the army? What sort of things were you getting in passing?

JONES: A good deal of it was not relevant to Desert Shield/Desert Storm. We were still doing a certain amount of standard work. Visitors were still visiting. Other plans and other information were ongoing. The department was working its diplomatic approaches. You would hear the results of it or you would see indirectly through reporting telegrams. Some of the events were on CNN, which was on TV in everybody's office all the time, regarding what approaches were being made. The Army really didn't have an input into this activity. The best I could do was to try to keep people informed as to what was happening to determine if they had missed something.

—**Barry McCaffrey**

Q: The conclusion of the Gulf War must have given a terrific boost to the feeling of the capabilities of the military.

JONES: Without any question. One of the observations by Carl Vuono was, "What a shame we had to have a war in order to show Americans how good their army is." It was a recognition that we really were incredibly good, so much better than people had thought we were. Up until then, the analogue had been Vietnam. The point was that Vietnam was almost twenty years in the past, and that the number of people that were on active duty who had had Vietnam service was surprisingly few. These people were for the most part senior military commanders. One of the men for whom I had remarkable respect was Barry McCaffrey. McCaffrey now is our drug czar. But McCaffrey, when I first encountered him, was a brigadier general on the Army staff in charge of operations and planning. He was assisted by another incredibly able man, Dan Christman, who currently is the head of the military academy at West Point. But the two of them had intelligence and energy that were remarkable, as capable as any two men that I've met anywhere. It was McCaffrey who was in charge of the Twenty-fourth Mechanized Infantry Division, which made the sweep around our left flank and really did the most dramatic part of the fighting for the war.

The consequence was a profound recognition that the combination of new equipment and new tactics, so-called air-land battle military tactics, had been amazingly successful. While, yes, we were using these skills against the Soviets' idiot cousins, the skills were indeed so overwhelming and so astonishing in their capabilities that I think there was a far greater sense of confidence about our ability to handle any threat anywhere, if we wished to go forth and handle it. But at the same time, people remained very careful about triumphalism. The Army staff was not a set of military muscle flexers. If you find muscle flexers, they're at a much lower level, where the general feeling is that you have to motivate the troops by bravado. But here again, I recall the mature steadiness with which so many of the soldiers who had microphones shoved in their faces by the media made mature and balanced statements. They would say, "Well, I'm afraid, but I have great faith in my men, my leaders, and my equipment. I am confident that we will be able to do what we're asked to do." This was not John Wayneism. It was in its own way a remarkable refocusing on what kind of military, including the Reserves, that we actually had on hand.

Q: At the end of this experience, the army was still focusing on the whole future. Both the Gulf War and the changes in Europe occupied them up to the time you were there, until '92.

JONES: Yes.

Q: Did Somalia come up on your radar at all?

JONES: No, Somalia just didn't matter. There were people I knew on the Army staff, such as Tom Montgomery, who later were engaged in Somalia. He was a lieutenant general dealing with a lot of the Somalia effort when he was there. But Somalia really wasn't on the army's radar.

Military Relations with China

Q: By the time you arrived on the scene, had relations with the Chinese mainland military been just cut off?

JONES: Yes, because of Tiananmen. There had been plans for senior U.S. military officials to visit. They had been scheduled, and there had also been plans for senior PRC [People's Republic of China] military officers to come and see us. All of those plans were put aside. Indeed, relationships with the Chinese embassy were, as a consequence, more restricted. They had beefed up their staff with the expectation that they were going to have a much more extensive and intensive relationship with the United States. But they just didn't. I was one of the people who could talk with them and meet with them. I had a steady series of lunches and dinners with Chinese military representatives. But this was all very casual. This was just a way of keeping the channel open.

Q: Did you find that the Chinese understood that this was going to be a down time?

JONES: Yes. It was one of those circumstances where, "Gee whiz, we wasted this administrative exercise by sending these two additional lieutenant colonel types here, and now we can't really use them. But okay, all right." Separately, we were engaged in several different sets of meetings with the Taiwanese military. Taiwan had a substantial and active group in Washington with a liaison office. There were regular, roughly annual, meetings to discuss what military equipment could be purchased and sold. We were always interested in being able to do as much as we possibly could with and for the Taiwanese. I won't say there was an open door, but there was real receptivity to them. In one amusing experience, there was a tenth anniversary commemoration of our agreement marked by a banquet. There were small "favors" (a tie with tanks and planes on it) distributed to attendees and we were told that in honor of the tenth anniversary, there would be ten speeches. I laughed—and then sat through ten speeches. My wife, knowing Chinese proclivities, was not surprised.

The Israelis—and Egyptians and Jordanians

Q: How about the Israeli connection? Was that at a higher level that bypassed and went through Congress?

JONES: There was an Israeli connection. To a degree, there was irritation with the Israeli military. In early 1990, the Chief of Staff of the Army made a trip to the Middle East—on which I accompanied him—to visit his counterparts. After first seeing the Reforger exercise in Germany, he went to Jordan, Egypt, and Israel. The Israelis wanted to brief him on a particular military topic—I assume it was a weapons exercise—and wanted to brief only him. He wouldn't take the briefing. He said, "If I can't have some of my people in with me, I don't want the briefing." They also expected a degree of cooperation that we didn't always accept.

There was no question that we had substantial respect for them in purely military terms. In the Middle East, we reached that conclusion during the walk-through of the countries we visited and with seeing the three armies; there was no question at all that the Israelis were head and shoulders and other dimensions above the Egyptians or the Jordanians. At the same time, they also were far more casual about their expertise. It was very Israeli, the way they went about their briefings and presentations to us. They had a string quartet come to play for the Chief at the formal dinner. The formal dinner was held in a hall that gave me more the sense that I was in a high school cafeteria than anything else. The four Israeli instrumentalists arrived in ordinary fatigues, winter fatigues, but just fatigues. They did it that way.

In contrast, the Egyptians put on a display of almost pharaonic excess, with a waiter behind each heavily carved and gilded chair for the formal dinner. At the same time, when they showed us their military expertise, it was no more than a training demonstration. It wasn't an exercise of one one-hundredth the professionalism that the Israelis demonstrated in the military exercise that they held for Vuono.

At the same time, we were also involved in tank production. One of the places that the Chief visited was a production facility that General Dynamics was assembling and building in Egypt. The line was being developed that was going to produce eventually about 500 M1s for Egypt.

Q: These are tanks.

JONES: Yes. These were Abrams tanks. This was a gigantic exercise both in financial and political terms. At that point, General Dynamics had already put $500 million into the facility. But it was also a real reflection of our effort to move and keep the Egyptians thoroughly out of the then Soviet-Russian orbit by replacing all of their old Soviet armor with American Abrams tank armor and then, at the same time, respond to their desire to gain the expertise associated with producing them themselves. So, instead of buying Abrams tanks from the United States, they were going to create this gigantic production facility that would produce them and then, perhaps in the longer run, permit them to sell them elsewhere in the Middle East.

The Israeli connection was there. During the Gulf War, the major effort was to keep the Israelis out of the war.

Q: I have interviews with Bill Brown, who was our ambassador there, and Chas Freeman, who was ambassador in Saudi Arabia. Chas Freeman was trying to keep the Saudis in and Brown wanted to keep the Israelis out.

JONES: The third person that you may talk to is Roger Harrison, our ambassador in Jordan, who, in effect, ruined his career by—I won't say by being an apologist—but by trying to explain why Hussein could not give the level of support to Desert Shield/Desert Storm that some of the other countries did. He attempted to explain to Washington exactly what was happening and that they should not belabor Hussein to the degree that we were clearly inclined to do. This was not something that Secretary Baker, or for that matter President Bush, wanted to hear. Harrison never got another embassy and retired fairly soon after the end of his ambassadorship in Jordan.

The Conference of American Armies: Western Hemispheric Armed Forces

Q: Is there anything else we should talk about during this period?

JONES: Let me talk a little bit about something that would have escaped my attention, or even my thinking at all, before going on the Army staff. That was an organization called the Conference of American Armies, the CAA. The CAA was an institution that absorbed a gigantic amount of time, almost a disproportionate amount of time, without any question, by members of the Army staff and the Chief of Staff of the Army personally. It is an organization in which the United States has tried to bring all of the other armies of Latin America into regular meetings, cooperative discussions, and exchanges of techniques. It is an attempt to develop a productive, effective alliance of armies throughout the hemisphere. This organization was of particular interest to me because it was the very first experience I had as the Chief's POLAD. I went to Guatemala for the meeting of army chiefs that's held every two years. It was interesting and informative. But then the next host for this meeting was to be the United States. As a result, for a good two years, we planned at a very high intensity to bring these senior military leaders to the United States and hold a four-day conference in Crystal City, Virginia. The Army staff set up an operation that absorbed twenty-five army officers and enlisted men headed by a very effective colonel, Leo Vasquez, and we planned it step by step, day by day, exercise by exercise.

Simultaneously, at this point, for this period of time, the executive for the CAA was the United States. All of the coordinative work, all of the briefings, the efforts to keep American armies on a high level of coordination, cooperation, and, to the degree possible, even military effectiveness, was run out of this group. This officer, Vasquez, and I spent a good deal of time together working on his projects and programs. Finally (and happily) this meeting ran for four days in the fall of 1991 and went off very smoothly and professionally. But what it also did was to prevent more trips by the Chief to Latin America, since he knew that all of these commanders were going to be coming to Washington during his time as Chief.

Indians and Pakistanis

Another topic of particular interest to me and the Army was an effort to develop better bilateral and trilateral relations with South Asia, with the Indian army and the Pakistani army. Here you had a situation where for decades we had been considered to be closer to the Pakistanis, and the Soviets closer to the Indians. Well, the Indians were no fools. They recognized that as the Soviet Union was in a state of implosion, they were going to have to engage with us. There was a visit by their Chief of Staff of the Army, General Rodriguez, who was Portuguese rather than pure Indian in origin, and a very clever, very articulate man who was able to quote both Winston Churchill and Yogi Berra. He came as an official visitor. Shortly afterward, the commander of the Pakistani army came. We had very productive and interesting discussions and meetings with them. One of our efforts was to see whether there was a possibility of greater exchanges and a closer army-to-army relationship between us and the Indians. To a degree, that effort was going to operate out of Hawaii with the Army forces there. These people were slowly trying to build a set of exchanges, joint training ventures, military meetings, briefings, students to one another's schools, and efforts of this nature.

Then the Chief of Staff of the Army, in one of the last trips I made with him, in May 1992 went to India and Pakistan. There was some hope that we might be able to serve as a conduit to develop improved Pakistani-Indian relations. The Chief, who was now General Sullivan, replacing Vuono, was willing to do this in Pakistan. He said, "If there is anything that I can do to foster this relationship, I'd be willing to go back." But as far as I know, it did not so transpire. Each side took the opportunity to complain to us vigorously about the nefarious attitudes, aspects, expectations, and approaches of the others. We got nowhere on that topic.

Unfortunately, relatively quickly after that visit, the Pakistani army chief died abruptly. No one was quite sure why he died, just that he fell over dead. His wife was convinced that he had been poisoned. They even went so far as to do autopsy-related tests on him. But in the end, it simply seemed that this very fit, very capable, very athletic man had just died. That took away one of the potential interlocutors. Before you knew it, we were back into circumstances where the Pakistani army had repoliticized itself, and there wasn't any opportunity for a U.S. interlocutor to assist in an engagement with India. At the same time, I am not sure whether the Indian military was able to take advantage of the opportunities for greater contact in dealing with the United States before their latest round of nuclear weapons testing.

Q: I would think that the Indians would find themselves by this time being somewhat disturbed that they had the Soviet Union as their supplier. The Soviet Union itself was going down. Also, confrontations between American equipment and Soviet equipment with the Israeli air force over Syria and the Gulf War, the Soviet materiel was showing badly. Of course, it was poorly manned. But at the same time, the material itself did not seem to be up to the caliber of the American.

JONES: I think you can say that that was a concern. But it wasn't one that they were expressing all that vigorously. If anything, you would have seen the other side of the coin: the Indians wanted to make sure that the Pakistanis didn't get more capable American equipment. Indian industrial ability has been rising. They are and were more and more capable of producing basic equipment themselves—of course, not just land-based equipment but other weaponry. For a long time, they thought they would be able to get, without any serious difficulty, the leftover materiel from the old Soviet Union. I have no idea how they equipped themselves and reequipped themselves in recent years other than knowing that their nuclear weapons systems increased. Obviously, they now have the capability to manufacture intermediate-range missiles as well.

The Clarence Thomas Affair and Resultant Workplace Attitudes

Q: Is there anything else we should talk about?

JONES: Interestingly enough, one of the things that struck me the most and ended by conditioning a certain amount of my own activity and thinking subsequently was the Clarence Thomas effort to get Senate approval of his appointment to the Supreme Court. From October 1991 onward, most senior officers and most officers had to alter their approach and relationships with any women on their staff and operate with even greater care. I was struck in retrospect at the intensity with which everyone was following the nomination hearing proceedings.

Q: We're talking about sexual harassment charges.

JONES: Yes. And how people were simply listening to the hearings day after day. I went from my office at one point to a reception and found that every single person at the reception had rather reluctantly left the reporting broadcast of the hearings to come to the reception. What it did was to change totally the casual nature of having a discussion one-on-one with a woman. It made me transform my personal style. Subsequently, any individual meeting that I had with a woman, I had to have a door open. If at all possible, I wanted to have a secretary in another room. It was a very, very defensive decision on my part to avoid being placed in a circumstance where I could be charged with something for which I had no guilt. It was reflected in discussions at that time. I think the rest of this decade has been a conditioning one for cultural and business attitudes.

CHAPTER 36

Oh Canada—A Defining Tour

Also at this point (in early 1992), I got the word that I had been assigned as the political minister counselor in Ottawa. I began my own preparations for going to Canada.

Q: You were in Canada from 1992 to when?

JONES: 1996.

U.S. Ambassadors in Canada

—Teeley

Q: You went to Canada as political counselor. Let's talk a little about the embassy first, in Ottawa. Who was the ambassador? What sort of a political reporting staff was there and how did that develop?

JONES: The ambassador [Peter Teeley] had also literally just arrived. Pete Teeley was interesting. He had a very close connection with George Herbert Walker Bush, having been a public affairs staffer in charge of some of his campaign press during the 1988 campaign. He had been in and out of government, but he was given the ambassadorial appointment and obviously would never have taken the appointment if he hadn't expected that the Bush presidency was going to continue into 1992-1996. Nevertheless, he had just arrived and was barely getting his feet on the ground at the same time that I had arrived. I had met him briefly in Washington when we both were invited to the National Press Club dinner. He was a very pleasant man, intelligent, thoughtful. At that juncture, he had a very young wife, who had been the press photographer for Bush at one point in his administration, and a couple of young children. Teeley was also a recovering cancer victim, so there was some additional poignancy associated with this man who was then in his early 50s with a very young wife and two young children.

In effect, and by summing up the Teeley administration before it began, it was one of the very shortest that you were likely to have. He left on February 20, 1993. During the time that he was ambassador, he was also out of the country a fair amount of time. His mother became quite ill while visiting Ottawa; she was medically evacuated, suffered extensively from pneumonia, and then died. So, I won't say that Teeley ever put a definitive stamp on the embassy. At the same time, there was a very substantial, one could say massive, turnover in the senior staff. Not only was there a new political counselor, but there was also a new economic counselor and a new agricultural counselor. The defense attaché also was new. The longest serving incumbent was the DCM.

Q: *Who was that?*

JONES: That was Todd Stewart. He stayed one more year, and then James Walsh replaced him.

—Blanchard

In the summer of 1993 the most interesting initial element was the arrival of the new ambassador, Ambassador James Blanchard, who was previously the governor of Michigan. He had an interesting background as well as the expectation that he was going to be the Secretary of Transportation rather than what he got. He subsequently wrote a book, *Behind the Embassy Door: Canada, Clinton, and Quebec* [1998]. It created a minor stir in Canada and had absolutely no resonance in the United States. Among other things, an observation he made which I have used subsequently is that Canadians and Americans view each other through a one-way mirror constructed along the border of Canada and the United States. Canadians looking south see everything that's happening in the United States, and we looking north see only our own reflection in the mirror.

Blanchard was one of the illustrations of why it is difficult to claim that only career professionals should be ambassadors. It's not that he was so much better than any career Foreign Service officer would have been as ambassador. It was simply that he was one of the people who could say, "Well, I'll talk to the president about that," and indeed could pick up the phone and call the president. I could pick up the phone and call the president, but the president was less likely to answer me than he would have been to answer Jim Blanchard.

The other circumstance that made it helpful for people in Ottawa, in comparison to people who had suffered under other political ambassadors, was that Jim Blanchard was a politician. Of all the personalities who become ambassadors but are not career ambassadors, whether they're academics or businesspeople or politicians, if I had to endure one as the political ambassador, I would prefer it to be a man who has been a politician. I draw that conclusion essentially because politicians realize that the staff is not their enemy. They have deal with civil servants when they were governors, senators, or whatever their elected position might have been, and essentially they realize that civil servants are there to serve the leadership of the day, and they will serve the leadership of tomorrow just as they served the leadership of yesterday. They aren't your enemy. They're pieces of functional machinery to get the job done.

The other side of it is that most politicians are likable. You rarely find a politician who is very unlikable—maybe Joe McCarthy was considered an essentially unlikable politician. Most politicians, however, when they go elsewhere in the world, still carry with them the essential aspect of electability—having people like them.

Q: Could you explain where Blanchard's power came from?

JONES: Blanchard's power came from being the first governor to endorse Governor William Jefferson Clinton of Arkansas for the nomination to be the Democratic candidate for president. Blanchard met Clinton relatively early on, was one of the people that supported him early, was the person that organized his campaign in Michigan, and he won Michigan, although Blanchard was defeated, subsequently, in the race for governor. It was a very close defeat, but he was still defeated. As a result, people tagged Blanchard to be one of the people in the Clinton administration. Indeed, Blanchard had been promised that he was going to be the Secretary of Transportation. He says this openly in his book detailing conversations with Warren Christopher, then co-director of Clinton's transition team, regarding his vetting for the position and anticipated announcement over the Christmas holidays. However, he found that he was not going to be Secretary of Transportation when there was an announcement on CNN that Pena was going to be the secretary. Blanchard professed in his book to having been "flabbergasted" by the announcement and the manner in which it was released. He was told quietly that there was just one white male too many in the Cabinet and, as a result, he lost out. They then came to him and said, "What do you want? What would you be interested in doing?" My understanding is that he was offered a number of ambassadorships, including the ambassadorship to Germany. He chose to be ambassador to Canada.

Subsequently, he said that he had always wanted to be ambassador to Canada, that he had had close relations with various Canadians, dealing as he did out of Michigan, and that this was a place that he knew something about intellectually and personally, having visited or traveled or met individuals who had been provincial premiers, and dealt with officials and issues of bilateral nature. There may have been a bit of "making lemonade from a lemon" as Secretary of Transportation was obviously a more prominent position, but ambassador to Canada at least permitted him to include "honorable" in his resume. As a consequence, he took that ambassadorial position. Also, for a while his wife worked in personnel at the White House. She, too, was reasonably well connected within the White House circle. So Blanchard, because he knew Clinton early, because he had connections within Congress (he had been a representative before he became governor of Michigan), and because he had spent some time at least with Clinton's staff, had respectable heft. He was able to call people around Washington, call people within the White House, and get a hearing on the issues that were important to him and important to Canada.

Ultimately, for both Canada and the United States, we both want ambassadors that can reach the most senior levels of their own government. In such instance, we can be sure that messages we deliver will not languish in mid level "in boxes" and we can be sure that important messages the ambassador delivers have the weight of senior official approval. Blanchard had that cachet and Canadians knew it. Likewise, the then Canadian ambassador in Washington, Raymond Chretien, was the nephew of Prime Minister Chretien (as well as being a professional diplomat) and his ability to reach "Uncle Jean" was undoubted.

Q: How did Blanchard bring himself up to speed when he arrived there? This is true of anybody—when you arrive in a new country, particularly as ambassador, and you've done some reading, but you go to your staff and ask what's up.

JONES: Here again, Blanchard deserves substantial credit for doing something that was very smart. He immediately started a full and comprehensive tour of Canada. He traveled for a significant period both west and east, hitting major spots, meeting each of the U.S. consuls and consul generals, and had the full range of high-level appointments with provincial premiers, senior politicians in the provinces, and other senior individuals in business, academia, and Canadian society. By following this approach, instantly, he would be in a position, and was in a position, to say, "Well, I met so and so at such and such a place" and, with the exception of virtually nobody else, to have a wider grasp of what was happening in Canada from having seen it on the ground. This isn't all that easy. Canada is continental size. It took probably, although he didn't travel every single day, much of a month of travel time. He did it in some sections. First he took a long western tour. Then he went to the Maritimes. He separately went into Quebec and to Ontario. But as a result of that, he gathered a gestalt of Canada that put flesh on the bones of fact and briefing papers and briefings that his staff had given him. He didn't take anybody other than his wife on these trips. He was met at each point by the consul generals in the areas in which he was going to travel. It worked quite well for him.

On Being the Political Counselor

As the political counselor, I had essentially a standard section. It had a labor counselor, two political officers, a political-military officer, and two secretaries. Both the labor counselor and the pol-mil officer were new as well.

The action within the political section was a pretty standard bifurcation of duties. On the one hand, it consisted of making démarches to the Ministry of Foreign Affairs and other Canadian agencies so that they understood what we wanted them to do (or at least they were able to appreciate what we were trying to do), or providing them a straight briefing on developments that we thought should be of interest to them. The other side of political section responsibility was our reporting and analysis of what was happening in Canadian domestic affairs and what was likely to happen. All of that analysis, of course, was not done just from the embassy. There were and still are consulates in Halifax, Quebec City, Montreal, Toronto, Calgary, and Vancouver. They provided a certain amount of additional provincial-level analysis and reactions from those parts of the country. The political section coordinated the overall reporting for the country through the consulates as well.

Q: When you arrived, how would you say the role of the Canadian embassy in Washington was? I would think you would all be in play together.

JONES: The Canadian embassy and the U.S. embassy each had a special set of problems. Essentially, our relationship with Canada is so close, and it meets in so many dimensions and so many facets, that sometimes it's the role of the embassy simply to try to catch up with what is happening in the other capital. You have a situation in which many of the senior people in both governments know and are comfortable enough with one another to pick up the phone and just call their counterparts. Since we don't even have international dialing code problems, you just pick up the phone, dial the local area code, and you can be in your colleague's ear that very moment.

But to answer your question, we did not deal specifically with the Canadian embassy in Washington any more than the Canadian embassy dealt with us in Ottawa. By definition, your embassy deals with their Ministry of Foreign Affairs. You end by knowing a little bit more sometimes of what was happening in Washington when you got a report from your Canadian colleagues. Getting a report from the State Department in Washington about what was happening at the executive branch level or within the White House was sometimes far more difficult—indeed, totally problematic—than getting some information on such a meeting from the Canadians.

Status of the Relations

Q: To get down to the substance, when you arrived there, how would you say the status of relations was? Then what were the issues you were dealing with?

JONES: Essentially, relations with the Canadians are almost by definition good. The Canadians have a major stake in maintaining good relations with us. They have a number of throwaway phrases associated with us, such as, "The Americans are our best friends whether we like it or not." The truth of it, however, remains that on better than 95 percent of all of our issues, the relationship runs very smoothly. Throughout most administrations, the overwhelming weight on the relationship is the economic rather than the political partnership. There are times when there are disconnects between administrations. That was particularly true during the Trudeau government era when there were a number of neuralgic issues between a Liberal government and a Republican administration.

But that was not the case initially for me. What we had in the Canadian government, at that point, was a progressive-conservative Tory government that had been in power since 1984, and the then prime minister, Brian Mulroney, had made a major point of being America's best friend. His throwaway phrase in that regard was that every morning when he got up he thanked God that he was living next to the United States—and he assumed that every morning the Americans woke up and thanked God that they were next door to Canada. But underlying that comment was the basic reality of a very strong relationship between the Republican administrations from 1980 to 1992 and the Tory government that existed in power between 1984 and the autumn of 1993. There were times when Prime Minister Mulroney was not just the first but the foremost in support for foreign policy in the United States—times such as when we removed Noriega from Panama, or earlier than that, when we directed air strikes against Qaddafi and Libya. He was front and center in promising Canadian support for the United States after Iraq's invasion of Kuwait. The baseline level of support for American foreign policy from Canada was very strong and very clear.

The problem, which will evolve over time, was that the Tory government was extremely unpopular and was in effect entering the fifth (and final) year of its mandate, hoping against hope that its fortunes would improve.

It was hanging on as long as it possibly could. The Canadian government is parliamentary in style, and it has a five-year period in which it operates between elections, with the ability to choose when it goes to the polls by its own volition rather than any preset electoral schedule. But, traditionally, most governments go to the polls at the four-year mark or around then. A government that is hanging on into the fifth year is one that is in very bad condition.

Unpopular Tories

Q: What were we seeing that made this government unpopular?

JONES: It was a combination of all of the strikes that you could possibly have against a government. First, it was running into a recession. Mulroney had promised that by endorsing the North American Free Trade Agreement [NAFTA] there would be great prosperity. Second, Mulroney had implemented a national sales tax called the goods and services tax, the GST. This was done for very sound financial reasons and, indeed, replaced another tax of essentially the same category and dimension. But this new tax was also identified clearly on the bottom of every sales slip, while the previous manufacturing sales tax had been buried within the total coast. So, you had a 7 percent national sales tax—a very painfully obvious sales tax, and one that was roundly disliked.

Then Mulroney had attempted to resolve the national unity question for Canada, a long-standing historic difference between English-speaking Canada and Quebec. One of his baseline commitments when elected in 1984 had been to address this problem and create new political arrangements to reinforce the Canada-Quebec relationship. He had undertaken that issue with energy, creativity, and failure. The first failure, which was called "Meech Lake" because it was designed at that location, was rejected by Quebecers. The second effort on constitutional reform to resolve the national unity problem was in process when I arrived. Instead of dealing only with Quebec affairs and problems, it was to address political/social problems Canada-wide in a comprehensive manner. But this effort was very divisive throughout Canada. That made the Mulroney government even more unpopular.

On top of that set of political/economic issues, there were style problems. The Mulroney government was viewed as at least somewhat corrupt. It was perhaps not more corrupt than normal and not corrupt on the level that you will find outside of Western democracies, but nevertheless there were enough people at a reasonably senior level who had struggled with malfeasance questions while in office that there was a popular impression that it was not an honest government.

Then, finally, Mulroney's personal style, one of a glad-handing, mellifluous-voiced exaggerator who dressed in tailor-made suits and commensurate footwear left people feeling that this was not Canadian, that he was too American in style. His wife also was always impeccably turned out (with perhaps not Imelda Marcos's extensive selection of shoes but nevertheless a very fine assortment of couturier goods and accouterments). This combination of circumstances had driven his popularity down into the low double digits. Mulroney used to joke about such polls and say that more people believed that Elvis was alive than were supporting him. That's essentially the core set of his problems with Canadians. Canadians really were in a position that they were simply waiting for the opportunity to pound the living daylights out of the government and the Tories and replace them. They were living "road kill." So, of course, the government, having no special desire to be pounded into sand, held on hoping, like Dickens's Mr. Micawber, that "something would turn up."

Dealing with the Government in Waiting

Q: From the embassy perspective, what did this mean for the United States? You knew the tidal wave was coming, more or less. But were we seeing what's in it or what's not in it for us?

JONES: Well, obviously, yes. My throwaway phrase in this regard is, "The time to get to know the government is when it's not the government." We could read the polls as well as anybody else. Part of our job was to go out and make all the contacts, connections, associations, and linkages we could with those we expected to be senior players within the coming Liberal government. This was just our job. We knew it was coming. My predecessor had been working on it. I simply plunged into the same kind of process of analysis and review. I oversaw the writing of an extended series of cables. For instance, I remember writing one six months ahead of time saying, "Prime Minister Jean Chrétien, what does this mean?" We explored topics of this nature and along these lines. We were always speaking with people who we knew would be key within the Liberal government about what course Liberal foreign policy would take or how Liberal defense policy would be managed. We had opportunities to meet with the people who became the senior members of the establishment. We had meetings with Chrétien, with other members of the establishment such as Sheila Copps, who became the deputy prime minister; John Manley, who became the minister for industry; Paul Martin, who became the finance minister; and just right on down the line of senior people in the Liberal government.

Q: With this group, were we seeing a different attitude toward the United States?

JONES: Well, yes. The Liberal government had at least on paper a far more skeptical view of American foreign policy. Ostensibly, they were saying that they wanted to review NAFTA, which was in its final stages for agreement. The existing free trade agreement or "FTA," was the result of the arguments associated with the 1988 election. The free trade agreement had been in effect, but it hadn't been producing the economic benefits that Canadians had believed it was supposed to produce. Just about everybody was in a mild recession. In the United States, it was that mild recession—"It's the economy, stupid"—that cost Bush his reelection. This circumstance is best described by the old saw that when the United States catches cold, Canada gets pneumonia, so far as economic downturns are concerned. The Canadian finances were poor. They were running significant deficits at all times. Unemployment was above 10 percent. Inflation was higher than that in the United States. There were a series of the kind of economic indicators that left people distinctly unhappy. The fact that the Liberal opposition, the Liberal Party, was saying things like, "We think that NAFTA should be renegotiated" was at least a warning signal.

—The Lloyd Axworthy Factor

One question was who would be the leading individual in foreign affairs. Well, the "shadow" foreign minister was Lloyd Axworthy, who was a very liberal skeptic of U.S. policies. When he ultimately became foreign minister in 1996—he did not become foreign minister immediately—U.S.-Canadian relations on many foreign policy issues became much more prickly and irritable. Knowing what his general policies were—he was a left-wing liberal from the Vietnam era with a PhD from Princeton, and his issues and interests were those of people who graduated from liberal schools in the 1960s—one could anticipate problems. Essentially, he personally believed that he knew better than we what USG policy should be—and never hesitated to tell us so.

Also, the Liberals were rather skeptical of U.S. policy, even as obvious a policy as resisting Iraqi aggression in Kuwait. They were quite critical of the Mulroney government initially. Eventually, they came around and gave support, but we saw that as rather halfhearted support. To be sure, the role of the Opposition is to oppose, but this position seemed more personal than philosophical. Canadian views on defense are rather feeble, but the Tory government at least verbalized a little more positively, while the very first thing that Jean Chrétien said he was going to do was to cancel the purchase of a major set of helicopters that were, and still are, very badly needed by Canadian forces. But he argued that these were "Cadillac, gold-plated helicopters" that were far too expensive, and he was just going to cancel these.

And there were other aspects in which we simply looked at a potential Liberal Canadian foreign policy and thought that it was going to be less supportive of U.S. foreign policy or U.S. economic interests in NAFTA than would have been the case if the Tories continued in office. We didn't say that the world was going to come to an end or that the 4,000-mile undefended cliché that exists between us was going to change dramatically, but we expected more problems with the Liberals.

Comments on Canada: Operating Environment

Q: Was this your first time serving in Canada?

JONES: Yes. I had not been to Canada since 1967, when I went to the Montreal Expo. My entire Foreign Service career and my entire career in government had never taken me to Canada, although I had met and dealt with Canadians while I was at NATO.

Q: Looking at Canada, one of the things that comes up often is the Canadian concern, "Poor little us and great big you. You've got to be nice to us." The other one is that it's been said that the Canadians really don't have any great sense of unity. We had our Revolutionary War and our Civil War and things that went across—real trials. The Canadians, it was sort of handed to them by the British government. This has caused a country without… There is no theme to the pudding.

JONES: That's more obvious from the outside than from the inside. One of the first points you were cautioned about when going to Canada was that Canadians did not consider it complimentary to say, "You're just like us." Indeed, if you look at the externals, they are very obviously similar. You have a first world, high-tech, freedom-loving, human rights—respecting, democracy in which both the major leadership elements of both countries speak English, understand each other's issues, and can pick up the telephone and dial directly and talk to each other. The similarities look more obvious than the differences. Yes, you're in Canada. You can get your automobile repaired. Water will be pure to drink. You can go to a hospital and, in contrast to much of the world, expect to get better rather than worse medical care. These points are all true. But in its core, I consider Canada very different from the United States.

Q: I'm going under the assumption that dealing with the Canadians, it was easy to get to see their officials and officials-to-be, that it was a fairly easy governmental structure to work with.

JONES: I would say that is correct. The level of access that official Americans had with official Canadians was very high. Of course there was a division as to whom you saw. The ambassador saw ministers; the DCM perhaps might do so in the absence of the ambassador. But outside of that restriction, among government officials and within normal Members of Parliament, individuals at that level, you could pick up the phone and ask for an appointment, and sooner or later you were likely to get that appointment.

People also spoke very frankly to you. They assumed a degree of confidentiality on your part, you assumed that your questions could be asked in a straightforward manner, and you normally got straightforward answers. This was as true among Quebecers as it was among English-speaking

French Canadians and English-speaking non-Quebecers. Quebecers, in particular, wanted the United States to understand exactly what Quebec wanted, exactly what it was trying to do, exactly how it was going to go about it, and also wanted to emphasize that it could do so without being a security, economic, or political concern to the United States. Wherever you went, you had a lot of access, particularly on political, national security, and defense issues. On issues that were of financial concern, they were more careful, more reticent, held their cards closer to their chest. These were issues and problems that were of very high financial value. But on the areas in which the political minister counselor was dealing, I would say that I was almost always able to get good access and clear indications of what Canada was interested in knowing and clear indications of what they were willing to do or not do.

Q: One knows that the Canadians are extremely effective and have been around for so long in Washington and they know the Washington game, in which the Department of State plays essentially a minor role. It's the White House, Congress, the media, maybe the think tanks. It's a diverse field. What was the game as far as our embassy in Ottawa was concerned? What were the places you had to touch?

JONES: The situation in many respects was completely different. Canadians find out very quickly, if they don't already know ahead of time, that getting the president on board is just part of their problem, and that 100 different senators and 435 congressmen can be individually very important on a special issue. In Ottawa, it's the reverse. Almost nobody counts except a senior minister, or somebody within the prime minister's office, or the prime minister himself. Individual Members of Parliament are sometimes referred to in a derisory manner as "potted plants" or "trained seals." They leap up and applaud during the day-to-day question period, discussion, and debate. But as individuals they are completely invisible 100 yards from Parliament Hill, as Prime Minister Trudeau memorably put it. The people that you need to know or need to have on board to deliver an answer are your senior mandarins within the specific bureaucracies or a minister or a member of the prime minister's office. These are not huge establishments. It's not as if you're working through anything like an American-style bureaucracy. One or two men in the prime minister's office might be the individuals who would be the key go-to persons so far as a difficult problem was concerned. Eddie Goldenberg has had this position with Prime Minister Chrétien throughout his entire prime ministership. He has been the prime minister's chief fixer, and presumably will be as long as Chrétien remains prime minister.

—Differences Between Canadians and Americans

Canadians are unnecessarily worried about their similarity to the United States. The core of the difference lies in the difference between the U.S. system of division of authority and balance of powers and the Canadian system of parliamentary rule, which is true across the country. A parliamentary system, without belaboring the details under these circumstances, is simply very different regarding the levers of control that are exercised, in the manner in which influence is delivered, and the process by which the population is governed. That point is defining.

As well as the difference in governance, there are obvious differences in the views that Canadians have toward how public health should be delivered; how crime should be handled and managed; what the right to bear or not bear arms should be; the degree to which aboriginals, which is the Canadian term for first nations, "Indians," should be compensated and assisted; and the emphasis—even greater than that in the United States—on the rights of women and minorities and the protection accorded these groupings. It's a very different society. It's a very different society in many of its facets and at its core.

Canadian Foreign Affairs Structures and Some Bilateral Issues

Q: Is it called the Ministry of Foreign Affairs?

JONES: It used to be External Affairs or "EXTAF." Now it's the Department of Foreign Affairs and International Trade [DFAIT].

Q: You got there in '92. How important were they from your perspective?

JONES: What I did had to be done with the Ministry of Foreign Affairs. My point, so far as the first half of my portfolio as political minister-counselor was concerned, was to deliver démarches and seek their support. By and large, the objectives that we were trying to accomplish were not really highly visible foreign affairs or foreign policy issues. A lot of topics looked as if they had just been resolved and consequently completed as issues. This was the "end of history" era.

One subject on which we were engaged was getting their participation in a maritime interception force, a Gulf interception force, in the Persian Gulf. This effort involved a series of ships that rotated and were inspecting traffic moving in and out of the area toward Iraq. We wanted the Canadians to provide a vessel and made a series of démarches in this regard. Eventually, they agreed to do so and continued the commitment. Over my tour in Ottawa, to skip ahead, we regularly went to them on foreign affairs—related issues for assistance that we hoped they would provide in Haiti or assistance that we hoped they would provide in Bosnia, in the way of contributions to joint multinational forces that were being created. I think that, more or less, we were successful.

There was one time that we were not successful, and that was when we attempted to persuade the Canadians not to withdraw from the international peacekeeping force in Cyprus. They had come to the conclusion that they had provided a battalion for about twenty-five years, and that twenty-five years was enough. Although we attempted to persuade them to stay because they had been very successful in their presence there, they decided that it was too large a continuing commitment to finance any further. They saw it as an issue that was obviously open ended, not likely to be resolved, and no longer having a level of tension that required them to be the peacekeepers. In effect, they were probably right in that judgment. In the intervening eight years, nothing has happened on Cyprus to gainsay their decision to depart. There was no horrible flare-up of fighting, and there has been no progress in resolving the standoff on the island. I was personally worried that the absence of peacekeepers from the Canadians might lead to a breakdown and a resumption of significant hostilities, but I was wrong.

Canadian Forces—The Status of the Canadian Military

Q: What about the Canadian military? How did we evaluate it? The world was changing. The Soviet Union was breaking up. But we were getting involved in Bosnia. We were looking around for solid troop commitments and to effect troop commitments.

JONES: This is an interesting question. It's one that I spent a fair amount of time studying. To a degree, I spent some time on it before going to Canada. One of the trips that I made with General Sullivan, when I was his foreign affairs advisor, was to Canada, to discuss and review Canadian forces. The estimates that we made of Canadian forces from the time I got there, which I made one of my personal areas of interest, were ones that were steadily negative. It was a judgment that we made with increasing regret.

We saw and recalled that in both World War I and World War II, Canadian military participation had been outstanding. In World War II, Canadians put over a million of their citizens into uniform out of a population of about twelve million, which was very directly comparable to the commitment that the United States made, which was about twelve million in uniform about of 140 million. As almost all of the Canadians who served were volunteers, it was even more remarkable. Canada didn't have conscription until almost the end of the war, and virtually none of the soldiers that went overseas were draftees. Canadian participation in World War II was really quite striking. At the end of the war, I believe they had something like the fifth largest army, the fourth largest air force, the third largest navy, and they were well-positioned to have been able to build nuclear weapons had they so desired. They had a heavy bomber force. They were operating at least one aircraft carrier. This was a very, very capable military.

Throughout the core of the Cold War, the Canadians put a very effective brigade into Europe that was there full-time. They had an air wing stationed in Germany. The brigade was a unit that I saw during a NATO Reforger exercise when I went to the field in Germany and saw various units, including the Canadian brigade. It was a fine unit. The Canadian expertise in peacekeeping was rooted in the fact that they were first and foremost good soldiers. It's certainly been one of my conclusions, and one of the conclusions by the military with whom I've dealt, that before you can be an effective peacekeeper, first you have to be a good soldier. But the Canadians, like everybody else around the world, with the collapse of the Soviet Union elected to take a peace dividend.

The amount of money in proportionate terms, and even in real terms, committed to Canadian defense fell steadily. Their force levels fell steadily. This was pointed out by military commentator after military commentator, including the man who led their forces in Bosnia under the United Nations mandate, Major General Lewis McKenzie, who very quickly noted that there were more Toronto policemen than there were Canadian infantrymen. It just went downhill all along the line. The Canadians had steadily reduced military capability in virtually all fields.

Canadians have a basic societal problem that has developed over the last fifty years that has become akin to the old Chinese saying that, "just as you don't make good steel into nails, you don't make good men into soldiers." Canada has virtually buried its very small military in penny-packet units spread out of sight of the population on small bases across the country. There is no social-political cachet to having been a former soldier. For example, no general officer has ever become prime minister. If you think of the number of generals who became president of the United States, there is simply no comparison between the political prospects for former military personnel in Canada and in the United States. When I arrived in Canada, there were, out of approximately three hundred Members of Parliament, perhaps no more than five people who had had military experience. In the United States, the number of people with military experience in Congress has steadily declined, but our World War II generation also became very much engaged in politics. Canada's World War II generation is not represented in their Parliament.

To a degree, that may be a reflection of the fact that politics in Canada is more of a young person's game than it is in the United States. You can get involved in Canadian politics at a lower level for less money than is true in the United States. Because the party system oftentimes creates a lot of safe ridings, or constituencies, if you can get into one of those, you are going to win. The party label is far more important than individual personalities in getting a candidate elected or defeated in Canada. But still, the point remains that Canadians seem to become politically engaged at a younger age, while we seem to wait until we've had a full career before we enter politics. Canadians will go into politics in high school in serious youth parties strongly associated with the individual national political parties. They can be running for office in their twenties. The burned-out, about to be defeated Tory Party that had been in office for eight years after its 1984 victory had most of its leadership quit and not run in the 1993 elections—but these were people in their forties or, at the most, their early fifties.

NORAD as a Keystone of the U.S.-Canadian Military Relationship

NORAD has been in effect since the 1950s. It has a U.S. commander and a Canadian deputy. They are responsible jointly to the heads of government of Canada and the United States. It was responsible for air defense over North America throughout the period of the Cold War. It has slowly grown into a system that is supposed to at least recognize and provide alert for any ballistic missile attack. It has also, however, been a point of question at times for Canadians as to whether they wish to continue this agreement, whether it sucks them into subordination to the United States, and whether it reduces Canadian sovereignty to have this agreement. This has been reflected in questions concerning how the agreement itself operates and how long they should renew the agreement for each time. What we did throughout a fair portion of the time that I was political minister-counselor was to work on NORAD Treaty renewal. This was batted back and forth between the Department of Defense, the Department of Foreign Affairs, and the U.S. government to try to find a formula and appropriate language that would get it done. Well, it got delayed and it got delayed. Although in theory it could have been one of the pieces signed when President Clinton visited in 1995, it ended by not really being agreed until March 1996, in an agreement that probably made the technical specialists a little happier but didn't really change the scope and thrust of the agreement from where it stood previously.

The Clinton Administration and the Canadian Government

Q: When the Clinton administration came in, what was your impression of how it dovetailed? The Clinton administration came in before the Tory government lost.

JONES: Yes. Of course, the Clinton administration was elected in November of 1992. It came to office in January 1993. The Tories were still in power and would be until October 1993. So there was a certain amount of overlap, and the Tories tried to develop a relationship with the Clinton administration. Mulroney did meet with the president. This was standard scheduling. The first foreign leader that American presidents usually meet has been the Canadian prime minister, even if very briefly. Mulroney was adroit enough so that, while it would have been obvious simply from looking at the circumstances that he would have preferred George H. W. Bush to have been reelected, he never said anything that was so publicly supportive of Bush during the campaign that it would have been impossible for the Tories to have a reasonable relationship with the Clinton Democrats. UK Prime Minister John Major, on the other hand, had made it more painfully clear than was appropriate that he wanted Bush to be reelected. So, there was a desire on the part of the Tories to have the best relationship they could have with the incoming administration. At the same time, it was very much in the Liberals' interest to try to get to people to Washington to sell their side of the case. After all, they said, "We are the government in waiting. We are going to be the government as soon as there is an election. Don't waste your time with these people." By and large, they were successful in making this point. We did what we could with the Tories as long as the government was in power. We were planning, expecting, analyzing, doing our biographic work, and doing studies that were designed to see what the new government was going to be like.

Q: On foreign policy issues, during this first period, did Cuba come up?

JONES: No, not really. Cuba was generally viewed, almost with a smile, as the way in which a conservative Tory Canadian government would differentiate itself from the United States. The Canadian policy toward Cuba, which is recognition and engagement, has not changed and has been the same as long as Castro has been the leader of Cuba. But we were not pushing them on Cuban issues at this juncture.

Q: Were we almost considering Cuba being a throwaway, and Canada, showing us how different they were, could hit us with that, and we'd shrug our shoulders and get on with more important things?

JONES: This was the point on which the Mulroney government would differentiate itself to its critics from those who said, "Oh, you're just a lackey of the Americans," and they would say, "No." There were other points of difference that they could find on specific African issues. They had been stronger and earlier in pushing for the elimination of apartheid and on not dealing with South Africa. It was not a question of the Canadians under the Tories invariably leaping up and saying, "Yes, sir!" to the Americans. Essentially, we didn't have a major problem with them holding this particular point of difference. We would have preferred it not to be the case, but it wasn't an issue that we were going to make primary in a relationship that was going so very well in so many other ways.

Q: In many ways, particularly in matters such as Cuba and Africa, the Canadians from our perspective didn't count for much anyway, did they?

JONES: Canada is at best a second-level power. Its presence around the world is very thin. They have points to make and they have issues on which they engage in Africa through what used to be the British Commonwealth, now just the Commonwealth, and they have a certain amount of leverage in these areas. But it's on the margins rather than primary. Working through UN peacekeeping operations, they had a presence in many places around the world. At this point, they took special pride in having participated in one level or another in virtually every single UN peacekeeping operation. You could say Canada was punching a little bit above its weight. It was a member of the G7, now the G8. It had done all of its peacekeeping. It could be seen by a number of countries as an interlocutor with the United States. Or, a country might imagine that if it can't really deal with the United States, maybe it could work an angle with the Canadians. There were times, although I can't put a finger on it for specifics, in which the Canadians would carry our water in areas where we were not going to be given anything other than a dismissive hearing by those involved, but in which our interests and those of the Canadians were not significantly different. The Canadians were willing to make points along the same lines that we would like to have heard. I wouldn't overestimate their weight, but I wouldn't just drop it out of hand.

National Unity and the Quebec Separatist Issue

There is also the essential difference between Canada and the United States regarding what the country's key problem continues to be which, for Canada, is national unity. We say that the United States solved its national unity problem, not in a way that is necessarily to be emulated, but in a bloody civil war. Nevertheless, following the Civil War, the United States changed in description from the United States "are" to the United States "is." Canada has never ultimately resolved this issue. Part of the problem is that Quebec could indeed be an independent country. There is no question that Quebec has the size, the resources, the economic strength, the skill of its population, and the quality of its government leadership to be a quite workable and effective small state of about eight million people whose trading-level relationship with the United States would be about eighth across the world. It could work. But whether it would be a smart idea for Quebecers to do this or whether it would be a very disruptive development, how long it would take to sort out these new circumstances, and the rest of their relationships with Canada and internationally, that's a completely different story. We can explore that at whatever length you wish later. But I don't consider Canada as a country akin to a themeless pudding.

Q: With Canada in these early days of your tour, how did we see the Quebec separatist movement? Did we see this as still being a viable possibility, or did we see this as beginning to fade?

JONES: If anything, we saw it beginning to rise. Although there had not been a referendum since 1980, the major efforts that the government had made to resolve the national unity question had either failed or were struggling desperately in the first year that I was in Ottawa. The Quebec government was run by the Liberals—a provincial Liberal party. The provincial political parties, although they may have the same name as the national parties are often very different from and independent of the national parties. But the *Parti Québécois*, the PQ, was strengthening. There was no question about that. The Liberals were weakening. You could say there was a reasonable to good likelihood that the PQ was going to win the next election, which would be held in 1994. As a result, I spent a fair amount of time dealing with the Quebec separatists and the *Parti Québécois*.

On the federal level, the *Bloc Québécois* (BQ) had just been formed. Their leader, Lucien Bouchard, had been a close personal friend of Brian Mulroney's, but broke with him over disagreements about how the Meech Lake accord was to have been drafted and why it ultimately failed. He took out of the Tories a group of about eight or nine Members of Parliament who were Quebecers, and he formed this small separatist party. The DCM and I met with Bouchard twice during the course of my first year there in an attempt to get to know who this man was, what he was doing, and how he struck us. He was very impressive. He had learned English in his forties. It was good, workable English. He was clearly an extraordinarily well-read man in English, not just in French. He was thoughtful, articulate, smart.

We didn't run around saying, "Well, he's going to do fantastically in the next election," but he was a respectable, very small party leader at that point.

On a more general basis, 1992-1993 was the last period before traditional Canadian three-party politics shattered completely. Canada in 1992 had three parties—a New Democratic Party [NDP], which is a socialist party; the Liberals; and the Progressive Conservatives, the Tories. You had this tiny splinter group of *Bloc Québécois*, which had broken off, who were Quebec nationalists/separatists. You had a single individual from the Canadian West, Deborah Gray, who represented the Reform Party. But after the 1993 election, which has continued in 1997 and 2000, although this is outside of my current purview for discussion, Canadian politics completely changed.

The Liberals are labeled the "natural governing party." Over Canada's history, they've probably run the country two-thirds of the time. When they get themselves into a position where there has been a hideous depression or they have been more than normally arrogant, Canadians have been willing to vote them out and turn to the natural opposition party. The natural opposition party normally consists of the West, a selection of dissidents within Quebec, and certain numbers of Ontario and Maritime province voters. But following the 1993 election, there was a group of regional parties with a regional opposition element: the Bloc Québécois, which held the majority of the Quebec seats; the Reform Party, which held the majority of seats in the West; a splintered social democratic party (the NDP), which had just become less and less relevant and more and more marginalized; and a very powerful Liberal Party.

Meech Lake and the Charlottetown Accord/National Referendum

Moreover, one of the major rocks on which Canadian politics of that era shattered was one of the first things that I encountered when I came to Canada: a national referendum, the first referendum in more than fifty years, on national unity. The government presented the Charlottetown Accord, designed to fix a substantial number of constitutional problems in Canada. It was an evolution from the Meech Lake Accord, which had been designed to fix only Quebec problems. The failure of that effort, however, prompted a decision that they had to address problems Canada-wide. Meech Lake had been approved by Quebecers, but it failed in several other provinces.

Q: The Maritime Provinces, didn't it?

JONES: Meech Lake failed in Manitoba and in Newfoundland. In Newfoundland, they had approved it and then the approval was withdrawn. In Manitoba, one man refused to give unanimous consent to continue the parliamentary session discussing it, and it ended without them ever taking a vote. But, nevertheless, there were serious problems in the review process for Meech Lake.

The emphasis consequently for the Charlottetown Accord was that they had to address problems nationwide regarding issues such as what level of senate reform there was to be, what the position of aboriginals should be, as well as specific problems associated with the role of Quebec within Canada. This collage of issues was brought to a national referendum. When the presentation was made initially, it had support across the board. With the exception of the Reform Party, every significant member of the power elite in Canada, all the major newspapers, as well as all of the national party leaders, all of the provincial party leaders and opposition parties—everyone supported it. But during the course of the campaign, a situation developed in which more and more people became less and less comfortable, not perhaps with the elements which might have been the goodies for others but on the elements that were supposed to be attractive to them. It was never enough or it was never done in the right way. On a province-by-province basis, it failed in all of the key provinces except Ontario. It failed in one of the four maritime provinces, in Nova Scotia. It failed in Quebec, much to the surprise of many people, who thought that then provincial premier (Robert Bourassa) would only have agreed to the referendum if he was confident that Quebecers would endorse it. It failed in the West. Canadian aboriginals, who voted on it separately, also rejected it. It was one of those situations in which all of the elites were on one side and the majority of the people were on the other. That, in effect, ended serious effort at constitutional reform for the rest of this decade.

There were developments after I left that I'm fully aware of because I follow events in Canada very carefully. But for the rest of the period of time in which I was in Canada, people were dealing with the ramifications of the failure of the national referendum. "Constitutional fatigue" followed the referendum effort, and there was a combination of irritation and anger in other parts of Canada because Quebec was being offered a special deal, and anger in Quebec because Canadians wouldn't give them the rights they believed they should have been normally accorded.

End of the Tories and the National Election

Q: This interview is dealing pretty much on the first year you were there. Any developments then that you would like to comment on?

JONES: Yes. The other point was that as we were seeing the Tory government play itself out, one of the issues that came up was, would Prime Minister Mulroney resign and give them a chance for a facelift, some revival? This was a major point of discussion. Indeed, you had a situation, as often happens in a parliamentary system, where nobody knows what the leader's plans are going to be. Every leader holds this decision as close to his vest as possible. The minute he indicates what his departure plans are, he's dead. He's not a lame duck; he's a dead duck. Well, Mulroney was so good at this tactic that in the departure interview Ambassador Teeley had with Mulroney (Teeley saw him around February 18), Teeley said in his reporting telegram that he would be amazed and flabbergasted if Mulroney did not continue in office. By February 24, Mulroney announced that he was resigning. So, you can see that Teeley, with years of American political experience—it wasn't as if he was some businessman or academic who became an ambassador, he was a political analyst/observer/political animal/media expert—was completely, totally, absolutely faked out by what Mulroney kept secret.

But then you had the next question: who was going to replace Brian Mulroney? You had an interesting contest within the Tories. They generated a good half dozen candidates. The leader from the very beginning was a well-regarded and carefully groomed woman, Kim Campbell. Although she was relatively new in politics—she had only been elected in 1984—she had held a series of good portfolios. She had been the justice minister, which in Canada is considered a key cabinet ministerial position. After that, she became the defense minister, which is not a very prominent ministry in Canada, but since she was the first woman to be the defense minister, it was also considered to be something of a plus. It was clear they were trying to give her a series of appointments that would lead her to being a respectable leadership prospect. Consequently, she was the frontrunner from the beginning.

But another, younger Tory, Jean Charest, was encouraged to run by Mulroney to provide a little competition. Charest had been not much more than a minister of sports. I think he might also have been the minister of health. But that, too, was not a very prominent position. He was not expected to give Campbell much opposition. But it turned out otherwise. Charest caught on by demonstrating a lot of young, enthusiastic, energetic, bilingual French-English capability. He looked right. He looked like the kind of man about which every young woman would tend to say, "Well, he's a teddy bear. He's not a sex object, but he's very nice." He was not threatening to any man, either, while at the same time he was an individual who, if not regarded as intellectually brilliant, at least could give a hell of a good speech, look very dynamic, and had that perfect Canadian combination of French-English bilinguality. By late March, during which period there had been a series of debates and a lot of organizational effort, there was something of a question as to whether the Charest "tortoise" would overtake the Campbell "hare." There were people that looked at Campbell and said, "Maybe we've made a mistake. If we had not all rushed to leap on her bandwagon, maybe we would have been better off to have gone with Charest anyway."

The party held a good, rousing, exciting, old-fashioned convention in Ottawa, and Campbell won; but she didn't win overwhelmingly. She won professionally because of the work that had been done in her favor by the team that had been assembled and put together beforehand, and because she very adroitly, at the last minute, made a compromise with one of the other candidates and got him with his votes to come on board with her. She had very little growth room, if she had not won on the first ballot as she did. As a result, we had Kim Campbell become the first female prime minister in Canada in early June.

Q: Starting in the summer of '1993, what were the issues that you were looking at and dealing with?

JONES: The primary issue for 1993 was when there would be a federal election and just how massive a defeat the Tories would absorb. It was clear, and had been clear even before I arrived in Canada, that it would have taken a substantial political miracle for the Tories to have been reelected in 1993. They had been in office for two terms. They came in because of a variety of Liberal disasters, and the Liberals had just worn themselves out as a party. However, during the eight years in which the Conservatives had been in control, they had put in a hated goods and services tax. They had run themselves directly into a depression, not by anything that they had done, but by the same bad accident of fiscal fate that "It's the economy, Stupid" defeated George H.W. Bush and also was driving the Tory conservative numbers down to virtually the single digits.

Mulroney had attempted with great energy and substantial goodwill to create a circumstance in which Quebec would sign on to the constitution. He reopened the constitutional question in line with his original campaign commitment in 1984 that he would bring Quebec willingly and eagerly back into full Canadian participation. In two substantial, even monumental, efforts, including the national referendum that I discussed earlier, he failed. The failure left Canadians even more irritated and divided than they had been previously, and left the Quebecers essentially highly alienated as a result of this effort. Then, finally, on top of that set of negatives, you had an endless sleaze factor. The Tories, having been out of power for many years, got back into the trough with all four feet—not just the one or two feet that you would normally expect in the trough. There were endless scandals of essentially minor nature, but they were sufficient to attrite popular approval and left the impression of a fundamentally dishonest party.

As for Brian Mulroney personally, although his glad-handing, almost bombastic style of speech and action went over well as an Irish politician in some areas, for others, it was excessive and hence offensive. Particularly there was the fact that he dressed with elegance and his wife was also very fashionably dressed and very prominent on the Canadian social scene. This approach generated a level of personal irritation to the effect that it was somehow not Canadian—as if being Canadian required being clothed "off the rack" and have a dowdy spouse. And as a final erroneous thought, he liked the United States. He gave the United States a great deal of specific and general support in a way that few Canadian politicians, and certainly no Liberal politician, would ever do.

Consequently, as I noted earlier, Mulroney resigned, and there was a party campaign in which Kim Campbell became the first woman ever to be prime minister in Canada. Of course, she then had to suffer the opprobrium of being "Mulroney in skirts," as Jean Chrétien put it, plus having all of the overburden that I earlier described. Although there was a flash of popularity associated with the novelty of having a feisty younger woman in charge of their country, she ran into the same problems that I have just outlined and a number of her own, as well. As a politician, she had advanced too fast. It would be as if Geraldine Ferraro somehow had become president, with all of the baggage that she might have had associated with it—and no real national leadership experience. Well, Kim Campbell had only been elected in 1984. She had never run a national campaign. She had held a couple of prominent ministries within the Mulroney administration—justice minister and defense minister, which were positions that Mulroney assigned her because the Tories wanted to give her a certain amount of exposure and experience. She was somebody that the leadership was grooming. With a Hail Mary pass—type of political maneuver, they made her Tory Party leader and consequently prime minister.

Q: This campaign was going on in 1993?

JONES: Yes, in the summer. They knew that an election had to be called. They have a five-year mandate, and the election had to be called by late 1993. Any Canadian party that goes into the fifth year of its mandate is a party that is in desperate trouble. Most of the time, they go for an election somewhere in the late three—to early four-year mark, and that is seen as the appropriate time. If you run your mandate into the fifth year, you are expected to lose.

Q: Were you telling the new ambassador, "Make your due obeisance to the party in power, but you'd better start getting close to the Liberals"? Was that just self-evident?

JONES: It was self-evident. It was something that you walked around and did all the meeting and greeting at the official level. I don't even know which of the senior Tories that were in government that Ambassador Blanchard did meet. It was during the summer and the government was closed both to enjoy the brief Canadian summer and campaign unofficially.

Since the government was closed and then almost immediately went into campaign mode, I'm sure he met some of the people who were ministers in the Campbell government, but most of them he wouldn't have met. For a good two years beforehand, the embassy was working full time to meet and cultivate the people that we anticipated would be senior leaders in the new Liberal government.

Q: You said something that strikes the difference between the American system and the British system, which the Canadians have to some extent, and that is the government was closed. In the United States, life goes on. When you say the government was closed . . .

JONES: What I meant was that Parliament was in recess just as Congress would be in recess. It was not that there was nobody at all minding the store, but that you did not have normal political activity in Ottawa during the summer. Their parliamentary recesses are longer than our congressional recesses—partly because the Canadians desperately want to enjoy their summers, given the depth and persistence of their winters.

Q: In the parliamentary system, it tends more to close down than in the presidential system, doesn't it?

JONES: Yes, because the parliamentarians are also the ministers. What you can do with a parliamentary system that you can't do with the American political system is largely identify from the shadow cabinet the people who will have prominent positions in the next government, assuming that it is the government. The phrase that I've always used is, "The time to meet the government is before it becomes the government." It is certainly far easier for political counselors, economic counselors, and so on to meet the key and senior members of the opposition in a country such as Canada than it is to meet ministers who are essentially the points of contact for the ambassador—and the ambassador reserves them to himself.

Q: Were you and your team putting together the new government and, were you able to get out and meet them?

JONES: Yes. This was just normal political work. You looked at the people that had the shadow ministry portfolios and you tried to get a chance to meet them and talk to them. You tried to get to meet people who were prominent and active within the Liberal Party, or who had been for a number of years, and the people who were deemed to be close to the prospective prime minister, part of his basic entourage, and at least develop points of contact. But these were all very standard. The man who is now deputy prime minister in Canada, John Manley, was simply a normal, standard Member of Parliament from an Ottawa riding, although he was considered to be a very smart man and was expected to have a cabinet position. So we obviously met him. The shadow foreign minister, Lloyd Axworthy, didn't immediately become the foreign minister. But within about three years after Chrétien won the election, he became the foreign minister. It was true for other senior people within the Chrétien establishment. They either became senior people within government or they were senior advisors close to him. By no means will I say that we met and knew them all, but we did have a fair number of solid contacts within what became the government, and we were able to make at least some reasonable judgments about what kind of people they were.

Prospects for Bilateral Relations with the Liberals and Liberal Attitudes

Q: Were you seeing trouble on the horizon with the new government coming in, which I take it, was working to keep itself somewhat separate from the United States?

JONES: You have a situation in Canada where they really have only one foreign relationship. That is with the United States. Their be-all and end-all in foreign affairs is their management of their relations with the United States—directed toward the benefit of Canada. Their A team is focused on dealing with their issues, problems, circumstances, and relationship with us. At the same time, our predominance in North America in the economy, on the continent, in the world is so massive that they have to get along with us. It's one of these realities that "we're best friends" whether they like it or not.

The relationship is one that has to work. They are our largest trading partner, but we are overwhelmingly their largest trading partner. Right now, the trade relationship is about two billion Canadian dollars a day each way. It's an enormous trading relationship. It's the largest trading relationship in the world. But it's even more important to the Canadians than it is to us. Something like 80 to 85 percent of their exports go to the United

States. This moved up over the years. I think it was 60 to 65 percent when I first arrived in Canada in 1992. But the free trade agreement and now NAFTA have stimulated trade to an extent that has been magnificently advantageous economically to the United States, Canada, and Mexico, but it has made Canada even more reliant upon the United States than was the case in the past. What we had was a situation where for eight years the relationship had been extremely good. Brian Mulroney in some instances was virtually our only supporting voice for some things that we did.

Thus while the role of the opposition in a parliamentary system is to oppose, there were times that we thought that the Liberals took more glee and more seriousness in their pointed opposition to what the United States was doing or intended to do than what would suggest that the relationship would be smooth, calm, and congenial. Indeed, the Liberals had talked during their election campaign about renegotiating NAFTA, which had been completed. At different times in the past, they had been pointedly critical or very slow to get on board in support of the U.S. effort to reverse the Iraqi invasion of Kuwait in 1991 for the Gulf War, and rather skeptical about the need to do so. Finally, they smartened up, but it was not something where they gave an instant response of support, such as "This could not stand; this must be changed."

Q: In a way, that one seems clear.

JONES: Yes.

Q: At least to a professional Foreign Service person. But was it visceral on the part of the Canadians that they just didn't want to get on board?

JONES: I honestly don't know, but I think to a degree it reflects the foreign affairs ignorance of the Liberals and the now prime minister Jean Chrétien. The foreign affairs ignorance has persisted. It has been consistent. He has little or no interest in foreign affairs, and less competence in it.

Q: This is Chrétien?

JONES: Yes. As prime minister and as leader of the opposition, Chrétien had and has very little sense for foreign affairs. I say that he has perfect pitch for domestic politics and a tin ear in foreign affairs.

Q: This brings up a point. How did the Canadians feel themselves? Did they feel themselves to be North Americans or Europeans? Bosnia brought a division there.

JONES: The Canadians view themselves now as North Americans. I think they have increasingly done so as their relationship with Europe distances, as the relationship with the United Kingdom declines, and as the United Kingdom grows closer to Europe. The Canadians in the late 1980s entered the Organization of American States as full members, which they had declined to do earlier. They had previously been observers. They had not really wanted to be associated with all those tin-pot dictators who were under American influence. They committed themselves within NAFTA—and, by joining the Organization of American States, even more so—to a continental North American view rather than a European view. By definition of their political attitudes, the Canadians had paid less and less attention to military concerns. With the end of the Cold War, they grabbed onto the peace dividend immediately; drove down their spending in defense both in real and in absolute terms to much lower percentages of their budget; pretty much withdrew all of their forces from Europe; and focused, to the extent that they continued to have any real military interest, on peacekeeping exercises either UN-related or not.

Q: How did we prepare ourselves for the election, and what happened?

JONES: We did not expect that there were going to be major problems, although these red flags were at least available for viewing. We thought it was going to be a situation, as is so often the case, of "where you sit is where you stand." It is much easier to oppose for the sake of opposition than it is, when you are in power, to change everything that has been done. We hoped and anticipated on the basis of the track record of U.S.-Canadian bilateral relations that we would have a reasonably good relationship.

In preparation for the election, which was in October once the "writ was dropped," which is their phrase for calling the election on a specific date, the political section did a comprehensive series of telegrams outlining how Canadian politics work, what the baseline descriptions of each of the parties were, where they stood, how they viewed life and politics. I set up a reporting schema by the consulates so that on a weekly basis they put in a short sketch as to how events were evolving in their area of responsibility. Then we followed the election campaign quite closely.

I had the interesting experience of joining the Liberal election entourage with a media seat for about four days. I rode on the campaign plane with them and the bus. These were transits around Ontario and Quebec. It was toward the very end of the campaign. This was something that I understand that embassy officers had done previously. The media buys a seat on the plane for a period, and the embassy bought a seat for me to travel with them. Previously, I had done some visits with Members of Parliament who were campaigning in local ridings and gone to some rallies to see how they were working and evolving. I saw Chrétien work while he was on campaign as opposition leader. I met and talked with people that I had known prior to the run-up to this campaign, and new people as well. This was an interesting experience. What I found was that Chrétien has an almost reflexive set of comments that are, if not absolutely hostile, at least strongly skeptical about the United States—things that he didn't need to say. He would make comments like, "We're not going to be the fifty-first state of America!" Who had invited him to be? "I'm not going to be Bill Clinton's fishing buddy," the reference being that Brian Mulroney had spent a fair amount of time with George H. W. Bush as a visitor and colleague and associations of that nature. Okay, that's fine, but were these relevant comments to make on campaign? And he didn't make them just once. He made them at every other campaign stop that he hit. Was this necessary?

Q: Did you find this hostility reflected by his members of the campaign staff that you came up against?

JONES: No, I won't say that this was an overwhelming aspect of the Liberal Party by any matter or means. They, too, are friendly, congenial, personable, and very approachable. I had tremendous access. Virtually anybody at almost any level in government or in the campaign would talk to you. Indeed, it was a skepticism that was evident in Mr. Chrétien, and it was also a skepticism certainly about American foreign policy and foreign affairs demonstrated by Lloyd Axworthy, who eventually became foreign minister. Mr. Axworthy is one of these people who, because he had a PhD from Princeton, is convinced that he knows how the United States should run its foreign policy better than we do. And he doesn't hesitate to tell us very loudly exactly how we should be doing it, why we should be doing it the way that he thinks we should, and does so in a way that is totally counterproductive for his own interests by prompting us to ignore him and his hectoring.

Q: *At the time, when Chrétien and company would talk about not wanting to be the fifty-first state, basically using the United States as the straw man on which to win some votes, did we treat this with a certain amount of a shrug because it didn't make much difference?*

JONES: We weren't belaboring this, and we certainly said nothing in public. It isn't our business to involve ourselves in their domestic politics. I think Canadians are always under the impression that Americans pay no attention to them at all and, consequently, they can say anything about us that they care to express. On the other hand, when someone's pissing down your back, you're sort of silly to call it rain. From time to time while I was on the trip, I made it clear to Chrétien's minders that I didn't think that that was a terribly productive line of approach. But I wasn't saying anything in public, and I wasn't saying anything to the other media on the bus or on the plane or anything of that nature. I just sat and listened and took note. But again, it was an illustration of the inner man, and not even necessarily affecting what we were predicting. We certainly were not predicting that there was going to be essential hostility in our foreign policy or economic relations.

Q: *We didn't think this was going to go back to Diefenbaker times.*

JONES: Or even to the earliest and most pointedly neuralgic Trudeau period, where there was very distinct hostility all the time. Of course, you could also say that so many things had changed that there were, almost by definition, going to be fewer points of controversy. Much of the controversy between the United States and Canada during the Cold War era was that, in their view, we were not being sufficiently supple in our relationship with the Soviet Union. After all, how could they possibly be an "evil empire" or be told that they should collapse and take down the Berlin Wall? That was just ridiculous. Of course, by 1993, there was no Soviet Union. Apartheid in South Africa had ended. There were no Contra battles going on in Latin America. There was a great deal of democracy where there had been a great deal of dictatorship in South and Central America. As a result, many of the points of conflict in foreign affairs between the United States and Canada had evaporated. Now, the fact that the U.S. policy on almost all of these issues had turned out to be correct is a point that the Canadians would never accept or admit. Nevertheless, the issues weren't there.

Q: It left them with Cuba.

JONES: Yes.

Q: Of all the issues, that's a throwaway.

JONES: Well, it's an issue on which we have—I won't say agreed to disagree, but since we have, in effect, disagreed on it for forty years, it remains a baseline/touchstone for Canadian foreign policy experts to differentiate themselves from their views on foreign policy with the United States. We thought then, think now, and will think in the future that the Canadians are on the wrong side of history so far as Cuba is concerned. As I politely told my Canadian colleagues, they had better advise their investors there to make all their money they can now because when the government changes, they certainly will not be the preferred investors in a new Cuban government. But okay, you make your choices. If the Canadian government continues to align itself with Castro's Cuba, that's their choice.

Results of the 1993 Election

Q: Let's go on with what you were up to.

JONES: We simply watched the election evolve and did our analyses as we went along. Of course, beforehand, I wrote the proverbial kind of predictive telegram of a smashing Liberal victory, and that's exactly what it was. It created circumstances in Canada that exist today. It virtually annihilated the Tory Party, which went from a majority of something like 160 seats—they had had an outright majority—to two seats. The prime minister and virtually every member of the cabinet were defeated. It left a Liberal government with a majority, and it shattered the opposition into these pieces: the tiny remnant of the Tories; a Reform Party, which grew from one seat to more than fifty seats and dominated the entire West; and the *Bloc Québécois*. That totally destroyed the Tories in Quebec.

The *Bloc Québécois* didn't gain a seat anywhere else, but it got enough seats to become the official opposition, which left a number of people scratching their heads, because the opposition is supposed to be the "loyal" opposition and this was a palatably, identifiably, and certifiably a disloyal opposition. This group was led by probably the most interesting and charismatic Canadian politician of the 1990s: Lucien Bouchard. He is one of these stormy petrels of politics who has ranged Churchill-like across parties, being different things at different times and then being the same thing again. He had been a senior member of the Tory government, a close friend of Brian Mulroney's, broke with Mulroney over one of the constitutional accord solutions (Meech Lake), and set up his own party, the *Bloc Québécois,* which was carved out of a hunk of the Tory party and a couple of Liberals. They had something like nine members. But in the 1993 election, they virtually swept Quebec, winning fifty-four of seventy-five seats. That put them in the very curious position of being the official opposition and, in theory, advancing the interests and attitudes of all Canadians in opposition, but by and large clearly devoted to the independence of Quebec. They were regarded as, and regarded themselves as, the vanguard in Ottawa to prepare for separation from Canada. What you had after the 1993 election was a province in Quebec that was headed by the Liberals on the provincial level but dominated by separatists on the federal level. It was not until 1994 that they had a provincial election that ousted the Liberals and put the *Parti Québécois* in power.

Preston Manning, Reform, and the Canadian West

But, back to the federal level, the other major winner from this election was the Reform Party. This was headed by another extremely interesting, charismatic, and highly intelligent Canadian politician, perhaps the second most interesting and intelligent politician in Canada in the 1990s, Preston Manning. Manning's view was that the West had been systematically disadvantaged and cut out of real power and authority in Canada at the federal level because of the manner in which the parliamentary system works. The parliamentary system rewards the provinces with the greatest population. If you don't have the population, you don't have the seats. If you don't have the seats, you don't have the influence. There is no substantive political equivalent to the U.S. Senate, where small groups of populations and small states can have a blocking power and influence at the federal level.

The Canadian West is less populated than Ontario and Quebec, and it has significantly less influence. The Tories had promised the West that they would bring them more into the center of power and authority. At the end, the Westerners, particularly as headed by the Reform Party, came to the conclusion, correctly, that the Tories had continued to pour their fiscal preferences into Ontario and Quebec. The Reform Party was sufficiently convincing that it changed the circumstance from one in which virtually all of the representatives in Alberta were Tories to a situation in which there were no Tories in Alberta, and every Tory in Alberta was defeated. Such also was the case in British Columbia, and less so in Manitoba and Saskatchewan, but there were Reform representatives in these provinces. Where the Reform Party failed completely and totally was east of the Ontario-Manitoba border. They had one seat in Ontario at that point and no seats in Quebec or in the Maritime Provinces. The political situation was such that the Conservative Party in Canada was now in three segments: the old Tories, the Reform Party, and the *Bloc Québécois*.

—The New Democratic Party

There is a socialist party, the New Democratic Party, in Canada and they, too, in 1993 lost a very substantial numbers of seats. They had forty-three seats going into the election and were reduced to about nine. So that, too, suggested the marginalization of the left and a decline of a real socialist view in Canada, partly because people hypothesized as a result of the end of the Cold War, the Soviets had failed politically, and there was a recognition that socialism wasn't working and had failed economically. The divisions that were manifested in 1993 have persisted through the present, and the present election, although the *Bloc Québécois* has declined somewhat and Reform changed its name, restructured itself, and gained a few seats. The Tories in two elections went up and then back down. It's a little hard to go anywhere except up when you have two seats. In the 1997 election, they went up to twenty seats. But then in the 2000 election, they declined to twelve seats, the minimum for official party status in Canada.

Q: What did we see was in it or not in it for the United States, this division of the West becoming quite discontented and not really attached to the government and then the Maritimes? Did we see any problems here for us?

JONES: Not at the initial juncture. It was simply a phenomenon that the Conservatives had totally and absolutely collapsed. They had been as thoroughly repudiated as virtually any party in democracy ever has been. In a longer view, the continued division of a conservative party has meant that the Liberals have totally dominated Canadian politics, and I have said that it's Liberals as far as the eye can see, so far as the predictability of Canadian politics well into the next decade is concerned. There simply is nothing and no likelihood of a coherent conservative rejoining that would make it possible to oppose the Liberals, who stride the center of the spectrum. They are what is called in Canada the "natural governing party," and they are an extremely effective political force. They will move slightly to the left or slightly to the right as economic, social, and other circumstances require and they win elections. They are extraordinarily effective politicians and they run by what used to be the maxim of the old Democratic Party in the United States: spend and spend, elect and elect.

Bilateral Relations with the Liberals after the 1993 Election

Q: Did they call their Foreign Ministry "External Affairs"?

JONES: It used to be called External Affairs or "Extaf." While I was there, they changed it to Department of Foreign Affairs and International Trade.

Q: Did that name imply anything?

JONES: It was meant to imply that there was a greater economic component in the Department of Foreign Affairs than in the past, but part of the decision to change the name was that "External Affairs" was close to being a Britishism, a legacy of the past that they wanted to modernize and update. And the Liberals also wanted to put their stamp on such bureaucracies.

Q: How did you find dealing with the professionals in those places? Were you dealing mainly with career Canadian diplomats when you were over there? Were these the experts, or did political appointees go down fairly far?

JONES: Political appointees really don't exist on the scale that they exist at in the United States, at least at the ministerial level. The political appointees will be involved in the prime minister's office and the Privy Council

Office. If you had to give a very rough analogy, you would say that this was equivalent to the White House staff and the NSC. These are people who have the position that can be characterized by the question: Where does the 800-pound gorilla sit? The 800-pound gorilla sits wherever it wants to sit. Eddie Goldenberg, a man who is a close personal, longtime associate of Prime Minister Chrétien, put his hand in any issue that he considered to be of importance. He was engaged in many bilateral U.S. issues. Goldenberg essentially is a very adroit fixer who wants to solve problems and move forward on these. He is not an ideologue. So you had someone such as Goldenberg involve himself at times in specific issues.

I knew and dealt with Goldenberg on occasion, but the people with whom I dealt were virtually invariably career professionals. They were very high quality. As I suggested to you earlier, Canada's primary requirement is the management of its relationship with the United States. Their frank emphasis is on management to Canada's benefit—not to mutual benefit. When they work it most effectively, they can leverage their position and our disinterest in certain areas to their advantage. Their people are invariably intelligent, well trained, hard working, and effective. They were also almost invariably quite straightforward. They gave you clear opinions of their position, and clear views of where our positions were, right or wrong. When they made démarches of their own, they were well-staffed, intelligently presented, good pieces of work.

Q: Were they working to repair a certain amount of the tenor of Chrétien, as far as foreign affairs go?

JONES: Remember also that during the initial period when I was political counselor, the foreign minister was Andre Ouellette. He was not out making waves. Lloyd Axworthy was consigned to an enormous and complicated bureau that overviewed health and human services and a wide variety of domestic topics of that nature, a whole variety of things for which he was not terribly well suited, but that was the ministerial assignment that he got. It's a very difficult, very complicated, enormous assignment. He didn't manage it very well, but he managed it.

Q: After the new government came in, from the point of view of our embassy, was there any adjustment? What was our goal?

JONES: Our first and primary focus was concern over NAFTA. It was an issue that the Liberals had made one of their key points in their campaign: they were going to renegotiate NAFTA. That left every person who had ever had any association with this agreement with their hand on their forehead wondering what this ostensible commitment was going to mean. Nobody knew exactly what it was going to mean. There was some upset in Washington about what this meant, how it was going to act out, how people were going to act as a result of it, and what the Canadians actually were going to do.

As it turned out, the Canadians and the Liberals made some minor suggestions, and had some very minor adjustments, as far as I can recall, in the final NAFTA text. Ambassador Blanchard played at least a reasonably helpful role in telling Washington fairly directly—and telling people within the White House and in the presidential entourage—to stay calm, don't get excited, let's wait this one out a bit. Blanchard met with Chrétien even before Chrétien officially assumed power as prime minister. Their transition is very quick. Their transition between a defeated government and a victorious government is a couple of days, not any extended period. We got the impression, at that point, that issues could be worked out, as they were. This was what we had hoped for and expected, but it was nothing about which we were assured. That uncertainty generated a degree of tension within the embassy where you expect something is going to work out, but you don't know because you have no control over what the other side eventually does. Of course, they were on record as saying that they were going to do something that would make what we wished to accomplish much more difficult. They didn't do it. That was helpful.

Q: As things kept rolling along, did you find that this new government was relatively easy to work with?

JONES: We just started back into our long laundry list of specific issues and problems on foreign affairs. The Liberals selected Andre Ouellette as foreign minister. He was not a career foreign policy expert either. He was essentially Chrétien's Quebec manager and a longtime Liberal. His foreign policy approach was pretty much to listen to his Foreign Ministry staff, so we were not faced with a lot of specific crises. Most of the crises we were *not* faced with were those crises that had evaporated after the Cold War, from the end of apartheid in Africa, significant increases in democracy in Africa and in Latin America, and the end of many of the guerrilla exercises that had been running either in Nicaragua or elsewhere. Since we didn't have these problems in which we would be doing one thing and the Canadians would be feeling that we should be doing another, we didn't have direct foreign policy conflicts.

The issues that were in play were primarily former-Yugoslavia exercises. For commentary on this topic, you really have to have be somebody who was an expert in Central Europe, Yugoslavia, and the former Yugoslavia to sort your way through who was doing what, to whom, and when. The Canadians had committed UN-subordinated forces in Bosnia and elsewhere for a good stretch of time. They continued to do so. By and large, they supported the efforts that we were attempting to stabilize one part of Former Yugoslavia or another. We were engaged in constant coordination on demarches and on policies for the area. The Canadians with whom I dealt were largely skeptical about greater involvement in the Former Yugoslavia and wanted to let the Europeans work it out to the degree that was possible.

Q: How did things flow after that?

JONES: The relationship was a reasonably straightforward, solid working relationship on the many individual démarches and issues in foreign affairs. This was simply a constant flow. We presented in the course of the year hundreds of démarches on issues of every dimension to the Canadian government, sometimes seeking their support, sometimes simply informing them of our views and positions, as is natural, standard consultation in foreign affairs.

—Cruise Missiles

One issue that did arise was on cruise missile testing. We had had a long-standing agreement with the Canadians to fly and test cruise missiles over certain areas of their northern provinces. This testing was designed so that we could perfect our terrain contour matching radar, as the terrain in Canada was a close approximate of the terrain over which such cruise missiles would have to fly for strikes against the old Soviet Union.

Essentially, the cruise missile agreement had expired. We thought it was still a useful agreement to have. The agreement had proceeded throughout the Cold War without difficulty, but there were, of course, always individuals who were critical of any such agreement with the United States, including environmentalists who claimed that it was scaring the elk. The politicians in Alberta who represented those areas were Reform Party politicians, and thus had no leverage in the decision making. Although we had been told that the Canadians were going to renew the agreement, three days before Secretary of Defense William Perry was due to visit, there was a conference of the Liberals in Ottawa. At that conference, the young Liberals voted that they should discontinue this agreement with the United States. The government decided that since the young Liberals had so said, that position was going to be government policy. Now, that to me was the limpest kind of excuse that I had ever heard from a government. It also was an embarrassment, certainly to the career professionals within the Ministry of Foreign Affairs and, to a degree, the Department of National Defense, because we had not been informed that this was going to be their policy prior to its public announcement just before SecDef arrived.

The Secretary of Defense was very gracious and just let it pass without comment. But it was illustrative of the manner in which the Canadian government can make essentially ideological one-in-your-eye decisions.

Q: Did you sense any pulling back on our side, saying, well, let's do what we have to, but let's not initiate anything new?

JONES: I wouldn't say that. You had a liberal Democratic administration in power in Washington and you had Liberals in Canada. They were more philosophically in tune than not. The issues that we were presenting and for which we were trying to get support were, by and large, straightforward issues that had little contention associated with them.

—Haiti

Over the next several years, one of the issues that we worked on most steadily and tried to find a solution for was that of the military dictatorship in Haiti. The Canadians had a certain domestic interest in Haiti. There were a fair number of Haitians who lived in the riding [parliamentary district] of Foreign Minister Andre Ouellette. These Haitians were strong supporters of the Liberal Party, so the Canadians had an interest in a positive resolution for Haiti's problems. We were groping, as we did for an extended period of time, with all of the issues associated with the military rule and the ouster of Aristide from Haiti. Consequently, we had a steady stream of cooperative efforts and consultations and policy discussions with the Canadians on how to manage the regime change in Haiti. The Canadians participated at a modest level in the force that eventually did oust the military dictatorship. They had, and may continue to have, a presence in Haiti in the way of RCMP [Royal Canadian Mounted Police] trainers for the Haitian police. These people, being French-speaking, had an entrée that many Americans would not. They also attempted to train Haitian police in Canada. They tried to encourage Haitians who were residents and even citizens of Canada to contribute positively to the success of a new regime in Haiti by returning to the country. Therefore, we were really pretty coordinated on such issues.

—A Much-Needed Civil Aviation Agreement

In a couple of other areas, although these were more frequently economic than political, we worked to improve the relationship. One in which Ambassador Blanchard had a particular interest was a modernized civil aviation agreement. He found, much to his displeasure, that it took an inordinate amount of time to get from Ottawa to Washington, notably that he had to fly through this or that place or fly on a very small plane. There simply was no convenient air connection between Ottawa and Washington. There had been repeated failures in attempts to modernize the civil aviation agreement, essentially because of Canadian aviation protectionism. Resolving this problem was one of Blanchard's efforts from the time he arrived. After quite an extended negotiation, we concluded an aviation agreement in February 1995 at the same time that President Clinton visited. You can see that it was at least a year-and-a-half effort on the part of Blanchard to get this particular problem solved.

—Salmon

Blanchard also worked on another one of the economic problems, the issue of Pacific Coast salmon. Here all I can do is say, in shorthand, that it's a problem of too many fishermen chasing too few fish. It has been a problem akin to that of softwood lumber, that is, one of the endless, repeating issues that come up on the laundry list. Out of our entire economic relationship of the magnitude that I've earlier described, maybe 5 percent can be characterized as problems of one sort or another. These problems constantly change, but some of them repeat. Among those problems are issues such as fishing, softwood lumber, and magazine publication. They are essentially economic. They don't become really political until they become very pointed or reach crisis level. But these were also problems on which the ambassador worked and about which I was somewhat aware, but I was not directly engaged.

Clinton's Visit to Canada: Some Atmospherics

American politics changed a bit with the November 1994 elections. That election left us in a situation where the Republicans for the first time in most people's living memory were in control of both houses of Congress. It left a very much weakened President Clinton. But at the same time, there had been preparations for a presidential visit to Ottawa. It would have been the first visit on a presidential level in quite some time. George H. W. Bush had never visited for whatever series of reasons—but I think they were Gulf War related. Through the first couple of years of his term, President Clinton had not made a visit. But an official visit was scheduled for late February 1995.

This decision generated all of the horror associated with any presidential visit. Anyone who has ever been a Foreign Service officer knows that the visit of a president, a visit that is not almost a spur of the moment visit or a visit that is not directed into a specific short, multilateral meeting, is just an endless disaster for the embassy associated with it. It's great glory and magnificent prominence, and just a tremendously unending workload for the staff and the group that comes.

At the same time, learning to love the White House staff, let alone the Secret Service, is not the easiest thing for either the embassy or the host country. Anyone who has ever borne up under the visit of the Secret Service knows that these are testosterone-charged confrontations between local security services and the Secret Service, most of whom would like to come armed like Rambo and have the local security services in the position of being Tonto to our Lone Rangers. Well, that doesn't go down very well in most areas, and it didn't go down very well in Canada either. As a result, in at least one instance of conflicting security views, the traditional laying of the wreath by the head of the state at the National War Memorial, which was within about a block of Parliament, was canceled because the Canadians refused to permit us to put snipers on all the building surrounding the monument. Ambassador Blanchard recounted one instance in which a driver and two huge security guards, one from the RCMP and the other from the Secret Service, were jammed into the front of the presidential limousine. While the Secret Service, of course, demanded that their person be present, the RCMP also claimed that it was responsible for the protection of a visiting dignitary in their country. There was always the question of just how much weaponry would be brought by how many people. In a Canada that is very significantly unarmed, the amount of weaponry that the Secret Service was going to bring—let alone the total numbers of the Secret Service that actually arrived—verged between impressive, awe inspiring, and ridiculous. But that depended, of course, upon the observer. Nevertheless, this was an exercise in which the president came, spoke to Parliament, had a variety of meetings, and brought his full American entourage with him. They had a variety of meetings. Certain agreements were signed, particularly the civil aviation agreement. Things worked out reasonably well.

There were a couple of clever elements to the parliamentary speeches, one of which was that the prime minister said that regardless of the president's current political circumstances, he should know that no president who had spoken before Parliament had ever failed to be reelected. President Clinton responded in an aside that showed just how intellectually quick he was: he said never had he so believed in the "iron laws of history" as he had after hearing what Prime Minister Chrétien had just said. He also took account of the fact that he had just delivered himself of one of the longest and most turgid State of the Union addresses ever made by saying that he promised that he would not speak as long as he had spoken before Congress in the State of the Union. Obviously, this ploy worked very well. The prime minister and the president had a good relationship. They had a boys' afternoon out with wives in a pleasant spot on the Rideau Canal, the canal being frozen at the time. Mrs. Clinton went ice skating on the canal, having had some ice-skating experience as a girl. They had a visit in which, according to Ambassador Blanchard, they went away considerably more upbeat in spirit than they had been certainly in the early days after the November election.

The other element of the visit of some interest to me was that I was responsible for Secretary Christopher and the monitoring of his work and his meetings. Unfortunately, after his first meeting, the secretary became ill and was hospitalized briefly in Ottawa, and Deputy Secretary Talbott took over for the meetings and circumstances that followed that.

This was a very successful visit. Perhaps all presidential visits are condemned to success. This had the same result.

Q: I think we've laid the groundwork for Quebec. Were there any major developments?

The Quebec Sovereignty Referendum

The concern and the obvious foreshadowing from the 1993 election was that events were headed to a constitutional crisis in Canada. We could see that a referendum was clearly coming for Quebec independence, as it was also very easy to predict that the Quebec Liberals were going to be defeated whenever they held provincial elections. That projected future meant that there was going to be a referendum on Quebec sovereignty. Consequently, that prospective development was what most focused our attention and what most interested us.

JONES: What I have mentioned is that we could see on the horizon the development of a referendum for Quebec sovereignty. This was a situation for which the groundwork had been laid. The foreshadowing came with the enormous majority and support given to the *Bloc Québécois* in 1993. Then we headed into an election in Quebec in 1994 in which it was very clear that the *Parti Québécois* was going to win. We anticipated this victory. Once again, we had spoken to many of the officials and leaders in the *Parti Québécois* and tried to get a sense for where they were coming from, where they were going, and how they intended to go about it. Here also you have a situation in which Canadian political leadership is almost across the board intelligent, hardworking, and intellectually and politically sophisticated, and they recognized what could be done by politicians in a North American twenty-first-century constituency.

We had a situation in which the PQ was also a known quality. It was not as if this was the first time they were seeking election in Quebec. They had been elected earlier and defeated earlier. While they expected to win the election in 1994, this was not an election being run by a bunch of wild-haired, wild-eyed fanatics who were headed toward cobblestone-erected barricades. These were a group of sophisticated individuals who represented a combination of political parties and views but were directed to obtaining Quebec sovereignty. I met with the man who at that time was the deputy head, the number-two man, in the PQ, Bernard Landry. He is now the so-called prime minister of Quebec. The woman who is now the head of their foreign affairs operation, Louise Beaudoin, and a variety of other PQ members have obtained substantial levels of influence in their party. Another man of particular interest is Jean-Francois Lisée, who wrote a book called *In the Eye of the Eagle* [1990], which was an extended and sophisticated compilation of American views on Canada and Quebec, constructed largely from FOIA [Freedom of Information Act] documents that probably should not have been released. Subsequently, we have been far, far more careful about what was released related to Canada. But what actually these documents and that book illustrated was that Quebec separatists are quite eager to tell Americans what they are going to do and why they are going to do it, because they don't want us disconcerted by developments. They want us informed rather than surprised. That was the case for me, and it was the case for other American diplomats prior to me and subsequent to me in dealing with these people and this party.

Q: The Quebec provincial election came in 1994

JONES: Yes, roughly October 1994.

Q: How did it come out?

JONES: It resulted in a very substantial victory for the PQ. It was not, however, as large a victory as they had anticipated and which the polls had suggested they would win. Because of the manner in which votes are distributed and ridings are gerrymandered, it gave them a substantially larger majority in Parliament, that they term the National Assembly, than they would have if it had been a straight differentiation of the vote. However, they did get a technical majority of the votes cast, and certainly a majority of the French-speaking Quebecers who voted, so they were very firmly in control of the government. As they had had previous members with experience in government, they were not starting from a ground zero of ignorance.

Their leader, Jacques Parizeau, was a sophisticated London-trained economist with very substantial skills both in politics and in economics and was a fine English speaker. Their earlier mentioned deputy, Bernard Landry, was also an economist and a lawyer who speaks three languages (Spanish, as well as reasonably good English). The head of their combination of culture and foreign affairs, Louise Beaudoin, is a French-trained but English-speaking, very effective spokesman for sovereignty.

Consequently, you had a group of people about whom you could say, "Well, we know they are headed toward a referendum." Their effort and their requirement was: "How do we hold a referendum that we're going to win? How do we marshal enough support, how do we organize ourselves so that we're able to win this referendum? It's the most important thing we're going to be doing. It's the objective that we've set out for. It was what Quebecers anticipated when they elected us. How do we go about it and do it?" They thrashed about trying to figure the best approaches and solutions, what question to pose, how to pose it in a way that would be one that was not merely "Do you support independence of Quebec with no relationship to Canada subsequently," the kind of question that the federal government in Ottawa would have posed. They wanted one that was more nebulous, one that implied a future relationship with Canada, one that suggested that it would happen only after an offer was made to the federal government for a renewed relationship or a radically changed relationship, one that was ambiguous in a way that would be interpretable in a positive light for them.

In the end, it didn't really matter what the question said. It meant that if you voted "yes," you were going to have an independent Quebec. If you voted "no," you were going to have the existing relationship. Some may think all of the intellectual fibrillation associated with how this went about perhaps was important, but I believe essentially it was unimportant. Likewise was the PQ's efforts to create and commission a series of complex studies. The studies were done, and then they were suppressed because they didn't like all of the answers that had come out of all of the studies.

It was a situation for which they had to mobilize support. You had a circumstance in which you could anticipate that better than 90 percent of the non—French speakers, those who were English-speakers, Anglophones—those who had originally spoken a language other than French or English were called Allophones—would vote against sovereignty. What percentage of the French-speakers, who were still better than 70 to 80 percent of the population, would vote against sovereignty was an unknown. What percentage of these Francophones would vote for sovereignty was likewise unknown—although polls indicated that a majority would support "yes."

Sovereignty has its attractions and its liabilities. While Americans can't see what possible attraction independence would have for Quebec—and why anyone would want to break up a country as successful, positive, and good to live in as Canada?—a certain basic percentage of Quebecers feel very much to the contrary. That percentage has always run at 30 to 40 percent. The job of sovereigntists was to boost it an additional 10 percent, from 40 percent to over 50 percent. Throughout 1994 and 1995, that was what they worked to do. We could see this coming like an avalanche rolling down hill. The only real question was when they would announce the referendum for and at what time? They selected, in the end, October 30, 1995.

I want to digress a little bit and talk about a special point: the devastating illness that Lucien Bouchard, the leader of the *Bloc Québécois*, suffered in December 1994. He was struck by necrotizing fasciitis, which in layman's terms comes out to "galloping gangrene" or a flesh-eating bacteria syndrome—an infection which has a very high percentage fatality. As a result of this, Bouchard went almost instantly to death's door. His leg was amputated. He made statements as he was going into the operating room that were translatable as, "Continue the effort. Continue the work." Here you had the man who was already considered to be the most dynamic prosovereignty politician coming out in a situation after his amputation as almost a heroic character. Some people referred to him as "Saint Lucien," and said that it had been a miracle that he had survived.

In any event, following the Clinton visit, we began to focus even more pointedly on the run-up to the referendum in Quebec. I was meeting regularly with the federal group in Ottawa that was monitoring how the federal government was going to handle and coordinate the "no" campaign, the "yes" campaign being run by the Quebec sovereigntists, and the *Parti Québécois*.

Separately, you had two umbrella groups in Quebec, the yes and the no campaigns. They had a variety of financial restrictions and controls associated with who could contribute money and how it came to them. As a result, one of the endless arguments was the degree of federal intrusion into what was the responsibility of Quebecers to determine; this controversy was one of the subthemes in the referendum. By early September 1995, the Quebec government announced the official question, which was a vague, elliptical question that had a variety of circumstances to it, including reference to a large document that had been developed beforehand regarding what circumstances had to be created for a new relationship between Quebec and Canada. The point still really was that if you voted yes, you were going to have an independent Quebec in one form or another. If you voted no, you would have a continuation of the existing circumstances.

What developed was that the early days of the referendum went quite badly for the yes forces. They did not get the bounce from a debate in their provincial national assembly that they had hoped for and anticipated. The ripostes by the provincial liberals had been sharper and clearer. The prosovereignty team was less effective in its own presentations. The fact that a group of studies associated with and commissioned for sovereignty had been suppressed was a negative for the sovereigntists. Generally, this campaign was not going well.

But in early to mid October, Lucien Bouchard, who had opposed having the referendum at exactly the time for which it was scheduled and who had been a secondary character in the campaign until then, was, in effect, brought to the fore and virtually given control of the remaining portion of the campaign. Bouchard had a career-year type of campaign. This was a man who had come back from death's door, who was viewed as a monumental figure, one whose efforts to survive were all but miraculous. He is a man who is not a natural politician. He had even been a rather poor politician in the early stages of his political career, but he developed communication and speaking skills that were as good as any Quebecer had seen in a generation. People just flocked out to see him. People rushed just to touch him. People went wild over him. He was able to say things that would have left a normal politician lying in the gutter like a dead dog. He said, in effect, "Well, Quebec's white women should be having more babies." Instead of saying, "My gosh, you racist sovereigntist pig"—the response wasn't quite the equivalent of, "Well, I'm bearing your baby"—but there was just no negative resonance. This was the kind of statement that an average politician could never have made and survived.

Bouchard, as a result, virtually single-handedly drove the yes vote up. He drove it up to the point where immediately prior to the referendum, the outcome was too close to tell. Quebec polling is very sophisticated. It's as good as polling anywhere in the world. These were polls done not by a couple of hundred people but oftentimes by well more than 1,000 out of a population of seven million. We were getting polling that should have been accurate to within 1 or 2 percent. But you had a problem in the polling. Although the yes vote was leading, and often leading by a significant percentage, four to six points, you had a significant number—15 percent or more—that would say they were undecided. Historically, the "undecided" weren't really undecided, but they weren't willing to say to a pollster what their viewpoint was. Their unspoken viewpoint was that they were federalists, that they would be "no" supporters. Historically, they had broken at two-thirds in favor of the federalists and one-third in favor of the sovereigntists. So it became an extremely difficult judgment call as to how it was going to work out. I made several trips to the Montreal area at the time, spoke several times to yes and no group leaders, including in particular to Bernard Landry.

Each side expressed confidence without being willing to say that, "Yes, we are sure that we are going to win." The weekend before the referendum, the embassy caucused on what the result was going to be. I said that the no vote was going to win, that the federalists were going to win; it was going to be very close but the federalists were going to win. I said that we should be able to send a telegram to the department making that prediction. The ambassador declined, suggesting a "too close to call and Canada will still be here on the morning of the thirty-first" type of telegram, which is the telegram that we sent.

The weekend before and the week prior to the referendum vote saw a great deal of action on everybody's part. The question of the position of the United States on this event was a key element, or certainly was viewed that way, by federalists and sovereigntists. We had had for a relatively extended period a set piece statement that we ended by calling the mantra. It was: "We have had an excellent relationship with a strong and united Canada. However, the choice of Canada is for Canadians to decide." This rendition is paraphrasing but provides the essential USG attitude. During the course of the referendum, in consultation between Canadians and Americans at a very senior level, there was the feeling that we should weigh in a little more strongly. This was certainly the position of Ambassador Blanchard. We orchestrated a statement by Secretary Christopher when Foreign Minister Ouellette visited Washington on October 18. The secretary came up with a statement that I still have at hand. He said, "The United States places great value on its excellent ties with a strong and united Canada. These ties have been carefully cultivated and a different entity could not take this type of relationship for granted." That unfortunately was a statement that was not sufficiently clear, or was reported in a muddled and mangled way in the press, so that it really wasn't clear what the secretary had said.

Since it really wasn't clear what the secretary had said, it was decided that more prominent, more pointed, words would have to be said. Here, too, we, and particularly Ambassador Blanchard, orchestrated at a presidential press conference on October 25 or 26 a statement in response to a planted question. The president said something that was viewed as a stronger endorsement of a strong and united Canada, and not being able to see how a country as successful as Canada would have a need to be changed. Unfortunately, that statement by the president came out at exactly the same time that Bouchard and Chrétien addressed national audiences regarding the referendum. So, while the president's statement was reported and had some media prominence, by no means did it have the weight or attention that it might have had if it had been delivered when something less dramatic than dueling spokesmen for the life of Canada was on national television.

As a result, although subsequent polls said that voters had taken into account the view of the United States on the referendum, there really isn't any indication as to how they felt about this statement. We don't know whether they divined that the United States didn't want this to happen, and therefore they voted that way, or they divined that the United States didn't want this to happen, which would have been clear to anybody with a fourth-grade education, and therefore voted in favor of it. We had a polling result that said that perhaps as many as 20 to 25 percent of Quebecers took this statement into account when they voted, but we have no idea *how* it affected them. It's just one of those interesting judgments that we were heard, but whether we were agreed with or simply heard remains unknown.

Also, this final week stimulated a major federalist rally in the heart of Montreal which was led by a number of Canadian politicians, in particular the Minister for Fisheries Brian Tobin, a very dynamic and energetic politician from Newfoundland, and others who gathered a "Canada loves Quebec" rally in the center of Montreal. This effort was designed to demonstrate to Quebecers the depth of federalist feeling and Canadian support for Canada from sea to sea to sea, and that Quebec was, in their view and in Canada's view, an integral part of Canada, and they should vote "no." There are people that feel that that the rally was a vast success. There are others that look at polls and say that it was a negative, at least according to some polls. But it happened, and it was part of a demonstrable campaign to rally support in favor of federalist Canada and for Quebec to remain in Canada. I didn't attend that rally but one of my political officers did. We sent him to Montreal to attend. He said that it was a dramatic and effective rally. I attended a rally that was held in Hull, Quebec, just across the river from Ottawa, on Sunday, October 29, immediately before the vote. That, too, even though it was conducted in a steady rain, was a major rally of thousands of Canadians who were attempting to demonstrate support for a united Canada and a Quebec that remained within that framework.

On October 29 in midmorning, I got a telephone call from Bernard Landry, who said that he just wanted to inform me that their polls now conclusively demonstrated that the separatists were going to win and that he wanted me to be aware of that fact ahead of time for whatever I wanted to do with it. During the course of the day, I informed the ambassador, the DCM, and the desk that this was the information that Landry had conveyed. The ambassador said—and he apparently conveyed this information also to the desk and to others in Washington—that at the federalist level, they were now convinced that they were going to win.

The result was about as close as it conceivably could have been. We sat and watched a very interesting mechanism for determining this vote. It was a fever thermometer that ran back and forth across the bottom of the television set as to where the vote was. It started significantly above the 50 percent line. Slowly during the course of the evening, it declined until the sovereigntists ended with 49.4 percent of the vote and the federalists got 50.6 percent of the vote out of something like a 93 percent turnout for eligible voters. You can see that it had been a very substantially mobilized society on an issue that as closely divided Quebecers as almost could have been possible.

As a result of that vote, the premier of Quebec, Jacques Parizeau, and his deputy said some nasty and bitter things. Parizeau was quoted as saying on the night of the election that they had been defeated by "money and the ethnic vote." While that judgment was accurate, it was certainly nothing that was acceptable to be said publicly either by sovereigntists or by federalists. Of course, you could have said that they were equally defeated by the number of French-speakers who didn't vote for them. But it was clear that probably something like 95 percent of the Anglophones and Allophones [in Quebec, a person whose native language is neither English nor French] had voted against them. Whether money had anything to do with it, certainly there was heavy campaigning by the federal government to retain a unified Canada. They would have been totally derelict in their duties if they had not done so. As a consequence, within something like a day, Parizeau resigned and then the question arose who would assume the leadership of the *Parti Québécois* and the PQ's government.

Although it appeared and was obvious that Lucien Bouchard was really the only choice, it took a stretch of time for reflection and consultation and other discussion before Bouchard actually moved from Ottawa to Quebec City and became premier of Quebec. Actually, the ambassador and I saw Bouchard the day that he left Ottawa finally, on something like December 13, 1995, and had one of these generally not terribly memorable conversations. Bouchard, however, said that he had just come from a long conversation with Jean Chrétien, which he didn't really reveal but said that it was much longer than he had anticipated having with Chrétien, and that he was indeed committed to the independence and sovereignty of Quebec.

In discussions, about which we did not know until they were revealed in his book, Ambassador Blanchard had held far more extensive high-level conversations with Canadian politicians and leaders than he conveyed to his senior staff. He also had a conversation with Preston Manning to the effect that Manning had asked how the Canadian debt should be handled if Canada separated, which is something that Blanchard revealed in his book, but which he had not bothered to tell anybody else, at least anybody that I knew, on the staff beforehand. This was certainly more revealing than would have been anticipated in a subsequent public account. Blanchard also said that subsequent to the referendum, he had a couple of conversations with Bouchard on how Canada and Quebec should resolve their differences. Again, to my knowledge, these were not reported, or if they were reported, they were reported in channels that I never heard, and I have never subsequently encountered anyone who had heard about these conversations, let alone any upshot from the conversations.

Aftermath of the Sovereignty Referendum

But we move now into 1996. At that point, people spent a good deal of time ruminating over what the next steps for Quebec would be. They pondered whether it would mean there would be another referendum in the near term, or whether it would be something in the further term; how Quebec and Canada would resolve their continued differences; and whether some of the promises that the Ottawa government had made (concerning giving Quebec additional powers and positions and circumstances) would come into effect for whatever reason.

Bouchard decided that what he wanted first to do was to prove that sovereigntists could demonstrate good government, that they had spent the first year of their mandate preparing for and really running this referendum, and that now, if they were going to be successful, they had to show that they were a real, working, effective government and worthy of an endorsement to be an independent country. That was the focus that he followed for the rest of the time that I was in Canada. There were polls that suggested that this was an effective approach, that he was gaining strength and sovereigntist support. There were sovereigntists, however, who were very skeptical and critical of Bouchard because he had never been part of the *pur et dur* [pure and hard] sovereigntist campaign, he had been in too many camps at too many times throughout his life, and they were never totally convinced that he was an absolutely committed separatist. It's almost like a man who has an absolutely beautiful, gorgeous, and attractive wife and can never quite become convinced that she is totally committed to him and is so critical and skeptical and suspicious of her that in the end he drives her away. Actually, in the end, Bouchard, although he ran and won an election in 1998, left Quebec and Canadian politics in 2000, partly because he was no longer interested in struggling with those who didn't believe that he was sufficiently committed to sovereignty or that his path to sovereignty would eventually get them there.

In any event, I continued as political counselor until the end of July 1996, doing the standard things that I had done until then. I left on August 1, 1996, and returned to Washington.

CHAPTER 37

Back to Washington—
End of Active Duty and into Retired Action

I spent time doing various assorted assignments. I did some work on benchmarking for the Department of State, what works best at other agencies, other companies, or organizations outside the Department of State. I worked for a stretch on human rights reports during the period of mid-October to the end of January 1997, the annual creation of the department's *Country Reports on Human Rights Practices*, assessing the status of human rights in countries around the world. I spent another stretch of time working on Freedom of Information declassification and review while on active duty. Then I retired, roughly at the end of January or early February 1998.

Q: After you retired, how have you occupied yourself?

JONES: It's been very busy. It's been even extraordinarily busy. My wife and I have produced a weekly for the National Coalition for Advanced Manufacturing. Its focus is on improving industrial productivity in the United States, research and development funding on the federal level for math and science in the United States, and efforts to improve the workforce skills of normal American labor so that the labor force of the twenty-first century can deal with the technology of the twenty-first century. We started this in January 1999 and have produced them for three years, fifty editions every year. Now we're well into another year of this activity. It's a sophisticated document drawn from Internet research every week, done in a *Wall Street Journal* style with one page of approximately eight summaries of important developments during the course of the week. Each one of these précis has a backup document associated with the précis on the front page; additionally there is a weekly selection of material in the form of government grants, Web sites, forthcoming conferences, and Internet publications that are associated with government, economic, and other associated aspects for productivity and general economic action.

Then I have continued to work as a WAE [when actually employed] reemployed annuitant/contractor equivalent for the Department of State. I worked and have worked for a number of years assisting to prepare the human rights report. I've done that through this year, which made it the sixth year that I had worked on them. I've also done a fair amount of declassification and review for a number of years.

I have published really quite extensively in Canada and the United States, with articles and columns in the *Foreign Service Journal*, in a number of Canadian publications from *Policy Options*, which is a publication associated with McGill, to an online magazine called *Ehgloo*, and probably about thirty to forty pieces in the Canadian equivalent of *The Hill*, a weekly called *The Hill Times*, in which I comment on Canadian-U.S. bilateral issues. I probably write and publish at least one piece every week.

Starting on April 1, 2002, I will begin another project in which I will be working with the State Department's historian as a contractor on a specialized project relating to the Middle East. This is an effort to put all the disparate material relating to the last two years of effort in the Middle East during the Clinton administration into chronological order: what was promised, to whom was it promised, how were the commitments made, and in what manner. This is going to be a classified study that will be available for further diplomatic effort as we continue our struggle to bring something that looks like peace, or at least a ceasefire, in the Middle East.

Q: *In other words, you're busy as hell.*

JONES: Yes. And I've also from time to time contributed my views on oral history with the good Mr. Kennedy.

Q: *I want to thank you very much.*

Edwards Brothers, Inc.
Thorofare, NJ USA
January 17, 2012